NATIONAL GEOGRAPHIC
TRAVELER
Costa Rica

NATIONAL GEOGRAPHIC

TRAVELER
Costa Rica

Christopher P. Baker

National Geographic
Washington, D.C.

Contents

Page 1: Blue-crowned
mot-mot
Pages 2–3: Birders thrill
to Costa Rica's avian
wonders.
Left: A national symbol:
intricate designs on an
oxcart wheel

How to use this guide

See back flap for keys to text and map symbols

The *National Geographic Traveler* brings you the best of Costa Rica in text, pictures, and maps. Divided into three main sections, the guide begins with an overview of history and culture. Following are nine regional chapters with featured sites that have been selected by the author for their particular interest. Each chapter opens with its own contents list.

The regions, and the sites within them are arranged geographically, each one introduced with a map highlighting the featured sites. Walks and drives, plotted on their own maps, suggest routes for discovering

an area. Features and sidebars give intriguing detail on history, culture, or contemporary life. A More Places to Visit page rounds off some of the chapters.

The final section, Travelwise, lists essential information for the traveler—pre-trip planning, getting around, communications, money matters and emergencies—plus a selection of hotels, restaurants, shops, activities, and entertainment.

To the best of our knowledge, all information is accurate as of the press date. However, it's always advisable to check in advance when possible.

Color coding

I I 0

Each region is color coded for easy reference. Find the region you want on the map on the front flap, and look for the color flash at the top of the pages of the relevant chapter. Information in **Travelwise** is also color coded to each region.

Reserva Biológica del Bosque Nuboso de Monteverde

www.cct.or.cr

🅰 101 E 2/3

✉ 6 miles E of Santa Elena

☎ 645-5122

💲 $$

Visitor information

Practical information for most sites is given in the side column (see key to symbols on back flap). The map reference gives the page number of the map and grid reference. Other details are address, telephone number, days closed, entrance charge in a range from $ (under $4) to $$$$$ (over $25). Other sites have information in italics and parentheses in the text.

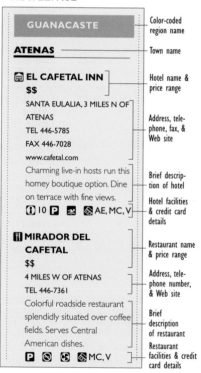

TRAVELWISE

GUANACASTE — Color-coded region name

ATENAS — Town name

🏨 **EL CAFETAL INN** — Hotel name & price range
$$

SANTA EULALIA, 3 MILES N OF ATENAS — Address, telephone, fax, & Web site
TEL 446-5785
FAX 446-7028
www.cafetal.com

Charming live-in hosts run this homey boutique option. Dine on terrace with fine views. — Brief description of hotel

🚹 10 🅿 🛉 🅰 AE, MC, V — Hotel facilities & credit card details

🍴 **MIRADOR DEL CAFETAL** — Restaurant name & price range
$$

4 MILES W OF ATENAS — Address, telephone number, & Web site
TEL 446-7361

Colorful roadside restaurant splendidly situated over coffee fields. Serves Central American dishes. — Brief description of restaurant

🅿 🚭 🍴 🅰 MC, V — Restaurant facilities & credit card details

Hotel & restaurant prices

An explanation of the price bands used in entries is given in the Hotels & restaurants section (beginning on p. 240).

REGIONAL MAPS

Road number

Point of interest

Important featured town

Map reference

Important point of interest

Adjacent region

Drive start point

- A locator map accompanies each regional map and shows the location of that region in the country.
- Adjacent regions are shown, each with a page reference.

WALKING TOURS

Direction of walk route

Walk route

Point of interest not on walk route

Red numbered bullets link site on map to descriptions in the text

Start point

Building outline

- An information box gives the starting and ending points, time and length of walk, and places not to be missed along the route.

DRIVING TOURS

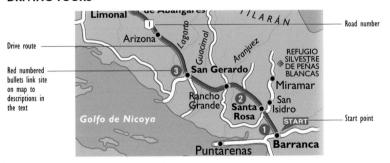

Drive route

Red numbered bullets link site on map to descriptions in the text

Road number

Start point

- An information box provides details including starting and finishing points, time and length of drive, places not to be missed along the route.

NATIONAL GEOGRAPHIC
TRAVELER
Costa Rica

About the author

After studying geography at the University of London and Latin American studies at the University of Liverpool, Christopher P. Baker settled in California and established a career as an award-winning travel writer, photographer, and lecturer. His many books include *The National Geographic Traveler: Cuba* and other guidebooks to Cuba, Costa Rica, Jamaica, the Bahamas, Turks & Caicos, and California. His enthralling travelog, *Mi Moto Fidel: Motorcycling through Castro's Cuba* (National Geographic Adventure Press), won the Lowell Thomas "Travel Book of the Year" award and the North American Travel Journalist Association's Grand Prize in 2001. He has a Web site at www.travelguidebooks.com.

History & culture

Pre-Columbian Indians used gold to create elaborate ornaments.

Costa Rica today

COMMON CLICHÉS ABOUT COSTA RICA PAINT A CANVAS IN TROPICAL HUES.
The background is of glorious emerald, teeming with colorful wildlife: rainbow-hued
scarlet macaws, electric-blue morpho butterflies the size of saucers, and the iridescent
green Holy Grail of neotropical birds, the quetzal. The settings are also familiar: sweeping rain forest, rugged mountains, fire-spitting volcanoes, and lonesome beaches
stretching along jungle-lined shores. All of these images fulfill the stereotype of Costa Rica
as a Lilliputian country proffering virginal nature on a Brobdingnagian scale.

These familiar impressions are real, and made
easier to confirm by the nation's size: about
the same as West Virginia or Nova Scotia and
only slightly larger than Switzerland. Costa
Rica has the advantage of being small enough
to explore end to end in a matter of days. A
more slothful pace lets you discover the full
kaleidoscope of wilderness wonders. The
diversity of terrain is remarkable, and the
landscape changes as if on a revolving hinge.

The Central Highlands are ringed by
mountains flanked by row upon row of glossy
green coffee bushes. Guanacaste is cowboy
country and provides a strong sense of the
past, while the Nicoya peninsula beckons with
diamond-dust beaches where turtles come
ashore to lay eggs. The Caribbean appeals for a
distinct culture rooted in a Jamaican heritage.
No less compelling is the rugged Pacific coast,
popular with surfers. The lagoons of the
Northern Lowlands boil with tarpon, and the
remote Talamanca massif is an unexplored
world where jaguars still roam free.

Virtually everywhere you will encounter
wildlife: Costa Rica boasts 5 percent of all the
known species on earth, including more
butterfly species than all Africa. Seeing the
wildlife is easy. About 25 percent of the
country is protected in wildlife reserves or
national parks. Local entrepreneurs have been
inventive in finding ways to make wildlife
viewing easy. The country boasts scores of
serpentariums, butterfly farms, and elevated
walkways through the rain-forest canopy. You
could spend a lifetime *oohing* and *aahing* over
the exotic flora and fauna.

Costa Rica, the most homogeneous society
in Central America, is set apart from its neighbors by its lack of indigenous culture. Visitors
will find no Teotihuacans, Tuxmels, or Tikals,
although Monumento Nacional Guayabo

continues to be excavated from the jungle and
promises to elevate Costa Rica's archaeological
standing. As capital cities go, San José is small
fry, but it boasts art museums and some phe-
nomenal gold and jade museums. It has
improved vastly in recent years, with a vibrant
night scene that is beginning to make even
sophisticates sit up and take notice.

Name your adventure! Costa Rica has
blossomed as a center for active pursuits from
angling to white-water rafting. A ten-day
highlights of Costa Rica itinerary might read
like a wish-list of tropical treats, beginning
perhaps with a birding trip in the Central
Highlands followed by an aquatic jungle
journey in Parque Nacional Tortuguero, a dip
in steaming hot springs at Volcán Arenal, hiking in Reserva Biológica del Bosque Nuboso
de Monteverde, a visit to Playa Grande to see
marine turtles nesting, a nature walk at
Manuel Antonio, whale-watching south of
Uvita, and ending with scuba diving off the
Península de Osa. Phew! What a tour! And yet
you would have only scratched at the surface.

TICOS

Costa Ricans—*los Costarricenses*, or *ticos*—are
unique on the isthmus. They know it, and are
proud of a distinct identity that owes much to
this country's relative prosperity and stability
in a region beset by poverty and turmoil.
Tenaciously proud of their country, ticos cling
to tradition.

Costa Rica's original inhabitants were the
two hundred thousand or so indigenous
peoples organized in disparate tribes. Most of
these peoples rapidly succumbed to disease
and the ruthless ways of 16th-century Spanish

**An indicator of geological youth, volcanoes
provide a dramatic backdrop to Costa Rica.**

conquistadors and were reduced to survivalist status. Whereas in neighboring countries Spaniards intermixed with the native peoples producing a large mixed blood population, Costa Rica, largely devoid of an indigenous base, has remained primarily European.

The early Spanish colonialists who came in search of gold and, frustrated, settled the Central Valley were joined, from the 18th century, by other European immigrants, notably Germans and Swiss peasant farmers who began to arrive in larger numbers in the 19th century, along with Italians, as the boom in coffee took hold. Widely dispersed in the countryside, they were quickly assimilated into the mainstream Spanish-speaking tico culture. On the Caribbean, African slaves had intermarried with Native Americans as early as the 16th century, resulting in mixed-blood Moskitos. Beginning in the 1870s, about 11,000 English-speaking Jamaicans also came as contract labor; they put down roots in the

Dominoes is an all-male pastime in Costa Rica's macho society.

Caribbean Lowlands and have managed to affirm their own colorful Afro-Caribbean identities. "White" highlanders looked down literally and figuratively upon their darker brethren; it was only in 1949 that blacks were granted citizenship and legally permitted to travel to and take work in the highlands.

Recent decades have witnessed a large influx of North Americans (around 35,000) seeking to retire in the sun, predominantly around Escazú, Santa Ana, and Alajuela.

Nicaraguans and other Central American refugees (around 250,000, about 6 percent of Costa Rica's population of 3.96 million) have arrived in the wake of warfare in their own countries, causing resentment among Costa Ricans. Easily recognized by their dark skin and Native American features, Nicaraguan refugees are treated with a general contempt

by their color- and class-conscious host culture. Most recently, French and Italians have begun to arrive and are primarily settling around the Pacific beaches.

WHAT MAKES TICOS TICK

The evolution of *criollo* (locally born) society differed markedly from that of neighboring lands, characterized by feudal land ownership and serfdom. In Costa Rica, the neglected settlers tilled their own lands and were equalized as peasant farmers, called *hermanticos* (little brothers) the name given to fellow citizens by the ruling cliques, who shared hardships and destitution (in 1719, the governor of Costa Rica complained that he, too, had to till his own land). In time, they became known by the diminutive: *tico*. Cut off from most outside influence by the forbidding terrain, they began to develop distinct traits—not least *ticismos*, a unique vocabulary and slang, and a profound aversion to conflict. The peaceable Costa

Rican way is based on compromise and a desire to please, known as *quedar bien* ("to be appealing"), using charm and humor and, often, avoidance. These sometimes surface-thin courtesies are endearing. But the temporizing ticos know that promises should never be taken as such. Regional blood runs thick. Frustration and resentment get bottled up and find their outlets in this otherwise pacific society in drunkenness, lunacy on the roads, and surreptitious acts of revenge.

The Basílica de Nuestra Señora de los Angeles in Cartago

Although tico society is not fraught with the tensions of neighboring nations, Costa Rica is far from egalitarian. It is riddled with elitist ways. "Whiteness" is considered an ideal, and many urbanites and members of the San José-based social elite look down on *campesinos* (peasants). Nonetheless, while 51 percent of the population is urban, the vast

majority of ticos retain ties to the land; Costa Rica has the highest rural population density in Latin America. The vast majority of rural folk live a simple life, tending coffee and cows in the highlands or as *vaqueros* (cowboys) in Guanacaste, where everyday life evokes the cowboy spirit. Tico society is far from urbane: The only true city is San José, the capital, which exudes the feel of an overgrown provincial town. Most other towns are regional market centers with their own subtle charm.

Standards of living

Costa Rica's annual per capita income in 2003 was $4,193, and its standard of living is exemplary in a region racked by destitution and disease. Both life expectancy and infant mortality are on a par with developed nations. The population enjoys free, albeit much-burdened, public education, and decent albeit inefficient health care, paid for by none-too-progressive taxation. The telecommunications system is the equal of anywhere in South America. The

average tico lives thriftily in a modest sized home with a small garden patch. But the regional disparities are great; the average income in the Northern Lowlands is less than 20 percent of the national average. About 20 percent of the population are *marginados* who live in humbling poverty, usually in wood-and-adobe huts in the countryside or on the fringes of the towns, in slum shacks hammered together from corrugated metal sheets and refuse.

Cattle are the lifeblood of Costa Rica's seasonally dry northwest region.

Indigenous peoples today

Costa Rica has around 40,000 indigenous people in a population of 3.96 million; about 1 percent of the total. The Indigenous Bill of 1977 guaranteed the eight indigenous tribes rights to self-government on their lands in which the government held title in trust. Today they live a reclusive, marginalized existence and are widely dispersed on 12 indigenous reserves in the Talamancas and the rugged mountains of the Pacific Southwest. Only in 1992 did the indigenous peoples receive citizenship, and they were permitted to vote for the first time only in 1994.

While the campesino views himself as a pioneer and the forest as a resource to be conquered, indigenous people see themselves as custodians of the forest and its interrelated inhabitants. Native Americans live in simple homesteads scattered around the reservations, much of it low quality land. The menfolk hunt in the forests and work the land, growing bananas, beans, citrus fruits, coca, and corn; and drink home-brewed *chica* (beer made of yucca or corn). The communities struggle to preserve vital elements of their traditional culture. Most wear Western clothes and speak Spanish. Few know their native language. Alcoholism and other social problems are rife. Their cultural integrity is further eroded by the efforts of missionaries working to break down their traditional religious beliefs.

Politically disempowered, these groups remain suspicious of outsiders and feel intense dissatisfaction with the National Commission for Indigenous Affairs (CONA), which has responsibility for their welfare. Despite the passage of laws intended to safeguard their heritage, the government continues to issue rights to powerful mining and logging entities that whittle away at the Native Americans' land. While not subject to the systematic persecution of Guatemala's indigenous peoples, Costa Rica's Native Americans suffer ongoing rights violations. Attempts have been made in recent years to provide greater self-sufficiency, including the first Native American bank in 1994, and an experimental iguana farm.

The Bribrí, who inhabit the mountains inland of the southern Caribbean, welcome visitors on a limited basis. Other groups are turning to tourism as interest in indigenous culture revives, although a permit is required from CONA to enter some reserves. A revival in crafts is nascent, and women of the Boruca and other tribes of the Pacific Southwest still dress in traditional garments. A renaissance of pride among the Chorotega of Nicoya finds its outlet in faithfully reproduced ceramics produced by the villagers of Guaitíl.

GOVERNMENT & POLITICS

The 1949 Constitution defines Costa Rica as a democratic republic run by an elected president and a 19-member cabinet, called the Council of Government. A president must be a secular citizen and traditionally could only serve one term (as of 2003, a president may serve two terms). Power rests with the Legislative Assembly, composed of 57 elected members *(diputados)* representing the country's seven provinces. Voting is compulsory for citizens aged 18–70 (though there are no consequences for those who choose not to vote). Elections are held on the first Sunday in February, every four years, and are overseen by a Special Electoral Tribunal whose members are elected by the Supreme Court judges and serve staggered six-year terms. Diputados are elected by proportional representation, with seats allocated according to the votes for each party. They serve four-year terms and may not be elected for consecutive terms. There is no higher chamber of review. The legislature's right to veto presidential decisions is a source of friction that occasionally results in rule by presidential decree. The Assembly sits in a handsome Moorish building overlooking the Plaza de la Democracía, in San José.

Costa Rica is divided into seven provinces: Alajuela, Cartago, Guanacaste, Heredia, Limón, Puntarenas, and San José. Each is run by a governor appointed by the president, while municipal councils run the day to day affairs of 421 *distritos* (districts) that make up the 81 *cantones* (counties) into which the provinces are divided.

Parties & personalities

Costa Rica traditionally alternates presidents every election, switching back and forth between candidates for the two great rival parties: the National Liberation Party (PLN) and Social Christian Unity Party (PUSC); victors, however, rarely win by more than 2 or 3 percent. The left-leaning PLN inclines toward welfare-state liberalism. The PUSC is made up of progressive conservatives who support business interests. The PLN traditionally holds a majority in the Legislative Assembly. Both parties are clannish.

Though party affiliations are defended fiercely, this has more to do with personal interest than philosophical sentiment. Costa

San José supporters greet President Abel Pacheco in 2002.

Rica's political process is mired in cronyism and it pays to show loyalty to one party or the other: Favors and contracts are dispensed liberally by the victorious side. Bribery and corruption are rife in a country whose politics has been dominated since independence by a small number of families. President Abel Pacheco (2002–) and his three predecessors have all been tainted by corruption scandals, and two—Miguel Ángel Rodríguez and Rafael Ángel Calderón—were jailed.

Public employees—25 percent of the work force—form the most powerful interest group; the well-paid bureaucracy is a crippling burden on the economy. Says one ticoism, "The government is a cash cow with a thousand teats and everyone wants a teat to suck." The interminable bureaucratic process has given rise to a whole class of workers called *despachantes*, who tackle the bureaucracy on behalf of others.

Pride in neutrality
Costa Rica declared neutrality in 1949 and has no armed forces. A heavily armed National Guard looks after the nation's security, backed by various specialized paramilitary police units. Pride in neutrality is reflected in the ticos' passive psyche. They not easily aroused to strong emotion or political passions about issues: "Don Pepe" Figueres (1906–1990), leader of the 1948 revolution, accused them of being as "domesticated as sheep." Issues get resolved by consensus—or, as frequently, get shelved to avoid conflict and thus fester unresolved. Harmony is more highly valued than discord, even at the cost of irresolution.

Post-independence politics has been marked by liberalism and stability. The country has had its fair share of *caudillos* (dictatorial leaders), but most redeemed themselves as proponents of progressive reform, and only three presidents have been military men. Ticos pride themselves on the "cleanliness" of their political process. Election day is a national holiday, which ticos turn into a grand fiesta. Elections are not marred by the violence and mayhem that has traditionally accompanied polling in neighboring countries (during elections, control of the police force reverts to the Special Electoral Tribunal to protect constitutional guarantees). Costa Rica's mainstream media is conservative. ∎

Food & drink

COSTA RICA BOASTS FINE DINING, CONCENTRATED OVERWHELMINGLY IN San José, where the restaurant scene plays all the notes on the international scale. Beyond the capital city, however, ticos are timid diners whose affinities are closely attached to homey peasant fare.

The ubiquitous staple of rice and black beans—*gallo pinto*— forms the backbone of local cuisines, or *comida típica*. Even breakfast, typically gallo pinto with scrambled eggs, isn't exempt from this rule. Served with fried plantains (Costa Ricans are fond of fried foods) and a basic salad of tomatoes and cabbage, gallo pinto becomes a cheap *casado*, or set special, sometimes served with *sopa negra*, a bean broth. Roast pork is the main meat staple. Both it and chicken are often roasted over coffee wood *(a la leña)* which gives it a smoky flavor. Many restaurants serve steaks *(lomito)*. Chewy is the rule, and rarely do beef dishes come up to par for North American tastes, although *lomito encebollado,* steak marinated with local Linzano sauce, is often delicious. Seafoods are relatively scarce away from the coasts, though shrimp and lobster dishes are widely available. In San José the fish of choice is *corvina* (sea bass), usually fried with garlic *(ajo)*. At seaside resorts you'll also find dolphin fish *(dorado)*, swordfish, and snapper *(pargo)*, almost always fried and served with white rice.

Corn finds its way into tortillas and corn pancakes called *chorreados,* and *tamales,* stuffed cornmeal pastries wrapped and baked

in corn leaf. Jalapeños and other hot spices are rarely used. Nor are vegetables, though they find their way into soups and stews, such as *olla de carne,* a meat and vegetable stew of potato, corn, yucca and gourds. The favored vegetable is plantain (a relative of the banana) served fried with almost any meal.

The Caribbean coast has its own unique flavor, one steeped in spices and coconut milk. Nowhere else in Costa Rica will you find *ackee* (a yellow fruit resembling scrambled eggs) and salted codfish on the breakfast menu.

Everywhere, roadside stalls are cornucopias of tropical fruits: mangoes, melons, papayas, pineapples, and many you may not have heard of, such as the *carambeloa* (starfruit), *marañon* (cashew fruit), and *pejibayes* (like tiny coconuts), all of which find their way into *frescas,* fruit blended with ice, water, or milk, and sugar. Milk is used in cheeses such as the mild white *queso blanco,* which frequently finds its way into deserts. *Tres leches,* a three layered custard flan is the national dessert, best followed by espresso coffee, drunk thick and sugared. *Café con leche* is coffee served with hot milk 50:50.

Other dishes to try include:

Arregladas: greasy puff pastries filled with beef, chicken or cheese.

Dulche de leche: a boiled milk and sugar syrup.

Empañada: turnovers filled with beans, meat and potatoes.

Palmito: soft heart of the *pejibaye* palm (not the fruit of the same name), popular in salads.

Costa Ricans are beer drinkers, and local lager-style brews (e.g. Imperial and Bavaria) are perfectly suited to the tropical climate.

Below: Campesino cooking forms the backbone of local fare.

Right: A supposed source of virility, turtle eggs are downed in many bars.

Bocas—snacks such as *ceviche* (marinated and spiced seafood) and thirst-inducing deep-fried *chicharrones* (pork rinds)—are usually served in bars. Wine is not popular, and imported wines, generally found in upscale restaurants, are expensive. The working man's drink is a potent clear white spirit called *guaro,* worth trying once. Local liquors are best avoided, although coffee liqueurs make good souvenirs. ■

Costa Rican history

WHEN CONQUISTADORS FIRST STEPPED ASHORE TO SUBJUGATE THE isthmus of Central America and claim it for Spain, the region was already a complex mosaic of cultures. The term Costa Rica first entered the European lexicon in 1522 when Captain Gil González Davila (died 1526) set out from Panama with a colonizing fleet to settle the region then known as Veragua. González and his men found Indian dignitaries adorned with gold, for which the conquistador coined the term "Rich Coast." Compared to its northern neighbors, however, the land was relatively sparsely populated; perhaps no more than 100,000 inhabitants occupied the densely forested and mountainous region at the time of first European contact.

FIRST PEOPLES

Little is known of the potpourri of indigenous people, who belonged to as many as 25 distinct and antagonistic groups that followed their own ways of life. The earliest occupants arrived from the north around 10,000 B.C., rather late in the day of human advancement following the first crossing by Hominoids of the Bering Strait around 60,000 B.C. Although these peoples came under the influence of the high civilizations of the Andes and Mesoamerica, the region remained a buffer zone and one whose meager population never evolved either the complex sociopolitical structures nor the monumental architecture of societies to the north and south. The peoples never unified to form a kingdom but remained under chieftains (caciques) who ruled over competing areas and whose names were adopted by the Spanish for each tribe.

People of the Northwest

The most developed group were the Choro-tega, who occupied today's Guanacaste following their arrival in the region around A.D. 500, displacing earlier and much simpler societies of which little is known. The Chorotega were influenced by the more advanced cultures of Mexico and Guatemala, initially the Olmec, and later by the Aztec and Maya, who dispersed south, imposing their culture on less advanced peoples. The name chorotega means "people who escaped." The details are shrouded in mystery.

The Chorotega lived in longhouses of wood and thatch inhabited by entire clans and centered on stone plazas where religious and civic ceremonies were held. The Chorotega constructed irrigation ditches and evolved an advanced agricultural society based predominantly on corn. They also cultivated cotton that they wove into dyed clothing. Among Costa Rica's indigenous peoples, only the Chorotega had a written language, and a calendar, both of Mayan origin. They spoke Nahua, an Aztec tongue and shared in common with their northern ancestors a rigid hierarchical system that included nobility and slavery, and a religious system based on bloodletting that included virgin sacrifice every full moon. The Chorotega were also noted for their distinctive ceramics, including phallic figurines, and anthropomorphic motifs of jaguars, frogs, and snakes in striking black, white, and red coloring. They also traded for jade with their northern neighbors and worked it into exquisite figurines using a string-saw technique.

The Highland cultures

The Corobicís, who lived in small bands as hunter-gatherers and agriculturalists, were the predominant group of the Central Highlands (Meseta Central). They traded gold with lowland tribes and became superb goldsmiths, leaving a legacy of exquisite amulets and statuettes depicting sacred idols, such as frogs. Although most groups lived in stockaded villages called palenques, the Corobicís built the only pre-Columbian town of note to have been discovered in Costa Rica: Guayabo, at the base of Volcán Turrialba. The settlement, which featured cobbled streets (calzadas), burial mounds, aqueducts and stone cisterns,

Lighting a votive candle, an adherent affirms her Catholic faith, which lies at the core of Costa Rica's culture.

dates from around A.D. 1000 and may have had a population of one thousand people. It was mysteriously abandoned about A.D. 1400.

The Cabécar and Guaymí inhabited the Talamancas further south and lived primarily as hunter-gatherers. Shamans were important in these societies, which lived in harmony with their environment and revered the jaguar.

The Coastal tribes

The Boruca, Chibcha, and Diquis in the southwest, and the Bribrí, Caribes, and KéKöLdi on the Caribbean shore, drew their influences from South American cultures. They were semi-nomadic hunters and fishermen and supplemented the bounty of forest and sea with yucca, squash, and tubers. The preeminent group, the Diquis of the Pacific Southwest, shared with the Chorotega a tradition of ritual sacrifice and slavery.

About 1000 B.C., the Diquis began crafting lithic spheres called *bolas*, often of immense size, perhaps for religious purposes. A major change in the culture occurred between A.D. 500 and A.D. 800 as a result of contact with the seafaring peoples of Colombia or Peru. At about this time, the Diquis began fashioning gold figurines and soon became skilled gold-smiths, making use of gold from the Península de Osa. It appears that there was little cultural exchange between these mainly matriarchal groups, who remained in a state of internecine warfare. Both men and women of the Boruca were warriors.

FIRST EUROPEANS

Christopher Columbus, the first European to reach Costa Rica, anchored off the Caribbean coast on September 18, 1502, during his fourth voyage to the New World. The Genoese explorer recorded signs of vast wealth in the region he called La Huerta ("The Garden"), creating high hopes for this newfound land.

The first attempt at colonization, in 1506, proved disastrous. Ferdinand of Spain appointed Diego de Nicuesa as governor of Veragua and financed an expedition to settle the Caribbean coast and discover the source of the Indian gold. Alas, the governor foundered off the coast of Panama and he and his troops were forced to hack their way north through the tormenting jungle. Their reception was less than welcoming and the expeditionaries were soon repelled by the ferocity of local tribes, sweltering swamps, and diseases—a fate that also awaited Gil González in 1522. After 1513, when Vasco Nuñez de Balboa (1475–1517) discovered the Pacific Ocean, the Spaniards focused their explorations along that shore. In 1524, Francisco Fernández de Córdoba established the first colony on the Pacific coast, at Bruselas, near present-day Puntarenas, but it too succumbed. New attempts at coloniza-tion were made, but the arrivistes failed miserably, driven one and all to despair and decimation by the cruel hardships of the New World.

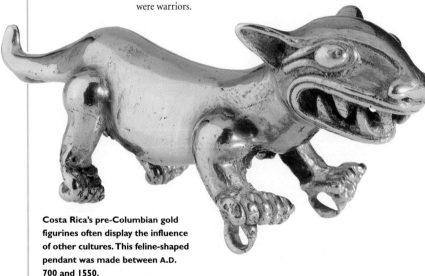

Costa Rica's pre-Columbian gold figurines often display the influence of other cultures. This feline-shaped pendant was made between A.D. 700 and 1550.

Destruction of local culture

The Spaniards were not on a holy mission: The conquistadors had set out in quest of gold and silver. In 1532 Pizarro found it in Peru and, a decade later, Cortes discovered the vast silver veins of Mexico. The Spanish found no source of gold in Costa Rica, so plundered the gold reserves of the indigenous peoples then began to enslave them to work in the foreign mines. Victims of the Spaniards' ruthless forays, the once-noble Indian populations of Costa Rica began their decline.

In 1543, the Captaincy-General of Guatemala was created incorporating all the lands from the Isthmus of Tehuantepec, in the Yucatán, to the swampy lowlands of southern Panama. Most of Costa Rica's indigenous peoples had by then been conquered, though the region languished as the Spanish consolidated their hold further north. In 1562, conquistador Juan Vásquez de Coronado (1523–1565) was appointed governor of Costa Rica. He established a settlement in the cool highlands and named it El Guarco (later Cartago)—Costa Rica's first capital. Although Coronado was a relatively benign conquistador, over ensuing decades, large land grants—*encomiendas*—were issued to Spanish soldiers, who received rights of vassalage over the indigenous peoples, who withered under forced labor. European diseases—smallpox, measles, tuberculosis—against which they had no resistance hastened their demise (the "Great Pandemic" of 1610–60 cut through the population like a scythe). The survivors fled to the interior mountains.

Spanish settlers found themselves without labor to work the rich soils. Conditions were thus lacking for the development of the feudal system imposed by the Spaniards elsewhere in the New World, based on large haciendas worked by slave labor. An exception was lowland Greater Nicoya (today's Guanacaste), which was administered as part of Nicaragua and where cattle haciendas evolved, worked by enslaved Chorotega. Without gold, which had already been stolen and shipped to Spain, or other items of value for trade with the homeland, Costa Rica's settlers were forced to sow their own lands for a livelihood. The region became a backwater full of poor farmers foiled in their hopes of becoming nobles.

Settlement

Settlements were meager and modest. When Volcán Irazú erupted in 1723, destroying Cartago, the lowly capital consisted of a single church and a few score houses made of adobe.

By the early 18th century, however, Costa Rica had evolved a viable agricultural base and the population expanded. Other towns began to take shape: in 1717, Heredia; in 1737, San José; and in 1782, Alajuela. The population remained far removed from central authority

In September 1513, Spanish conquistador Vasco Nuñez de Balboa was the first European to see the Pacific Ocean.

and evolved free of the rigid social and color distinctions that developed in neighboring countries, where miscegenation between Spaniard and Indian produced large mixed blood *(mestizo)* populations. In Costa Rica, intermixing of the races was limited, and this resulted in in large numbers of poor white farmers and the absence of a resentful mestizo class subject to the abuses of the established white aristocracy.

On the Caribbean Lowlands, a separate

cultural scene had evolved. English, Dutch, and French pirates and merchantmen had for three centuries raided and traded along the shores of the "Spanish Main." Piracy had driven the Spanish to close their port at Puerto Limón in 1665, choking legal trade and fostering a rise in smuggling and the evolution of English-run ports for precious hardwoods beyond the limits of Spanish authority.

The Cinderella colony received little official attention and never having felt the stern hand of colonial rule, remained aloof from the bitter independence movement sweeping through Spain's American empire by the close of the 18th century.

INDEPENDENCE & WEALTH

When independence for Central America came on September 15, 1821, on the coattails of Mexico, it took a full month for the news to reach Costa Rica, where a provisional council elected to accede to the new nation of Mexico.

Time of turmoil

It was a time of confusion. Throughout the isthmus, battles raged between disparate interests competing to shape national boundaries. In 1823, the four provinces of Guatemala, El Salvador, Honduras, and Nicaragua formed a federation—the United Provinces of Central America—with its capital in Guatemala City and autonomy for individual states (Panama became a part of Colombia).

The decision sparked a brief civil war in Costa Rica: The conservative leaders of Cartago and Heredia favored maintaining alignment with Mexico; the more progressive gentry of Alajuela and San José were federalists. On April 5, 1823, tensions boiled over into a battle at Ochomongo in which the federalists were victorious. Costa Rica then joined the United Provinces.

It was a poor fit. Central America descended into a cycle of civil wars and rule by repressive *caudillos* (strong-men leaders) representing the interests of elites. In Costa Rica, however, institutional rule had never been consolidated and the gains of economic prosperity were shared among a relatively classless society. Democratic institutions emerged that permitted resolution of social tensions through reform.

Consolidation & coffee

In 1824, Costa Rica named teacher Juan Mora Fernández (1784–1854) its first head of state. He established a trend for progressive, liberal political leadership that would characterize the nation as it evolved apart from its reactionary neighbors. Internal rivalry resurfaced in 1835 when forces from the three subordinate towns attacked San José, which won the War of the League and consolidated its status as Costa Rica's capital city. Tensions within the United Provinces resulted in its dissolution in 1839, one year after Costa Rica's benevolent dictator Braulio Carrillo (1800–1845)—best known for establishing civil legal codes and an orderly public administration—had withdrawn from the federation and declared independence.

At the time, coffee drinking was all the rage in Europe. Costa Rica's pattern of rural small-holdings combined with conditions of climate and terrain in the Meseta Central proved conducive to coffee cultivation, which Mora and Carrillo had sponsored by issuing land grants, luring European immigrants who brought fashionable liberal ideals. By 1830 high-grade coffee—*grano de oro* (grain of gold)—was already the nation's prime export. Coffee income was used to prettify San José with neo-classic buildings. Earnings were spread throughout the farming community, but the immensely profitable coffee trade coalesced in the hands of a few "coffee barons"—*cafeteleros*—who began to dominate the political scene. In 1849 they ousted the nation's enlightened first president, José María Castro (1818–1892), replacing him with one of their own, Juan Rafael Mora (1814–1860).

Invasion & militarism

Mora served two terms marked by economic prosperity. His second was highlighted by an unlikely invasion. U.S. President James Buchanan wanted to build a canal across Nicaragua, whose government was charging what to the U.S. government appeared an exorbitant fee. Backed by Buchanan, a brash Tennessean named William Walker (1824–1860) landed in Nicaragua in June 1855 with a band of mercenaries. He toppled the government, established himself as president, and in November 1856, invaded Guanacaste. President Mora was victorious over Walker's

The coming of the railroad in the 1800s boosted the fortunes of the banana industry. By the end of that century, Costa Rica produced more bananas than anywhere else in the world.

motley toughs at La Casona (in today's Parque Nacional Santa Rosa). Walker fled to Rivas in Nicaragua, where a Costa Rican drummer boy called Juan Santamaría gave his life torching the fort where Walker was hiding, earning a posthumous distinction as a national hero.

The war ushered in a period of militarism as politically ambitious cafeteleros used self-styled generals to attain power. In 1870, General Tomás Guardia (1831–1882) seized power as a reformer. He established a viable central government, tamed the cafeteleros and their military cronies, used coffee-tax revenues to fund civic construction, and promoted a railroad linking San José with the Atlantic to facilitate the transshipment of coffee. The railroad, built against almighty odds at the cost of 4,000 lives (mostly imported Chinese and Jamaican labor) and completed in 1890, was the accomplishment of Minor Keith (1848–1929), a determined North American who planted bananas on concessions wrangled from the government. By 1899 Costa Rica was the world's leading banana producer. Keith's

company evolved into the United Fruit Company, an overlord of Central American economies in ensuing decades.

Democracy affirmed

In 1889, President Bernardo Soto (1854–1931) stood for reelection. The nation's first honest election with popular participation produced an upset victory for Soto's opponent. When Soto refused to step down, the people took to the streets and enforced their decision. The democratic process was still tenuous and marred by presidents who whittled away at the Constitution or exiled rivals to extend their rule. The army remained in its barracks—until 1917, when President Alfredo González Flores (1877–1962) proposed a system of progressive taxation and the cafeteleros prompted Minister of War Federico Tinoco (1868–1931) to seize power. Tinoco was a bullying dictator who suspended the constitution. But Costa Rica's educated populace would no longer accept oligarchic caudillos. Tinoco was ousted peacefully by a demonstration led by women and high-school students, ushering in another period of peaceful liberal leaders. Democracy had been affirmed.

CIVIL WAR & REFORM

Old-style paternalism had failed to alleviate the social ills of the relatively prosperous nation. Many people lived in destitution, a

Three brothers who fought with revolutionary hero José María Figueres meet their mother in Cartago.

situation worsened by the Great Depression in the wake of the Wall Street crash of 1929, and by the stranglehold that the United Fruit Company—by now a powerful force—held over its workers, fueling a virulent four-year strike initiated in 1934 against "Big Fruit."

In 1925, *sigatoka* (a fungal disease) and Panama disease had begun to devastate the banana plantations, and many Afro-Caribbeans, facing unemployment and starvation, turned to cacao and fishing; this was the beginning of desperately hard times for the Caribbean region. A series of illegal labor strikes paralyzed Costa Rica. Change was needed.

Calderón sets the stage

It came in 1940s, when Rafael Angel Calderón Guardia (1900–1970) became president and promulgated a series of much-needed reforms that included progressive taxation, a social security system, and a Labor Code that established workers' rights. Calderón, a deeply religious man, earned the ire of the rural-based upper classes, including cafeteleros of German origin who resented government seizure of their land when Costa Rica declared war on Nazi Germany. Calderón's massive public spending programs coincided with a stymied economy that combined to produce rapid inflation, whittling away his support with the poor. When the 1944 election came around, he wed himself to an unholy alliance with the Communists and Catholic church. The triumvirate formed the Social Christian Unity Party (PUSC). Meanwhile, labor leaders made an unlikely pact with the business and rural elites and, joined by urban intellectuals, formed the Social Democratic Party.

Calderón's hand-picked successor, Teodoro Picado (1900–1960), served an uneventful four-year term (1944–48) and in 1948, Calderón stood again for election. Tensions were rife; violence broke out on the streets. Unexpectedly, a third-party contender, Otilio Ulante (1891–1973), won the election. Calderón claimed fraud. That night, the building holding the ballot papers went up in flames, and the Calderonista congress annulled the election. On March 10, 1948, Costa Rica erupted in civil war. The truth of ensuing events is mired in mythology.

War of National Liberation

José María Figueres, an ambitious revolutionary, later affectionately known as "Don Pepe," had been planning a coup for years and had been exiled to Mexico in 1942 for his firebrand ways. He was permitted to return in 1944, but immediately launched a bid for the violent overthrow of the government. He founded a ragtag army—the National Liberation Armed Forces—that trained at his mountain farm in Santa María de Dota. The election debacle was a godsend. Figueres' insurrectionists swept down off the mountain and quickly took Cartago and Puerto Limón. The ill-trained government army of 500 men was armed by Nicaragua's right-wing Somoza regime and included machete-wielding banana workers. For 40 days the two forces skirmished, leaving more than 2,000 (mostly civilians) dead. As Figueres' forces prepared to strike at San José, the government's paltry standing army surrendered.

Figueres established the grandiloquently named Founding Junta of the Second Republic. Calderón was exiled, while many of his followers were executed along with leading leftists and labor leaders. Then Figueres surprised everyone by disbanding the army and declaring neutrality. He saw himself as a crusader against Communism and corruption. He banned the Communists, drew up a new constitution, and launched a whirlwind of social reform. He abrogated Costa Rica's apartheid laws, gave women the vote, nation-alized the banks and insurance companies, and established presidential term limits and an independent body—the Electoral Tribunal—to oversee future elections. Then he handed power to Otilio Ulate as had been agreed and stepped down. "Don Pepe" was hailed as a national hero and went on to win two terms as president (1953–57 and 1970–74) as leader of the PLN, which he founded in 1951. Figueres earned the wrath of his long-time enemy, Nicaraguan dictator "Tacho" Somoza. Their two nations had a brief skirmish in 1955, when Nicaraguan troops attacked Guanacaste, meeting a pathetic demise at La Casona.

MODERN TIMES

Immediate post civil-war politics were marked by political stability and economic prosperity. PLN governments followed conservative, pro-business agendas, while the welfare state was vastly expanded by the Social Democrats, until it reached every sector of society and subsidies consumed 40 percent of the national budget. By the 1970s, 25 percent of the work force was employed by the state. Economic stagnation set in. A massive currency devaluation added to woes caused by crippling inflation and by the devastating fall in worldwide prices of coffee, bananas, and sugar, Costa Rica's three largest exports.

The economic crisis was worsened by the Nicaraguan crisis, which consumed the region for one long, dark decade.

War & peace

During the 1970s, Nicaragua's Sandinista National Liberation Front (FSLN) launched a war to topple the right-wing Somoza regime. The government of Costa Rican President Rodrigo Carazo (born 1926) permitted the Sandinistas to set up shop in Costa Rica. When Somoza's air force struck across the

José María "Don Pepe" Figueres, "Savior of the nation," visits his lumber mill. He dis-banded the army in the late 1940s.

border, Carazo tried to close the Sandinistas' camps, but also cut diplomatic relations with Nicaragua and seized the Somoza family's estates in Guanacaste.

On July 19, 1979, the tables turned. The Sandinistas swept into Managua. Right-wing Somoza supporters flooded Costa Rica and found support with wealthy ranchers in Guanacaste. The exiles coalesced to form the Nicaraguan Democratic Front (FDN), better known as the "Contras." Costa Rica's new president, Luís Alberto Monge Álvarez (born 1925), struggled to remain neutral, but the economy was a shambles and the U.S. was pressuring Monge to commit to the Contras.

Soon the CIA was building airstrips and supply bases close to the Nicaraguan border; and U.S. military specialists were militarizing the Costa Rican police forces. The Sandinista air force was bombing Contra bases, and paramilitary groups—supported by right-wingers in Monge's government (1982–86)—were committing acts of domestic terrorism meant to implicate the Sandinistas. Costa Rica was edging dangerously away from neutrality.

In February 1986, a liberal economic lawyer named Oscar Arias Sánchez (born 1914) became president. He kicked out the Contras and worked ceaselessly for peace in the isthmus (El Salvador and Guatemala were also wracked by internal strife). In February 1987, Sánchez presented a peace plan. The Reagan administration tried to nix it. But the five Central American presidents signed up. Sánchez earned the Nobel Prize. In a speech to U.S. Congress, Sánchez announced that the Costa Rican people "are convinced that the risks we run in the struggle for peace will always be less than the irreparable cost of war."

Putting the house in order

The war destabilized Costa Rica. Around 250,000 Nicaraguan refugees had flooded in, draining scarce resources. International confidence had also suffered, resulting in a capital flight and a 60 percent drop in trade. The country was bankrupt

Throughout the 1960s, 1970s, and 1980s, Costa Rica had funded its development through massive loans. In September 1981, Costa Rica became the first country in the world to default on its loans, causing a banking crisis throughout the Americas. By 1989, with a 5 billion dollar national debt, Costa Rica had the dubious distinction of being the world's largest per capita debtor. A stiff dose of economic austerity was needed to put Costa Rica back on course.

In February 1990, Rafael Angel Calderón Fournier (born 1949), a conservative lawyer and son of the reforming president, was inaugurated on the fiftieth anniversary of his

Visitors get a bird's-eye view of Monteverde's rain-forest canopy. Costa Rica has set aside almost 30 percent of its land as parks and preserves.

father's inauguration. He initiated measures to curb Costa Rica's massive deficit and debt. His tenure was marred, in 1991, by a massive earthquake that killed 62 people; and, in 1992, by condemnation in a U.S. law court for Costa Rica's onerous labor practices.

Calderón was succeeded by José María Figueres (born 1954), son of the elder Calderón's nemesis. Under pressure from the International Monetary Fund and World Bank, Figueres continued the austerity program, which was painful for a people used to handouts. With inflation rampant, 100,000 people took to the streets in 1995—the largest demonstration ever in Costa Rica. In July 1996, Hurricane César devastated the region. A summit of Central American leaders in May 1997 provided a ray of sunshine: President Bill Clinton attended, the first U.S. president to visit Costa Rica since John F. Kennedy in 1963.

A series of government scandals tainted Figueres' administration. He was replaced in February 1998 by wealthy businessman Miguel Angel Rodríguez, whose bid for the presidency in 1994 unearthed his own involvement in a tainted-beef scandal. Dr. Abel Pacheco of the center right Social Christian Unity Party was elected president in 2002 in a historic second round presidential election.

Corruption, nepotism, and crime are major concerns. Burglary and petty theft are endemic and, since Noriega's ousting in Panama in 1989, Costa Rica is evolving a reputation as a drug transshipment center.

Despite these problems, the country has managed to avoid sinking into the turmoil that surrounds it, drawing tourists in increasing numbers (tourism is Costa Rica's largest foreign income earner, generating 1.45 billion dollars in 2004, when 1.48 million tourists arrived). Big-name hotels have sprouted on waterfront property, adding a touch of resort life to a destination known primarily for more rugged attractions, notably stupendous scenery, active adventures, exotic flora, and wonderful wildlife.

The country has also proved attractive to high-tech investors, as well as foreign retirees, lured by clean air and political stability. While the early years of the 21st century have seen an economic boom, scandals involving the four most recent presidents have somewhat tainted the gloss. ∎

Land & landscape

MOUNTAINS DOMINATE COSTA RICA, A POCKET-SIZE PRODIGY THAT PACKS a potpourri of other terrains, landscapes, and climates into its 19,652 square miles (50,900 sq km). Nowhere is the country more than 175 miles (280 km) wide, and nowhere more than 300 miles (480 km) north to south—totaling an area equal to three ten-thousandths of the world's land area. Yet Costa Rica seems to contain the entire world within its small compass, whisking the surprised visitor allegorically on a world tour, from cool Swiss alpine forest to steamy Amazonian lowland jungle. A glance at a map explains why. Costa Rica lies at the thread-thin southern end of the Central American isthmus separating two dramatically disparate continents. It is also a land between seas: The Caribbean Sea and Pacific Ocean are separated by a mountain backbone that is still being pushed skyward by awesome tectonic forces that erupt in volcanoes and earthquakes.

A majority of the population lives in the Central Highlands, most within towns that cluster on a temperate plateau, the Meseta Central, that lies within a few hours' drive of beach and ocean. Though the country lies wholly within the tropics, vast extremes of elevation and relief spawn a profusion of climates and microclimates. The result is a spectacular amalgam of vegetation and wildlife. Costa Rica, a meeting point for the biota of North and South America, is crowded with exotic flora and fauna.

THE VOLATILE EARTH

Costa Rica lies at a critical juncture where four of the earth's crustal plates converge and crumple. These plates, interconnected pieces resembling a cracked eggshell, are powered in their jostling movement by currents deep within the earth's molten core and wrestle one another until one or other gives way. Costa Rica sits atop the Caribbean plate. Its arch contestant is the Pacific's Cocos plate, which shoves against it from the east and nosedives beneath it, sparking cataclysmic earthquakes and fueling volcanoes that spew out magma (molten rock) produced by the stupendous friction. The Costa Rican landmass is relatively young—only around three million years ago was it thrust upward from beneath the sea by the Cocos' dynamic burrowing. The tectonic movement has further fractured the earth along fault lines. Mega-quakes frequently rattle the country, such as the 7.4 shocker that struck on April 22, 1991, heaving the Caribbean shoreline upward and leaving coral reefs high and dry.

VOLCANIC VERTEBRAE

Costa Rica's lush green shawl drapes itself over a spine of volcanoes that march south from the Nicaraguan border, studding the landscape with perfect cones that look as if they've fallen from their own postcards. These volcanoes are part of the 9,000-mile (14,500 km) chain of mountains that runs along the western edge of the Americas from Alaska to Tierra del Fuego. Of the 42 active volcanoes in Central America, Costa Rica has seven. These are found in three distinct ranges, or *cordilleras*, arrayed northwest to southeast: the Cordillera de Guanacaste, the Cordillera de Tilarán, and the Cordillera Central, the latter a string of four volcanoes—Poás, Barva, Irazú, and Turrialba—that encircle the Meseta Central. Set between the Guanacaste and Tilarán chains is windswept Lake Arenal.

Many of Costa Rica's threatening giants are ephemerally user-friendly: At two of them, Poás and Irazú, visitors can drive to the crater rims and peer into the bubbling bowels. Both Poás and Irazú recently awoke from their slumbers and periodically boil over in small but intense eruptions. At restless Poás, a mini-volcano is being birthed within a mile-wide caldera—the largest collapsed crater in the Western Hemisphere. On Rincón de la Vieja and Miravalles, in Guanacaste, steaming vents have been harnessed for geothermal electricity. The most sensational sight is youthful Volcán Arenal, an archetypal cone that thrills visitors with almost daily eruptions (a Hollywood

Gazing into the active crater of Poás volcano is an awesome experience.

favorite, it starred most recently in Michael Crichton's *Congo).* On upper slopes, mists veil cloud forest, as at Monteverde which encompasses eight ecological zones.

MESETA CENTRAL

Around two-thirds of Costa Rica's population lives in the Meseta Central, a huge scalloped valley that basks in eternal springtime in the heart of the temperate Central Highlands at an average elevation of 5,000 feet (1,524 m)

above sea level. The plateau measures 50 miles (80 km) across and 25 miles (40 km) north-south and nestles beneath the gentle volcanic slopes of the Cordillera Central to the north and the dauntingly sheer, forest-clad slopes of the Talamancas. It is divided in two by a low range of hills, the Cerro de la Carpintera. San José and its *nouveau riche* suburbs dominate the larger and more populous level valley to the west of the hills, where most of the nation's major towns are found; the smaller

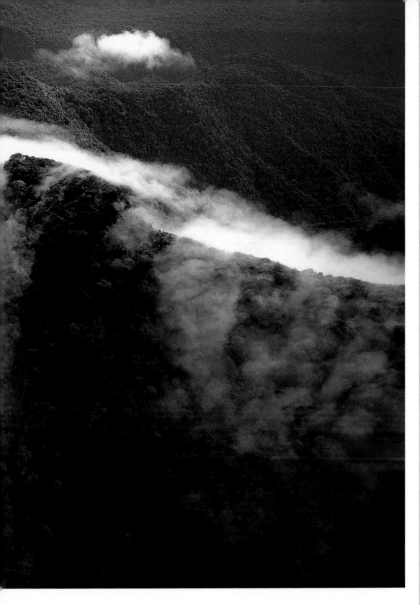

Cartago valley slopes gently eastward before falling steeply through the valley of the Río Reventazón—very popular with white-water rafters—to the Caribbean Lowlands.

The climate is idyllic. Sunshine pours down year-round (temperatures average a balmy 74° F, 23° C), combining with reliable and modest rainfall and rich volcanic soils to metamorphose the Meseta into the rich bread-basket of the nation. Sugarcane dominates the valley floor, rippling in the constant light

Clouds shroud a ridgetop on Volcán Irazú, blanketed in dense, tangled cloud forest.

breeze like folds of green silk. The lower slopes are intensely farmed for coffee, with dairy farms, horticultural gardens and strawberry patches situated on the cooler, higher slopes that gradually merge into lush montane forests where eco-minded visitors can hike through cloud forests on the flanks of mist-shrouded volcanoes.

TALAMANCA MASSIF

Massive, dauntingly rugged, the Talamancas induce humility. They dominate the southern half of the country and consist of a chain of mountains extending along a northwest-southeast axis from the Meseta Central into Panama. Here are Costa Rica's highest peaks. Rising to 12,526 feet (3,818 m) atop Cerro Chirripó, the Talamancas separate the Caribbean from the Pacific. These great *cerros*, or peaks, are folded in serrated pleats with vast valleys nestling in between. Moisture-laden winds racing in from the east dump their cargo and bruised clouds swirl ominously about windswept summits so cold that trees cower. Towering and sodden, they have been little explored although cross-hatched by pathways known only to Indians who live in remote reserves on the lower slopes. A lush green shawl drapes over this rugged spine. Much of the velveteen jungle is protected within Parque Internacional La Amistad—a

refuge for endangered wildlife. The montane forest merges with cloud forest on higher slopes, where stunted dwarf forests meld into *páramo*, high mountain grasslands.

PACIFIC NORTHWEST

Costa Rica's dry quarter defies the image of Costa Rica the green. Humpbacked, floppy-eared Zebu cattle munch savannas that shimmer gold in the searing sun, and cowboys register a poignant effect on the landscape.

A chromatic sunset gilds the roughly hewn Pacific coast at Dominical.

The region, lowland Guanacaste, averages less than 20 inches (50 cm) of rain per year—this in the lee of volcanoes whose sodden eastern slopes soak up as many feet. Rivers that form oases for wildlife spill down from the curving slopes and loop through the parched lowlands of the Tempisque basin to merge in watery Parque Nacional Palo Verde, a spectacular haven for birdlife. Patches of rare dry forest burst into Monet-colored blossom year-round. Mere morsels of the great forests that were felled for cattle following Spanish settlement, these remnant tracts are easily explored at Parque Nacional Santa Rosa, where La Casona evokes Costa Rica's turbulent past relations with Nicaragua. A chain of sleepy and historic cowboy towns—Liberia, Cañas, Bagaces—speckle the Inter-American Highway, while Puntarenas, a motley port city extending along a thread-thin peninsula, is a gateway to the Nicoya peninsula by ferry across the Golfo de Nicoya. The peninsula is lined on its Pacific coast with stunning beaches swept by surf and warm currents that bring ashore marine turtles. The country's only white-sand beaches are here—draws for a bevy of upscale resorts and golf courses whose emergence in recent years have lent a new cachet to the region. The warm waters of the Gulf of Papagayo teem with gamefish, yet another angle on adventure, centered on the sportfishing resort of Playa Flamingo. And spelunkers can explore the limestone caverns at Parque Nacional Barra Honda.

PACIFIC SOUTHWEST

This zone is made up of valley, mountain, and coast. To the east, the Río General—popular with whitewater rafters—powers out of the Talamancas and has carved a broad trough—the Valle de El General—that is an important center for fruit plantations south of San Isidro. The valley was brought into the mainstream only in the 1950s, when the Inter-American

Highway linked it with San José and Panama, drawing immigrants, including Italians whose influence is paramount in the hilltop town of San Vito, in the southerly Valle de Coto Brus. A narrow range of mountains between valley and warm fecund sea rises precipitously in the north to create a narrow littoral quilted by palm plantations and, further south, a coastal plain swathed in bananas. Beaches are backed by jungle where birds flash their bright colors and monkeys cavort in the trees, as at Parque Nacional Manuel Antonio, a tiny emerald where coral reefs and diamond-dust beaches enclose a rare swathe of humid forest teeming

Ticos relax in the thermal waters of Tabacón hot springs, where water is heated by magma from Volcán Arenal.

with wildlife. Rainfall increases to the south, reaching a peak on the overwhelmingly green Osa Peninsula. Osa's Parque Nacional Corcovado is a sodden refuge for jaguars, scarlet macaws, and hardy hikers. Nutrient-rich offshore waters draw humpback whales to the Bahía de Coronado, and game fish to the Golfo Dulce where sportfishermen are lured to funky Golfito, an old United Fruit Company town that now attempts to attract business with its duty-free zone. Laid-back Zancudo is among scores of beaches favored by surfers. Uninhabited Isla Caño, 10 miles (16 km) offshore, boasts pre-Columbian remains. And Isla del Coco, about 300 miles (480 km) southwest of Costa Rica and part of the Galapagos chain, offers superb scuba diving.

THE NORTHERN & CARIBBEAN LOWLANDS

Lush forests extend across the vast *llanuras*—flatlands—of northern and eastern Costa Rica like a soggy carpet. The undulating plains are drained by countless rivers that cascade down from the mountains and flow into the Río San Juan, forming the Nicaraguan border. Other rivers drain into Refugio Nacional de Vida Silvestre Caño Negro, teeming with feisty gamefish, crocodiles, and birdlife. Much of the forest has been felled during recent decades for cattle, and international fruit companies are tightening their grip, pushing citrus and banana plantations up against the remaining forest. Tortuguero and Barra del Colorado, two ramshackle Caribbean hamlets, where the Río San Juan meets the sea, are sportfishing centers. Parque Nacional Tortuguero and Refugio Nacional de Vida Silvestre Barra del Colorado, are channel-laced forest reserves where wildlife is viewed from canoes. The Caribbean coast sashays south from Barra to the Río Sixaola and the Panama border. The shore is lined by gray-sand beaches hemmed in by the sea and by the crowding Talamancas. Puerto Limón, a disheveled port, is the only town of significance, while the villages of Cahuita and Puerto Viejo preserve Afro-Carib culture, drawing surfers and younger counter-culture vacationers. The Northern Lowlands are served by the Ciudad Quesada and by Fortuna, gateway to Parque Nacional Volcán Arenal and Tabacón Hot Springs. ■

A conservation ethic

DESPITE SPIRALING POPULATION GROWTH AND UNSUSTAINABLE ECONOMIC practices—logging, ranching, large-scale commercial agriculture—that have diminished Costa Rica's forest cover by 60 percent during the past 400 years, the nation has banked 28 percent of its land in national parks and reserves, a larger percentage than any other country on Earth. They are grouped into 11 Regional Conservation Units (RCAs) that create corridors for migratory wildlife by linking adjacent national parks. Every major ecosystem is represented, safeguarding natural treasures for ecotravelers to enjoy.

DIMINISHING FORESTS

To the casual visitor, Costa Rica looks like an endless lush swatch of green. In fact, forest destruction is occurring at a frightening rate, much of it illicitly by loggers driven by immense profits in hardwoods. Where trees fall, rains cause wholesale erosion. The effect of lost forest is felt throughout the biological kingdom, where the survival of countless species (including jaguars, tapirs, and macaws) is at risk.

More than 95 percent of the lowland dry forests were felled during the colonial era to make way for cattle ranches. The 1960s and 1970s were particularly devastating to the rain forests of the Northern Lowlands, as vast

tracts were felled to raise beef for the U.S. market. The rate of deforestation has slowed in recent years. Nonetheless, fruit companies continue to whittle away at lowland rain forests, and squatters edge up against protected forest, which they destroy with slash-and-burn agriculture.

SAVING WHAT REMAINS

Costa Rica is at the forefront of attempts to create sustainable revenue from tropical forests, and boasts 11 Regional Conservation Areas (RCAs), with 24 national parks and more than 120 wildlife refuges, biological reserves, marine parks, and similarly protected

Newly hatched olive Ridley turtles make a dash to the sea. Only about one percent will survive to adulthood.

areas. Ecotourism is a boon; more private reserves are being opened to public visitation. A conservation ethic is beginning to take hold among the local population, many of whom see the forest as an economic resource. In the modern world, Costa Rica's forests must earn their keep to survive. Harvesting ornamental plants and raising tree-dwelling iguanas for meat are among the schemes introduced by dozens of conservation organizations within Costa Rica to give local communities a vested interest in preservation. International bodies such as the Nature Conservancy, World Wide Fund for Nature, and U.S. Agency for International Development now sponsor creative forest management projects such as "debt for nature" swaps, where Costa Rica "swaps" part of its national debt (duly discounted) for a guarantee to safeguard a specific amount of forest. The Costa Rica government has also promoted reforestation, although these secondary forests are mostly of single species such as teak, and do little to restore native ecosystems, which take many hundreds of years to replenish themselves.

A MIXED REPORT CARD

It is a fine balancing act. Many national parks are being degraded by too many feet, while hotels squeeze parks such as Manuel Antonio against the sea. Although the scale has tipped toward greater integrity and enforcement in recent years, lack of funding and poor management bedevil the beleaguered National Park Service and the Forestry Department, which are tainted by corruption; entrenched political interests have a toehold in fighting conservation, and illegal logging and hunting continue with connivance of NPS personnel.

The situation has been complicated by the emergence of large-scale luxury resorts concentrated in dry northwest Nicoya, where new golf courses are draining the aquifers. The temptation to build bigger was resisted for many years, but the Calderón administration (1990–94) abandoned ecological principles established during preceding governments, paving the way for wanton disregard for protective laws. Even raging rivers have become battlegrounds as ICE, the nation's electricity agency, taps into their power by building hydroelectricity dams. ∎

The lush environment

NATURE LOVERS SPEAK IN HYPERBOLES, USING TERMS LIKE NIRVANA FOR the Garden of Eden called Costa Rica. Though it lies strictly within the tropics, between 8 and 11 degrees north of the equator, the country claims twelve distinct ecological zones, spanning tidal mangroves and dry deciduous forest to tropical rain forest and even subalpine grassland, called *páramo,* atop the windswept heights of the Talamanca massif. Costa Rica offers some surprises: Cactuses stud desert-dry pockets of the northwest, where hardy zebu cattle range parched savanna bordering wetlands where crocodiles bask on mudbanks, motionless as logs. This is a veritable hothouse of biodiversity. Acre for acre, Costa Rica is as species rich as anywhere else on earth. Around 5 percent of all known species on earth slither, skip, or swoop through the varied habitats, including one tenth of all birds known to man. The extraordinary biodiversity stems from Costa Rica's position at the juncture of two major continents; over eons, life-forms from both have migrated across the narrow land bridge and adapted to constantly varied local relief and climate. In this arena of intense competition they have diversified remarkably to survive. No wonder travelers who are tired of just seeing pictures of jaguars, quetzals, and three-toed sloths flock here like migrating macaws.

HOTHOUSE DIVERSITY

In the tropics, temperatures are relatively constant, for the sun shines directly overhead throughout the year, while drenching downpours and an annual rainfall in excess of 100 inches (250 cm) maintain a constant high humidity that fosters the luxuriant growth. Lush to the point of saturation, Costa Rica is a botanical breeding ground of stupendous proportion. Its 800 or so species of ferns, for example, far outnumber the whole of North America. Costa Rica is particularly rich in orchid species; about 1,400 have been identified so far. Orchids are found from sea-level to the heights of Cerro Chirripó, and with flowers ranging from less than one millimeter across to pendulous petals spanning 20 inches (50 cm). The greatest diversity is associated with rain forests, where orchids steep in year-round moisture. Around 90 percent of orchid species are epiphytes, or "air plants," (plants that root on other plants but are not parasitic) which thrive in the compost deposited on the limbs by decayed forebears and draw moisture by dangling their roots in the air. Whole colonies of epiphytes live atop the massive boughs, which often resemble vast galleries. Other epiphytes include bromeliads, which have evolved tightly wrapped leaves that act as miniature cisterns, trapping water and leaf litter that decays and donates its nutrients to the plant. Costa Rica has in excess of 2,000 species of bromeliads, which reach awesome sizes—some species measure as much as 4 feet (1.2 m) across.

ECOLOGICAL ZONES

Costa Rica's varied landscapes are classified into 12 ecological "life zones," identified in 1947 by internationally renowned tropical forest biologist Leslie R. Holdridge (1907–1999). Each zone is characterized by a distinct combination of terrain, climate, and life form. While the canvas is overwhelmingly green, Costa Rica's ecological zones include dry deciduous forest and subalpine grasslands. Various gradations exist in-between.

Mangroves and wetlands

Costa Rica's variegated coastline is rimmed by silted strips colonized by mangroves, halophytic plants (a terrestrial species able to survive with its roots in salt water) that thrive on alluvium scoured from the inland mountains and carried to the coast, where the silt is rinsed from the slow-flowing rivers and forms land. Five species of mangroves grow at the juncture of land and sea, notably along the coast of Gulf of Nicoya (particularly the

A red-eyed tree frog epitomizes the beauty of Costa Rica's miraculous fauna.

Support group: Buttress roots of a ficus tree at Hacienda Barú

mouth of the Río Tempisque), the delta of the Río Terraba, the shores of Golfo Dulce, and in the brackish lagoons of Tortuguero and Gandoca-Manzanillo, where variant mangrove ecosystems—*jollilos* and *orey*, respectively—have evolved. Veined with braided channels, they provide a rich haven for animal life. Their unprepossessing appearance disguises an intricate and vital environment where vast numbers of wild creatures—not least, crocodiles—thrive, protected from the encroachment of man. Migratory waterfowl, wading birds, and small mammals abound in the shallows and tidal creeks at low tide, thriving on the agglomeration of amphipods, marine worms, crabs, mussels and other living organisms that inhabit the watery sloughs and, in turn, thrive on the decayed vegetation and other material washed down by the rivers and brought in from the sea and trapped amid the dense thickets of plant roots. Decaying leaf litter is reworked by bacteria into detritus that feeds a legion of marine species to be consumed in turn by larger creatures in a world of astounding profligacy.

Inland, Costa Rica's two prime wetland ecosystems are Caño Negro, in the Northern Lowlands, and Palo Verde at the mouth of the Río Tempisque. These soggy regions are congenial to the tastes of wild aquatic birds and shelter a variety of migrant birds and other wild creatures—crocodiles, monkeys, deer, peccaries, coatis, ocelots—that is the equal of any other environment in Costa Rica. The wetlands flood in rainy season and contract to mudflats in dry season. Streams and rivers wind among these vast aquatic systems, forming interconnected channels and broad lagoons that draw tens of thousands of waterfowl and other exotic birds.

Rain forests

Rain forests, which mantle the equator, are among the most complex ecosystems on Earth. More than 50 percent of *all* known living species on the planet can be found in tropical rain forests, in a band 10 degrees north and south of the equator. Biologists recognize at least 13 distinct types of rain forest, ranging in subtle differentiations from the lowland jungle, a high-canopied riot of green so densely shaded that little undergrowth grows on the floor, to high-mountain cloud forest, choked by low-story epiphytes and thick undergrowth. Differences are determined by differences in altitude, rainfall, and soil conditions.

Thus, the same latitude in Costa Rica may be marked by tropical evergreen rain forest on the Caribbean coast and seasonally dry evergreen forest on the Pacific shore, sharing a sodden environment, near constant, stifling humidity and heat, and an overwhelming profusion of plant life. All rain forests receive in excess of 100 inches (250 cm) of rainfall per year; typically lowland rain forests may receive up to 300 inches (750 cm)! Premontane wet forest is found at higher elevations, as in rain-soaked Braulio Carrillo and Tapantí National Parks, where conditions are cooler. Pockets of mist-soaked tropical montane rain forest, or "cloud forest," swathe the mountainsides at elevations around 4,000 feet (1,220 m), where branches drip with mosses and galleries of epiphytes thrive in the constantly humid conditions. At the highest elevations, as atop Poás and Irazú volcanoes, stunted trees cower before chill wind-driven rains.

The true lowland rain forests that smother the *llanuras*—flatlands—of the Atlantic lowlands, the Osa Peninsula, and the eastern flanks of the Talamancas are of Gothic proportion, with trees soaring upward for 100 feet (30 m) or more before merging like a crowd of giant umbrellas. Their flattened, mushroom-shaped crowns touch to form a great green canopy so dense that you might imagine yourself able to walk across it as if it were solid ground. The canopy is shaded by mammoth trees—emergents, such as the kapok (*Ceiba pentandra*)—that soar past their neighbors like great Corinthian columns. Height is paramount in the competitive search for light. Most trees have long, straight limbless trunks with branching not occurring until 60 or more feet (18 m) from ground level. These branches form an understory. Some emergents tower as much as 100 feet (30 m) above the canopy. The lowland rain forest is a multi-layered labyrinth (see illustration pp. 180–81).

The canopy, which is subject to the passage of clouds, wind, and storms, has a wholly separate climate than the forest understory and the shrub-covered floor below, for the canopy is so dense that rainfall may take many minutes to reach the ground, if at all. Similarly, only about 10 percent of sunlight reaches the ground, where the vegetation is consequently sparse. The lack of sunlight precludes growth so that the saplings of many high canopy species stop growing once they reach about 10 feet (30 m) in height, then wait until a tree falls before erupting into explosive growth with the sudden burst of sunlight. Forest floor species have adapted crafty techniques to seek out and make the most of the subaqueous light. In clearings, plants put out broad leaves to soak up the sun, such as the "poor man's umbrella" (*sombrilla de pobre*), whose leaves like elephant ears make perfect cover in downpours.

Whereas in temperate zones, forests are marked by whole "neighborhoods" of one or two tree species, rain forests are a veritable free-for-all of hundreds of species intermingled—from cecropia trees favored by muppet-like sloths to towering mahoganies favored by loggers.

A single rain-forest tree may play host to around 100 other species of smaller plants, such as ferns, vines, and bromeliads. In the hot and humid tropics, plants grow and reproduce year-round. Dead leaves decompose and nutrients are quickly recycled and sucked back up to the forest canopy and reabsorbed, unlike in temperate zones where tissue break-down is slow and nutrient-rich humus builds up a thick layer of soil. Since tropical soils are thin, most tree species have adapted and spread their roots wide for balance and maximum nutrient uptake; the emergents, unsecured by the intertwined canopy, have evolved great flanges, like rocket fins, to overcome their inherent instability. Vines twine up and around their hosts like serpents around Eden's tree, often reaching several hundred feet in length as they coil along branches and between trees, knitting the canopy together. The strangler fig is an arboreal boa that works in the opposite direction. It germinates in the forest canopy and sends down tendril roots, which anchor to the forest floor and send up nutrients. As the roots envelop the host tree, they literally suffocate it until it dies and decomposes, providing added sustenance and leaving a cylindrical, free-standing fig.

Dry forests

On the eve of Columbus's landfall, the lowlands of the Pacific Northwest were swathed in dry deciduous forest, which covered a greater expanse than did Central America's rain forests. These forests evolved in the five-month seasonal drought that befalls Guanacaste in November, when the sun beats down hard as a nail and trees shed their leaves to conserve water.

Trees in dry forest rarely rise more than 40 feet (12 m) and are relatively sparsely distributed, making wildlife viewing easy; anteaters, monkeys, and scarlet macaws are noteworthy and numerous. The open-crowned canopy rises above a secondary layer of trees with smaller crowns, and thorny scrub and grass at ground layer. Epiphytes are missing in any profusion, though a few evergreens and palms dot the landscape. The dry forests bloom in a seasonal palette of Cézanne colors: the jacaranda in purple, the *poró* in bright orange, and the *corteza amarillo*—Guanacaste's state flower—in yellow, often exploding synchronistically, with all the members of a single species bursting into bloom on the same day before dropping their petals like colored confetti strewn on the ground. Trees blossom one after another in a strict cycle: the rose-pink *pouí* in January, for example, followed by the pastel-pink *tabebuia rosea* in March and the vermilion *malinche* in April. When the rains return in April or May, the dry forest buds afresh.

During the colonial era the Spanish destroyed vast areas of forest for cattle, decimating dry forests from Panama to Mexico. In Costa Rica, only around 200 square miles (520 sq km)—about two percent—of the original dry forest cover remains in a threadbare patchwork in Guanacaste and Santa Rosa National Parks and the Tempisque Basin.

TROPICAL MENAGERIE

Costa Rica is a cornucopia of botanical and zoological treasures. The National Institute of Biodiversity, which is attempting to identify every plant and animal species in the country, estimates there are at least one million species. Anteaters, coatis, iguanas, monkeys, birds by the hundreds, and insects in tens of thousands, colorful as creatures in a Rousseau painting and often to be seen within fingertip reach. Seeing the wildlife isn't always easy. Often patience is called for. It is a rare visitor indeed, for example, fortunate enough to see an elusive jaguar on the prowl.

Mammals

Costa Rica claims only around 200 species of mammals, of which half are bats—including vampire bats and a giant fishing bat which scoops up fish with its claws while on the wing. Most mammal species are shy and rarely seen by casual visitors.

The cats are well represented, notably by jaguars, ocelots, pumas, and extremely rare margays and oncillas—both spotted like cheetahs—and dark brown jaguarundis. Superb climbers, cats can sometimes be seen racing up tree trunks to chase down arboreal rodents and monkeys scampering along the high branches. All six cat species are both endangered and elusive.

Far more easily seen are the four species of neotropical monkeys found in all lowland and mid-elevation habitats. Descendants of Old World monkeys that migrated across the Bering land bridge eons ago, the New World species are noted for their long prehensile tails. The large, leaf-eating black howler monkey is the most common species—and the most noticeable: The males frighten tourists with their loud roars, announcing their territorial fiefdoms, particularly at dawn and dusk. The small, omnivorous, black-and-white-faced capuchin monkeys are also easily spotted play-acting among the branches, notably at Parque Nacional Manuel Antonio, where their presence is guaranteed. The diminutive, orange-hued squirrel monkey *(tití),* though endangered, is gregarious and groups of 40 or so family members are not unusual. By contrast, the long-limbed, copper-colored spider monkey is a solitary critter that faces severe deprivations from loss of habitat.

Sloths *(perozosos)* are commonly seen moving in treetops at a pace close to rigor mortis using their powerful arms and curved claws. Costa Rica has two species: the three-toed sloth and the smaller, nocturnal Hoffman's two-toed sloth. These leaf-eaters have huge stomachs to process large quantities of fairly indigestible food, which can remain

The *corteza amarilla* typifies the explosion of colors that occurs in Guanacaste's dry season.

in their stomachs for up to one week. Their metabolic rate is correspondingly slow; the animal even garners heat from direct sunlight, much like cold-blooded reptiles. Sloths typically spend 18 hours a day sleeping and digesting their meals. They do not wash much, and their shaggy fur is tinted green by algae and inhabited by bugs.

Two species of raccoon *(mapache)* are found in Costa Rica: The white-faced northern raccoon is found throughout the moist lowlands, while his dark-faced crab-eating cousin confines itself to habitats along the Pacific coast. More ubiquitous—it is one of the most frequently seen mammals—is the coati *(pizote)*, which can be easily identified by its panda-like ringed eyes, brown coat, and ringed tail, which the animal craftily uses to thwart predators: When attacked, it rears up, stuffs its tail between its legs and waves it in front of its face, so that predators will attack the tail and get slashed in the eyes in return. Smaller, nocturnal, tree-climbing cousins in the raccoon family are the olingo, cacomistle, and kinkajou.

In addition to two squirrel species and around 40 species of rats and mice, Costa Rica claims two neotropical rodents of note. The large, brown agouti *(guatusa)* is a dainty forest-dwelling creature that resembles a large tailless squirrel with long, slender legs. Different subspecies have evolved with both darker and lighter coloration as adaptations to either wet or dry forest habitats. The agouti and its nocturnal cousin, the paca *(tepezcuintle),* which resembles a large guinea pig, are traditionally hunted by campesinos for meat and are now endangered. The timid tapir *(danta),* a distant relative of the elephant, also once roamed far and wide but has been brought to the point of extinction by hunting. More intrepid hikers may chance upon these trunk-snouted animals high in the mountains, drinking at volcanic lakes, and in remote sections of Corcovado and the Talamancas.

Other mammals include Costa Rica's three species of anteaters, which subsist solely on a diet of ants, scooped up with a long sticky tongue; and two species of armor-plated armadillos. Coyotes and foxes abound as do

The elusive jaguar is a symbol not only of Costa Rica but of environmental health worldwide.

rabbits, and two species of opossums represent the marsupials (mammals whose embryonic offspring are reared in an external pouch). Peccaries *(sainos)* are also numerous. These fearsome wild pigs roam in herds and grub up roots and other foods from beneath the topsoil. Although they normally shy away from human presence, aggressive males have been known to attack people. Several kinds of skunk are also common, including the fierce badger-like grison; and the sleek, chocolate-brown tayra, a 3-foot-long (0.9 m) giant that hunts rodents and small deer and can be found in both lowland and highland habitats. Manatees—endangered marine herbivores that resemble tuskless walruses and have a spatulate tail in lieu of flippers—inhabit the watery recluses of Parque Nacional Toruguero and Refugio Nacional de Vida Silvestre Gandoca-Manzanillo, where a rare dolphin endemic to the region, the *tucuxí*, inhabits the lagoons. Otters are commonly seen in lowland rivers, notably in the waterways of Tortuguero and the adjacent Refugio Nacional de Vida Silvestre Barra del Colorado.

Amphibians and reptiles

Amphibians and reptiles thrive in the hot, damp tropics. Costa Rica claims around 160 species of the former and 220 or so reptile species, of which 162 are snakes, though only 22 species are poisonous.

Frogs abound, including gaily colored poison-dart frogs (the dendrobatids) hopping among the forest litter secure in their Day-glo livery—red as lipstick and blue as the morning sky—meant to scare predators. About 20 species of Costa Rican frogs produce deadly toxins. Recent years have witnessed a wholesale decline in frog and toad populations, including the demise of the golden toad, a diminutive wonder discovered at Monteverde only in 1964 but already considered extinct. Many frogs have adapted to life away from large bodies of water; some have evolved suction-cup feet and taken to a life in the trees, where they lay their eggs in the cisterns of bromeliads.

Snakes are ubiquitous in Costa Rica. Most snakes, such as the chunk-headed snake with elliptical cat-like eyes, are fairly small and feed on nesting birds, small rodents, and lizards. Others, such as the commonly seen boas, can grow up to 10 feet (3 m) in length. Pythons are often spotted along riverbanks, glowing yellow or iridescent green, snoozing in sensuous coils on a branch. The viper family includes the much-feared, burnished brown fer-de-lance (tercioelo), waiting with jaws of death for passing fodder. This aggressive giant accounts for three-quarters of all snake bites in Costa Rica, and almost all deaths. Most other fatalities are due to the brightly banded coral snakes, which have a distinct venom (all other snakes produce the same venom).

Costa Rica's river estuaries and lowland waterways are favored by American crocodiles (cocodrilos), which reach lengths of up to 15 feet (4.5 m). Their diminutive cousins, caimans, rarely grow beyond 6 feet (1.8 m). Crocodiles have suffered mightily from hunting during four centuries. Protected since the 1970s, they are making a comeback, particularly in the Río Tárcoles and Refugio Nacional de Vida Silvestre Caño Negro.

Ubiquitous throughout Costa Rica, the tree-dwelling iguana inhabits both wet and dry lowland forest and can grow to 3 feet (0.9 m) in length. Cloaked in scaly armor, it presents a fearsome appearance but is quite harmless to humans. The spiny-tailed iguana is green, though males turn orange during the November–December mating season; the smaller ctenosaur is dun-colored. The dozens of smaller lizard species are highlighted by the Jesus Christ lizard, a resident of the Pacific Lowlands, named for its ability to run across water on its hind legs.

Many visitors to Costa Rica come in hope of seeing marine turtles laying their eggs. It's easily done at any number of beaches on both Caribbean and Pacific coasts. The females of five species of turtle come ashore here at various times throughout the year. The green turtle is most easily seen at Tortuguero. Leatherback turtles, the largest reptiles on earth (they can weigh up to a ton) nest at Playa Grande in Nicoya. The most exhilarating sight is to witness the synchronized nestings (arribadas) that take place at Refugio Nacional de Vida Silvestre Ostional, where tens of thousands of olive Ridley turtles swarm ashore during full moons from July to December.

Insects

Costa Rica's insect fauna is incalculably rich— from the microscopic flower mite, which hitches a ride inside the nostrils of hummingbirds, to true giants such as the 3-inch-long (7.5 cm) rhinoceros beetle, named for the fearsome horn on its head. Tens of thousands of species await identification. The kingdom comes into its own at night, when the moths and beetles take wing and the forests resound to a cacophonous chirruping and croaking. Guanacaste is particularly rich; when seasonal rains strike the region, the insect fauna explodes. More than 1,000 species of butterflies—one-quarter of the world's total—flit about the country in a never-ending kaleidoscopic ballet of color. The undisputed monarch of the butterfly realm is the saucer-sized, neon-bright morpho flashing its electric blue wings. Subspecies differ in coloration according to locale; one rain-forest canopy species is iridescent red. Another stunner is the owl butterfly (Caligo memnon), a 6-inch (15 cm) giant whose underwing coloration resembles a pair of owl eyes, flashed when the butterfly is threatened.

Of the thousands of species of ants, the most intriguing are the leaf-cutters, which farm mushrooms underground using mulch chewed from leaves stripped from trees. Costa Rica even has army ants, fearsome colonies that number in millions and sweep through the countryside, terrorizing and devouring any living thing in their path.

Birds, birds, birds!

It's remarkable to think that one-tenth of all known bird species in the world inhabit this little patch of land. Of the 850 or so species found here, at least 600 are permanent residents, including 51 species of humming-birds whose exotic names—fiery-throated hummingbird and scarlet-thighed dacnis, for example—you may never recall but whose beauty you will remember forever. Humming-birds are found throughout the nation in cloaks of shimmering cerulean blue, purple, and green.

Equally ubiquitous are parrots, of which Costa Rica has 16 species, from diminutive green parakeets to giant scarlet macaws like flying rainbows plunging between the high

branches. Large colonies of scarlet macaws are easily seen at Corcovado and Manuel Antonio national parks and Reserva Biológica Carará. These monogamous birds are often seen flying in pairs. The smaller, predominantly green Buffon's macaw is found only around Tortuguero and the Northeastern Lowlands. Both species are endangered due to habitat loss. There are several private institutions in Costa Rica that have active breeding programs to release macaws back to the wild.

Another dazzler is the quetzal, the crown jewel of the cloud forest and the sole reason that many visitors flock to Costa Rica. This pigeon-sized beauty—one of 10 species of trogons in Costa Rica—boasts iridescent emerald feathers. The male woos potential mates with a fiery blood red chest and a sweeping, forked tail up to 24 inches (60 cm) long. They're easily seen at Monteverde, where in springtime the birds descend to lower altitudes and perform acrobatic mid-air mating displays. Visitors should listen for their mournful two-note whistle. That eerie metallic *bonk* resounding through the cloud forests is the call of the three-wattled bellbird.

Keel-billed and chestnut-mandibled toucans, with their banana-like beaks, are common in habitats throughout the country. Their sharp-beaked cousins, the toucanets and aracaris, are no less flamboyant. Another colorful favorite of birders is the motmot, which has a racquet-like tail and lives in a hole in the ground.

The list goes on and on. Costa Rica has 25 species of doves and pigeons. The small, stub-winged tanagers, exotically colored in flame reds and sky blues, are represented by 50 species. There are 78 species of flycatchers, 52 species of warblers, 22 species of wrens, and some 50 species of raptors, which feed on everything from crabs (favored by the black hawk) and fish (beloved by ospreys) to monkeys, a favorite snack of the locally extinct harpy eagle, reduced to remote parts of Corcovado and the Talamancas. Four species of vultures *(zopilotes)* pick at roadkill and other carrion; count yourself lucky to spot the mighty king vulture.

Cattle egrets, blazing white, are found nationwide and easily seen in pastures and along riverbanks. The remaining 25 species of stilt-legged waders include herons; storks such as the massive jabiru; the roseate spoonbill, with its spatulate bill and shocking pink plumage, nowadays confined to the safety of Caño Negro and Palo Verde; and three species of ibis. Costa Rica's wetlands are especially rich in avian fauna, as they lie directly beneath the Pacific migratory flyway. They attract waterfowl—coots, ducks, grebes, teal—in such numbers that the rush of their wings sometimes sounds like the roar of a jet-engine. Marine birds include cormorants and anhingas, with serpentine necks, as well as boobies which can be seen in Bahía Salinas and Golfo de Nicoya, where the mangroves prove ideal nesting sites for frigatebirds which, with their long sinister wings and forked tails, hang like kites in the wind. Ironically, given this wealth of avian fauna, the national bird of Costa Rica is the somewhat drab robin, a dull-colored species locally known as the *yiquirro,* with bright red eyes. When the male breaks out in song in the spring mating season, local lore says he is calling the rains.

Marine life

The tropical waters that form both Costa Rica's coasts are a pelagic playpen (notably the Pacific) where scuba divers can swim eye-to-eye with whale sharks, manta rays, and groupers, and anglers can cast their lures for the billfish that cruise the offshore waters year-round. The Golfo de Papagayo and Golfo Dulce are particularly rich in gamefish, such as marlin, dolphin fish, tuna, and wahoo. The top draw for experienced divers is Isla del Coco, where hammerhead sharks school in unsurpassed numbers.

In the coral-laced waters off Manuel Antonio and in Bahía Ballena, a whirligig extravaganza of fish play tag among their plots of limestone real estate, while stingrays flap slowly over the ocean bottom. Smaller coral reefs exist off Cahuita and Gandoca-Manzanillo in the Caribbean, and off Isla del Caño. Humpback whales gather seasonally to feed and mate in the warm, nutrient-rich waters of Bahía Ballena, providing exhilarating eye-to-eye encounters for whale-watchers. ■

To see life at sea, take a dive at Isla del Coco.

The cultural scene

COSTA RICA'S MODERN NATIONAL SYMPHONY ORCHESTRA RISES TO THE standard of its stunning venue: the Teatro Nacional (National Theater) in San José. But otherwise, Costa Rica is relatively culturally underdeveloped, and the nation has sought in vain for a pre-Columbian legacy to stimulate a modern renaissance. The sterility can be explained by Costa Rica's benign colonial history, because social tensions have always been a spark for vibrant cultural expression. This peaceful nation thereafter suffered from a creative paucity, with the exception of a few native crafts.

The nation has long been dismissed as a cultural backwater. The entire cultural scene, including dance and theater, was for a long time moved by the national sense of a brotherhood of lowly, country-based ticos. For example, visual art struggled to break out of a traditional straitjacket of portraying idyllic rural scenes.

In recent years, however, Costa Rica has begun to evolve a new confidence as artists cast aside rigid norms. The nation's young, up-and-coming artists and woodcarvers are following the examples of American artists-in-residence, whose success owes much to their freedom from the constraints of a campesino-based national identity and spirit.

The ceiling of the Teatro Nacional's lobby depicts an idyllic scene from the 19th-century heyday of coffee.

villages, usually with a volcano for backdrop. The school evolved in Escazú and neighboring Santa Ana, southwest of San José, which remain an informal artists' enclave.

This art of *casitas* (little houses) was derided by the next generation of artists, who by the 1950s were experimenting in abstract styles. Modernist and en vogue contemporary styles have since found their way into a more mature artistic expression, and today Costa Rica's crop of current young artists display an eclectic world vision. In recent years, artists such as Isidro Con Wong (born 1931), have won international acclaim. Wong's works—described as "magic realism"—fetch up to $35,000 apiece on the world market. Rafa Fernández (born 1935) is another magic realist, specializing in erotic female images. And Zapote's Rolando Castellón, former director of the New York Museum of Modern Art and today curator of Costa Rica's Museum of Contemporary Art, is known for his 3-D art.

Plastic arts

Sculpture has never been a strong suit in Costa Rica, although the pre-Columbian influence can be seen in a tradition of jewelry work and an outpouring of splendid gold and silver adornment. Contemporary jewelry styles owe much to traditional indigenous forms, such as animist figurines.

The nation's most famous sculptural piece dates back to 1936, when sculptor Francisco Zuñigo (1912–1998) unveiled a stone carving of a mother suckling her child. The piece, called "Maternity," can be seen today outside San José's Maternidad Caritas maternity clinic. It was ridiculed by local critics who derided it as looking more like a cow than a woman, causing Zuñigo to leave for Mexico. His "Evelia con Batan" stands at the entrance to San José's Centro Nacional de Artes y Cultura.

Tourism has sparked a revolution in crafts, notably in wood carvings inspired primarily by Escazú's Barry Biesanz. Sarchí, however, is the undisputed center of crafts. Here, Costa Rica's clichéd wooden oxcarts called *carretas* are still made and gaily decorated in floral

In performing arts, too, dance and theater companies have broken away from their traditional bonds, especially in the realm of contemporary dance.

Visual arts

Until recent years, there was little energy to Costa Rican art, which has lacked the passionate, visceral, socially engaged formats of other Latin nations. Artists have struggled to Houdini out of a straitjacket of stylized Costa Rican landscape that developed in the late 1920s based on depictions of campesino life. The so-called Group of New Sensibility was influenced by the French Impressionists and headed by Teodorico Quirós (1897–1977). The movement's legacy remains preeminent today in paintings, including miniatures, showing adobe dwellings and cobbled rural motifs, including miniatures intended as garden ornaments or as domestic liquor carts for the home. Sarchí is also the main center for other craft items and traditional wooden furniture hewn from hardwoods including mahogany, lignum vitae, and rosewood.

Santa Ana is famed for its earthenware. And at Guaitíl, in Nicoya, a renaissance in Chorotega pride finds its outlet in much-sought-after pottery. Members of the Boruca tribe make traditional musical instruments, wooden masks, and handwoven textiles. And the womenfolk of Bahía Drake, in the Pacific Southwest, still make *molas*, decorative hand-sewn appliqué.

Literature

Unlike other Latin American cultures, the dispassionate ticos are not a particularly literate people, despite a high literacy level. Only a fistful of writers make a living from the profession, which is dominated by parochial themes. Costa Rica's literary style is insipid and the country has yet to produce a writer of international note.

Injustice and social turmoil are the grist for great literature and Costa Rica has lacked both; it is notable that the singular literary work to gain broad recognition is *Mamita Yunai*, a story decrying the injustices wrought by the United Fruit Company upon Costa Rica's banana workers, by Carlos Luis Fallas (1912–1996). Likewise, the acclaimed *El Eco de los Pasos* by Julieta Pinto (born 1922) had the 1948 civil war as its theme. The works represented in a lone anthology of literary works by twentieth-century Costa Rican authors, *Costa Rica: A Traveler's Literary Companion*, are prosaic and anemic.

Theater

Ticos enjoy theater so much that the country boasts more theaters per capita than any other country in the world. This dates to the turn of the 20th century, when drama became part of the school curriculum and an influx of South American playwrights boosted theatrical for-tunes. San José's tiny theaters offer a mix of comedy, mime, and avant-garde, drawing the residents of San José every night except Mondays. The nation's oldest theatrical group, the Little Theater Group, performs in English.

Music & dance

Costa Rica is the southernmost of the *marimba* countries—those owing much to the Africa-derived xylophone *(marimba)* that forms the base of native music throughout Central America. It is no surprise then that Guanacaste, where the native tradition remains strongest, provides the impetus for traditional music and dance, typified by the national dance: the *punto guanacaste*, a toe-and-heel stomp for couples. Pre-Columbian instruments, such as the *quijongo* (a gourd amplifier attached to a string bow) are still used to accompany the Spanish guitar. Traditional dancing is based on the stylized Spanish *paseo*, with men and women alternately circling each other, accompanied by much *"yip-yipping"* and tossing of hats and scarves. It is now mostly performed at tourist venues by such groups as Fantasía Folklórica.

The traditional Latin *peña*, where intellectuals gather and share poems and music, is strong among the educated middle class. On the classical front, however, Costa Rica has been neither an inspirational locale nor a breeding ground for composers and instrumentalists. The Teatro Nacional hosts the National Symphony Orchestra, formed in 1970, which draws middle-class *Josefinos* (resi-dents of San José) during the April to Novem-ber season. Several minor classical and choral groups also perform.

Younger ticos have forsaken traditional forms of music and dance for the modern dance hall. Latin rhythms draw them to discos where hip-swiveling merengue, cumbia, and salsa are the music and dance forms of choice. On the Caribbean coast, where musical influences derive from Jamaica, reggae's Bob Marley is king. Reggae, a modern phenome-non, has displaced traditional musical forms such as the *sinkit* and *cuadrille*, colonial island carry-overs based on banjo and drum.

Jazz has gained in popularity in recent years and finds its major outlet in the annual International Festival of Music, each August. No national style has evolved, although it is a bravura, macho style with trumpeters playing the highest notes and pianists going as fast as they can go. The Southern Caribbean Music Festival in February also offers jazz side by side with reggae and classical music. ∎

Almost parochial in scale, Costa Rica's capital city clings to its provincial feel, with plenty of small museums and art galleries, pocket-size plazas, and intriguing edifices from the halcyon days of coffee.

San José

A mountain backdrop silhouettes the city.

San José

PERCHED AMONG A CRESCENT OF MOUNTAINS, SAN JOSÉ ENJOYS AN enviable setting in the heart of the Meseta Central at 3,773 feet (1,150m). In many ways it is an ideal locale. The compact city of around 300,000 enjoys what *National Geographic* dubbed one of the three best climates in the world, with temperatures that hover around 70°F daily year-round and rainfall limited mostly to short-lived showers and occasional downpours, May to October. Pleasantly small-scale as Central American capitals go, San José clings tentatively to a provincial feel despite sprawling suburbs that now claim 1.3 million residents—one third of the nation's total.

San José can never be called colonial quaint. The city was founded as late as 1737 and as capital cities go, has relatively few colonial architectural glories. The main commercial boulevards are little strips of America, with neon signs blaring the offerings of fast-food outlets, car dealerships, strip clubs, and shopping malls. The city—which is made up of a set of distinct districts called *barrios*—has not entirely shaken off its village feel, however. In many ways it remains a working-class city where social life is based around the local *pulpería*, or corner store.

COFFEE CULTURE

Throughout its first century of existence, San José endured as a humble village of simple adobe structures. But its position in the heart of the fertile valley was advantageous, and by the 1820s it had grown to equal the then-capital Cartago in size. In 1823 the city seized the standard after a brief civil war, and the town took on the role of capital. San José prospered as coffee took hold on the surrounding slopes. Parks, plazas, and fine public buildings rose up as a result of this prosperity, and the city's nouveau riche *cafeteleros* (coffee-trading barons), who looked to Europe for inspiration, adopted the French-inspired New Orleans and Port-au-Prince (Haiti) style for their new homes.

The years following World War II saw rapid growth, and the city's infrastructure has been hard-pressed ever since to keep pace with the the changes. Beyond the touristed core, central San José is a chaos of ugly modern buildings, decrepit sidewalks, open sewers, and potholed streets. Crime has risen dramatically in recent years, and gangs of youths called *chapulines* operate like Fagin's street urchins, so that visitors are well advised to leave valuables in their hotel safe. Crowds elbow their way along clogged streets that teem with overflowing markets, lottery sellers, and sidewalk vendors who hawk items from underwear and candies to petty trinkets. Pedestrians are forced to fend off a noisily honking armada of buses, trucks, motorcycles, and taxis that belch out a pall of fumes that hangs over the streets.

ARCHITECTURAL RENEWAL

Nonetheless, San José has an undeniable charm and many visitors end up with a fondness for *chepe*, as the city is colloquially known. Most sites of interest lie within a few blocks of the Plaza de la Cultura, which is ground zero for any downtown exploration. On weekends the heavy traffic thins and Josefinos, the residents of San José, take to strolling along the pedestrian-only Avenida Central and the half dozen plazas shaded by mauve jacarandas. The Ministry of Culture has applied some elbow grease in recent years, and managed to put a polish on the previously run-down plazas and to the fistful of notable edifices, such as the Catedral Metropólitano.

Most tourists find that San José can be fully explored in two days, after which you will be ready to escape to the country. This is easily done. Coffee fields edge up against the city, so that one has the feeling that the countryside is close at hand. San José's position means that it provides a splendid base for day trips throughout the Central Highlands, either by rental car or organized excursion.

Popular destinations from the capital include the Butterfly Farm, Café Britt Coffee Plantation Tour, Poás Volcano, Orosi, the Rainforest Aerial Tram, and the artisans' center, Sarchí. ■

Area of map detail

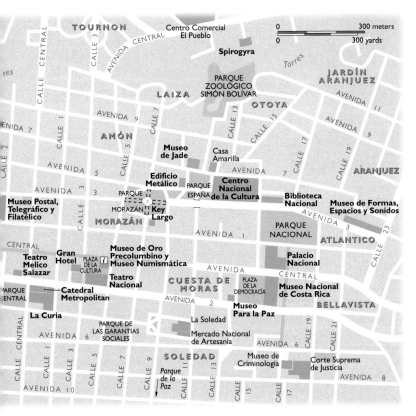

The city core

Visitor information
🗺 See map pp. 56–57
✉ Calle 5, Ave. Central/2
☎ 223-1733

Teatro Nacional
🗺 See map pp. 56–57
✉ Ave. 2, Calle 3
☎ 221-1329
🕐 Closed Sun.
💲 $

ALTHOUGH SAN JOSÉ OFFERS SUBURBAN TEMPTATIONS, the city's main sights of interest are concentrated in a compact core laid out in a grid, which makes exploring easy. Use Avenida Central as an axis to find major nodes of interest sprinkled handily along its route. A good place to start is Plaza de la Cultura, not least for the main visitor information bureau accessed on the east side.

PLAZA DE LA CULTURA

The nondescript Plaza de la Cultura is the center around which life in San José whirls. Hemmed by Calles 3 and 5, it lies at the heart of a pedestrian-only shopping zone extending seven blocks along Avenida Central. The plaza is a gathering spot for youth, and jugglers and musicians entertain the crowds on weekends. A clock tower and fountain stand at the junction of Avenida Central and Calle 3.

On the east of the plaza, on Calle 5, steps lead to the subterranean **Museo de Oro Precolombino,** *(closed Mon.; fee),* the gold museum, best explored using the audio-taped self-guided tour. Some 2,000 pieces of pre-Columbian gold jewelry and life-size figures adorned in gold glitter under spotlights. The

Museo Numismático adjoins *(for visitor information, see Museo de Oro Precolombino),* with coinage dating back three centuries.

On the south side is the neoclassic **Teatro Nacional,** the jewel in Costa Rica's architectural crown. It owes its origins to a fit of local pique when operatic prima donna Adelina Patti (1843–1919) bypassed Costa Rica during a Central American tour in 1890. The ruling clique promptly voted a tax on coffee exports to pay for the construction of a theater in the style of the Paris Opera House, sumptuous enough to tempt the Paris Opera to perform *Faust* at the inauguration in October 1897. Statues of the Muses of Dance, Music, and Fame decorate the Renaissance facade. Beyond the pink marble foyer, the Intermezzo has a colorful mural of an idyllic coffee harvest, while in the lavish triple-tiered auditorium naked deities prance across the ceiling.

Above: A pre-Columbian gold figurine
Right: San José's downtown streets pulse like veins of the city.

Museo de Oro Precolombino
www.museosdelbano central.org
🗺 See map pp. 56–57
✉ Calle 5, Ave. 2/Central
☎ 243-4202

Do you know the way in San José?

A venidas (avenues) run east-west in San Jose. They ascend in odd numbers north of Avenida Central, and in even numbers south of it. *Calles* (streets) run north-south; they ascend in odd numbers east of Calle Central, and in even numbers west of it. Street addresses and numbers are rarely used (many Josefinos would be hard pressed to name the street they live on).

Instead, general addresses are given: Avenida 1 between Calles 6 and 8, for example, would be written as "Avenida 1, Calles 6/8." Often addresses are stated in relation to a well-known "landmark," such as "100 meters east and 200 meters south of Coca-Cola," a reference to a bus depot that is still referred to by the name of a defunct bottling factory. ■

Museo de Jade Marco Fidel Tristán

- See map pp. 56–57
- Ave. 7, Calles 9/11
- 223-5800, ext. 2584
- Closed weekends
- $

Right: A pre-Columbian effigy in the Museo de Jade Marco Fidel Tristán evokes the strength of a long-lost civilization.

Orthodox style, looms to the east, replacing an original structure toppled by an earthquake in 1821. It boasts an ornate altarpiece. Attached is the rugged and mellowed **La Curia** (*not open to the public*), built in 1887. The Archbishop's Palace is fronted by a quaint garden pinned by a bronze statue of Monseñor Bernardo Augusto Thiel Hoffman, second bishop of Costa Rica (1880–1901).

Parque Central's north fringe is Avenida 2, the city's busy main thoroughfare, dominated by the neoclassic facade of the **Teatro Mélico Salazar** (*tel 222-2653*), built in the 1920s and named for Costa Rican tenor, Melico Salazar

Contemporary mural at the National Museum of Art

The theater and the landmark **Gran Hotel** open onto tiny **Plaza Mora Fernández,** where marimba bands frequently perform. The hotel lobby has a 24-hour casino fronted by the balcony of the **Café Parisienne,** a popular spot for watching life pass by.

PARQUE CENTRAL

This bustling plaza draws ticos to converse and flirt beneath the guanacaste trees and domed bandstand, where concerts are given on Sundays. The city's blue-domed **Catedral Metropólitano,** erected in 1871 in an austere Greek

(1887–1950). The marble lobby is supported by Corinthian columns that extend into the delightful theater café. The *teatro* is occasionally used as a setting for classical and folklore-related concerts.

PARQUE MORAZÁN

This small park, between Avenidas 3 and 5 and Calles 5 and 9, is pinned by the domed Temple of Music and makes a quiet retreat. Named for Central American federalist Francisco Morazán (1800-45), the park features statues and busts of Latin American notables including the South

American liberator, Simón Bolívar (1783-1830).

The area to the south forms a mini red-light district serving the tourist trade. Many visitors choose to pop into **Key Largo** to sample the bordello-style flavor that belies the beauty of the turn-of-the-century mansion featuring exquisite stained-glass work and a metal crest crowning the roof.

Parque Morazán is bordered to the east by tree-shaded **Parque España,** featuring busts of conquistador Juan Vásquez de Coronado (1500–1553) and Queen Isabella of Spain (1830–1904). Songbirds roost in the densely packed trees. To the northwest is the green **Edificio Metálico** *(private)* made in Belgium of prefabricated metal and shipped to Costa Rica in 1892. Now a school, it took four years to weld together.

To the north is the glass-fronted INS Building. On the 11th floor is the **Museo de Jade Marco Fidel Tristán.** You'll find a superb collection of pre-Columbian jade jewelry and carvings, plus ceramics and stone *metates,* stools used for grinding corn with a pestle.

PLAZA DE LA DEMOCRACIA

San José's largest square, 400 yards (365 m) east of Plaza de la Cultura, is a lugubrious affair laid out in 1989 for the Hemispheric Summit. It is highlighted by a small cascade and a bronze statue of "Don Pepe" Figueres (1906–90). It is well worth taking time to shop for homespun crafts and Guatemalan textiles in the tiny market that sits at the foot of the sloping plaza.

To the east, the castle-like, ocher-colored Bellavista Fortress overshadows the plaza. Riddled with bullet holes from the 1948 civil war, like a vision from *Beau Geste.* Today the fortress is home to the **Museo Nacional de Costa Rica,** which traces the nation's historical and cultural development using exhibits illustrating topics that range from religion to geology and archaeology. A room dedicated to pre-Columbian gold and jade is the highlight.

On the plaza's southwest corner, the **Museo para la Paz** is dedicated to the cause of peace and displays former president Oscar Arias' Nobel Peace Prize.

San José swirls around the vortex of Parque Central and its simple cathedral.

Museo Nacional de Costa Rica
www.museocostarica.com
🅰 See map pp. 56–57
✉ Bellavista Fortress, Calle 17, Ave. Central/2
☎ 221-4429, 257-1433
🕓 Closed Mon.
💲 $

Museo para la Paz
www.arias.or.cr/museo.html
🅰 See map pp. 56–57
✉ Avenida 2, Calle 13
☎ 224-1919
🕓 Closed Sat. & Sun.

A domed band-stand crowns Parque Central.

Centro Nacional de la Cultura
- See map pp. 56–57
- Ave. 3, Calles 15/17
- 255-3638
- Closed Sun.–Mon.

Museo de Formas, Espacios & Sonidos
- See map pp. 56–57
- Ave. 3, Calle 21
- 222-9462
- Closed Sat.–Sun.
- $

Costa Rica's seat of government is a handsome whitewashed building off the plaza, on Calle 15. The Moorish-style **Palacio Nacional,** housing the Legislative Assembly, began life in 1912 as the would-be-home of presidential candidate Máximo Fernández (1858–1933). He lost but magnanimously offered his house to the victor, Alfredo Gonzalez Flores (1877–1954).

PARQUE NACIONAL

All levels of society take to San José's largest inner-city park—at the west end of the city, between Avenidas 1 and 3—at lunchtime and on weekends, when it is pleasant to stroll beneath shade trees and palms that vibrate with bird song.

The white marble **Monumento Nacional** proclaims the victory of the Central American nations in 1856 over William Walker (1824–1860) and his *filibusteros* (mercenaries). It was cast in the Rodin studios in Paris and stands atop a granite pedestal with bas-reliefs. Costa Rica's national hero, the drummer boy Juan Santamaría, stands in effigy at the park's southwest corner. To see

the monuments, go during the daylight because it is best to avoid the park at night

The **Biblioteca Nacional** *(tel 221-2436, closed Sat.–Sun.),* the nation's main library, lords over the park to the northwest, on Avenida 3.

Across the street is the **Centro Nacional de la Cultural,** containing the **Museo de Arte y Diseño Contemporaneo.** This features collections of art from throughout Latin America. The gallery is housed in a former liquor factory dating from 1887, which is also home to two theaters and the office of the Ministerio de Cultura.

The **Museo de Formas, Espacios y Sonidos** (the Museum of Forms, Space and Sounds) is housed in the ornate Atlantic train station built in 1907 on the northeast corner. Three salons offer interactive displays that invite you to run your fingers over sculptures or listen to the sounds of more than two dozen instruments. The eclectic displays include scale models of the old station and other important historical sites, plus instruction in the plastic arts. ∎

Parque Sábana & nearby

Parque Sábana is a bucolic retreat situated in the heart of the city.

WEST OF DOWNTOWN, AVENIDA CENTRAL OPENS UP INTO a wide boulevard, Paseo Colón, sloping gently uphill to Parque Sábana de Metropólitano. Paseo Colón epitomizes the modern mayhem of San José with its billboards, supercharged neon advertisements, and pandemonium of honking traffic culminating, eventually, in the pacific counterpoint of leafy Sábana.

A stroll along Paseo Colón puts you in touch with San José's busy main artery. Step south along Calle 24 and after 440 yards (400 m) you will arrive at the **Cementerio de Obreros,** on the south side of Avenida 10. Here the wealthy of past decades vied for immortality on a grand scale. This exercise in pious excess makes for intriguing browsing among the flamboyant mausoleums, vaults, and tombs embellished with angels, griffins, cherubs, and other ornamentation.

The west end of Paseo Colón bumps up against **Parque Sábana de Metropólitano,** with grassy expanses, tree-lined jogging trails, and a miscellany of sports facilities. The bucolic, yet disheveled retreat overlays the old airport, and the former terminal is today the **Museo de Arte Costarricense,** displaying many of the nation's finest artworks, ranging from pre-Columbian artifacts through robust contemporary pieces, including a superb collection of wooden sculptures and woodcuts. To the rear, the **Jardín de Esculturas** displays pre-Columbian and contemporary sculptures, including those by such leading artists as Francisco Zuñiga.

Tucked off the southwest corner of Parque Sábana is the **Museo de Ciencias Naturales La Salle,** which spans the natural science world with more than 22,500 exhibits. A dinosaur exhibit in the foyer features life-size T-rex, Torosaurus, and Utahraptors. ∎

Museo de Arte Costarricense
www.cr/arte/museos.html
🅼 See map pp. 56–57
✉ Calle 42 & Paseo Colón
☎ 222-7155
🕐 Closed Mon.
💲 $ (free Sun.)

Museo de Ciencias Naturales La Salle
🅼 See map pp. 56–57
✉ 100 yards W of Colegio La Salle, Calle Lang
☎ 232-1306
🕐 Closed Sun.
💲 $

Walk around Barrios Otoya & Amón

This walk explores two contiguous *barrios*—Barrio Otoya to the east and Amón to the west—that form the city's historic district, replete with Victorian-era mansions squeezed into narrow one-way streets in a hilly area north of Avenida 7. The region contains much of the city's finest domestic architecture built by cafeteleros inspired by the en vogue French style of New Orleans and Martinique. Until a few years ago, many of these mansions were ready to face demolition. The area has been popularized in recent years by the wealthy class, including hotel owners, who have conjured beautiful mansions into homey inns. A few of the streets are steep, but the ambling is peacefully pleasant.

Begin the walk at the **Legación de México ①,** a neoclassic stone gem in a splendid state of repair 50 yards (45 m) northeast of Parque España, on the edge of Barrio Otoya. Immediately west, pause to admire the ornately stuccoed facade of the **Casa Amarilla ②,** the "Yellow House," an 18th-century edifice in neo-baroque style bequeathed to Costa Rica by Andrew Carnegie to serve as the Pan-American Court of Justice. After later doing duty as the Residencia Presidencial and as the Asemblia Legislativa, it now houses the Ministry of Foreign Relations. The ceiba tree that looms over the west side of the building was planted by President John F. Kennedy in 1963. It is not open to the public.

After visiting the **Museo de Jade Marco Fidel Tristán** (see p. 61), turn up Calle 11, which snakes uphill to Avenida 9. Turn left and walk downhill one block past the **Hemingway Inn** to Calle 9, where you should peek inside the **Hotel Don Carlos ③** (see p. 242), an exemplary wooden home, blending art deco and neoclassic elements with ornamental grillwork in colonial style. Built as the residence of President Tomás Guardia (1832–82), this gracious charmer is now run by art connoisseur Don Carlos Balser and brims with pre-Columbian treasures and Sarchí oxcarts. An exquisite ceramic in the lobby shows a quintessential bucolic scene—a theme that plays along Avenida 7 as you continue downhill past walls inlaid with hand-painted tiles depicting coffee pickers and the like.

One block west, to your right at the corner of Calle 7, in Barrio Amón, is **La Casa Verde de Amón ④,** which is intriguing for its antique detailing and a soaring lounge skylit by a stained-glass atrium *(tragaluz)*. This stately mansion is made of red pine imported from New Orleans in exchange for a shipment of coffee. It received a UNESCO award in 1994 for the restoration that retains the Victoria claw-foot tubs and includes poster beds, and even a centenarian grand piano in the lobby.

VICTORIAN FLAVOR

Continue west along Avenida 9, lined with examples of low-slung aristocratic wooden houses in "Caribbean Victorian" vernacular, with detailed wainscoting and extensive decorative touches. At Calle 5, to your right, note **Le Chambord,** another splendid home, and farther along Avenida 9, **Casa Morisca,** influenced by Moorish fashion. Turn right at Calle 1 and right again onto Avenida 11. At the corner of Calle 3 on the west side of the street, you will pass the **Castillo del Moro ⑤,** colloquially called the Bishop's Castle after archbishop Don Carlos Humberto Rodríguez, for whom it was built in 1925. The crenelated structure was inspired by Moorish design, with extravagant touches such as hand-painted tiles adorning a dome, rows of keyhole windows, and intricate plaster decoration. On the east side is the **Britannia Hotel ⑥** (see p. 241), which was built in 1910, and is one of several neo-Victorian mansions within 100 yards (90 m) to metamorphose into hotels.

Follow Avenida 11 east to its terminus at the entrance to **Parque Zoológico Simón Bolívar ⑦** *(tel 223-1790, $),* immediately east of Calle 7. By international standards—and Costa Rica's reputation for wildlife welfare—the zoo is appalling, retaining many of its tiny cages dating to 1916. But at least you will get a good sense for the wildlife that can be more appreciatively seen in the wild.

Return to Avenida 9 via Calle 7, stopping at **TeoréTica,** an avant-garde art space where

The quaint Casa Amarilla now houses the Ministry of Foreign Affairs.

exhibitions and workshops are held in a restored mansion. Then, climb east 150 yards (137 m) up Avenida 9 and turn left on Calle 11 to admire the statue of a *campesino* on the patio of the mansion at number 980.

To end your walk, follow Avenida 9 to Calle 15, where **Café Mundo** ⑧ serves cappuccinos and other beverages in one of the most beautiful restored houses in the city. ■

📖 See area map pp. 56–57
▶ Legación de México
🔄 1.22 miles (1.95 km)
🕘 90 minutes
▶ Café Mundo

NOT TO BE MISSED
- Casa Amarilla
- Hotel Don Carlos
- Café Mundo

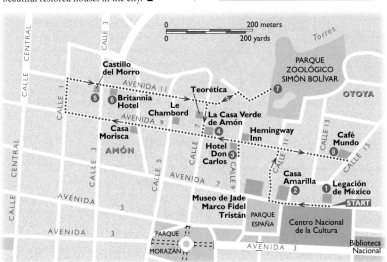

More places to visit in San José

CENTRO COSTARRICENSE DE CIENCIAS Y CULTURA

The turreted "castle"—a former peniten-
tiary—situated atop the hill at the north end
of Calle 4 is today the unlikely venue for the
Galería Nacional, a repository of avant-
garde works of art displayed in the converted
jail cells. Its **Museo de Niños,** or children's
museum, spans themes ranging from astrono-
my to communication and provides a solid,
entertaining education of interests to adults
and children alike. A state-of-the-art theater,
the Auditorio Nacional, has performances.
Its foyer features a notable contemporary
sculpture—Imagen Cósmica—by Jorge
Jiménez Deredia.
www.museocr.com ⓜ See map pp. 56–57
✉ Calle 4, 100 yards N of Ave. 9 ☎ 238-4929
🕐 Closed Mon. 🅂 $

**The vendors in San José's markets sell
everything from fresh produce to trinkets.**

EDIFICIO CORREOS

Constructed in 1917 in eclectic style and highlighted by an ornate green facade, the Postal
Building is one of San José's most dramatic
structures. It functions as the nation's central
post office and as the Museo Postal, Telegráfico
y Filatélico (on the second floor). This small
museum is a curiosity for its collection of early
telegraphic and telephonic equipment. It also
has a philatelic display. The Edificio Correos

faces a small plaza with a statue of Juan Mora
Fernández, the nation's first president (1824-28).
ⓜ See map pp. 56–57 ✉ Calle 2, Ave. 1/3
☎ 223-9766 🕐 Closed Sat.–Sun. 🅂 $

MERCADO CENTRAL

There is no more truly Costa Rican experience
available in San José than a visit to this cen-
trally situated market built in 1880. Crowds
work their way through a dizzying warren of
narrow alleyways lined with cobblers, saddle
shops, artisans' stalls, trinket-sellers, florists,
fruit-sellers, and fishmongers all attended by
vendors screaming for attention. Guard your
valuables closely in these crowded conditions.
Be sure to dine at one of dozens of tiny *sodas,*
eateries favored by ticos and offering traditional meals for a pittance.
ⓜ See map pp. 56–57 ✉ Ave. Central, Calles
6/8 ☎ 295-6104 🕐 Closed Sun.

PUEBLO ANTIGUO

This theme park is a mixture of Colonial
Williamsburg and Disney World, offering re-
creations of an idyllic past, with urban, rural,
and coastal sections, staffed by ticos in period
costume. In the milking shed children can
help milkmaids fill their pails. Horse-drawn
carriages ply the streets of the make-believe
village. Marimba bands perform and folk
troupes re-create historical scenes. Craft shops
and restaurants complete the experience.
Pueblo Antiguo is part of Parque Diversiones,
a fairground with roller coasters, water slides,
and other rides.
www.parquediversiones.com ⓜ See map pp.
56–57 ✉ 200 yards E of Hospital México
☎ 231-2001 🕐 Closed Mon.–Thurs.
🅂 $$$$$ (four-hour tour)

SPIROGYRA

To immerse yourself in a lepidopteran world,
step inside the 420-square-yard (350 sq m)
netted butterfly garden of Spirogyra, home to
more than 30 species of butterflies. Displays of
live chrysalis and caterpillars provide context.
www.infocostarica.com/butterfly ⓜ See map
pp. 56–57 ✉ 100 yards E and 150 yards S of
Centro Comercial El Pueblo ☎ 222-2937
🅂 $$ ■

B lessed with a climate of eternal spring and summer, this mountain-rimmed region offers colonial antiquities, coffee fields, butterfly farms, bubbling volcanoes, and cloud forest roamed by wildlife.

Central Highlands

Traditional oxcart wheel

Central Highlands

BEAUTY LIES AROUND EVERY BEND IN THE SUBLIME, TEMPERATE CENTRAL Highlands, a region of forest- and coffee-cloaked mountains cradling a broad fertile valley—the Meseta Central—some 40 miles (64 km) long by 20 miles (32 km) wide. There are many attractions, not the least sweeping vistas. Touring is facilitated by roads that span the Inter-American Highway and spiderweb even the highest slope. And no place is too remote to find lodgings—which range from rustic mountain hostelries to modern architectural stunners rising over the coffee fields like Hollywood stage sets.

Many visitors explore the Central Highlands for the sheer pleasure of varying vistas, which grow more dramatic with height. You have no need for your own wheels—organized excursions are offered from San José—but a rental car provides the flexibility to stop for snap-shots and serendipitous treats. Everything of interest lies within a three-hour drive of San José, although the narrow roads are appallingly potholed and deteriorate in places into rutted tracks that your vehicle ascends only with wheezing difficulty.

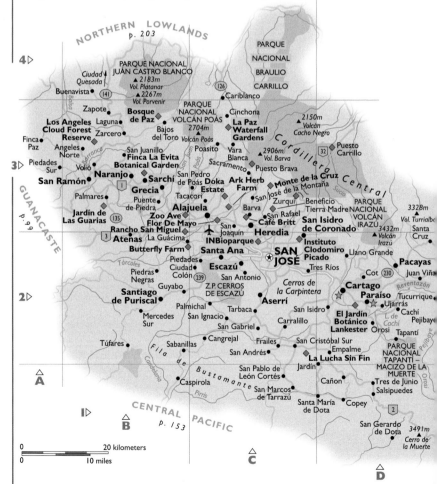

The inter-montane Meseta Central—central plateau—is roughly wedge-shaped: broad to the west and narrowing to the east, averaging in elevation around 3,000 feet (914 m). The Meseta Central is bisected by a relatively low, north-south mountain range, the Cerros de la Carpintera, rising immediately east of the capital city. The valley is flanked to the south by the Talamancas, dauntingly rugged and cut through with valleys that invite exploration. To the north, a series of volcanoes—notably Poás, Barva, Irazú, and Turrialba—poke up in a row, forming the Cordillera Central that reaches 11,260 feet (3,432 m) atop Irazú. Their slopes ascend gradually like the concave curves of an arithmetic equation. Poás and Irazú still fume, although most days their bark is worse than their bite and you can climb to the top for daunting views into the burbling bowels.

Area of map detail

THE CARIBBEAN
p. 217

Lajas
Monumento   Parque
Nacional   Vibarona
Guayabo   Chitaria
Turrialba   1617m
CATIE   Pavones   Cerro Tigre
    La Suiza
        Tuís   Bayo   RESERVA
Hacienda   Pacuare Moravia
Attiro   Platanillo   INDÍGENA
                        Chirripó
                        Abajo
              CHIRRIPÓ
    Chirripó Arriba
        2378m
        Cerro
        Tsuitebeta

SOUTH CENTRAL
p. 187

E   F

You can also thrill to the sparkling highland sunshine and crystal clear air. The lower flanks are cloaked in coffee bushes—the *sine qua non* of the highland economy—shaded by *erythrina* trees and aligned in trim rows. At cooler heights, coffee gives way to dairy farms, strawberry patches, and *viveros* (flower farms) where tropical flowers grow under swathes of black cloth. To the east, Irazú's lower slopes are quilted in "market gardens" growing potatoes and carrots. Corn, sugarcane, coffee, and macadamia plantations dominate the fertile valley floors. On the upper slopes, mists swirl through pines and oaks festooned with mosses and epiphytes typical of conditions atop the continental divide—perfect for spotting quetzals and three-wattled bellbirds.

The region has always been a breadbasket. Pre-Columbian people tilled the soil and thrived. Although they were swiftly decimated following the arrival of the Spanish, their legacy remains in stone at Monumento Nacional Guayabo. The broad-leaved forests that originally cloaked the land were cleared during colonial times by yeoman farmers. The quintessential highland vignette remains the farmer in rubber boots, machete by his side, leading an ox-drawn cart or a herd of cows down the road. Church spires pinpoint scores of rural villages lined with colorful wood and adobe houses fronted by neat-trimmed lawns. The plateau shelters about 70 percent of Costa Rica's population, concentrated in three historic cities—Alajuela, Heredia, and San José (see pp. 55–66)—crammed together. To the east sits Cartago, the original capital city, commanding the Reventazón Valley at a lower elevation than the main valley, which narrows eastward too and falls ever more steeply as the Cordillera Central and Talamancas crimp together. The eastern, windward slopes of the mountains are rain-sodden. Tapantí and Braulio Carrillo National Parks are perpetually wet havens of lush forest echoing with birdsong. Hikers might even spot pumas and tapirs. The Butterfly Farm, Zoo Ave Wildlife Conservation Park, and a dozen other roadside venues offer wildlife viewing for less intrepid souls. Cloud forests close to the mountain crests prove exhilarating for hikers hoping to glimpse quetzals. ■

Escazú & Santa Ana

Escazú

🅰 68 C2

**Biesanz
Woodworks**
www.biesanz.com

✉ Belo Horizonte,
2 miles E of Calle
León Cortes

☎ 289-4337

🕐 Weekends open by
appointment only

THE SOARING HILLS SOUTHWEST OF SAN JOSÉ ARE A dramatic setting for hip Escazú, which combines Old World charm and contemporary chic. This bewitching town is beloved by expatriates and wealthy ticos alike for its luxury living, trendy restaurants and nightclubs, and well-stocked shopping plazas. Escazú is only 3 miles (4.8 km) west of Parque Sábana and central San José (and linked to them by the Carretera Próspero Fernández expressway), yet it manages to retain yesteryear's beguiling campesino spirit. It also offers an array of B&Bs, and the rugged outdoors lies at its doorstep. Santa Ana, 5 miles (8 km) west, offers a more reclusive, old-fashioned appeal.

TRIPTYCH TOWN

Escazú sprawls haphazardly up the northern slopes of its namesake mountain, **Cerro Escazú.** At the base of the hills, close by the freeway, is **San Rafael de Escazú,** the trendy, modern section full of deluxe condominiums and villas, restaurants, the **Costa Rica Country Club** (*members only*), and upscale shopping areas such as the **Multiplaza** (see p. 258), Costa Rica's largest mall. Incongruously in San Rafael's midst is a grassy plaza with a gleaming white colonial-style church built in the 1930s. The hip restaurants and nightclubs draw the crowds at night. The hilly upscale suburb of **Belo Horizonte,** northwest of San Rafael, is a center for charming country inns plus **Biesanz Woodworks,** where carvers conjure masterly hardwood bowls and boxes under the genius-level guidance of Barry Biesanz.

Calle León Cortes, the main road, leads a mile uphill to **San Miguel de Escazú,** the tranquil heart of Escazú laid out around its own colonial-era square. This is the original town and one of the oldest settlements in the nation, dating back to at least 1711 when a chapel was built as a nucleus for an adobe hamlet. Many of the red-tile-roofed homes are extant;

likewise the red-domed 1799 church commanding the square and fringed at its base by a strip of blue to ward off witches. Don't be surprised to see cattle or ox-drawn carts laden with coffee beans being led through the streets.

Calle 1 snakes sharply upward 2 miles (3.2 km) to the smaller community of **San Antonio de Escazú,** where rolling clouds swirl around the church. Every second Sunday in March, the square is the focus for an annual fiesta, the **Día de Boyeros,** when traditional gaily colored oxcarts (*carretas*) parade in honor of the *boyeros* (oxcart drivers), and young girls and women put on traditional garb.

SANTA ANA

The Carretera Próspero Fernández sweeps west beyond Escazú and drops to **Santa Ana,** in a vale whose warm microclimate has fostered a bloom of flower farms and honey-producing apiaries. This town of simple adobe and wooden homes is also a center for ceramics, as at **Cerámica Santa Ana** (*tel 282-6024*) where pottery is still made using kick-wheels.

Three miles (5 km) southwest of Cuidad Colón, **Hacienda de Rodeo** (*tel 249-1013*) offers equestrian lessons and tours. Trails

here go into primary forest that adjoins the **Universidad de Paz** *(tel 249-1511),* dedicated to fostering harmony in the world. The university's botanical garden is filled with statues and busts of famous pacifists.

SYLVAN AND SYBARITIC RETREATS

To enjoy the incredible vistas take to the steep coffee-clad hills above San Antonio de Escazú, cloaked at upper heights in mists that swirl through the native forests of the **Cerros de Escazú,** a protected zone good for hiking. With a keen eye you might spot sloths, monkeys, or even pumas amid the dense forests dripping with Spanish moss.

The sybarite in you might indulge in a spa treatment at **White House Hotel** (see p. 245), overlooking San Antonio with vistas across the Meseta Central. This Greek Revival hotel replete recalls *Gone with the Wind.* It features Scarlett's Fountain of Youth Spa offering treatments from aromatherapy to massage. ■

Barry Biesanz conjures one of his magical wooden creations on a lathe.

Cerros de Escazú

✉ El Cedral, San Antonio de Escazú

☎ 228-0183

Of brooms and *brujas*

Some 60 witches are said to live in Escazú, the *bruja* (witch) capital of Costa Rica. "Any woman who lives in Escazú long enough eventually becomes a *bruja,*" claims Doña Estrella, a town matriarch and self-acknowledged kindhearted witch in a town where they are openly accepted.

Yet evil spirits are said to abound here, too. Among them is La Zegua, a maiden whose enchanting beauty belies her true nature: Men who make love to her discover that she has turned into a horse. And many older residents still believe that the Río Tiribi is haunted, and that the evil monkey Mico Malo attacks those who dare to cross the Los Anonos bridge at night.

Local musician Lencho Salazar relates the legends of the *brujas.* ■

A world of butterflies

At times the Costa Rican countryside resembles a storm of sweetpeas as butterflies float by in endlessly colorful streams. The nation has around 1,250 species, more than the whole of Africa and one in ten of all known species worldwide. Most of these winged insects are as beautiful as the denizens of an exotic harem—from *Riondinidae* with metallic gold wings to the electric-blue morphos, the neon narcissi of the butterfly world.

Morpho glory

There is nothing common about the morpho, colloquially called *celeste común*, which ranges from sea level to 4,500 feet (1,370 m) and zigzags through the forest with a great loping gait along flyways that follow the route of others, like cars on a highway. The 50 or so species range from satiny red to the teals of a Maxfield Parrish sea. The bluest of all morpho species are found on the Caribbean coast.

The morpho's dun-colored underwings are uninspired but when it takes off it displays its iridescent upper wings like a flashing sign. The exotic flash serves as a dinner bell to flycatchers and jacamars, for whom the morpho is a favored tidbit.

Color with a purpose

There is a purpose to bright coloration. Take the Heliconids, a family whose chromatic schemata—normally black speckled in red, white, and yellow—advertise their foul taste: As caterpillars, they gorge on leaves containing cyanide. The strategy works so well that edible species mimic Heliconids by adopting their liveries. Slight variations in coloration serve as flags so that potential suitors can distinguish their perfect partners from among the subspecies. The females of some Heliconid subspecies release pheromones while in the chrysalis, drawing male butterflies to mate with them before they emerge.

Many species of Lepidoptera migrate to mate. With the onset of rainy season around May, the countryside is a never-ending ballet as millions of insects flutter from lowland to highland. The iridescent green and black *Uranidae* flaps its way between Mexico and Bolivia, a distance of 34 degrees latitude. The *Uranidae* is often mistaken for the swallowtail butterfly, which it mimics. Butterflies are experts at guile. One species of moth even mimics a wasp! Even caterpillars are expert tacticians. The larvae of the giant swallowtail (*Papilio cresphontes*) mimic bird droppings and give off an appropriate stench. Another resembles the head of a viper.

A mime troupe

Some species blend with their backgrounds, such as the cream owl butterfly (*Caligo memnon*), whose wings up to 6 inches (15 cm) wide provide superb camouflage. While the upper wings are an attractive blue-gray, the undersides are mottled brown and gray and have yellow "eyes" complete with black pupils and white spots resembling reflected sunlight, so realistic that when opened they look like the face of a wide-eyed owl. They are relatively static by day, but with dusk they take to the air and flit about the forest in search of rotting fruit. The cream owl butterfly is found at elevations up to 3,500 feet (1,070 m), especially on the Pacific side.

The devilish *caligo* caterpillar can grow to 5 inches (13 cm) long; it has horns on its head and a forked tail. Caterpillars exist to eat and grow. "Butterfly larvae are a mouth with chewing mandibles and a long body to house a long gut," says P.J. DeVries, author of *Butterflies of Costa Rica.* Lacking jaws, butterflies use a proboscis to feed on juices—nectar, decaying fruit, or decomposed carrion.

Population densities vary by habitat and seasonality, but all habitats have significant increases in populations in June and July. In general, you will see more butterflies on sunny days. At least one species of butterfly is nocturnal, though most are diurnal and more active by morning. See moths at night when many species gather at light sources.

To learn about butterfly ecology, visit a butterfly "farm," most of which are live exhibits. There are more than a dozen in the country. The Butterfly Farm (see p. 75) at La Guácima, near San José, is the largest butterfly breeding center in the Western Hemisphere. ∎

Above: Camouflaged as poisonous thorns, a snake, and an owl, butterflies and their larvae are creative in self-defense.

Right: Unlike most butterflies, the morpho does not owe its coloration to pigmentation. Morphos are brown, but their scales have a complex structure that absorbs all colors of the spectrum except blue, making them appear that color.

Alajuela & around

Alajuela

🅐 68 C3

Museo Cultural y Histórico Juan Santamaría

www.museojuansantamaria.go.cr

☎ 441-4775

💲 $

ALAJUELA, A SMALL REGIONAL TOWN FOUNDED IN 1676, lies at the base of Volcán Poás a mile north of the Juan Santamaría International Airport and 13 miles (21 km) northwest of San José. Although hardly a calling card in its own right, it is a splendid base for exploring Poás and there are several key sites tucked amid the waves of coffee that wash against the town on all sides.

The main attraction is the **Museo Cultural y Histórico Juan Santamaría** *(closed Mon.)*, to the northwest in the old city jail. Its meager collection tells the tale of the William Walker saga in 1856 in which Juan Santamaría, Alajuela's drummer-boy hero, gave his life (see p. 27). Cultural programs are offered in a screening room. You can request in advance to see an English-language video about the saga. A statue of the young hero stands in the **Parque Juan Santamaría** at corner of Calle 2 and Avenida 2.

The town bustles on Saturday, when you should visit the compact **Mercado Central,** where all manner of produce is sold within the tight, shaded warren.

The soccer team, La Liga, is a source of local pride. You can catch a game on weekends at Avenida 7 and Calle 13.

THE SLOPES OF VOLCÁN POÁS

North of Alajuela, the land rises incrementally toward the forested summit of Volcán Poás. The drive is superbly scenic as you wend up through coffee fields hugging the convex slope. Higher up the coffee fields thin out, replaced by a quilted patchwork of strawberries and ornamental plants grown under black shade nets, while Holstein dairy cattle munch contentedly on lime green pastures. The aromatic smell of log fires scents the crisp air, drawing you to eat at any of several

Juan Santamaría's statue in his park

Flor De Mayo

www.hatchedtoflyfree.org

🅐 68 C3

✉ Rio Segundo de Alajuela

☎ 441-2658

🕑 By appt.

💲 Donation

Alajuela, "Costa Rica's second city," is colloquially called the "City of the Mangoes" for the trees that shade **Parque Central,** officially the Plaza de General Tomás Guardia but known by local wags as Park of the Dead Doves for the old men who gather to gossip and watch the pretty girls pass by.

The body of ex-president Guardia is buried in the simple metal-domed cathedral, dating from 1863, on the park's east side.

rustic restaurants that serve traditional peasant fare, such as roast pork and chicken. At **Poasito** you can continue north to Parque Nacional Volcán Poás or east to Vara Blanca and the Catarata La Paz (see p. 98).

ANIMAL WORLDS

You'll be enthralled by a visit to **Flor De Mayo,** a 7-acre (2.8 ha) estate and breeding center for endangered green and scarlet macaws, at Río Segundo de Alajuela, 2 miles (3.2 km) southeast of Alajuela. Here Richard and Margot Frisius, founders of the Amigos de las Aves foundation, breed these majestic birds for release into the wild in an attempt to counter the devastation wrought on macaw populations by a combination of poaching and habitat loss. An educational visitor's center offers a prelude to watching the young birds careening across the vast flyway. Visits are by appointment only.

Scarlet macaws are also bred at **Zoo Ave Wildlife Conservation Park** (tel 433-0989), situated in the tony suburb of La Garita, west of Alajuela. This 142-acre (57 ha) zoo is a haven for in excess of 100 species of birds, including quetzals, curassows, cranes, and dozens of toucans. Recreations of natural habitats are home to all four species of native monkeys, as well as crocodiles, and other enthralling beasts. Injured and confiscated wildlife are tended at a rescue center, though it and the breeding center are off-limits.

Another must-see is the **Butterfly Farm** at La Guácima, about 2 miles (3.2 km) south of the airport. Around 30,000 pupae are bred and exported each year to zoos around the world—the offspring of some 60 native species of butterflies that are allowed to flap freely through a lush world secured by netting. Pathways guide you through this fascinating lepidopteran world.

A video and the farm's erudite guides enlighten visitors about the complex relationships between the insects and their host plants, and about butterfly life cycles from egg to adult. You should be given the

Richard Frisius with two macaws

chance to witness the astounding metamorphosis from caterpillar to flying insect as a butterfly wriggles free of its chrysalis.

Two miles (3.2 km) north of La Guácima, **Rancho San Miguel** (tel 438-0849, www.ranchosanmiguel .co.cr) offers a chance to ride Andalusian horses at this stud farm, where dressage tuition is also offered. The highlight is the thrice-weekly show, when the beautiful horses perform. ■

Zoo Ave Wildlife Conservation Park
www.zooave.org
🅰 68 B3
✉ Dulce Nombre, 2 miles E of the Inter-American Hwy.
💲 $

Butterfly Farm
www.butterflyfarm.co.cr
🅰 68 B2
✉ 400 yards S of Los Reyes Country Club, La Guácima
☎ 438-0300
💲 $$

The Western slopes

THE CLASSIC TOURING CIRCUIT TAKES IN THE WESTERN Highlands, coffee and dairy country par excellence laced with small artisan and market towns lining the Inter-American Highway and Carretera 3, two parallel routes that weave through the region, ascending gradually toward the western rim before beginning their plummeting descents to the Pacific and the Northern Lowlands. The vistas over the Central Valley are stupendous.

GRECIA

This compact market center, founded only in 1864, is known for its twin-spired **metal church,** which was imported from Belgium in 1897 and now commands the palm-shaded main plaza. The somewhat dour rust-red exterior of the edifice belies the handsome wooden interior, which features pendulous glass chandeliers and a soaring marble altar—a fanciful confection in stone.

Be sure, too, to stop in at **World of Snakes** on the old Alajuela road, where more than 300 live snakes are exhibited in glass-fronted cages. The Austrian owners breed snakes for sale and use educational labeling and guided tours to shatter commonly held negative stereotypes about snakes, replacing them with a healthy respect for these ecologically vital reptiles. A "petting" program encourages children to handle non-venomous snakes.

SARCHÍ

A staple on the beaten tourist path, this agricultural town—divided into Sarchí Norte (the main town) and Sarchí Sur (the artisan center) about 0.6 miles (1 km) further east—is also renowned as Costa Rica's center of crafts and fine furniture despite being firmly in the grip of commercialism. The main road is lined with souvenir stores selling leather and wooden items—from handsome bowls of lignum vitae ("wood of life") and classic wood-and-leather rockers to miniature hand-painted oxcarts, Sarchí's hallmark and also a national symbol.

You can see oxcarts being made and adorned at **Fábrica de Carretas Joaquín Chaverrí** *(tel 454-4411)* in Sarchí Sur. Although many artisans now produce tawdry kitsch, others remain true to tradition; be sure to visit **Taller Eloy Alfaro** *(tel 454-4131),* two blocks north of the main street in Sarchí Norte, where you can watch Señor Alfaro conjure traditional oxcarts and yokes intended for use in the fields.

Grecia
🅜 68 B3

World of Snakes
✉ 0.5 mile E of
    Grecia
☎ 494-3700
💲 $$

Sarchí
🅜 68 B3

Left: The church in Grecia is made of steel plates.

The rambling town is cusped by coffee-clad vales, a magnificent setting with a photogenic appeal enhanced by the town's quintessential floral motif adorning whitewashed adobe buildings and the blush-pink **church** in the main square of Sarchí Norte. The church has an impressive vaulted ceiling.

Try to visit Sarchí in the first week of February for the town's lively fiesta.

BOSQUE DE PAZ

North of Sarchí is a narrow winding road that climbs up the western flank of Volcán Poás and, beyond the cloud-shrouded saddle between Poás and Volcán Platanar (7,162 feet, 2,183 m), plummets precariously down to **Bajos del Toro,** a scenic Shangri-la secreted in its own valley. This remote farming community provides access to the 960-acre (390 ha) **Bosque de Paz,** a private nature reserve whose mountainous rain-soaked terrain is a veritable Noah's Ark of safeguarded wildlife. Trails offer an opportunity to spot scores of rare birds such as curassows and black guans. Big cats, which give people a wide berth, prowl through the lush forests in search of brocket deer and primates, including howler monkeys, capuchins, and the endangered spider monkeys.

The reserve lies at the foot of **Parque Nacional Juan Castro Blanco,** a 35,230-acre (14,260 ha) swath created in 1995 to protect the precious montane rain forest and

An artist adds decorative touches to a traditional oxcart wheel.

Bosque de Paz
www.bosquedepaz.com
- 68 B3
- Bajos del Toro, 7 miles N of Sarchí
- 234-6676
- By appointment
- Call for details

cloud forests of Volcán Platanar. The park is cut through by trails but otherwise has no facilities—perfect for hardy hikers.

AROUND NARANJO

The countryside west of Sarchí appeals mainly for its uplifting vistas. Three miles (4.8 km) west of Sarchí is **Naranjo,** an important market town sitting astride Carretera 3 and alluring for its comely church supported by Corinthian columns. Next comes the regional center of **San Ramón,** 7 miles (11.2 km) farther, on the western rim of the Meseta Central and gateway to Puntarenas and Guanacaste. Market gardening is important hereabouts and the town's Saturday **farmer's market** *(feria de agricultor)* is well worth a stop. So too is the centenarian metal church, which was made in Germany, shipped to Costa Rica and welded together in situ.

The Inter-American Highway skirts San Ramón, which sits immediately to the north, and **Palmares,** a mile (1.6 km) to the south. Palmares is renowned for its colorful mid-January **fiesta,** which

features rodeo-style bullfights and all the fun of the fair. Also here is the largest orchid collection in the country, consisting of some 40,000 blooms, can be enjoyed at **Jardín de las Guarias,** the private garden of Javier Solórzaro Murillo, at Cocaleca, a mile (1.6 km) south of Palmares.

AT THE CREST OF THE CORDILLERA

You could be forgiven for imagining yourself in Switzerland as you drive along Carretera 141 between Naranjo and **Ciudad Quesada** (see p. 212), a center of the local dairy industry that clings to the mountainside. The mountains fall away to the Northern Lowlands via a breathtaking switchback.

Midway between Naranjo and Ciudad Quesada is **Zarcero,** a pretty village whose simple **church** is fronted by a leafy arbor running through a **topiary park** that resembles a circus. The gardener responsible, Evangelisto Blanco, wields his pruning shears like an artist's paintbrush, conjuring up such smile-inducing spectacles as an elephant with light bulbs for

Parque Nacional Juan Castro Blanco
🗺 68 B3
✉ Bajos del Toro, 8 miles N of Sarchí
☎ 460-7600
💲 $$

San Ramón
🗺 68 B3

Jardín de las Guarias
🗺 68 B3
✉ Cocaleca, 1 mile S of Palmares
☎ 452-0091
🕐 Call for details
💲 Call for details

eyes, and a cat riding a motorcycle atop a hedge. All around, black-and-white Holstein cattle chomp on emerald green alpine meadows and even many of the farmsteads hint at Swiss provenance.

From San Ramón, lonesome Carretera 702 climbs north up the mountain slopes and 12 miles (19 km) above the town, where it begins its looping drop to the Northern Lowlands. You'll want to stop at the **Valle Escondido Lodge** *(tel 231-0906)*, a vivero (flower farm) suspended in a cleft of the valley that offers hiking and horseback rides into the surrounding cloud forest. The **San Lorenzo Canopy Tour** is here as well; its restaurant has stunning views over the cascading valley.

For a fuller immersion, detour to the **Los Ángeles Cloud Forest Reserve,** a private 2,000-acre (810 ha) reserve ranging from 2,100 feet (640 m) to 5,400 feet (1,650 m) in elevation. More than 200 bird species, plus monkeys, and cats such as ocelots and even jaguars await visitors on guided hikes from the rustic and enchanting **Villablanca Cloudforest**

Lodge (see p. 245), perched on the very edge of the continental divide, the hotel offers Hansel-and-Gretel-style cottages with wood-burning fireplaces. A steel cable 600 feet (182 m) long is slung between the treetops to grant a bird's-eye view of wildlife on a **canopy tour** through the forest. The property is part of an expansive dairy farm owned by ex-president Rodrigo Corazón and features a delightful chapel adorned with colorful tiles.

ATENAS & AROUND

The charming town of Atenas on Hwy. 3, 8 miles (13 km) south of Palmares, has a truly sublime climate. The town plaza boasts an exquisite church and is surrounded by venerable wooden homes. The **Monumento a Los Boyeros,** located on the east side of town, commemorates the days when Atenas was a major stop on the *camino de carretas,* the old coffee route to Puntarenas.

For a breathtaking view over coffee fields toward the Gulf of Nicoya, break your journey at **Mirador del Cafetal** on Hwy. 3 5 miles (8 km) west of Atenas. ∎

Zarcero's quaint church viewed through an arch of its topiary park

Los Ángeles Cloud Forest Reserve
www.villablanca-costarica.com
🅰 68 B3
✉ 5 miles E of Angeles Norte
☎ 461-0300
💲 $$

Grano de Oro

Costa Ricans call coffee *grano de oro*—the grain of gold—with good reason. The humble bean lifted the nation out of obscurity two centuries ago, bringing wealth to countless subsistence farmers and to the country as a whole. The slopes and steep vales of the Meseta Central are patterned in endless rows of dark green corduroy, coiling along the hillsides like snakes.

Coffee bushes, native to Ethiopia, came to Costa Rica from Jamaica in 1779; they turned out to be Costa Rica's economic salvation. The rise of coffee in Central America coincided with the demise of slavery in the Caribbean, which threw the islands' industry into chaos. Jamaica—at that time the world's largest coffee producer—was quickly displaced by Costa Rica, whose climate and rich volcanic soils proved perfect for coffee cultivation.

The coffee plant grows best in well-drained soils at elevations of 2,500 to 3,500 feet (760 to 1,070 m), with nearly constant temperatures between 59 and 82°F (15–28°C) and a distinct wet and dry season. The Meseta Central met these conditions as well as anywhere in the world. On the Central Highlands a particular combination of aspect, slope, soil type, and climactic conditions combined to produce a distinctly flavored coffee—mellow and aromatic, with a hint of acidity—that international coffee connoisseurs soon acclaimed as one of the best in the world. Economically, a dry season aided the Costa Rican harvest; it was also propitious for the transportation of the beans down the mountains via mule train to the port of Puntarenas, whence a three-month journey via Cape Horn delivered the beans to java-thirsty Europe.

For Costa Rica's subsistence farmers, the coffee was a commercial godsend—and one on which no taxes were levied. Soon everyone was growing the grano de oro (in the early 1800s there was even a law that required every tico household to grow coffee bushes in its yard), which by 1829 had established itself as the nation's *numero uno* income earner. Thus prosperity came to Central America's erstwhile paupers.

Small farmers dominated production and took their fair share of wealth. But the real profits lay in the processing and trade, which quickly coalesced into relatively few hands. Costa Rica gained its first social and political elite—the cafeteleros (coffee barons). Even today there are only 95 coffee mills *(beneficios)* in the country, although some 80,000 producers grow coffee on approximately 270,000 acres (110,000 ha).

Coffee remained the nation's prime source of income until 1991, when world coffee prices plummeted and the grano de oro was toppled from its pedestal by both bananas and tourism, causing economic distress in the industry. Coffee's fortunes have continued to decline; production has fallen from 2.5 million bags in 1997 to 2.12 million in 2003. Nowhere else in the world do coffee producers attain such high productivity per acre. Ideal conditions are enhanced by the propagation of high-yielding plants and intensive production techniques. The highest quality coffee grows at higher elevations, where beans take longer to mature and are more robust and aromatic, with less caffeine.

The seeds are planted in nurseries and nourished until, as yearlings, they are planted out in rows that follow the contours of the mountain slopes under shade trees or tousled bananas, which fix nitrogen in the soil. Shaded coffee bushes are more productive. The glossy green bushes will begin fruiting by their fourth year (carefully tended, a coffee bush will bear fruit for up to 40 years), announced at the onset of rainy season by the appearance of tiny white blossoms that scent the air with a jasmine-like fragrance. The beans are surrounded by lush green berries that turn blood-red by November—the time of the seasonal harvest. Then families and children take to the fields bearing large wicker baskets.

The hand-picked beans are shipped to beneficios, where the fleshy outer layers are removed to expose the beans, which are blow-dried or spread out in the sun in the traditional manner. The leathery skins are then stripped away; the beans are roasted, sorted, vacuum-sealed, and finally shipped to market. Java! ■

Above: A coffee grower harvests beans on his marginal riverside plot. Right: The fragrant white blossoms and plump red berries of *coffea arabica* are favored as ornamentals.

Left: A basket of hand-picked beans awaits delivery to a beneficio. Costa Rica's coffee harvest is maintained in traditional style using hand-woven wicker baskets.

Heredia & Volcán Barva

HEREDIA AND ITS SURROUNDINGS EXUDE THEIR OWN beauty. The pull defies gravity, luring you inexorably up the slopes of Volcán Barva, where emerald pastures give way to pine and merge into the mystical cloud forests that shroud the uppermost slopes of Parque Nacional Braulio Carrillo. On weekends, the inhabitants of San José also head north, seeking cozy cottages warmed by log-burning hearths and rustic restaurants where simple fare is cooked over coffee-wood fires.

HEREDIA

This former coffee capital of Costa Rica, 7 miles (11.2 km) northeast of San José, dates from 1706 and is affectionately called "City of the Flowers." At its core is the atmospheric **Parque Central** dominated by the venerable **Basílica de la Immaculada Concepción,** erected in 1797 and featuring bells imported from Cuzco, Peru. The handsome tree-shaded plaza proffers a panoply of historic attractions, including the circular brick fortress, **El Fortín,** erected by president Alfredo González Flores (1914–17). Note the gun slits that open outward so that bullets ricochet into the fortress— a military heresy that speaks volumes for Costa Rica's innocence in such matters. Flores lived across Calle Central in what is now the **Casa de la Cultura,** housing a small museum and art gallery.

The east side of town is dominated by the campus of the **Universidad Nacional,** its surrounding area bustling with coffee shops. The bougainvillea-lined suburb of **San Joaquín de las Flores** is famous for its traditional Easter Parade.

Near **Santo Domingo de Heredia,** southeast of town, is **INBioparque,** the headquarters of the Instituto Nacional de Biodiversidad. In addition to housing a collection of millions of species of flora and fauna, this educational facility has static and interactive exhibitions on tropical ecology. Trails go through a butterfly garden and re-creations of habitats.

BARVA

Exquisite and endearing, this historic village 1.5 miles (2.4 km) north of Heredia lures visitors to its narrow streets lined with old adobe homes adorned with grill windows and terra-cotta roofs. At its heart is the **Iglesia de San Bartolomé de Barva,** built in 1867.

The **Ark Herb Farm** *(tel 239-2111, $),* at Santa Barbara de Heredia, about 2 miles (3.2 km) northwest of Barva, spreads over 20 acres (8 ha) of hillside carpeted with nearly a thousand species of medicinal and culinary herbs raised for export. Trails weave among the redolent herb beds, shrubbery, and fruit orchards. Guided tours are offered.

To see an example of adobe construction and learn about campesino culture at the turn of the 19th century, pop into the **Museo de la Cultura Popular,** housed in the former home of Alfredo González Flores at **Santa Lucía de Barva,** midway between Heredia and Barva.

Barva is surrounded by a sea of coffee, much of it belonging to the estates of **Café Britt,** Costa Rica's preeminent producer of export-quality coffee. Café Britt offers a highly recommended educational

Heredia
🅰 68 C3

Casa de la Cultura
✉ Ave. Central, Calle Central, Heredia
☎ 260-1619

INBioparque
www.inbioparque.com
✉ 1.5 miles SW of Santo Domingo de Heredia
☎ 507-8107
💲 $$

Barva
🅰 68 C3

Museo de la Cultura Popular
✉ Carretera 126, 1.5 miles NW of Heredia
☎ 260-1619
💲 $

tour that features a multimedia presentation and includes the roasting plant and tasting room where visitors learn the fine art of coffee discernment. Guided by professional actors in traditional garb, visitors see amusing skits that blend the tale of an evolving love story, the nation's development, and the evolution of coffee. Cafe Britt's nearby **Beneficio Tierra Madre** coffee farm and processing mill is adorned with murals celebrating the "golden bean" and welcomes visitors eager to learn about the process.

VOLCÁN BARVA

On weekends and holidays, Josefinos hit the slopes of Volcán Barva due north of Heredia, where mountain resort communities such as **San José de la Montaña** and the **Reserva Monte de la Cruz** offer cabins nestling amid the pines. Temperatures grow chillier with altitude as roads lined with

impatiens curve past alpine meadows and pine, cypress, and oak forests draped with ferns, orchids, and Spanish moss. It is easy to imagine yourself in the Tirol, a notion enhanced by the Tyrolean architecture that is so popular here.

The finest example of transplanted Alps is to be found above **San Rafael de Heredia** at the **Hotel Chalet Tirol** (see p. 245), which looks like a set from *The Sound of Music*. The hotel has a superb French restaurant and in summer hosts the **International Music Festival,** with classical concerts in the Salzburg Theater.

Hiking at these upper heights is stupendous. The trails lead through cloud forest reserves such as that of **Cerro Dantas Wildlife Biological Center** *(tel 274-1997)*, which has an ecological center, educational trails, and guided hikes by community members. ∎

The grotto of the 1767 Basílica de Barva draws those seeking miracle cures.

Café Britt
www.coffeetour.com
🅰 68 C3
✉ Carretera 126, 1.25 miles NW of Heredia
☎ 260-2748
💲 $

Beneficio Tierra Madre
www.beneficiotierramadre.com
🅰 68 C3
✉ San Rafael de Heredia
☎ 277-1600
💲 $$

Parque Nacional Volcán Poás

Parque Nacional
Volcán Poás
www.sinac.go.cr
📍 68 C3
☎ 482-2165
💲 $$

THE MOST DEVELOPED OF THE COUNTRY'S NATIONAL parks protects the most dramatic of the region's volcanoes, which rises above the northwest Meseta Central. On clear days you can see both the Caribbean Sea and the Pacific Ocean from its summit. Peering down into the crater may evoke the same sensations that virgins of pre-Columbian times felt moments before they were tossed in as sacrificial lambs to the gods.

The steaming innards of Poás put you on edge.

The 13,838-acre (5,600 ha) Parque Nacional Volcán Poás is centered on the eponymous 8,871-foot-high (2,704 m) volcano, whose main crater collapsed eons ago to form a mile-wide (1.6 km) caldera. You can drive all the way to the summit. A 300-yard (275 m) walk from the parking lot leads up to the viewing terrace 600 feet (183 m) above the awesome cauldron, where fumaroles hiss, a sulfurous pool bubbles, and smoke is disgorged from a 300-foot-high (90 m) mini-volcano that has been thrown up in recent decades. You may get a whiff of sulfur fumes, which can at times be sufficiently acidic for the park to be closed to visitors.

The feisty giant, still intermittently active, entered its most recent volatile phase in the early 1990s.

The main crater burbles and belches persistently; occasionally it spews violently, frightening the farming communities that litter its slopes.

Poás also has two minor craters, both extinct, snoozing beneath lush green blankets. One, **Botos,** has a jade-colored lake reached via the **Botos Trail.** The cloud forest surrounding the lake can now be accessed via the **El Canto de los Aves** trail. The forests resound with the songs of sooty robins and toucanets, as well as the melodious two-note whistle of resplendent quetzals. Fiery-throated hummingbirds also flit past, and you are sure to see the endemic Poás squirrel.

Plan to arrive early to beat the clouds that blanket the chill heights by midmorning. Bring warm clothing to shield yourself from the wind whistling over the continental divide. As the most visited park in the country, Poás is popular on weekends with ticos who disdain the wondrous silence. If possible, visit midweek.

The **visitor center** shows a scale model of Poás; its exhibits provide a good explanation of the processes at work. Audiovisual presentations are given on Sundays. The 23-mile (37 km) drive from Alajuela, featuring a summit road that winds like a coiled python, is half the fun; for those without independent transport, excursions leave daily from San José. Check for times and prices with local tour operators there. ■

Parque Nacional Braulio Carrillo

Parque Nacional Braulio Carrillo

🅰 68 C4

✉ Hwy. 32, 14 miles NE of San José

☎ 233-4533, ext. 25

💲 $$

RUGGED TO THE POINT OF BEING ALMOST IMPENETRABLE, Parque Nacional Braulio Carrillo protects a precious watershed on the windward side of the Cordillera Central—a massive tract of pristine wilderness spanning five life zones less than a 40-minute drive from the metropolis of San José. Permission is required for camping.

raulio Carrillo is a 108,970-acre (44,100 ha) swatch of endless dark green cloaking the flanks of **Volcán Barva** (9,534 feet, 2,906 m) and **Volcán Cacho Negro** (7,053 feet, 2,150 m), and ranges from windswept cloud forest at higher elevations to lowland rain forest in the soggy Northern Lowlands barely 100 feet (30 m) above sea level. Given the park's size and elevation range, temperatures differ markedly, though rainfall is a near constant and nowhere less than 10 feet (3 m) per year.

Hiking the rugged trails is a guaranteed way of seeing wildlife, including more than 500 species of birds, from quetzals to toucans, and almost 150 mammal species, including jaguars, peccaries, pumas, monkeys, and tepezcuintles (a giant rodent, also known as the paca), the park mascot.

The park is easily accessed by Highway 32—the Guápiles Highway—whose construction in 1978 resulted in the park's creation. Access is from the **Zurquí ranger station,** on the highway 13 miles (21 km) northeast of San José, where there's an **information center.** There is also access from the lowlands at the **Puesto Carrillo ranger station,** on the Guápiles Highway; and with a rugged four-wheel drive from the west, and from the south via the **Puesto Brava ranger station,** above **Sacramento,** requiring a daunting first-gear ascent. ∎

Riding the Rainforest Aerial Tram lifts visitors into treetop life.

Rainforest Railway

F ew fun-fair rides are as thrilling as a 90-minute, mile-long (1.6 km) excursion through the forest canopy aboard this open-air aerial tram, in a private tropical wet forest reserve abutting Braulio Carrillo. The trip reveals details of everyday life in the treetops, where 75 percent of all rain-forest species dwell. You can view monkeys eye-to-eye while dangling as high as 200 feet (60 m) above the forest floor. Says Dr. Donald Perry, who conceived the tram: "We like the idea of putting people in cages, not animals." ∎

Rainforest Aerial Tram

www.rainforesttram.com

🅰 205 E1

✉ Rara Avis, Hwy. 32, 30 miles NE of San José

☎ 257-5961

💲 $$$$$

Cartago

ALTHOUGH CARTAGO, THE NATION'S ERSTWHILE CAPITAL
and today its second largest city, offers meager attractions, a fistful of
top-class sites lie nearby, the surrounding countryside is enrichingly
scenic, and the city is a starting point for stupendous drives up Volcán
Irazú, through the Orosi Valley, and along the mountain ridge that
leads south to Cerro de la Muerte.

Cartago
🅜 68 D2
**Visitor
information**
✉ Cartago Chamber of
Commerce, 30 yards
E of Las Ruinas de
Cartago
☎ 591-4785
🕐 Closed Sun.

Cartago, Costa Rica's oldest
settlement, was founded in 1563
by conquistador Juan Vásquez
de Coronado and remained the
nation's capital until 1823, when
it lost the Battle of Ochomongo
to San José. It is hardly a beautiful
city and long ago ceased to wear
its history on its sleeve. Most of
the colonial edifices have literally
fallen victims to earthquakes
(most recently 1910), and nearby

Volcán Irazú frequently spews ash
on the city.
    The parochial city, at the
eastern base of the Cerros de la
Carpintera, 16 miles (26 km) east of
San José, retains its role as religious
capital, symbolically represented by
the ruins of **Iglesia de la
Parroquia,** in a tree-shaded plaza
at Avenida 2 and Calle 2. The
nation's preeminent church, the
blue-and-white **Basílica de**

El Jardín Botánico Lankester

🗺 68 D2

✉ Hwy. 1, Paraíso

☎ 552-3247

💲 $$

A dramatic blood-red heliconia is a highlight of El Jardín Botánico Lankester.

Nuestra Señora de los Ángeles, stands foursquare in the main square at Avenida 2 and Calle 14. It was built in of steel with a concrete stucco surface in 1929 in Byzantine style following the collapse of its precursor in 1926. The stunning interior of glistening hardwoods boasts exquisite stained glass. A steady stream of supplicants kneel and pray to **La Negrita,** the nation's *mulatta* (mixed-blood) patron saint to whom local superstition ascribes miraculous cures. She resides in an 8-inch-high (20 cm) effigy set in a gold-encrusted shrine above the main altar. In the basement, to the rear, the **Cripta de la Piedra** shrine is a veritable mini-museum of *promesas,* or votive offerings, left by worshippers as thanks for prayers granted. In the southeast corner, supposedly curative waters seep from a tiny cavern.

EL JARDÍN BOTÁNICO LANKESTER

This 27-acre (11 ha) garden, at **Paraíso,** 5 miles (8 km) east of Cartago, protects an invaluable collection of neotropical flora that is one of the largest in the Americas, including its pride and joy—more than 700 species of orchids. The gardens also abound with palms and bromeliads, effusive as a Pisarro painting, drawing butterflies and birds by the thousands. Peak blooming is in springtime.

The gardens are named for the founder, Charles Lankester Wells (1879-1969), an Englishman who worked to collate a representative corpus of Central American flora. The garden, established in 1917, later passed to the North American Orchid Society, and is today owned and maintained by the University of Costa Rica. ∎

OROSÍ VALLEY DRIVE

Orosi Valley drive

Southeast of Paraíso, 5 miles (8 km) east of Cartago, Carretera 224 drops sharply into a Shangri-la canyon edged to the south by the dauntingly forested flanks of the Talamanca mountains. The rivers that drain the vale have been dammed to form Lago de Cachí, around which the road loops. This tour makes a circle that begins and ends in Paraíso, passing two precious colonial churches and many intriguing stops en route.

At the main square in Paraíso, turn south off the main highway—Carretera 10—and follow the looping road 1.5 miles (2.4 km) to the **Mirador Orosi** ❶, offering views over the valley and set in a park run by the ICT (Instituto Costarricense de Turismo). Shortly beyond, the road begins to slalom the ski-ramp route into the canyon. At the foot you're instantly immersed in coffee, with shiny-leafed bushes to all sides.

The road wends through the coffee fields and beyond the **Río Aguacaliente** deposits you in the picturesque village of **Orosi** ❷ (visitor information, tel 533-3333), backed by broodingly forested hills. On your right you pass the **Iglesia de San José de Orosi,** a charming little church built in 1743 whose thick adobe walls and beamed roof have withstood many an earthquake. Its ascetic interior, with a terra-cotta floor and wooden gilt altar, was recently restored. Adjoining is a small **Museo de Arte Religioso** (tel 533-3051, closed Mon.) containing religious art, chalices, and other ecclesiastical icons plus colonial furniture. Photography is not permitted.

Continue four blocks south and one east to the hillside **Balnearios Termales Orosi,** (tel 533-2156), offering relaxing bathing in well-maintained thermal mineral pools, which abound in the valley. Immediately south of the village you'll pass the **Beneficio Renex** coffee-processing plan (no tours). The plant sits at a junction for Parque Nacional Tapantí-Macizo Cerro la Muerte (see p. 98). Turn left and cross the **Río Grande de Orosi** via a narrow suspension bridge (a nominal toll is collected on Sundays). On the far bank is the **Hotel/Restaurante Río Paloma** (tel 533-3128), specializing in dishes of local trout.

Turn left immediately beyond the river and trace its course along a deteriorated section of road. After about 4 miles (6.4 km) pick up the pavement again as the road swings along the southern shore of **Lago de Cachí** ❸, which attracts waterfowl. The lake was created in the 1960s when the Río Reventazón was dammed for hydroelectricity. It is becoming popular for fishing and boating offered at **La Casona del Cafetal** (tel 533-3280), a lakeside coffee farm that also offers hiking and horseback riding and a restaurant with marvelous views.

Continue east less than one mile (1.6 km) to the rough-hewn **Casa El Soñador** ❹ ("House of the Dreamer," tel 577-1186), a wooden and bamboo structure adorned with primitivist carvings—the whimsical creations of the late Macedonio Quesada, whose sons continue the tradition of conjuring twisted coffee-tree stumps into carvings. Two miles (3.2 km) farther, the road turns west and crosses the **Presa de Cachí** (Cachí dam) ❺, pointing you back to Paraíso. After about 5 miles (8 km) you'll see signs for **Ujurrás** ❻, renowned for its ruined church—**Iglesia de Nuestra Señora de la Limpia Concepción**—on the fringe of the lake. The church dates from 1681 but was abandoned in 1833 when the valley flooded. Today it sits amid lawns fronted by giddily colorful flowers. It is the setting every third Sunday in April for a pilgrimage from Paraíso, which awaits at the top of a scenic climb. ■

- 🗺 See area map pp. 68–69
- ▶ Paraíso
- ↔ 19 miles (30.4 km)
- ⏱ 3 hours
- ▶ Paraíso

NOT TO BE MISSED

- Iglesia de San José de Orosi
- Casa El Soñador
- The ruins at Ujurrás

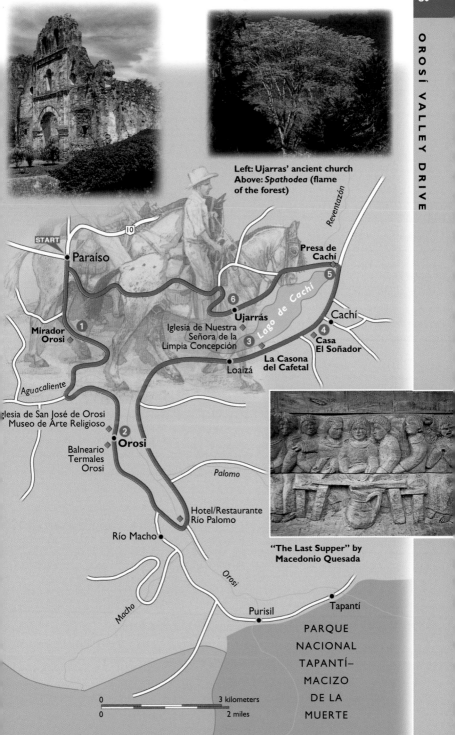

Left: Ujarras' ancient church
Above: *Spathodea* (flame of the forest)

START

10

Paraíso

Presa de Cachí

5

Mirador Orosi 1

6

Ujarrás

Lago de Cachí

Cachí

Iglesia de Nuestra Señora de la Limpia Concepción 3

4

Casa El Soñador

Loaizá

La Casona del Cafetal

Aguacaliente

Iglesia de San José de Orosi
Museo de Arte Religioso

2 Orosi

Balneario Termales Orosi

Palomo

Hotel/Restaurante Río Palomo

Río Macho

"The Last Supper" by Macedonio Quesada

Orosi

Macho

Purisil

Tapantí

PARQUE
NACIONAL
TAPANTÍ–
MACIZO
DE LA
MUERTE

0   3 kilometers
0   2 miles

Parque Nacional Volcán Irazú

VOLCÁN IRAZÚ LOOMS OVER BOTH CARTAGO AND THE Reventazón Valley, rising to the north as steadily as the line created by a logarithmic equation. For anyone with a head for heights, a drive to the top offers sublime rewards. On clear days, the view takes in the shimmering waters of both the Caribbean and the Pacific.

Parque Nacional Volcán Irazú

🗺 68 D2/3

✉ 22 miles NE of Cartago

☎ 551-9398

$ $

Volcán Irazú (11,260 feet, 3,432 m) is an active volcano and made international news on March 13, 1963, when it erupted the day that President John F. Kennedy arrived in Costa Rica for an official visit. A resulting mud storm left highland dwellers ankle-deep in volcanic mud, obliterating the coffee crop but enriching the countryside for years to come. Irazú's last major hiccup was in 1996. In more benign moods, the giant welcomes visitors.

The volcano is the centerpiece of its namesake national park, created in 1955 and encompassing 5,705 acres (2,300 ha) of primary forest, including cloud forest. A 22-mile (35 km) drive from Cartago leads to the barren, windswept summit. As you climb upwards, the views grow ever more panoramic until it is all you can do to keep your eye on the serpentine road. On the lower flanks you'll pass through trim little farming communities, like colorful pointillist dots on the emerald green canvas. Although dairy farming is predominant, the area is Costa Rica's main center for market gardening: the indecently rich slopes are a patchwork of fields growing vegetables such as carrots, potatoes, and legumes.

The volcano—whose name means "thunderpoint" and is derived from the indigenous word *ara-tzu*—has twin craters. The smaller of the two, the 300-foot (91 m) deep **Diego de la Haya** crater, cradles a mineral-rich lake that changes hue from jade green to blood red. Fumaroles steam in the larger crater, which yawns 900 feet (275 m) deep.

It is foggy and chilly up here most of the time. Bring a sweater and jacket to brave the wind that beats down the vegetation, such as stunted dwarf oaks that cling low to the ground. Don't be put off from below by the clouds swirling near the summit, for it is quite possible to climb above the clouds and emerge in the sunlight, giving you views of the crater with the clouds far below.

For your own safety, stick to the marked trails. Out of respect for the fragile ecosystems, refrain from following the illicit paths that have been trampled by visitors who chose to ignore the signs warning not to approach the dangerously unstable rims of the craters. Because the clouds normally thicken as the day progresses, mornings are usually the best time to visit.

Mountain rabbits, squirrel, and even armadillo and coyotes can be seen scurrying across the ashy plains, while birds such as the ruddy nuthatch, night sparrow, and masked woodpecker swoop by within fingertip reach.

The **ranger station** is 1.25 miles (2 km) below the summit, where facilities include picnic benches and a mobile *soda* that serves snacks. Short trails tempt the hardy hiker.

Take warm, rainproof clothing to guard against inclement weather. Also, plan on stopping in at the **Restaurante Linda Vista** (*tel 386-9097*) for hearty fare. ∎

Opposite: Volcán Irazú and the larger of its two craters are breathtaking in scale.

Valle de Reventazón

DRAINING LAKE CACHÍ, THE RÍO REVENTAZÓN FALLS
through a narrow valley, tumbling ever more steeply to the east as the
land steps toward the Caribbean Lowlands. Hemmed between the
sheer face of the Talamancas and the steep yet gradual slopes of
Volcán Turrialba, the area is given short shrift by tourists though it
offers appeals a-plenty.

At its heart lies **Turrialba,** a
somewhat nondescript town in a
broad valley swaddled in sugarcane,
citrus, and macadamia plantations.
Turrialba was once a major way-
stop on the old highway between
San José and the Caribbean, and
has been left high and dry since
construction of the Guápiles
Highway and since the demise of
the Atlantic Railroad in 1991. It's
now best known as the launching

point for white-water rafting trips.
 Worth a visit is **CATIE** (Centro
Agronómico Tropical de Investi-
gación y Enseñanza), a 2,150-acre
(870 ha) research center devoted to
the investigation of tropical agriculture and husbandry. Plants here have
been culled from around the globe.
Visitors can witness the results of
breeding experiments with animals
and crops. Trails offer superb birding.
Visits are by prior arrangement,

though some tour operators offer excursions from San José.

Nearby is **Hacienda Atirro,** a sugarcane, macadamia, and coffee farm that can be explored on horseback. Tours can be arranged from **Casa Turire** (see p. 246), a sublime hotel that also serves as a watersports center for **Lago Angostura.** This 633-acre (256 ha) lake was created by Proyecto Hidroeléctrico Angostura, a recently completed (and controversial) project that tapped the Río Reventazón (Exploding River) for energy by building the country's largest dam and hydroelectric plant. The lake now draws waterfowl, and much of the surrounding land is being rehabilitated to create wildlife habitats and natural forest, providing an ecological link with the forests of the Talamancas.

Turrialba is a base for rafting on the **Río Reventazón,** which plunges through a remote canyon and is considered a classic whitewater run. It is also the place to arrange excursions to **Volcán Turrialba** (10,919 feet, 3,328 m), a dormant giant reached with four-wheel drive via **Santa Cruz** or **Santa Teresa.** You can hike up to the summit, which boasts three craters and cloud forest; make the rustic **Volcán Turrialba Lodge** (tel 273-4335) your overnight base.

MONUMENTO NACIONAL GUAYABO

The nation's most important archaeological site pales beside the great Mexican and Guatemalan ruins, yet nonetheless is impressive for its setting amid the jungle at the base of Volcán Turrialba.

The settlement, which may have housed up to 1,000 people, was occupied between 1000 B.C. and A.D. 1400, when it was mysteriously abandoned. The monument covers 540 acres (218 ha), mostly tropical wet forest, which is gradually being peeled back to reveal a vast cobbled pavement *(calzada).* Trails lead to a lookout point above the excavated village featuring still extant stone cisterns, working aqueducts, and circular terraces *(montículos)* on which conical bamboo structures were built. A self-guided walk leads down from the **ranger station** past petroglyphs and around the montículos, where lizards scuttle amid the bleached ruins.

The surrounding forests are rich in fauna and superb for birding: Oropendolas and aricaris are particularly numerous.

INTO THE TALAMANCAS

East of the Río Reventazón, Carretera 232 cuts into the flanks of the Talamanca mountains, deteriorating all the while until about 20 miles (32 km) east of Turrialba, beyond the hamlet of **Moravia del Chirripó,** you arrive at the threshold of **Reserva Indígena Chirripó,** a remote indigenous reserve that makes a good base for expeditions into the dauntingly rugged **Parque Internacional La Amistad** (see pp. 198–199), a haven for wildlife extending south into Panama. The reserve receives few visitors and it is a good idea to go with a guide, which can be hired in Moravia del Chirripó.

At **Tuís,** midway between Turrialba and Moravia, a rugged dirt road leads north 10 miles (16 km) to the remote hamlet of **Bajo Pacuare,** the traditional starting point for rafting trips on the **Río Pacuare.** Reservations for rafting should be made in advance with local tour companies such as Costa Rica Expeditions and Ríos Tropicales (see p. 261). ■

Casa Turire

🅰 69 E2

✉ Carretera 225, 8 miles SE of Turrialba

☎ 531-1111

Monumento Nacional Guayabo

www.sinac.go.cr

🅰 69 E2

✉ 12 miles N of Turrialba

☎ 559-0099

🕐 Closed Mon.

💲 $$

MOUNTAIN RIDGE DRIVE

Mountain ridge drive

To travel this 45-mile (72 km) route between Cartago and the Cerro de la Muerte opens up some of the most spectacular vistas in the entire country. The rich profusion of scenic views—not to mention a chance to escape the heat of the lowlands atop the northern extent of the ridge-cleated Talamancas—makes amends for the poorly engineered road.

Linking the valleys of the Meseta Central and El General, this section of the Inter-American Highway (Hwy. 2) exposes visitors to the highest mountains accessible by road, to dwarf forests, and to cloud forest reserves where a quetzal sighting is nearly guaranteed.

The Inter-American Highway was built in the 1950s to link the nations of the Central American isthmus. Remarkably, for most of its length the nation's main arterial highway is an unlighted, shoulderless, narrow two-laner. Exercise extreme caution: Many of the grades are steep, and the road is twisty and subject to fog. Slide areas and potholes are frequent, and big-rig trucks are common. Three-lane passing zones may occasionally provide opportunities for uphill traffic to pass slower vehicles. Pass with care as downhill traffic often rips down this lane. Set out early in the morning to beat the clouds and to ensure that you'll be safely back in the valley well before dusk.

Note: In the rainy season (May–Nov.) clouds settle over the mountains, obscuring the beautiful panoramas.

Two miles (3.2 km) south of Cartago at **San Isidro 1**, you begin to climb. The long and winding road rises to **Vara de Roble 2**, where Highway 222 falls westward to Santa María de Dota. The views down the mountain are sublime—and they grow more so as you ascend another 2 miles (3.2 km) to **Empalme 3**, your last chance to buy gas. Orchards are plentiful and fruit stalls line the route. Lime-green pastures cling to the slopes, forested with pines and native oaks. Roadside trout farms offer fishing and horseback rides.

Continue to the Km 58 marker, where the yellow church of **Cañon 4** is a good place to stop to admire the breathtaking vista westward over forest-clad valleys and mountains. You are now atop the crest of the continental divide. A rugged dirt road leads eastward 2 miles (3.2 km) from the church to **Genesis II Cloudforest Preserve and Wildlife**

Refuge 5, where some 14 miles (22 km) of trails grant access to rare native white forest bordering Parque Nacional Tapantí. The birding is superb; more than 200 species have been recorded, including hummingbirds, toucanets, quetzals, and trogons. Lodging is available at Genesis and other rustic mountain retreats.

Settlements begin to thin as you continue uphill through the **Reserva Forestal Río Macho** and the **Iyöla Amí Cloud Forest Reserve,** protecting rare, 500-year-old cipresillo oaks and aguacatillos, a favorite food for quetzals. A curiosity at the Km 76 marker is the **Casa Refugio de Ojo de Agua 6**, a refuge hut—now a meager museum—used by traders in the days before a road over the mountains existed.

The road levels out some as you approach the Km 80 marker, where a side-road spirals sharply westward into the valley of the **Río Savegre.** The detour is worthwhile. The rocky road drops 2,100 feet in 9 miles (640 m in 14.5 km), depositing you in the hamlet of **San Gerardo de Dota 7**, tucked into a valley fulsome with orchards, trout-filled streams, and a large population of quetzals. The **Savegre Biological Reserve** (740-1028) welcomes visitors curious to see and learn about these elusive birds.

Return to the main road and continue south the final 3 miles (4.8 km) to the Km 85 marker, where a path leads uphill one mile (1.6 km) to the windswept summit of **Cerro de la Muerte** (11,450 feet, 3,491 m) **8**. The "Mountain of Death" is named for the many campesinos who froze to death hauling produce over the mountain for sale in San José. You are now above tree line; shrubs skulk close to the ground, and the peak is covered by peaty bogs and *páramo* grasses. The road continues 2 miles to a truck stop, **Las Torres 9**, whence it begins its dizzying descent into the Valle de El General. ■

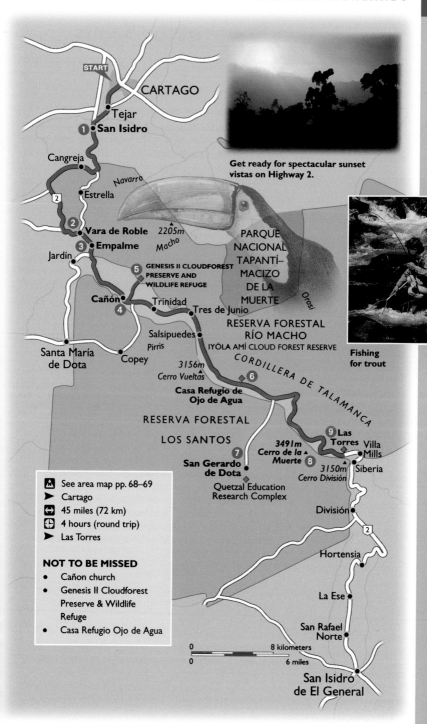

START

CARTAGO

Tejar
1 San Isidro

Cangreja

Estrella

2

Navarro

Get ready for spectacular sunset vistas on Highway 2.

2 Vara de Roble   2205m
3 Empalme   Macho

Jardín

5 GENESIS II CLOUDFOREST
PRESERVE AND
WILDLIFE REFUGE

Cañón   Trinidad
4   Tres de Junio

PARQUE
NACIONAL
TAPANTÍ–
MACIZO
DE LA
MUERTE

Orosi

RESERVA FORESTAL
RÍO MACHO

Salsipuedes
Pirris   IYÖLA AMÍ CLOUD FOREST RESERVE

Santa María
de Dota   Copey

CORDILLERA DE TALAMANCA

3156m
Cerro Vueltas

6

Casa Refugio de
Ojo de Agua

RESERVA FORESTAL

LOS SANTOS

7   3491m   9 Las
San Gerardo   Cerro de la ▲   Torres   Villa
de Dota   Muerte   8   Mills
3150m   Siberia
Quetzal Education   Cerro División
Research Complex

Fishing
for trout

División

2

Hortensia

La Ese

San Rafael
Norte

San Isidro
de El General

🏔 See area map pp. 68–69
▶ Cartago
🔁 45 miles (72 km)
🕐 4 hours (round trip)
▶ Las Torres

NOT TO BE MISSED
• Cañón church
• Genesis II Cloudforest
  Preserve & Wildlife
  Refuge
• Casa Refugio Ojo de Agua

0   8 kilometers
0   6 miles

Route of the Saints

NAMED FOR THE VILLAGES THAT SPECKLE THE RIDGES south of San José, this off-the-beaten-track region offers superlative vistas as the roads rise and dip over forested highland cleats and through vales full of orchards releasing choice aromas. It makes a fabulous day-long trip as you savor the calm poetry of green glens and felicitous silence broken only by the braying of a mule or the distant chiming of a church bell.

Coffee berries

Superbly situated on the northern face of the **Cerro de Escazú** mountains, **Aserrí,** 7 miles (11.2 km) south of San José on Highway 209, has a fine church, although it is better known locally for its rustic roadside restaurants serving campesino fare grilled over wood stoves and offering mesmerizing views across the Meseta Central toward the distant volcanoes. Beyond **Tarbaca,** Highway

222 drops eastward toward the whitewashed village of **San Gabriel;** at dusk it glistens like hammered gold from the sunlight slanting in from the west. East of **San Cristóbal Sur** you can visit **La Lucha sin Fin** ("The Endless Struggle") the mountain farm where "Don Pepe" Figueres trained his army for the 1948 revolution. Today, as a museum, it has trails and a **hemp-rope factory** *(tel 544-1410),* open to visits.

The **Fila de Bustamente** rises south of San Cristóbal, the slopes green with coffee, the major crop surrounding the pretty villages of **San Pablo de León Cortés** and **San Marcos de Tarrazú,** which has as its beacon a domed hilltop church sheathed in white light like a celestial glow. Finally you reach **Santa María del Dota,** where the road swings north and begins to crawl up the mountain to the Inter-American Highway, offering stupendous views back into the valley. ■

Quetzals

The resplendent trogon, better know as the quetzal, is an exotic and elusive species that draws many birders to Costa Rica. Its iridescent emerald plumage is so luxuriant that Mayans worshiped it as a god called Quetzalcoatl, or the Plumed Serpent. The endangered pigeon-size bird is common at elevations of 3,500 feet (1,070 m) associated with cloud forests. The male boasts a chest of brilliant crimson and trailing tail feathers, sinuous as feather boas and put to good use in its mating displays. The quetzal prefers the avocado-like fruit of the *aguacatillo,* which it plucks from below in mid-flight. ■

**Opposite:
The Holy Grail
of tropical birds,
the quetzal**

More places to visit in the Central Highlands

DOKA ESTATE

For an authentic "Coffee 101" experience, head to this working coffee farm and *beneficio* (coffee processing mill) on the slopes of Poás volcano. Twice-daily guided educational tours take visitors into the fields and roasting facilities, ending with coffee-sampling in the tasting rooms. The Vargas family has owned the 4,000-acre (1,600 ha) estate since 1929, although the *beneficio* dates from 1893. It is the oldest working water-powered mill in the entire country.
www.dokaestate.com 🅰 68 C3 ✉ San Luis de Sabanilla de Alajuela, 7 miles N of Alajuela ☎ 449-5152

FINCA LA EVITA BOTANICAL GARDEN

This splendid botanical garden, created by the Kientzler family who grow tropical flowers for export, fills the grounds of a former coffee plantation on the outskirts of Sarchí. Birds, especially motmots, abound. Paved paths are inlaid with decorative stones. Visitors can get lost in a small maze. Guided tours are offered.
🅰 68 B3 ✉ 2,625 feet (800 m) N of Stadium, Sarchí Norte ☎ 454-4956 💲 $$

INSTITUTO CLODOMIRO PICADO

Colloquially called the "snake farm," the institute—part of the University of Costa Rica—is dedicated to research on snake ecology. The center is named for Clodomiro Picado Twight, a 19th-century Costa Rican graduate of the Pasteur Institute who pioneered research into immunizations and serums. Scientists here "milk" the snakes for serum.
🅰 68 C2 ✉ Hwy. 216, 1 mile SW of San Isidro de Coronado, 10 miles NW of San José ☎ 229-0344

LA PAZ WATERFALL GARDENS

Named for the Catarata La Paz ("Peace Waterfall"), this private nature reserve offers well-maintained trails that lead to a series of waterfalls, overhung by suspension bridges. You can actually walk behind the La Paz cataract (rainwear is provided). The falls are a series of cascades that tumble in tiers for some 3,000 feet (915 m) down the eastern flank of Volcán Poás, culminating in the narrow namesake falls. A visitor center and local nature guides explain rain-forest and cloud-forest ecology, and an orchid garden and butterfly garden entertain. A restaurant serves *típica* (traditional) fare.
www.waterfallgardens.com 🅰 68 C3 ✉ Hwy. 126, 5 miles N of Varablanca and 23 miles N of Alajuela ☎ 482-2720 💲 $$$

MUSEO DE LAS CARRETAS

Costa Rica's traditional motif, the oxcart, both decorative and functional, is displayed at this small museum in a venerable adobe home in Desamparados, on the outskirts of San José. Other aspects of traditional campesino life are also described here.
✉ Hwy. 209, 2 miles S of San José ☎ 259-7042 🕐 Closed Mon. 💲 $

PARQUE NACIONAL TAPANTÍ-MACIZO DE LA MUERTE

This 15,024-acre (6,080 ha) national park covers mountainous territory ranging from 3,600 feet (1,100 m) to 8,832 feet (2,692 m) and protects the pre-montane and montane rain forest blanketing the precipitous northern slopes of the Talamancas. Trees such as giant mahoganies, Spanish cedar, and ficus thrive in the persistent rains, which average 300 inches (75 cm) a year, feeding numerous pummeling waterfalls. The park teems with wildlife, including anteaters, monkeys, ocelots, jaguars, otters, poison-arrow frogs, tapirs, and almost 300 bird species, including quetzals, which are often seen near the ranger station. The park is easily accessed using well-marked trails.
🅰 68 D1/2 ✉ 23 miles SE of Cartago ☎ 771-3297 💲 $$

PARQUE VIBARONA

Giant boas hiss like kettles as you step into their cages at this family-run serpentarium. More snakes, some of them deadly venomous, reside in glass cages. You can witness the snakes being fed live tidbits. Trails lead into the adjacent pre-montane wet forest.
🅰 69 E2 ✉ Hwy. 10, at Chitaría, 15 miles E of Turrialba ☎ 538-1510 💲 $ ■

S tudded by a string of volcanoes, Costa Rica's cowboy country abounds in dramatic landscapes, from dry deciduous woodlands to mist-shrouded cloud forests. Guanacaste's unique culture owes much to its Chorotega Native American heritage.

Guanacaste

Guanacaste tree

Guanacaste

IT'S EASY TO UNDERSTAND WHY GUANACASTE HAS BECOME ONE OF THE country's premier attractions, drawing visitors to its untamed splendors. The region is bounded on the east by a group of green-swathed volcano forming the Cordillera de Guanacaste and Cordillera de Tilarán. You can hike to their summits, where jaguars and tapirs still forage on the densely forested flanks. The rivers that tumble out of these steep mountains flow down to rolling flatlands, forming a vast alluvial plain drained by the Río Tempisque, which empties through swampy wetlands into the Golfo de Nicoya. The great river—the nation's longest—defines one side of the huge, horsehead-shaped Península de Nicoya, enclosing the gulf to the west. From beaches to birding, horseback riding to high-mountain windsurfing, Guanacaste is humbling in its diversity.

The province is named for the gargantuan *guanacaste* tree—the national tree—also known as the "ear pod tree" for its pendulous pods. This stately giant is unmistakable, being as broad as it is high and spreading its languorous branches low to the ground, providing pools of shade that suck in all manner of living beasts retreating from the ravaging heat. Guanacaste is the nation's dry quarter. In summer the sun beats down hard as a nail and Guanacaste broils relentlessly. No rain relieves the region during this period (November through April), so that the dry deciduous forests and savannas of the lowlands thirst, bringing forth bright blooms beloved by myriad insects.

Historically the region developed apart from the rest of the nation, as befits its distinct physical nature. As part of Nicaragua, a province within the Captaincy General of Guatemala during the Spanish colonial era, the land was cleared of its dry forests at an early stage and developed into huge cattle haciendas worked by enslaved Chorotega, the most vibrant indigenous tribe of its day. A cowboy culture still clings to the reins and although the Chorotega culture was virtually annihilated, the Native American influence is clearly seen in the broad, bronze-skinned faces of Guanacastecans. The region was legally united with the rest of Costa Rica only in 1858 and has always felt strong affinities with Nicaragua.

You can savor the magnificent scenery without leaving the Inter-American Highway, which cuts through the region. National parks and wildlife reserves line the north-south route. Branch roads, many unpaved, probe east and west, leading to such varied treats as misty Reserva Biológica del Bosque Nuboso de Monteverde; bubbling mud pools on Volcán Miravalles; the wetlands of Palo Verde, where you can hunt crocodiles and roseate spoonbills from a boat with a camera; and fish-filled Laguna de Arenal, set like a jewel in a trough dividing the two cordilleras.

Cattle ranches invite visitors to try their hand in the saddle. Mountain biking is more and more popular. And hiking—be it backpacking into the upland wilds or tamer tramping along a superb network of wildlife trails at Santa Rosa and Monteverde—truly puts you in the landscape. You can even tread boardwalks through the treetops. Waterborne options range from windsurfing on windwhipped Laguna de Arenal and Bahía Salinas to docile rafting trips on a wildlife-lined river.

The Inter-American Highway threads its way from one dusty colonial town to another, where *sabaneros* (cowboys) trolling lassoes at their side gather for annual fiestas held in *retornos de toros* (bullrings). Then the horsemen preen and show off the fancy footwork of their steeds at *topes*—lively horse parades—while every macho male with enough guts (or sufficient alcohol in his veins) leaps into the bullring to play tag with a snorting *toro*.

Nowhere else in Costa Rica will you see so much color. The national costume, music, dance, and the national fare originate in Guanacaste, where Costa Rica's cultural traditions are kept alive.

Tourism has blossomed in recent years, thanks partly to the opening of the nation's second international airport west of Liberia. ■

NICARAGUA

Santa Cecilia

cienda ocentes   Brasilia   Hacienda

San José   4

487m án Orosí
1659m Cerro Cacao

Dos Ríos
1806m
Volcán Rincón de la Vieja   1916m
Volcán S. María
PARQUE NACIONAL RINCÓN DE LA VIEJA

Canalete

Aguas Claras

2028m Volcán Miravalles

NORTHERN LOWLANDS p. 203

Santa María
Curubandé ★
San Jorge   Guayabo
Fortuna
ZONA PROTECTORA MIRAVALLES

Bijagua

ereceda
Liberia   1916m

Volcán Tenorio
PARQUE NACIONAL VOLCÁN TENORIO

Salitral

Pijije   CARRETERA   Bagaces   6   Tierras Morenas
RESERVA BIOLÓGICA LOMAS DE BARBUDAL
INTERAMERICANA   142
Montenegro
REFUGIO DE VIDA ILVESTRE DR. LUCAS DRÍGUEZ CABALLERO
Cañas

Tilarán

L. de Coter   Jardín Botánico Arenal
Arenal   Arenal Hanging Bridges
Laguna de Arenal   Tabacón Resort
Presa Sangregado   1633m
Volcán Arenal   ▲ 1100m
Volcán Chato

Arenal Observatory Lodge ◆
Arenal Rainforest Reserve & Aerial Tram
PARQUE NACIONAL VOLCÁN ARENAL

Hacienda Palo Verde ◆   Bebedero
San Miguel
Reserva Santa Elena

PARQUE NACIONAL PALO VERDE

NICOYA p. 129

Las Juntas de Abangares   145   Santa Elena
RESERVA BIOLÓGICA DEL BOSQUE NUBOSO DE MONTEVERDE
BOSQUE ETERNO DE LOS NIÑOS

Solimar   Palma   Limonal
San Buenaventura   18   Pueblo Nuevo
Colorado   Abangaritos
Arizona   Ecolodge San Luís & Research Station
Guacimal

CENTRAL HIGHLANDS

2▷

C △

Refugio Nacional de Vida Silvestre La Enseñada
Manzanillo
Pájaros
San Gerardo
Finca Daniel Adventure Park
Unión
Peñas Blancas

AS p. 67

Reserva Biológica Isla Pájaros
Golfo de Nicoya
Rancho Grande   San Isidro
Santa Rosa
144   Miramar
Chomes
Pitahaya
Esparza
Jesús María
Puntarenas
Barranca
Caldera
San Mateo
Orotina
Mahogany Park

Punta Caldera   Z.P. TIVIVES
San Pablo de Turrubares
PARQUE TROPICAL TURUBARI

D △

E △
CENTRAL PACIFIC p. 153

F △

San José

Area of map detail

0   30 kilometers
0   20 miles

Puntarenas & Costa Pájaros

Puntarenas
🅰 🍴 ⓘ
**Visitor
information**
✉ Puntarenas Chamber
of Commerce, 1st
floor, Oficina INC,
Blvd. Casa de la
Cultura
☎ 661-2980

**Museo Histórico
Maritino**
www.museocostarica.com
✉ Ave. Central, Calles
5/7
☎ 661-5036
💲 $

THREE MILES (5 KM) LONG BUT BARELY FIVE BLOCKS WIDE, the anomalous sea-girt city of Puntarenas is somewhat of an ugly duckling. Jutting into the Golfo de Nicoya at the tip of a pencil-thin peninsula, it makes an ideal springboard for maritime leaps to Nicoya by ferry or for day-long forays to Isla Tortuga. The mangrove-rimmed gulf shores lure binocular-laden birders, while inland the grasslands and tropical moist forest can be explored via canopy tours and even an aerial tram.

Puntarenas, 75 miles (120 km) west of San José, traces its lineage back to 1524, when conquistador Francisco Fernández de Córdova (1490–1526) founded an ill-fated settlement. In time it grew to be the nation's major port for coffee export, but a gradual demise set in after the completion of the Atlantic Railroad in 1890. For a while, the town had a viable conch-pearl fleet and drew Josefinos to bathe at its *balnearios* (swimming pools). Josefinos of modest means still flock to the brown-sand beach that runs unbroken for 7 miles (11 km) from **Boca de Barranca** to the tip of the spit.

Cruise ships call at the nearby

COSTA PÁJAROS

Pelicans—herons—frigate birds—ibises. Bird watching is the name of the game along the "bird coast," the inner gulf shoreline which stretches north from Puntarenas up to the mouth of the Río Tempisque. Small crocodiles called caimans also lurk in the dense reeds and mangroves. To get a look at them, head to **Refugio Nacional de Vida Silvestre La Enseñada,** which encompasses 940 acres (380 ha) of lagoons, creeks, and forest in the midst of a cattle and salt farm. A short way offshore, brown pelicans and other seabirds have colonized a rocky islet that is protected as **Reserva Biológica Isla Pájaros.** Only biologists may go ashore here, but you can view it from a boat.

THE HINTERLAND

Inland from Puntarenas lies **Orotina,** a town renown for its ceramics and fruit stalls that line Highway 3. Orotina is gripped in a pincer by the **Río Jesús María** and **Río Cuarros,** which spill into the Gulf of Tivives. This wetland ecosystem supports crocodiles, monkeys, and all sorts of fabulous birds. Many of these species can be seen at the nearby **Mahogany Park,** where you can flit between the soaring trees on a zipline cable.

At San Juan de Mata, four miles (2.5 km) east of Orotina, **Parque Tropical Turubari** is an adventure theme park that sprawls across almost 500 acres (200 ha). The scenery ranges from tropical garden to primary forest. Some of the highlights in the park are a butterfly farm, a canopy tour, an aerial tram, and horseback riding.

For an added kick, the "Sensational Cable" whisks you down a steep-angled zipline as you dangle prone in harness, arms widespread, like a bird. ∎

port facility of **Cárdenas,** but most passengers bypass the town. Still, if it's funky charm you are seeking, you will find plenty in the weathered wooden homes and in decrepit fishing boats tethered to equally decrepit piers. Ongoing development aims at beautifying the forlorn city. The small **Museo Histórico Maritino** *(closed Mon.),* in the 19th-century jail, traces the city's history with displays spanning pre-Columbian times to the building of the Atlantic railroad, and the coffee industry. The jail was a family residence and later served as the military command post and Casa de la Cultura. The **Paseo de las Turistas** boulevard makes an intriguing walk along the gulf shore. The north of the spit faces a mangrove-lined estuary that is a great spot to see roseate spoonbills.

Refugio Nacional de Vida Silvestre La Enseñada
www.laensenada.net
101 D2
1.5 miles S of Abangarito, off Hwy. 132, 11 miles W of Hwy. 1
289-6655

Mahogany Park
www.canopytour.com
10 miles E of Orotina
257-5149
$$

Parque Tropical Turubari
www.turubari.com
Turrubares, 4 miles E of Orotina
250-0705
$$$

Inter-American Highway drive

Highway 1, Costa Rica's umbilical cord to its neighboring states, sweeps through Guanacaste like a Roman imperial highway, linking historic cowboy towns. It is a magnificent drive, with the scenery gathering northward like a series of Hollywood stage sets making irresistible compositions for your camera.

Linking San José with Nicaragua, the road leads to sublime vistas of savanna ranged by sabaneros, with cattle against a backdrop of cloud-crowned volcanoes to the east. Side roads lead to national parks and wildlife reserves, but the beauty of the surrounding countryside—and the ugly quality of the road—may make you miss your turnoff.

The route described is a 128-mile (205 km) journey with only three traffic lights. The highway is mostly a fast two-laner; arrow-straight stretches unwind for miles, tempting motorists to speed. Don't do it! Traffic cops sit beneath shade trees, training their radar guns on unwary speedsters. Other caveats: Some potholes are big enough to swallow a Zebu; oncoming cars tend to swerve into your lane at inopportune moments; and behemoth, hell-bent trucks hurtle up and down the highway.

(Drive starts on page 106.)

Zebu cattle are hardly cowed by Guanacaste's extreme heat.

Lago de
Nicaragua

See area map pp. 100–101
Barranca
128 miles (205 km)
3–8 hours, depending on stops
La Cruz

NOT TO BE MISSED
- Las Pumas cat zoo
- Liberia
- Parque Nacional Santa Rosa
- La Casona

1806m
Volcán Rincón
de la Vieja

PARQUE
NACIONAL
RINCÓN
DE LA VIEJA

**This night-blooming cactus
is found in dry forest habitats.**

Buena
Vista
Mountain Lodge
& Adventure Center

C O R D I L L E R A   D E   G U A N A C A S T E

2028m
Volcán
Miravalles

1916m
Volcán Tenorio

Liberia
Salto
Salto

Tenorio

Corobicí

**La Casona, a traditional
Costa Rican farmhouse**

Laguna de Arenal

Bagaces

7

Montenegro

Corobicí

Cañas

Centro de
Rescate
Las Pumas

Tilarán

6

Piedras

San
Miguel

Cañas

C O R D I L L E R A   D E   T I L A R Á N

Santa
Elena

Monteverde

PARQUE
NACIONAL
PALO
VERDE

Tempisque

Bebedero

Lajas

4

Limonal

5

**Las Juntas
de Abangares**

Arizona

Lagarto

Guacimal

Aranjuez

REFUGIO
SILVESTRE
DE PEÑAS
BLANCAS

Miramar

3   San Gerardo

San
Isidro

Rancho
Grande

2   Santa
Rosa

Golfo de Nicoya

1

START

Puntarenas

Barranca

0		20 kilometers
0		10 miles

Big wheels: Fancy hubcaps become status symbols in a culture fixated on social position.

Begin in **Barranca ❶,** at the interchange of Highway 1 and Highway 27, the junction for Puntarenas (west), Jacó (south), and San José (east). This heavily trafficked southern section is a bit of a roller-coaster and gives a foretaste of the beauty that lies ahead, with the western slopes of the Cordillera Tilarán pressing upon the road. After 4 miles (6.4 km), at **Santa Rosa ❷,** you will pass the turnoff for Miramar and Refugio Nacional de Vida Silvestre Peñas Blancas. The road continues to dip and rise beyond **San Gerardo ❸,** where it becomes pinched between the hillsides of **Río Lagarto** valley, with long glades of trees leaning over the road like kissing lovers. The long grade descends to an iron-framed bridge over the river, 16 miles (26 km) north of Barranca. The turnoff for Monteverde is here, one hundred yards (90 m) south of the bridge, poorly marked and well hidden. Slow down well before the bridge in either direction: *Túmulos*—road bumps—lie across the road and should *not* be hit at high speed.

Eight miles (13 km) farther turn off for **Las Juntas de Abangares ❹,** a somewhat self-consciously attractive village strong on history tucked into the folds of the mountains, 4 miles (6.5 km) northeast of Highway 1. The town is famed for a gold rush that began in 1884 when nuggets were found in these hills, and *oreros*—miners—flocked from the four

corners of the world to seek their fortunes. A patined bronze statue in their honor stands in a triangular plaza on the northeast side of town. A pint-size old steam train, *María Cristina,* sits in the main plaza.

Highway 1 edges north along the foothills, with the parched golden grasslands of the **Llanos San Pedro** to the west grazed by hardy humped cattle, ashen-colored and well-muscled, standing fixedly in the magnesium light like bovine figures on a Cretan urn. Rounded hillocks dot the plain. Deciduous trees speckle the scene in a pallet of pastels: yellow *cortexa amarilla,* scarlet *poró,* and bright orange *spathodea,* locally known as the Jesús Cristo tree because it blooms blood red at Easter. You will notice the heat building as you move north, with the warm air parting ahead of you like an unfolding blanket.

Beyond **Limonal ❺,** where Highway 18 peels off westward for the Río Tempisque ferry and the Península de Nicoya, continue straight 13 miles (21 km) to whitewashed **Cañas ❻** *(tel 669-0042),* a cowboy town par excellence and the gateway to Parque Nacional Palo Verde, Tilarán and Laguna de Arenal. On the far side of town is **Centro de Rescate Las Pumas** *(tel 669-6044),* where Costa Rica's six species of cats—cougars, jaguars, jaguarundis, margays, ocelots, and "tiger" cats—prowl safely behind chain-link fences. The zoo takes in orphaned and injured cats and others confiscated from private owners and hunters. A stone's throw north, the highway crosses over the 25-mile-long (40 km) **Río Corobicí.** Fed by dam-controlled runoff from Laguna de Arenal, it flows even in the midst of drought, and is popular for float trips—which are good for birding and for seeing howlers monkeying around above in the branches of stately mahoganies and ceiba trees. Rafting the river with **Safaris Corobicí** *(tel 669-6091)* takes several hours, and if time is short you can watch from the veranda of the roadside **Restaurante Rincón Corobicí** (see p. 246), a good spot for sea bass or local fare.

Beyond Cañas the road opens up, swinging northwest and gaining distance from the **Cordillera de Guanacaste** so that three volcanoes—Tenorio, Miravalles, and Rincón de la Vieja—are in glorious view, rather like a procession of monarchs. The sky is usually an exhilarating clear, deep blue; clouds pour up over the mountains from the Caribbean before burning off under the searing heat of the sun.

Continue north to **Bagaces 7**, where Parque Nacional Palo Verde is signed to the west. The park is administered along with other regional parks and reserves as the **Area Conservación Tempisque** (see p. 112) whose administrative office is beside Highway 1, opposite the Palo Verde junction. Bagaces, which is also the gateway to Zona Protectora Miravalles, is intriguing for its old adobe houses. More appealing by far is **Liberia 8**, 15 miles (24 km) farther north, the capital city of Guanacaste and another cowboy town known as the "Ciudad Blanca" (White City) for its dazzling white buildings. If low on gas, you should fill up at one of four stations at the junction with Highway 21 (which takes you to the airport and Nicoya).

The final 33 miles (53 km) steal the show, with breathtaking landscapes seen fleetingly through gaps in the deciduous trees that flare with seasonal blooms. You are now in the heart of cattle country, hot as Hades in summer when a searing breeze rustles the grasslands that carpet the billowing flatlands, like a gently undulating sea of chartreuse. **Volcán Rincón de la Vieja** (5,925 feet, 1,806 m) looms massively to the east, tempting you to tackle the blindingly white roads of exposed

ignimbrite that lead to cattle haciendas where horseback rides are offered, and to the ranger stations that are gateways for hiking in Parque Nacional Rincón de la Vieja.

For an intriguing side trip, 11 miles (18 km) north of Liberia turn northeast from the highway. After 8 miles (13 km), you'll arrive at **Hotel Borinquen Mountain Resort Thermae & Spa** (see p. 248), a spa facility built around bubbling mud ponds good for rejuvenating thermal treatments. Monkeys abound in the surrounding forest. Nearby, the **Buena Vista Mountain Lodge & Adventure Center** *(tel 661-8158)* is a ranch that offers horseback rides, a 0.6 mile-long (1 km) canopy tour, and a 1,312-foot (400 m) water slide, plus occasional rodeos. Rustic yet charming cabins are available, and *típico* meals can be savored.

Farther north are the steep nipples of **Cerro Cacao** (5,443 feet, 1,659 m) and **Volcán Orosi** (4,879 feet, 1,487 m) piercing the eastern sky. They are accessed from **Potrerillos,** 15 miles (24 km) north of Liberia, with a police check-point at the junction. The two volcanoes are encompassed within **Parque Nacional Guanacaste** (see p. 126), a 208,800-acre (84,500 ha) expanse that spans the highway and tethers several disparate ecologically independent parks and reserves, including **Parque Nacional Santa Rosa** (see p. 127), accessed from Highway 1 about 5 miles (8 km) farther north and a must-see on any tourist's list. Wildlife viewing in Santa Rosa is staggering; more than 100 mammal species include jaguars, ocelots, tamanduas, coatis, and three species of monkeys, plus a rainbow assortment of birds, all easily seen in the sparse dry forests. The park wears Costa Rica's history on its sleeves, too, at an old farmstead called **La Casona,** now a museum dedicated to the battle fought here in 1856.

From here, the traffic thins and it is a special joy to zip along with the sun pouring down its warm rays, mantling the tousled palms and low-slung guanacaste trees in pools of sunlight and shadow. At last you reach **La Cruz 9,** a sleepy town 14 miles (22 km) from the Nicaraguan border. A left turn at the town plaza in La Cruz leads 100 yards to a vantage point over **Bahía Salinas** with great views. ■

Monteverde

THE JEWEL IN THE CROWN OF CLOUD FOREST RESERVES, Monteverde is generously blessed with bucolic beauty. Its immense popularity has spawned contiguous forest reserves and a gamut of nature attractions that combine with Monteverde's world-renown to draw tens of thousands of visitors annually.

The community that translates as "Green Mountain" squats upon a plateau 3,500 feet (1,065 m) above sea level near the crest of the Cordillera de Tilarán; a vertiginous, bone-shaking road leads up to it from the Inter-American Highway. The setting is idyllically pastoral, with incandescent light intensifying the emerald greens of the mountain pastures grazed by black-and-white Holstein cattle. Ethereal mists swirl overhead and the crisp alpine climate is a constant interplay of drizzle and warming sunshine.

The heart of things is the village of **Santa Elena.** There is no village of Monteverde as such. Instead, this community of farmsteads sprawls upon the hillside that rises east of Santa Elena, accessed by paths that branch off the steep dirt road that leads to the cloud forest reserve for which Monteverde is famous. The community was founded in 1951 by U.S. Quakers who fled the draft and chose Costa Rica because it was neutral. They brought with them 50 Jersey cattle and after clearing forest for pasture, they established a cheese-making industry—still the bedrock of the local economy, as *cuaquerismo* (Quakerism) is of the local culture. Visitors are welcome to attend the Wednesday morning assemblies in the Friends' Meeting House.

The Quaker settlers have been at the forefront of conservation since Monteverde's inception: The kernel of today's world-famous cloud forest reserve was founded in 1972 jointly by the community and by scientists who sought to protect the watershed and the unique species for which it provides a habitat. The contiguous communities have also been leaders in efforts to educate local children. The Centro de Educación Creativa, a local school for grades 1 to 12, has an environmentally based curriculum. **The Monteverde Cloud Forest Ecological Center** *(tel 645-5390)* in Santa Elena, and the **Monteverde Conservation League** *(tel 645-5003)* work to educate youngsters in ecology, and train youths as naturalist guides in an effort to move tico families away from destructive practices and toward tourism-related income derived from conserving their green heritage. And the **Monteverde Institute** *(tel 645-5053)* offers local farmers and families courses in local ecology and lifestyle.

Art is also vibrant here. Venues such as **El Sapo Dorado** (see p. 248) put on live musical performances. The **Monteverde Institute Community Art Center** has workshops with themes from basketry to woodturning from January to August with local craftsfolk.

THE LONG AND WINDING ROAD

A narrow, serpentine road leads 3 miles (4.8 km) uphill, eastward from Santa Elena ending at the entrance to the Reserva Biológica del Bosque Nuboso de Monteverde. The route—a quagmire in wet season and cloudy with dust during

Mist cloaks the ridge-top forests.

Monteverde
🅐 100 E2

Monteverde Institute Community Art Center
www.mvinstitute.org
✉ Monteverde
☎ 645-5053

Serpentario Monteverde
www.snaketour.com
✉ 400 yards E of Santa Elena
☎ 645-6002
💲 $$

rare dry spells—is lined with attractions plus more than a score of charming wooden mountain lodges with roaring log fires to add to the homey alpine ambience.

To learn about amphibians and reptiles that can be encountered in the reserves, visit **Serpentario Monteverde** to see poison-arrow frogs, chameleons, and more than 20 species of snakes, including the fearsome fer-de-lance—safely behind glass. There are more than 500 species of orchids on display at **Orquídeas de Monteverde,** an exquisite garden specializing in miniatures such as *Playstele jungermanniodes,* the world's smallest flower, best seen with the aid of a magnifying glass (thoughtfully supplied). And the **Ranario de Monteverde** (*100 yards/90 m N of Monteverde Lodge, 645-6320, $*) is a

herpetarium displaying frogs and other amphibians.

Over 500 species of butterflies flit about these hillsides and forests. You'll find more than 40 species at **Monteverde Nature Center & Butterfly Gardens,** where North American biologist Jim Wolfe oversees a huge netted garden and two greenhouses that re-create three distinct natural habitats. The "Garden of the Butterflies" features an educational nature center, library, and weather center as well as exhibits of other colorful insects. Visit early-to-mid-morning.

The Monteverde community has been making its famous cheeses since 1953 at **La Lechería,** the cheese factory. Fourteen types of cheese are made, including Monte Rico, the local bestseller. A trail beside the factory leads uphill 400

Orquídeas de Monteverde
✉ 0.75 mile/1.2 km E of Santa Elena
☎ 645-5510
💲 $$

Monteverde Nature Center & Butterfly Gardens
✉ 400 yards/360 m W of Hotel Heliconia
☎ 645-5512
💲 $

La Lechería
www.monteverde.net
✉ 2.5 miles/4 km E of Santa Elena
☎ 645-5436
🕐 Tours at 9 a.m. & 2 p.m.

The Sky-Walk provides a perfect vantage point for viewing wildlife in Reserva Bosque Nuboso Santa Elena.

Reserva Biológica del Bosque Nuboso de Monteverde
www.cct.or.cr

🏔 101 E 2/3
✉ 6 miles E of Santa Elena
☎ 645-5122
💲 $$

Reserva Bosque Nuboso Santa Elena
www.monteverdeinfo.com/reserve.htm

🏔 101 E 2/3
✉ 4.5 miles NE of Santa Elena
☎ 645-5390
💲 $$

yards (365 m) to the **Sarah Dodwell Watercolor Gallery** (see p. 258), where the acclaimed local artist displays her works, which hang in many hotels and homes nationwide. You can admire and purchase other fine artwork at the **Hummingbird Gallery** (see p. 258), named for the scores of rufus-tailed, violet saber-winged, and fiery-throated hummingbirds that zip in to feed on the patio of the gallery, where nature slide shows are given.

RESERVA BIOLÓGICA DEL BOSQUE NUBOSO DE MONTEVERDE

This internationally acclaimed reserve straddles the Continental Divide. Its upper-elevation forests are cloaked year-round in swirling mists formed by humid Caribbean trade winds condensing as they are forced up and over the ridge crest. The reserve encompasses 25,730 acres (10,400 ha), covering eight distinct life zones on both the Caribbean and Pacific slopes. The diversity of flora is astounding—from dwarf cloud forest atop the mountains to bamboo forests and even swamp forest in poorly drained areas. Zoological treasures include more than 100 mammal species, not the least all five species of cats, plus howler and capuchin monkeys, deer, and sloths. There are 400 species of birds, including 30 species of hummingbirds, and the endangered three-wattled bell-bird (named for the worm-like wattles that hang down from its beak). About 100 breeding pairs of quetzals also nest within the reserve, migrating to lower levels during the spring mating season.

The reserve is run by the Tropical Science Center of Costa Rica, which regulates visitor numbers and maintains the boardwalks that lead into the reserve. More rugged trails punch down the Caribbean slopes into true wilderness, spilling out in the Northern Lowlands. You can rent rubber boots to ease exploration. Guided nature hikes are offered, and well-versed nature guides can be hired.

THE OTHER RESERVES

The **Reserva Bosque Nuboso Santa Elena,** which is owned and administered by the Santa Elena community, protects 1,440 acres (580 ha) abutting Reserva Biológica del Bosque Nuboso de Monteverde to the northwest. It has most of the same species as the larger reserve, plus some of the endangered spider monkeys, which are absent at the Monteverde reserve. You can hike well-maintained trails or take to the air on a **Sky-Walk** *(tel 645-5238, $$)* and follow half a mile (0.8 km) of "pathways" and suspension bridges through the treetops, while the **Original Canopy Tour** *(tel 645-5243, $$$$$)* lets you glide through the treetops in a harness attached to a pulley.

The **Bosque Eterno de los Niños,** to the east and south of the Monteverde reserve has grown to more than 50,000 acres (20,200 ha). Funded by schoolchildren from around the world and administered by the Monteverde Conservation League, it encompasses a similar range of terrain and flora and fauna to Santa Elena. Trails and facilities for visitors are minimal.

Sendero Bajo del Tigre ("Jaguar Canyon Trail") grants access to a 44-acre (18 ha) portion of the reserve and features a forest habitat that's distinct in the region. It is especially good for seeing quetzals in springtime; they are easily spotted in the relatively mist-free environment. There is an arboretum and self-guided interpretive trail, and kids will enjoy the Children's Nature Center, with both live and static exhibits.

Nearby, the **Finca Ecológica Wildlife Refuge** is a 40-acre (16 ha) private reserve where trails grant access to montane moist forest and where coatis, capuchin monkeys, sloths, and countless bird species are easily seen with a guide.

Four miles (6.5 km) of trails crisscross the **Paradise for Bellbirds** *(tel 284-8590),* another private reserve situated between Santa Elena and Monteverde, and renowned for its large population of three-wattled bellbirds, whose distinctive call—a metallic *bonk*—sounds hauntingly through the forests. **Selvatura,** abutting the Reserva Bosque Nuboso Santa Elena, grants a similar entrée to a wildlife-rich world with treetop boardwalks, a zipline canopy tour, and guided nature hikes along forest trails. Here is the **Jewels of the Rainforest Bio-Art Exhibition,** featuring dramatic displays of arachnids and insects, comprising the largest such private collection in the world. ■

Discovered only recently, the golden toad may already be extinct.

Golden toads

In 1967, an endemic species of vermilion toad was discovered in the Monteverde cloud forest. The discovery of *Bufo periglenes* helped spark the creation of the preserve. Only the diminutive inch-long (2.5 cm) males are gold; the much larger females are black, speckled with vermilion and yellow. The last sighting was in 1988. This sudden demise has struck amphibious species worldwide. ■

Bosque Eterno de los Niños
- 🅐 101 E2
- ✉ 2 miles E of Santa Elena
- ☎ 645-5003
- 💲 $$

Finca Ecológica Wildlife Refuge
- ✉ 300 yards W of Hotel Heliconia
- ☎ 645-5554
- 💲 $

Selvatura
- www.selvatura.com
- ✉ 4 miles NE of Santa Elena
- ☎ 645-5929
- 💲 $$$

Parque Nacional Palo Verde

BIRDERS FLOCK TO RUGGED AND REMOTE PALO VERDE, A marvelous repository of avian fauna at the mouth of the Río Tempisque, named for the green-barked *palo verde,* or horseshoe bean tree. Combining wet and dry ecosystems, it supports not only vast flocks of waterfowl but crocodiles and mammals that are easily seen in the sparse vegetation.

A snowy cattle egret stands out against a dry Guanacastecan forest.

Parque Nacional Palo Verde
🅰 101 C2/3
✉ 18 miles SW of Bagaces
☎ 671-1290
💲 $$

Area Conservación Tempisque
☎ 659-9194 or 671-1290
💲 $

Organization for Tropical Studies
www.ots.ac.cr
☎ 240-6696
💲 Tours from $$$$

The 32,266-acre (13,057 ha) park encompasses 15 distinct habitats from mangroves, grassland, and scrubland, to tropical dry forest. Together with the Refugio de Vida Silvestre Dr. Rafael Lucas Rodríguez Caballero and Reserva Biológica Lomas Barbudal, which abut it to the north, and Parque Nacional Barra Honda to the southwest, it forms the **Area Conservación Tempisque,** a vast arena of sun-baked limestone ridges, marshes, and seasonally wet floodplains best explored in dry season, when the trees that have evolved to resist the debilitating drought (November to March) shed their leaves and thirsty wildlife congregates at waterholes.

This oasis in the heart of the rain-starved Tempisque Basin is fed by the Río Tempisque and its mangrove-lined tributaries, forming an aquatic haven for birds—more than 300 species of neotropical birds roost or nest here. Following the rainy season, the alluvial plains flood, attracting in the region of 250,000 migratory ducks, teal, geese, and other waterfowl to winter alongside their native cousins. In the midst of the river, **Isla de Pájaros** boasts particularly prolific and unusual bird life. Rarely seen great curassows are here in numbers. So are anhingas and such long-legged waders as roseate spoonbills, white ibis, wood storks, and the world's largest stork, the jabiru. Palo Verde also boasts the only permanent colony of scarlet macaws to inhabit a dry environment.

Trails lead to depressions that fill with water to become freshwater lagoons where birds and mammals gather at dawn and dusk. The park headquarters is situated in the old **Hacienda Palo Verde,** which is surrounded by mango trees that draw peccaries, white-tailed deer, coatis, and monkeys to feast. Anteaters and armadillos abound. You can see crocodiles, motionless as logs on the muddy banks. There are modest archaeological sites within the park, some in caverns gouged from limestone cliffs.

Local companies arrange guided natural history tours, as does the **Organization for Tropical Studies,** which maintains a biological field station here *(tel 661-4717).* It's impossible to explore in wet season other than by boat. Boats leave from Puerto Humo, on the riverbank 17 miles (27 km) east of Nicoya township on the Península de Nicoya. ∎

Dry forest reserves

COSTA RICAN NATURALISTS HAVE WORKED HARD TO preserve the last vestiges of the dry forests that were so much a part of the environment in pre-Columbian days. Their chief success has been the establishment and maintenance of the Reserva Biológica Lomas Barbudal, where the native woodland habitat supports a thriving range of wildlife.

Reserva Biológica Lomas Barbudal
🗺 101 C3
✉ 4 miles SW of Pijije (Km 221) on the Inter-American Hwy.
☎ No phone (call 671-1062 for conservation office in Bagaces)
💲 $

A fire prevention ranger surveys the forest from a watchtower.

CONTIGUOUS WILDERNESS

Palo Verde adjoins two contiguous wilderness regions. To the north is the remote and infrequently visited 18,172-acre (7,353 ha) **Refugio de Vida Silvestre Dr Rafael Lucas Rodríguez Caballero,** (administered jointly with Lomas Barbudal) which offers the same array of wetland and dry habitats and their associated wildlife. The refuge extends north to **Reserva Biológica Lomas Barbudal,** enshrining 5,631 acres (2,279 ha) and protecting precious remnants of the dry deciduous forest that once encompassed most of the Tempisque Basin. The Río Cabuyo flows through the "bearded hills" reserve, named for the mosses that drape from tree branches, feeding lush riparian forest and drawing wildlife to its banks. There is a small **information center** and **museum** at the entrance beside

the river. Nature trails lead from here to swimming holes.

Many endangered tropical hardwoods still thrive here: the appropriately named cannonball tree, mahogany, Panama redwood, rosewood, and sandbox, whose tart fruit is favored by scarlet macaws, which call in from neighboring Palo Verde. Yellow-naped parrots and chicken-like great curassows, popularly hunted by campesinos for food, are among the many other bird species commonly seen, as are monkeys and a host of other mammalian frugivores that gorge on the seasonal fruits. The three parks form a vital migratory route for wildlife and are particularly renowned for their huge insect populations, including hundreds of moth species and more than 250 bee species, important pollinators for the flowering trees, which burst into often synchronized blooms in the midst of drought. ■

Around Laguna de Arenal

Jardín Botánico Arenal

www.junglegold.com

🗺 101 D3

✉ 2.5 miles E of Nuevo Arenal

☎ 385-4457 or 694-4305

🕐 Closed Oct.

💲 $

FRINGED BY EMERALD MOUNTAINS, LAGUNA DE ARENAL IS a svelte platinum gem of entrancing beauty, enticing camera-toting visitors seeking pleasure in its picture-postcard appeal and proving the adage that a fine jewel is made complete by its setting.

Costa Rica's largest inland body of water occupies a depression that forms a gap between the Cordillera de Guanacaste and Cordillera de Tilarán. The lake, covering 48 square miles (124 sq km), lies to the east of the continental divide at an elevation of 1,798 feet (548 m) above sea level. It is topped by mountains shimmering every shade

Volcán Arenal looms above its namesake lake.

of green in the clear light. To the south and west great carpets of green pasture unfurl down to the cobalt waters. To the north, primary tropical wet forest clambers up the steep slopes, dark and foreboding and raucous with the screeching of monkeys and birds. To the east, reflected in the silvery lake is the black, smoking peak of Volcán Arenal, brooding ominously between fits of pique.

Although the natural depression dates back about two million years, the lake was created by engineers in 1973 when a 290-foot-long, 190-foot-high dam (88 m by 58 m)—

Presa Sangregado—was built at the eastern egress, where the Río Arenal begins its cascade through a narrow gorge dropping down to the Northern Lowlands. The 20-mile-long, 3-mile-narrow (32 km by 5 km) lake inundated several pre-Columbian sites plus the sole settlement in the valley. It is caressed by near constant winds that whip up from the Caribbean and become compressed as they push through the gap. The howling winds, which can reach 60 mph (96 kph) in winter are beloved of windsurfers. They also drive the wind-turbines that have been erected atop the continental divide. Anglers too find their lures in machaca, mojarra, feisty guapote, or rainbow bass, that give a good run on the end of a line. The *Rain Goddess* (see p. 260) now offers multi-day fishing trips.

Laguna de Arenal lies 18 miles (29 km) east of Highway 1 on well-paved Highway 142, which leads via the trim agricultural town of **Tilarán** (on the western flank of the continental divide) to the lake around which it curls clockwise. The windswept western shore makes a perfect venue for the **Tilawa Viento Surf Center** (see p. 262) and **Tico Wind Surf Center** (see p. 262) from which active outdoorsy types set out to skim over the waves on their boards. For a diversion follow the signs to **Lago de Coter**, 3 miles (4.8 km) northwest of Laguna de Arenal. This much smaller body of water has been adopted as its own by the **Eco-Lodge** *(tel 257-5075)* offering all

manner of outdoor activities together with a small butterfly farm.

Capping the north shore is the small town of **Nuevo Arenal,** created in 1973 when its precursor was drowned with the lake's creation. This side of the lake is otherwise uninhabited except by the lakeside lodges spawned by the tourism boom. Immediately east of the town, the forested slopes crowd in with a murky closeness and the pavement gives out, growing more deteriorated with every mile; often the narrowing causeway is blocked entirely by mud sluiced down from the rain-sodden hillsides. Some stupendous vistas are thrown in as a reward for perseverance.

To catch your breath, stop in at **Toad Hall** (see p. 247), a café and general store where, ensconced in a hammock on the hillside veranda, you can savor divine desserts which are served as accompaniments to the incredible views.

A TROPICAL EDEN
The British are experts at gardening, whether at home or in adopted homelands. Take, for example, **Jardín Botánico Arenal,** the brain child of an Englishman,

Michael LeMay, who has been assisted by Costa Rica's rich volcanic soils and climate in creating a work of art on the hillside. Some 2,200 species of native plants are represented; anthuriums and heliconias spring up beside gingers, orchids, and other pretty natives.

Nature's Eden can be explored at the **Arenal Rainforest Reserve & Aerial Tram,** on the forested slopes southeast of the lake. A tram whisks visitors to a mountainside platform for stupendous views of the lake and volcano; for an adrenaline-charged return to Earth, try a zipline tour across the canyon. ■

Top: Jardín Botánico Arenal is a colorful frame for picture-perfect Laguna de Arenal. Above: Consistent high winds draw windsurfers.

Arenal Rainforest Reserve & Aerial Tram
www.arenalreserve.com
▲ 101 D3
✉ 14 miles W of La Fortuna
☎ 479-9944
🕐 Closed Oct.
$ $$

Parque Nacional
Volcán Arenal

**Parque Nacional
Volcán Arenal**
⚠ 101 E3
✉ Hwy. 142, 10 miles/
  16 km W of
  Fortuna
☎ 461-8499
💲 $$

COSTA RICA'S MOST DRAMATIC ATTRACTION IS KNOWN FOR the regularity of its eruptions, providing grandstand views of its fiery fury. The environs offer soothing hot springs and fabulous hiking.

Volcán Arenal (5,389 feet, 1,643 m) is a quintessential cone and the focus of this national park, one of 16 protected reserves that make up the Arenal Conservation Area, spanning 12 life zones (see p. 42). The 26,690-acre (10,800 ha) park boasts two volcanoes; Volcán Arenal's minor sibling is **Volcán Chato** (3,609 feet, 1,100 m), a dormant cone with a pea-green lagoon within its collapsed crater.

Arenal began to emerge about 1,000 years ago, pushing up like a great molehill. Understandably, pre-Columbian Indians considered it to be sacred. It barely hiccuped during the colonial era, then on July 29, 1968 a fateful earthquake awakened the slumbering giant, which exploded, decimating the nearby town of Tabacón. It has simmered ever since and barely a day goes by without a minor eruption; there are usually smoking cinder-blocks rolling down the slopes. It is especially spectacular at night, when the pyrotechnics appear like a giant firecracker and red-hot lava oozes down the steep slopes. Visitors are never assured of seeing an eruption, however, as clouds frequently obscure the summit. The best times are from around midnight to dawn and in dry season.

You can buy an interpretive map-guide at the **ranger station,** which lies one mile (1.6 km) south of Highway 142, 2 miles (3.2 km) east of Laguna de Arenal and 10 miles (16 km) west of Fortuna, in the Northern Lowlands. Five separate trails lead to washes of lava fossilized by the sun. The **Arenal Observatory Lodge** *(tel 692-2070)*, on the slopes of Volcán Chato, offers spectacular views, plus a museum on volcanology.

Río Tabacón's waters provide soothing hot springs best enjoyed at **Tabacón Resort** *(tel 460-2020, www.tabacon.com)*, 1.5 miles (2.4 km) east of the park entrance, where mineral pools and a hot-water cascade have been laid out amid gardens. Nearby, **Arenal Hanging Bridges** *(tel 253-5080)* has a series of suspension bridges through the rain-forest canopy and trails in the 618-acre (250 ha) forest reserve. ∎

Exploring the flanks of Volcán Arenal by horseback

Volcán Tenorio & Zona Protectora Miravalles

THE TWIN VOLCANOES TENORIO AND MIRAVALLES LIE within a few minutes drive of the Inter-American Highway yet a world away in their brawny, thick-forested, aloof appeal.

Mud pools gurgle up at both Tenorio and Miravalles.

Mantled in savanna on the lower western slopes, montane rain forest at mid-elevations, and above by mist-haunted cloud forest, these contiguous volcanoes offer a lush, pristine, wildlife-rich world seen by few tourists. Wear hiking boots and prepare for the steep trails and you will be rewarded with enthralling treasures. Monkeys—white-faced capuchins and howlers—abound, as do sloths, agoutis and pacas. Visitors are as likely to see ocelots, cougars, or jaguars here as anywhere else in the country.

Parque Nacional Tenorio can be reached from the Inter-American Highway north of Cañas via Highway 6, which dips and rises 21 miles (34 km) northeastward to Bijagua, nestled between the volcanoes. **Heliconia Ecolodge** *(tel 470-0115),* a biological research station and eco-lodge, makes a perfect base for exploring Volcán Tenorio. The arduous **Lago Las Dantas Trail** deposits you atop the volcano at 6,256 feet (1,916 m), where tapirs *(dantas)* reliably show up at dusk to sip at the crater lake. Another trail leads to a waterfall of the **Río Celeste** and thence to burbling mud-pools and fumaroles.

The best way to reach **Zona Protectora Miravalles** is from Bagaces by Highway 164, arching over the volcano's western haunch. Miravalles (6,653 feet, 2,028 m) is known for its sulfur springs, fumaroles, and bubbling mud pots, easily seen at **Las Hornillas,** where the Costa Rican Institute of Electricity harnesses super-heated vapor for geothermal energy. To bathe in the thermal waters, head to **Centro Turístico Yökö,** with swimming pools and a whirlpool spa at the foot of the volcano. ∎

Parque Nacional Volcán Tenorio
- 101 D3/4
- 21 miles NE of the Inter-American Hwy. off Hwy. 6
- 695-5180
- $$

Zona Protectora Miravalles
- 101 D4
- 23 miles NE of the Inter-American Hwy. off Hwy. 164
- 695-5180
- $$

Centro Turístico Yökö
- 2.5 miles E of Guyabo, Hwy. 164
- 673-0410
- $

Volcanoes

Volcanoes are the primary vents in the earth's crust through which hot molten rock—magma—wells up from the mantle of liquid rock beneath the crust. There are more than 600 active volcanoes in the world today. Costa Rica has seven—another 60 are dormant or extinct—making it one of the most volcanically active areas of the world.

Volcanoes are associated with the movement of rigid sections of the earth's crust, or lithospheric plates, that ride atop the asthenosphere (mantle) made of hot, plastic rock—a process called plate tectonics proposed by the German geophysicist Alfred Wegener in 1915 and adopted by earth scientists in the 1960s. The major and minor plates pull apart or press against one another. Convection currents rise from deep within the earth's interior, much like a pot of boiling water, to fuel the process, bringing molten material to the surface and forming necklaces of fire along the fractured joint lines.

There are two types of volcanoes. Basaltic formations, such as those of Hawaii and Iceland, are normally associated with rifts in the earth's crust, as in mid-ocean ridges, where the plates are pulled apart by convection. The runny magma tends to pour steadily from the volcano. Costa Rica's volcanoes are andesitic types,

Cocos plate

Caribbean plate

Subduction trench

Far left: Gentle steam seeps from the summit of Volcán Arenal.

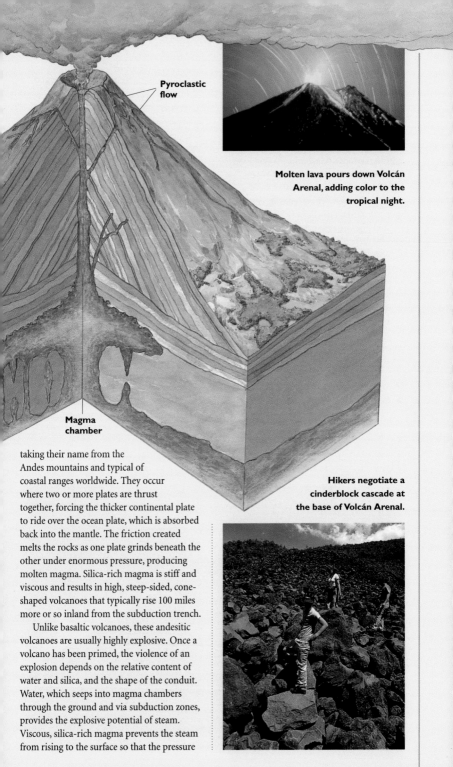

Pyroclastic flow

Magma chamber

Molten lava pours down Volcán Arenal, adding color to the tropical night.

Hikers negotiate a cinderblock cascade at the base of Volcán Arenal.

taking their name from the Andes mountains and typical of coastal ranges worldwide. They occur where two or more plates are thrust together, forcing the thicker continental plate to ride over the ocean plate, which is absorbed back into the mantle. The friction created melts the rocks as one plate grinds beneath the other under enormous pressure, producing molten magma. Silica-rich magma is stiff and viscous and results in high, steep-sided, cone-shaped volcanoes that typically rise 100 miles more or so inland from the subduction trench.

Unlike basaltic volcanoes, these andesitic volcanoes are usually highly explosive. Once a volcano has been primed, the violence of an explosion depends on the relative content of water and silica, and the shape of the conduit. Water, which seeps into magma chambers through the ground and via subduction zones, provides the explosive potential of steam. Viscous, silica-rich magma prevents the steam from rising to the surface so that the pressure builds like a pressure-cooker. Silica-rich magma also tends to clog quickly, plugging the vent like a cork in a champagne bottle. When a dome is plugged by solidified lava, the magma becomes supersaturated with pressurized steam until the volcano is at breaking point; it then ruptures explosively at its weakest spot. Sometimes the explosion may occur via a fissure to the side. When blasted laterally from the volcano, the lava appears as a *nouée ardente* (glowing cloud), a super-heated avalanche of steam, red-hot ash, and poison gases that can roar downhill with the force of a thermonuclear explosion.

Vegetation for many miles around is often bowed down by blankets of hot mineral-rich ashes that eventually are transformed into fertile soils. The vast quantities of dust and energy released sometimes spawn great clouds above the volcano charged with lightning and triggering tremendous storms that dump immense torrents of rain on the mountain.

At other times, the walls protecting a crater lake may rupture and the waters cascade downhill, turning into a massive avalanche of mud—called *lahores*—which can be up to 100 feet (30 m) deep laden with trees, boulders, and other debris, as destructive in its power as a runaway locomotive.

Volcanoes can lie dormant for centuries before announcing their awakening with a long series of burbling mutterings that grow gradually stronger and more ominous. There may initially be emissions of sulfurous gas, followed by puffs of steam, a series of small earth tremors, and clouds of ash. Then— *BOOM!* The mountain detonates either at once or in an ongoing series of thunderous explosions that may end in a cataclysmic detonation. In lush tropical settings such as Costa Rica, such pronounced eruptions often set off stampedes of wildlife, so that any settlements in their path of flight become overrun with ants, centipedes, and a variety of venomous snakes.

Several volcanoes, such as Miravalles and Rincón de la Vieja, are associated with features such as the fumaroles and boiling mud pools that occur where rainwater seeps into the porous ground above the volcano's magma chambers. The water in the permeable ground thus becomes super-heated from below like a giant boiler, with water temperatures reaching 5,000°F. Rising back to the surface, the water begins to boil as pressure is released, emerging in great vents of steam or bubbling mud pools, or mingling with cool groundwater to form hot springs, like those at Tabacón on the flanks of Volcán Arenal. ■

Sign of an active giant, Arenal puffs clouds of smoke and ash on a daily basis.

Liberia

STRIKING FOR ITS SIMPLE ADOBE ARCHITECTURE, THIS whitewashed provincial capital resounds to the clip-clop of hooves, providing an intriguing sun-bleached way-stop beneath the gaze of Rincón de la Vieja volcano and handily situated as a springboard for Parque Nacional Santa Rosa and the Península de Nicoya.

The venerable Iglesia La Agonía attests to the antiquity of Liberia, the charming provincial capital of Guanacaste.

Liberia is without a doubt the most colonial of Costa Rican cities, redolent with its own unique charm that owes much to its historic core of red-tile-roofed buildings made of ignimbrite, a diatomaceous rock as white as burning magnesium for which Liberia is known colloquially as the Ciudad Blanca, or White City. Many venerable old homes feature *puertas del sol*, corner entranceways with doors on two sides as an effective air-vent system.

Situated at the heart of Guanacaste and cattle country, Liberia is wholeheartedly a cowboy town and plays host to several lively fiestas, when townsfolk dress up in traditional garb for the parades, mariachis serenade, and rodeos provide entertainment. The liveliest fiesta is the **Día de Guanacaste,** on July 25, which is a celebration of Guanacaste's independence from Nicaragua in 1812. The festive spirit is resurrected in early September for **Semana Cultural.**

The town sprawls eastward from the Inter-American Highway and is accessed along a broad tree-shaded boulevard, Avenida Central, which features a life-size bronze cowboy statue, the **Monumento Sabanero** *(Calle 10)*. The avenue slopes gently past the peaceful tree-shaded main plaza *(between Calles 2 & Central)*—featuring a historic church and the old town hall, or *ayuntamiento,* locally called the **Gobernación,** which is topped by a fluttering Guanacastecan flag—and ends at the **Iglesia La Agonía** *(Calle 11),* an enchanting antique church simply adorned within. The church dates back to 1854. Time your visit for mid-afternoon—the only time the church is open—when women gather daily for the rosary. Be sure to stop in, too, at the **Casa de la Cultura** *(Ave. 6 & Calle 1, tel 666-1606, closed Mon.).* This charming example of typical Guanacastecan colonial architecture houses both

Liberia

🗺 101 C3

Visitor information

✉ Ave. 6 & Calle 1

☎ 666-1606

🕐 Closed Sun.

💲 $

All comers can jump into the ring to prove their bravado before a raging toro.

the regional tourist information office and the **Museo de Sabaneros,** in which weathered saddles and other memorabilia pay homage to local cowboy culture.

The old city jail, one block east of the plaza, still functions as such, and boasts crenelated towers at each corner. The Comandancia (police station), on the northwest side of the plaza, displays a large archaeological collection. Calle Central, east of the plaza, has been renamed **Calle Real** and boasts many fine colonial structures.

A lively setting to relax in is the **Hacienda La Chácara** (see p. 261), a cattle ranch and sugarcane farm where sabaneros and hostesses in traditional dress serve up a cocktail of typically Guanacastecan music, dance, and food, with bull-riding thrown in to boot. Visits to this Fiesta Brava can be arranged through the Casa de la Cultura.

Liberia has taken on an increasingly important role in recent years, following the opening of the Daniel Oduber International Airport, 7 miles (11 km) west of town. It is mostly used by charter flights delivering package vacationers to the beaches about an hour away. ■

Rodeos

Costa Rica's cowboy *(sabanero)* culture has been part of the traditional Guanacastecan way of life for centuries. Just as in North America's Wild West, breaking wild broncos was a part of the daily routine, while riding bulls served to prove a sabanero's manhood—a tradition kept alive at *fiestas cívicas*, where *recorridos de toros* (bull rodeos) are everyone's favorite part of the entertainment. The sabaneros ride the enraged bulls bareback and display their rope-handling skills, accompanied by much whooping and hollering and *yip-yip-yipping*. Costa Rica does not practice bull-fighting in the Spanish tradition. However, scores of ticos regularly pour into the ring to show their bravado—usually fueled by an excess of *chicha*, the local brew made of fermented corn—by running in amongst the wild bulls and taunting them with sticks and electric prods. ■

Parque Nacional Rincón de la Vieja

THE VELVETEEN CONE OF RINCÓN DE LA VIEJA ("OLD woman's corner") makes a theatrical backdrop that dominates the landscape of northern Guanacaste and offers active travelers a variety of invigorating attractions within the 34,800-acre (14,080 ha) park.

Parque Nacional Rincón de la Vieja
www.acguanacaste.ac.cr
🅰 101 C4
✉ 16 miles E of Liberia
☎ 666-5051
💲 $

This volcano is the grandest of fiery giants that make up the Cordillera de Guanacaste. The park spans an elevation range of 5,000 feet (1,525 m) and protects markedly different vegetation on its rain-soaked Caribbean and seasonally parched Pacific sides—from savannas to montane rain forest and upper-level dwarf cloud forest. Rain clouds from the Caribbean cloak its summit, spawning swift rivers that radiate in every direction, gouging deep ravines into its concave sides.

The volcano has two peaks—**Rincón de la Vieja** (5,925 feet, 1,806 m) and **Santa María** (6,256 feet, 1,916 m). The nine craters include the Rincón peak's bowl-shaped, gently steaming **Von Seebach crater**—a reminder that this is an active volcano that occasionally hiccups.

Casona Santa María is an adobe farmstead housing the park headquarters and an exhibition. The hacienda was purchased by Costa Rica's national park service from former U.S. President Lyndon Johnson. It and the **Las Espuelas** (Las Pailas) ranger station, farther north, can be reached from Highway 1 via dirt roads.

Much of the volcano's lower western slopes are occupied by working cattle haciendas, providing lodgings and horseback riding. Key among them are **Hotel Hacienda Guachipelín** (see p. 262) and the **Rincón de la Vieja Lodge** (see p. 248), which offers a canopy tour where you can traverse the forest canopy in a harness. Highlighting the many mammal species are tapirs, to be seen at higher elevations. ■

Rincón de la Vieja on a quiet day. On another day, you might catch the active volcano smoldering.

A walk to the top of Rincón

The soaring mass of Rincón de la Vieja draws hardy hikers up its jungle green sides in search of rare wildlife and the satisfaction of ascending the summit. Hot springs, mud pools and "ovens"—evidence of vibrant geothermal activity—make diverting landmarks along this rewarding two-day walk. Take a tent and sleeping bag for the night on the mountain.

It is a straightforward hike, beginning at the **Casona Santa María ❶** Ranger Station, on the southwestern side of the volcano. There is a basic camp site 400 yards (365 m) from the hacienda, where it is also possible to sleep in the basic dormitory-style accommodations in the ranger's *cabina* by prior arrangement *(tel 661-8139 or 233-4160).* You will need to bring your own sleeping bag and blanket. From here it is an 8.3-mile (13.3 km) hike to the summit, with an elevation gain along the way of 3,614 feet (1,100 m).

Head out along the old roadway that leads west from the ranger station. After half a mile (0.8 km) you pass the **Sendero Bosque Encantado ❷** ("enchanted forest trail") on your left, making an interesting side excursion into old growth forest that abounds with orchids, including *guaría morada,* the national flower. The main trail continues 0.6 miles (1km) to another side trail marked **Aguas Thermales ❸** ("hot springs"); you should save your visit for the return journey (when you will be better able to appreciate a soothing celebratory soak). About 2.5 miles (4 km) farther along take the right-hand trail, uphill, at the Y-junction. The landscape opens up at the top and you can make a short detour—marked as **Pilas de Barro ❹** ("mud pots")—to where boiling mud explodes in great belching bubbles and the super-heated mineral-rich pools are tinged with a rainbow of colors. Stay away from the overhanging edges of the pools; they are often insecure underfoot.

Continuing along the main path, you will pass through former cattle pasture that is being slowly regenerated with native forest. Steam rises mystically over the treetops, luring you along another short trail to your right that deposits you at **Las Hornillas ❺** ("ovens"), where *fumaroles* (vapor geysers) hiss like kettles, spitting up odoriferous steam and gases—hydrogen sulfide and sulfur dioxide.

Again, use caution when walking around the "stove pipes." The main trail continues, ascending more steeply, half a mile (0.8 km) to the **Río Colorado ❻,** where there is a basic campsite on the riverbank. Just beyond is the **Las Espuelas Ranger Station ❼,** sometimes called Las Pailas, 4 miles (6.4 km) from Santa María. You can pitch tent here. Plan on getting up around sunrise and ascend to the summit in time to beat the clouds, which generally tend to form in mid-morning.

It is a 6-mile (10 km) ascent through pre-montane and montane rain forest festooned with bromeliads and epiphytes, including hundreds of the park's renowned orchid species. The forests vibrate with birdsong; look for the turkey-like black guan, a raucous bird that hops about in the branches. The trail snakes upward through bamboo then stunted dwarf forest near the edge of the tree line. About 3 miles (5 km) above Las Pailas, you will pass a meager campsite—set amid the gnarly copey clusia, a cloud forest species with waxy leaves that scent the air with perfume. You are now only a few hundred yards below the ridge, attained by a scramble up loose lava scree. **Von Seebach crater ❽** is half a mile (0.8 km) away. The way is marked by cairns, but it is easy to lose the trail when the clouds set in, whipped up by a cold wet wind swirling about the summit like a mad maypole.

🏔 See area map pp. 100–101
► Casona Santa María
↔ 8.3 miles (13.3 km)
🕐 2 days (one night on mountain)
► Laguna las Jilgueros

NOT TO BE MISSED
- Aguas Thermales
- Pilas de Barro
- Von Seebach crater

Volcanic eruptions occasionally obliterate the summit trails.

With luck, the sky will be scintillating blue overhead and the last 1.5 miles (2.5 km) across the lava-strewn saddle to the smoking summit of **Volcán Rincón de la Vieja** will be clear. You can revel in the vast views, which are phantasmagoric in their infinity, with the Pacific and Caribbean shimmering on hazy horizons. With proper planning, you might camp on the beach at **Laguna los Jilgueros ❾**, which is southeast of the Von Seebach crater, and surrounded by a ravaged moonscape like a scene from Dante's *Inferno*—there is a chance at both dawn and dusk to watch super-shy tapirs drink at the pea-green lake

that sits in the saddle between the Von Seebach and Rincón craters.

This hike is best tackled in the dry season (November to April), with January to April the best months. Ticks and other biting insects inhabit the thick elephant grass that can grow as tall as your shoulder. It is recommended that you wear long pants tucked into socks, especially around campsites. Take insect repellent, sleeping bags, good camping gear, and warm, water-repellent clothing (as much as 200 inches—500 cm— of rainfall douses upper elevations each year). ■

Canopy tours are a popular way to explore the rain forest.

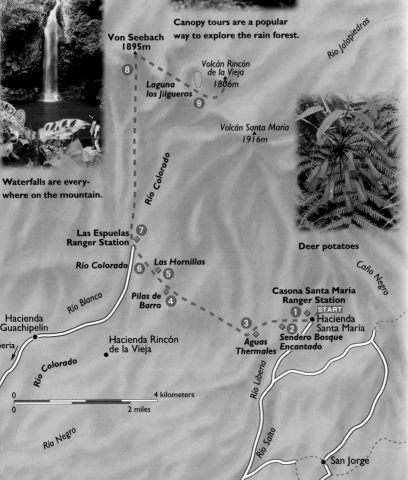

Waterfalls are everywhere on the mountain.

Deer potatoes

Shell games: Armadillos are at home in the dry forests of Guanacaste.

Parque Nacional Guanacaste

WELLSPRING OF THE RÍO TEMPISQUE, THE WATERSHED OF the Orosí and Cacao volcanoes was protected in 1989 and enshrined in this national park, a rugged, rarely visited world devoid of tourist services and appealing to those with a spirit of adventure.

Parque Nacional Guanacaste

🄰 101 B4

☎ 666-5051

💲 $$

The keystone in the 2,742,810-acre (1,110,000 ha) **Guanacaste Conservation Area**—an amalgam of contiguous parks and reserves—the 207,560-acre (84,000 ha) Parque Nacional Guanacaste is a mosaic extending from lowland savanna to cloud forest atop its two volcanoes: **Orosí** (4,879 feet, 1,487 m) and **Cacao** (5,443 feet, 1,659 m). Much of the cattle range at their western base is being returned to dry deciduous forest in an effort to fuse the disparate native habitats and create migratory corridors for the parks' profuse wildlife.

The main entrance to the park is via **Quebrada Grande**, accessed from Highway 1 at Potrerillos via a 6-mile (10 km) dirt track. Beyond **Gangora**, hike 3 miles (5 km) to the **Cacao Field Station** on the south side of Cacao at 3,350 feet

(1,021 m). From here, you can hike through cloud forest, spying for wildlife as you head for the summit, 1.5 miles (2.5 km) beyond Cacao. Another trail slopes down through montane moist forest and seasonally dry moist forest where **Maritza Field Station** links to Highway 1 by a trail from the Cuajiniquil turnoff. Maritza, the main ranger station, has basic dormitories. You can hike to the summit of Orosí via **El Pedregal**, an archaeological site where pre-Columbian petroglyphs peer through algae and mosses on the **Llanos de los Indios**, the "plain of the Indians."

On the Caribbean side, the **Pitilla Field Station**, set in pre-montane rain forest (good for birding) is reached via a dirt track from **Santa Cecilia**, 18 miles (29 km) east of Highway 1. ■

Parque Nacional Santa Rosa

THIS NATIONAL PARK, THE FIRST TO BE ESTABLISHED IN Costa Rica, boasts an abundance of human and natural history. Seagirt on two sides, Santa Rosa is framed by fine beaches washed by rugged surf. Good camping facilities help make this one of the country's most appealing wildland attractions.

Parque Nacional Santa Rosa
🅰 101 B4
✉ 4 miles W of Hwy. I, 20 miles N of Liberia
☎ 666-5051
💲 $$

Its 122,350 acres (49,512 ha) enfold 10 distinct habitats, home to about 115 mammal species and more than 250 species of birds—all easily seen amid the predominant landscape of dry deciduous forest, where anteaters, iguanas, deer, and howler, spider and white-faced monkeys are preyed upon by five species of cats, including rarely seen jaguars. In the scorching heat of the dry season, the forests explode in vibrant color, birds and beast gather at precious water holes, and wildlife viewing is easy for patient and silent visitors.

The park is divided into two separate sections. To the south is the larger **Santa Rosa sector,** where armored vehicles rust amid tall grasslands west of the entrance gate in memory of an ill-fated invasion by Nicaraguan troops in 1955. Close by, and setting for the park headquarters, is a replica of **La Casona,** where in 1856 Costa Rica's ragtag army of peasant soldiers routed William Walker and his mercenary toughs (see p. 27). The venerable hacienda—the original was destroyed by arsonists in 2001—houses a museum.

Numerous rails branch out from La Casona through the dry forest. **The Naked Indian Trail,** named for the gumbo-limbo trees whose peeling bark exposes a red trunk, makes an easy loop; the **Los Patos** trail is good for spotting rare mammals. Visitors with rugged four-wheel drive vehicles can descend the 8-mile (13 km) track to **Playa Naranjo,** which

is flanked by headlands and beloved of surfers for its tubular waves. Nearby Playa Nancite is off-limits to visitors, for here one of nature's miracles plays out each summer as Ridley turtles—as many as 10,000 at a time—swarm ashore en masse to lay eggs. Crocodiles lurk leery-eyed in the mangrove swamps that back the shore.

To the north is the **Murciélago sector,** which extends along the Santa Elena peninsula. Few visitors call at the white-sand beaches that shine like diamonds beneath the sun. Bring camping gear. Pelicans and frigatebirds wheel overhead. **Hacienda Murciélago,** once owned by the Nicaraguan Somoza family, was the site for Oliver North's secret airstrip during the Contra era. Fisherman will take you out to the **Islas Murciélagos** (Bat Islands), renowned for their superb diving potential. ■

The blue iguana thrives in the dry forests of Santa Rosa.

More places to visit

BAHÍA SALINAS
Several fine beaches line this flask-shaped bay, including the sugar-white Playa Pochotes which is backed by glistening salt pans picked upon by wading birds, and mangroves where crocodiles lurk. The bay is enfolded to the south by Punta Descartes, which opens to the northwest and garners winds off the open sea making it a nirvana for windsurfers, who are served by the Eco-Wind Surf Center *(tel 679-9380)* and Kite Surf Center *(tel 679-0218)*. A few rustic fishing hamlets remain, tethered to a hard life at sea. A craggy isle covered with drought-resistant shrubs—**Refugio Nacional de Vida Silvestre Isla Bolaños**—studs the bay. This island is a protected nesting site for frigate birds, American oystercatchers (it is their only known nest site), brown pelicans, and boobies. The island is off-limits to visitors.
 68 B5   ✉ 4 miles W of La Cruz

Sally Lightfoot crabs migrate to Manzanillo beach to mate.

ECOLODGE SAN LUÍS & RESEARCH STATION
This private research center of the University of Georgia welcomes tourists to its 165-acre (67 ha) reserve and working farm in the small hamlet of San Luís, whose residents are being integrated into a project to develop a model for sustainable development. Montane wet forest and cloud forest provide opportunities for birding and viewing wildlife on foot or horseback, and visitors are welcome at the research facilities for lectures and classes on local ecology, or to help out in the fields. A wide range of participatory educational workshops is offered, as are cultural activities, for both resident students and ecotourists. Accommodation is available in comfortable *cabinas* and bungalows.
www.ecolodgesanluis.com ⓜ 101 E2 ✉ 5.5 miles SE of Santa Elena ☎ 645-8049

FINCA DANIEL ADVENTURE PARK
This 66.7-acre (27 ha) private ranch and fruit farm, in the hills north of Miramar, west of Refugio Nacional de Visa Silvestre Peñas Blancas, offers magnificent views down over lowland Guanacaste. Trails and a canopy tour through montane cloud forest reveal monkeys, and quetzals are commonly seen. Horseback rides lead to cascades and the Bambú Private Ecological Reserve; guided tours are given to historic gold mines where visitors can pan for gold. Mountain biking trips also are given to nearby coffee farms.
www.vistadelgolfo.com ⓜ 100 E2 ✉ 2.5 miles N of Miramar on Hwy. 44 ☎ 639-9900 💲 $

HACIENDA LOS INOCENTES WILDLIFE CONSERVATION & RECREATION CENTER
A former cattle ranch that covers 2,600 acres (1,052 ha), Los Inocentes is dedicated to ecotourism. It lies at the northern base of Volcán Orosí, on the edge of Parque Nacional Guanacaste, in the transition zone between moist and dry forest. The hacienda is being restored to a natural state. Guided tractor tours, hikes, and mountain biking are offered, as are guided horseback rides on the flanks of the volcano. Parrots and howler monkeys screech, and scarlet macaws fly free here.
www.losinocenteslodge.com ⓜ 101 C5 ✉ 10 miles E of Hwy. 1, on Hwy. 4 between La Cruz and Santa Cecilia ☎ 679-9190 🕐 Guided tours 💲 $$$$$ ∎

The glint of diamond-dust beaches and the gleam of emerald golf courses have created a tourism gold rush for Nicoya, bringing new panache to an otherwise sleepy region known for its superb sportfishing, scuba diving, and surfing.

Nicoya

The hawksbill turtle has a beaklike mouth.

Nicoya

SAND AND SEA ARE THE NAMES OF THE GAME IN SUNNY NICOYA, A mountainous crab-claw peninsula that hooks around the Golfo de Nicoya, endearing itself to visitors with the appeal of its white-sand beaches—unique in the nation—and a six-month dry season when the sun dances incandescently on a sea which has blue sky pouring into it. A handful of resort villages offer their own brands of refuge or adventure. Certain coastal stretches remain beyond the pale; these are difficult to access in rainy season in anything other than a four-wheel drive vehicle, but guarantee a laid-back lifestyle where you can ease into a hammock and enjoy watching howlers monkeying around in lush treetops overhanging the surf. Notable among Nicoya's wildlife treats are marine turtles which can be seen laying their eggs. Water sports are well developed. And golf courses have multiplied in recent years, attached to the deluxe beach resorts that are attracting a new breed of traveler to Costa Rica.

Northeastern Nicoya is an undulating plain fringed by wetlands fed by the Río Tempisque, fabulous for birding and opening into the island-studded Golfo de Nicoya. The plain narrows southward along its mangrove-lined shore. The region's few towns speckle well-paved Highway 21 which runs north to south down the plain, east of the low-slung, deeply incised mountain range that dominates Nicoya, much of which has been denuded for cattle ranching, the predominant industry since early colonial days. Prior to the depredations of the Spanish, the peninsula was the center for the Chorotega culture, whose legacy can be seen today in distinctive pottery. The hamlet of Guaitíl is at the center of a renaissance in Chorotega culture.

Modernity has come late to the region. Local life still revolves around fishing and ranching, and Nicoya moves at a sleepy bucolic pace. A half-dozen burgeoning resort settlements dot the rugged shoreline, though Tamarindo is the only coastal town of significant size or sophistication. While all of San José seems to descend at weekends and holidays, Josefinos tend to flock to a fistful of beaches, and visitors find it relatively easy to escape the madding crowd. This is despite the fact that three quarters of the nation's hotel rooms are here, concentrated along Nicoya's sugar-white northern beaches. The sands gray further south, where the dry season is less pronounced and forests thicken and cascade down to the shore, lush and lovely and teeming with wildlife. Two experiences stand out: watching leatherback turtles nesting at Playa Grande, and witnessing the awesome spectacle of the *arribadas*—the synchronized nesting of battalions of Ridley turtles that storm ashore at

Playa Ostional at predictable times every year. Parque Nacional Marino Las Baulas and Refugio Nacional de Vida Silvestre Ostional protect these precious havens. Reserva Natural Absoluta Cabo Blanco and Refugio Nacional de Vida Silvestre Curú, both tropical moist forest environments in southern Nicoya, protect their own wildlife wonders.

Recent years have brought an explosion of construction. For better or worse, large-scale resorts are changing the face of the region. Bahía Culebra is shaping up to become a mini-Cancún—the result of a contentious decision during the Rafael Calderón administration (1990–94) to target the untapped deluxe beach vacation market. The Gulf of Papagayo Project stalled in the mid-1990s under charges of environmental abuse and corruption, though the dust seems to have settled and the project is moving ahead under a more careful surveillance. The nation's second airport—the Daniel Oduber International Airport—was opened in 1996, creating access for package-tour vacationers.

New golf courses offer relaxed pleasures, though they are draining the aquifers in this drought-plagued region. Watersports make a big splash. Waves pump ashore, providing thrills for surfers. Despite low visibility, scuba divers rave about eye-to-eye encounters with giant groupers and other locomotive-size fish. And sportfishing is world-class, centered on the Golfo de Papagayo where marlin run thick and fast, with Playa Flamingo the major marina. Ashore, spelunkers can escape the searing heat of summer in cool caverns at Parque Nacional Barra Honda.

Most of the roads that link coastal hamlets are unpaved and, in dry season, covered with fine dust. Some rivers still need to be forded—all part of exploring sleepy Nicoya. ■

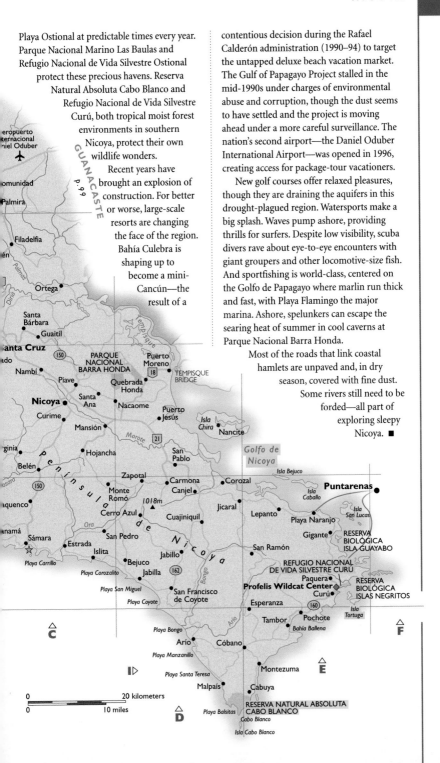

Golfo de Nicoya

Golfo de Nicoya
🅜 131 D/E3
Visitor information
☎ 685-5417
📧 Coonatramar R.L.
(Naranjo): 661-1069;
Naviera Tambor
(Paquera): 661-2084
💲 $ for ferry

THE ISLE-STUDDED, MANGROVE-FRINGED GOLFO DE NICOYA is a slender sleeve of shallow water separating the Península de Nicoya from mainland Guanacaste, exposing mud banks during low tide and forming an aquatic haven for bird life.

Settlements are few along its banks, where mangroves swathe vast acres, fed by the Río Tempisque whose sediment-laden waters pour into the gulf. The river mouth offers stupendous birding and the chance to see crocodiles.

The largest and most northerly of the gulf isles is **Isla Chira,** a favored nesting site for frigate birds, which hang in the sky like kites on invisible strings. Roseate spoonbills and other stilt-legged waders grub about in the mud flats and salt pans—*salinas*—from which a few hardy inhabitants eke a living extracting salt. Precious nesting sites of brown boobies, frigate birds, and other seabirds are also protected on scrub-covered **Isla Guayabo** and **Isla Negritos,** two tiny isles at the mouth of the gulf. Guayabo, uniquely, is a winter nesting site for peregrine falcons.

Both isles are off-limits to visitors. Dolphins and whales can sometimes be spotted cavorting in the open waters.

Isla San Lucas, off the southeast tip of Nicoya, was once a sacred burial place for pre-Columbian Indians, whom the Spanish conquistador Gonzalo Fernández Oviedo massacred on the island. In the 19th century its barren wastes were turned into a hellish prison. Ghosts seem to haunt the forlorn isle. Visits to the ruins can be arranged with cruise-tour companies in Puntarenas.

Tempisque bridge, opened in April 2003, spans the wide mouth of the river, linking Highway 1 with the Península de Nicoya. Other ferries operate between Puntarenas and **Playa Naranjo** and the village of **Paquera,** providing access to southern Nicoya. ∎

Roseate spoonbills feed in the mudflats of the Golfo de Nicoya.

Parque Nacional Barra Honda

RIDDLED WITH STYGIAN CHAMBERS LIKE HOLES IN SWISS cheese, Barra Honda offers cavers an exciting challenge. Not all of its appeals are subterranean, however; above ground, its hiking trails thread a wonderful, wildlife-rich world of dry forests.

Parque Nacional Barra Honda

🏔 131 C/D3

✉ Hwy. 18, 10 miles E of Nicoya

☎ 686-6760

🕐 Caves closed May—Nov.

💲 $$

Stalactites drip from the ceiling of the Terciopelo Cave in Barra Honda park.

Unique in the nation, Barra Honda comprises a 5,670-acre (2,295 ha) wilderness of pitted limestone uplands that rise west of the Río Tempisque flood plain and from which eons of weathering have carved out caverns. During the dry season you can make arrangements via the national parks service to go into many of the 42 caverns that have been explored so far. You will need appropriate gear.

Many caverns boast spectacular dripstone formations. In the **Santa Ana Cave,** for example, glistening stalagmites and stalactites fill the **Hall of Pearls.** The **Terciopelo Cave,** accessed by a thrilling 100-foot (30 m) roped descent, contains "The Organ"; when struck, this stone fills the cave with haunting chimes. **Mushroom Hall** is named for its flat-shaped formations. It's fun to project your imagination onto the crystal structures—a lion's head? entwined lovers?—in

the **Hall of the Caves.** The **Nicoya Cave** contains pre-Columbian remains dating back two millennia.

Barra Honda is ideal for terrestrial exploration, too: Its convoluted trails stipple the hilly, scrub-covered landscape. You can get trail maps and hire a guide at the ranger station. **Cerro Barra Honda** (1,459 feet, 445 m) offers a tremendous vantage over the country spread out below. Take plenty of water, as well as a camera to capture any anteaters, monkeys, scarlet macaws, or other exotic denizens of the relatively open dry forest.

The caves boast their own "homegrown" species; among them are endemic blind fish and salamanders that have adapted to absolute dark. The bats here have created the chiropteran equivalent of the Augean stables, depositing so much guano that one cave is called **Pozo Hediondo**—"Fetid Pit." ∎

Mangroves

Mangroves are halophytes—plants that exist in salty conditions—although they also thrive in fresh water. Five species—black mangrove, buttonwood mangrove, red mangrove, tea mangrove, and white mangrove—are found in Costa Rica, and each has evolved its own unique method for ridding itself of salt—from secreting it through leaf glands to preventing it from being taken up by the roots. One of the greatest pleasures in exploring coastal Costa Rica is in learning about this distinctive tropical habitat.

The glutinous mud that mangroves call home is so dense that it contains almost no oxygen. The mud is also acidic, and the nutrients upon which mangroves feed lie not deep down but near the surface, where decomposing organic debris drops from above or is deposited by the receding tides. Thus, most mangroves form aerial roots, drawing oxygen in through spongy bark and giving the appearance that the mangroves are walking on water. Black mangroves differ, preferring to send forth underground roots that sprout long lines of offshoots, called pneumatophores, that stick up from the ground like upturned nails.

The tangled spiderweb of interlocking roots helps stabilize land, protecting it against erosion by waves while acting as a pioneer land builder by filtering out the silt brought down to the sea by Costa Rica's turbulent rivers. The nutrient-rich muds foster the growth of microorganisms that form a food source for larger species, such as shrimps and snails. Many creatures live on the buffet, including stilt-legged wading birds that pick tiny, shrimp-like amphipods from the glistening mud. The redolent mangroves are also important nesting sites for cormorants, pelicans, kingfishers, and frigate birds, which deposit their guano atop the mud, fertilizing

Crab

Kingfisher

Red mangrove

Frigatebirds

the mangroves and speeding their growth.

Mangroves also serve as aquatic nurseries for creatures such as oysters, sponges, crustaceans, fish, and even stingrays and baby sharks. So important are these habitats for marine species that the destruction of mangroves has an inordinately harmful effect on the marine ecosystem.

Raccoons, lizards, and snakes abound too, as do insects, including a species of mangrove ant that is only found here. Many animal species are unique to mangroves, such as the yellow mangrove warbler (Dendroica petechia), an insectivorous migrant present from August to May; and the arboreal mangrove tree crab (Aratus pisonii), a leaf-eater that is stalked by another arboreal crab species, Goniopsis pulchra, and is thereby forced to spend a life away from water in the crowns of the mangroves.

Mangroves propagate swiftly, and often establish new colonies far removed from the parent plants—this is thanks to a splendid reproductive system. The mangrove blooms briefly in spring, then produces a fruit from which sprouts a fleshy seedling shaped like a plumb bob. This pendulous seed, which can grow to a foot (30 cm) in length, germinates on the branch then drops like a dart. At low tide, they stick upright in the mud and instantly send out roots. Seeds that hit water float on the tides like half-filled bottles. They are astoundingly hardy and can survive sea journeys of several hundred miles, often traveling for a year or more before touching a muddy shore, where they anchor themselves and begin a new colony.

A seedling can grow two feet (60 cm) or more within its first year. By its third year it has grown to become a mature bush and begins sprouting seeds that establish themselves around the parent's prop roots. Within a decade a mangrove colony has been formed and the process of silting is well under way as the colony creeps farther and farther out to sea. As the land builds up in their lee, they may eventually strand themselves high and dry and die on land of their own making. ∎

Anhinga

Raccoons

Black mangrove

White mangrove

Black mangrove

Fer-de-lance

Mangrove fern

Yellow mangrove warbler

Button-wood or gray mangrove

The solemnity of Catholic processions finds form in Nicoya's Easter festivities.

Heartland of the Chorotega

NICOYA'S HEARTLAND MAINTAINS A REGIONAL PRIDE AS the wellspring of a newly resurgent Chorotega heritage. The countryside is still worked in the traditional manner: Ox-drawn plows and carts are familiar icons tended by campesinos in soiled cotton linens and straw hats, each with a machete and a gourd canteen by his side.

Nicoya
🗺 131 C3

By some accounts the oldest town in the country, **Nicoya,** administrative capital of the region, serves agricultural communities for miles around. A settlement existed here and served the same purpose prior to arrival of Spanish conquistador Gil González Dávila (died 1526), who named his colony for the local Chorotega Indian chief. Nicoya was the center of the Chorotega culture, and well-defined trade routes radiated as far as Nicaragua. The nation's oldest extant church—

Iglesia de San Blas—is here, a squat 16th-century adobe affair on the tree-shaded main plaza. The town comes alive each December 12 for the **Festival of La Virgén de Guadalupe,** a celebration that combines Catholic beliefs with the Chorotega legend of *La Yequita,* which tells of two brothers spared by a mare from killing one another over a Native American princess. The are no other attractions, but the town has several banks, a hospital, and other key services.

Above right: Nicoya's Iglesia de San Blas is one of Costa Rica's oldest churches.

Santa Cruz, astride Highway 21 and 12 miles (19 km) north of Nicoya, is renowned as the "Folkloric City" for its civic fiestas each January 15 and June 25, when beer and *chicha* (corn liquor) flow freely, citizens kick up their heels by dancing the Punto Guanacasteco, and the bullring resounds to the cheers of spectators. **Plaza Bernabela Ramos** has some notable statues plus a ruined colonial church and the modern building that has replaced it.

GUAITÍL
There is a splendid charm and vitality to this hamlet, 7 miles (11 km) southeast of Santa Cruz. Guaitíl is zero milestone in the renaissance of Chorotega cultural pride, and local residents carry proudly the dark, robust facial features of their Indian forebears. The village, which squats amid parched cattle country, is lined with stalls of pottery made in the traditional manner: turned on wheels and fired in wood-fueled, open-hearth kilns, finished with jade grinding stones that local matriarchs believe have magical powers and painted with animal motifs.

The artists are organized in cooperatives. Visitors are welcome to stop at family workshops where the homespun craft is performed in front yards beneath spreading shade trees. The **Eco-Museo de la Cerámica Chorotega** opened in 2005 in the adjoining village of San Vincente, where an annual festival celebrating the pottery tradition was initiated that same year. ■

Santa Cruz
🗺 131 C4
Visitor information
✉ One block S of Plaza de los Mangoes
☎ 654-4123

Jade
The pre-Columbian Chorotega were masters at crafting jade. They used the string-saw carving technique, in which a hole is drilled and a string is inserted through it, then repeatedly drawn back and forth like a saw. This enabled them to create detailed figures of jaguars, frogs, crocodiles, eagles, and humans; the latter were often shown engaging in the most worldly of pleasures. Archaeologists have found no local source for the semiprecious stones, which more advanced northern cultures introduced to the Chorotega around 400 B.C. ■

Sunset at Playa
Hermosa: So
that's why they
named it "Beauti-
ful Beach"!

The northern beaches

CUPPED BY BAYS AND COVES GILDED WITH A DUSTING OF
sugary beaches, northern Nicoya's rugged shoreline—the nation's
laid-back "riviera"—provides a variety of choices for vacationers
seeking sun, sand, and sea. All of Costa Rica's ubiquitous nature
highlights are on hand.

Northern beaches
🏕 130 B4/5

Easily accessed from Liberia along
well-paved Highway 21, Nicoya's
northern beaches extend southward
from the Bahía Culebra to Bahía
Tamarindo in scalloped relief, set in
deep basins which are separated by
scrub-covered headlands. The nation's major resort developments
are concentrated here. Playa Flamingo, Playa Hermosa, Playa
Tamarindo, and the all-important
Bahía Culebra are nodes for the
burgeoning flock of self-contained
upscale resort complexes that are
reshaping the face of the region.
Between them are lesser resorts
where local fishing communities
cling to a simple life by the sea.
Sportfishing, scuba diving, and
surfing are favorite pastimes. And
golfing is new to the region—a
contentious use of precious water
and a source of growing conflict
between government and local
communities concerned about the
effects of tourism on their lives.

Weekends and holidays get
crowded, when Josefinos flood
lemming-like from the capital to
sun themselves and swim in the
surf conjured by the breeze from
the warm Prussian-blue sea. Be
warned, because the most popular
beaches get terribly littered in the
wake of these weekend invasions.

BAHÍA CULEBRA
This massive horseshoe-shaped,
cliff-rimmed amphitheater is held
in the pincers of **Punta Ballena,**
to the south, and **Península de
Nacascolo**—an archaeologically
precious region of pre-Columbian
sites—hooking around to the

north. Its setting is dramatic and the sublime vistas across its aquamarine waters are made more so by the dramatic backdrop of Rincón de la Vieja volcano looming to the east.

The previously uninhabited Bahía Culebra is at the center of the largest development project attempted in this part of the Central American isthmus. The Gulf of Papagayo Project, named for the vast gulf into which the bay opens, was initiated in 1993 by the Rafael Calderón administration with ambitions to push Costa Rica into the big league of resort tourism—with 15,000 hotel rooms, two golf courses, self-contained residential communities, a massive marina, and other resort facilities. Most of the score of beaches that nestle in coves that rim the bay between rocky headlands have been earmarked for development. The administration let developers ignore environmental restrictions: bulldozers were plowing willy-nilly over protected mangroves and pre-Columbian settlements, for example. After corruption probes and a legal moratorium, construction has proceeded under more conscientious scrutiny.

Take your pick from several completed resort hotels at **Playa Arenilla** and **Playa Buena** to the south, and **Playa Manzanillo** and **Playa Nacascolo** to the north. The opening of the **Four Seasons Resort & Golf Course** *(tel 696-0000)* in 2003 brought a new cache to the project. Nearby, the **Witch's Rock Canopy Tour** offers a zipline jaunt through the forest.

AROUND PLAYAS DEL COCO

Playas del Coco is a small fishing village popular with tico youth who pack in as tightly as sardines on weekends and holidays to tan their bodies, play volleyball, and flirt beneath the palms. Their informal hang-out is the small central **plaza,** ringed by bars. Pelicans perch on the fishing boats anchored in the mile-wide horseshoe-shaped bay. The noisy partying climaxes in January with the civic fiesta with beauty contests, rodeos, and a lot of over-the-top revelry.

White sand lines the protected cove at Playa Flamingo.

Witch's Rock Canopy Tour

✉ 22 miles W of Liberia

☎ 666-7546

💲 $$$$

To the north lies **Playa Hermosa,** a gray-sand beach with tide pools at the northern end, where the headland is commanded by a large condominium and hotel complex. The beach is in the throes of development yet manages to retain its laid-back appeal. This is enhanced toward its southern end by nets that drape old fishing smacks drawn up on the sands. Farther north, on the southern cusp of Bahía Culebra, lies **Playa Panamá,** offering grand views and a choice of moderately priced to deluxe accommodations. You can camp beneath the brazilwood and sarno trees, and hike inland 600 yards (550 m) to the community of **Panamá** along a dirt road good for spotting wildlife.

A dusty dirt road leads 2 miles (3 km) south from Playa del Coco to **Playa Ocotal,** a secluded gray-sand beach blessed with tide pools and known as a base for sportfishing and scuba diving excursions in the Golfo de Papagayo. The snorkeling is good, particularly at Las Corridas where sea horses float among the soft corals.

AROUND PLAYA FLAMINGO

No, there are no flamingoes in Costa Rica, and this beach resort is also called **Playa Blanca**—White Beach—particularly by promoters. In combination, its coruscating sands and setting are as alluring as any other beach in the nation. The stunning mile-long scimitar of silver lamé unspools within the cusp of rocky headlands speckled with luxurious villas of wealthy ticos and gringos (foreigners).

Despite the presence of a fistful of modest resort hotels, the colloquial title of "Acapulco of Costa Rica" belies the paucity of nightlife and other tourist facilities. Nonetheless, Flamingo has a large marina and is Nicoya's main center for sportfishing.

The commercial development extends along Bahía Potrero, whose gray sands sweep north to the rustic fishing hamlet of **Potrero** and, beyond a rocky headland, to white-sand **Playa la Penca,** backed by a vital mangrove estuary good for spotting monkeys, coatis, iguanas, roseate spoonbills, and parrots amid the rare saltwater forest. The dirt road dips and rises, eventually depositing you at **Playa Pan de Azúcar,** a splendid cove with **Isla Santa Catalina,** a precious nesting site for seabirds such as bridled terns, offshore.

The explosion that has come to Nicoya's beaches has hit the funky fishing hamlet of **Brasilito,** a mile (1.6 km) south of Flamingo, with megaton force. This community has been forced into the modern era by the construction of the **Paradisus Playa Conchal Beach & Golf Resort** (see p. 249), set immediately south of the village at **Playa Conchal,** a half-mile-long (0.8 km) beach of powdered sugar shelving into warm turquoise waters ideal for snorkeling. It is actually composed of pulverized seashells. Water sports are available. The spectacular 18-hole golf course, studded with lagoons, is a creation of visionary designer Robert Trent Jones Jr. Alas, much of the wildlife that formerly inhabited the dry forests hereabouts has been chased away.

From **Huacas,** 4 miles (6.4 km) south of Brasilito, a dirt road leads west via **Matapalo** to **Playa Real,** a secluded gem of a beach hidden within the cusp of headlands. There are tidal pools for wading, and a rugged islet attached to the shore by a short isthmus provides a nesting site for pelicans that perch on rustic fishing boats that bob in the bay. ∎

Parque Nacional Marino Las Baulas

THIS MARINE NATIONAL PARK ENCOMPASSES A STUNNING long beach white as flaming magnesium and known as the preeminent nesting site for leatherback turtles. Waves pound ashore all year, drawing the surfing cognoscenti.

Parque Nacional Marino Las Baulas protects 1,100 acres (445 ha) of Pacific shore-line and an additional 54,000 acres (21,850 ha) out to sea, safeguarding environments vital to the endangered leatherback turtle, whose females lay their eggs on **Playa Grande.** The females come ashore to lay during the cool nights, October to May, preferring full moon—a boon to tourists who can watch the awe-inspiring spectacle under the scrutiny of local guides. This magnificent white-sand beach unfurls along the north shore of **Bahía Tamarindo** and suits the leatherback's need for a deep-water approach that minimizes the distance it has to crawl to nest.

The park's creation in 1990 is seen as a victory over commercial egg poachers, including members of the local community who today derive their livelihood protecting the turtles for ecotourism income. Visitation is regulated.

Nonetheless, developers have been permitted to erect hotels abutting the beach, boosting the numbers of trampling feet. To learn about turtle ecology, call in at **El Mundo de la Tortuga,** a superb museum with audio visual displays.

Dry forest and mangroves behind the beach are laced by trails good for spotting monkeys, birds, and crocodiles. ■

Parque Nacional Marino Las Baulas
🅰 130 A/B4
✉ 5 miles W of Huacas & 35 miles W of Liberia
☎ 686-4967
🕐 Turtle watching Oct.–May
💲 $

El Mundo de la Tortuga
✉ 200 yards inland from the beach
☎ 653-0471
🕐 Call for details
💲 $$

Heeding age-old instincts, a female leatherback drags her ponderous bulk onto the beach.

Leatherback turtles

The world's largest reptile traces its lineage back to the antediluvian dawn. Males can grow to 10 feet (3 m) in length and weigh 2,000 pounds (900 kg)—and yet their brains weigh less than an ounce (28 g)! Other marine turtles have external carapaces made of flattened ribs; the leatherback has an internal skeleton and a leathery exterior of thick, cartilaginous skin.

The giant reptile roams the oceans, often diving to 4,000 feet (1,220 m) in pursuit of its favorite food—jellyfish, which it seizes with jaws that operate like a pair of scissors. The leatherback, insulated from extreme cold by a thick layer of fat, is powered by huge flippers and tapered for streamlined motion, aided by longitudinal ridges that act as keels. ■

Marine turtles

Seven species of marine turtles *(Chelonidae)* roam the world's oceans, from the diminutive Ridley, which rarely grows to more than 30 inches (75 cm) long, to the Cadillac-size leatherback. Turtles are creatures of grace and speed in water, with a remarkable physiology—including an external skeleton and toothless jaws that act like a paper cutter—dating back 200 million years, proving an incredible ability to adapt and endure.

Loggerhead
47 inches

Hawksbill
35 inches

Leatherback
74 inches

Adult turtles face capture in shrimpers' nets, or by commercial pirates. And turtles choose to nest on beaches beloved of hotel developers.

Turtle populations are endangered throughout their range thanks to man's depredations. Several species are nearly extinct. Following the discovery of the New World, turtle meat became a staple of seamen cruising these waters. Turtles were harvested to cater to Europe's taste for turtle soup. The green turtle population has been so reduced that only three major nesting sites remain in the region.

All the major nesting sites in Costa Rica are now protected, yet turtle populations continue to face domestic pressures. Raw eggs, valued for their reputed aphrodisiacal properties, are imbibed in local cantinas to bolster libidos, and nest-poaching still goes on despite laws against taking eggs. Other thieves partake of the banquet; coyotes, raccoons, peccaries, coatis, vultures, frigate birds, and crabs snatch up hatchlings as they flail their way to the sea.

Nature's miracle

Adults are known to navigate vast distances, often crossing oceans, on foraging forays. Males spend their entire lives— up to half a century—at sea; only the

Olive Ridley
30 inches

Green
49 inches

Opposite: Guided by an internal compass, a green turtle follows its destiny.

Green
hatchling

Leatherback
hatchling

Olive Ridley
hatchling

Hawksbill
hatchling

Loggerhead
hatchling

A biologist releases olive Ridley hatchlings from a study nest at Playa Nancite.

females return to land. Each female returns to shore every two or three years, usually by night and during high tide—often at full moon—to ease her climb up the beach.

After finding a spot above the high tide mark, she uses her front flippers to scoop a hollow and digs a pit with her back flippers. In this she lays an average of 107 spherical, golf ball-sized eggs. "There is a great deal of biology packed into that figure," said turtle expert Dr. Archie Carr (1909–1987). "The whole race and destiny of the creature are probably balanced at the edge of limbo by the delicate weight of that magic number." Any fewer and predators prevail and the species wanes.

Once the first egg drops, she will proceed with egg laying oblivious to any intrusion. After shoveling the sand back and thumping it down with her body, she flings sand wildly about to hide her nest, then heads back to sea and, if no longer producing eggs, swims off. If she is still receptive, she will remain near shore where the males take turns mounting her. Females often nest several times in one season.

Whither the youth?
After incubating in the warm sand for around seven weeks, the eggs hatch. Hatchlings are usually the same gender in each nest, due to the temperature of the sand (cooler for males), with 2-3°F making the difference. They emerge from their eggs together, dig their way up to the surface, and wait until night to make their mad dash to the sea.

Baby turtles are programmed to head for the ocean horizon and easily become disoriented by other lights, so that hotel guests who leave their lights on often find baby turtles at their door. Once at sea they continue to paddle maniacally for several days. The hatchlings swim off, and are rarely seen until some come back as big as a chest of drawers.

Recent genetic evidence bears out the long-held belief that turtles return to their own natal beaches. How they accomplish this navigational feat is far from clear.

Turtle viewing
Five species of turtle lay their eggs on Costa Rica's beaches, and can be seen nesting at any time of year. Leatherback turtles come ashore October to April at Playa Grande in Nicoya, at Refugio Nacional de Vida Silvestre Gandoca-Manzanillo on the southern Caribbean shores, and in lesser numbers elsewhere. Green turtles can be seen at Gandoca-Manzanillo and at Parque Nacional Tortuguero, where as many as 5,000 turtles come ashore between June and November. The most awe-inspiring site is the *arribada* (see page 147), or mass nesting, of olive Ridley turtles occurring at Playa Ostional and Playa Nancite (off limits) in Nicoya, where tens of thousands of turtles swarm ashore during full moons, between July and December. Hawksbill turtles nest singly and in far smaller numbers at select beaches throughout the nation, and loggerhead are found on the Caribbean shore. ∎

Tamarindo

THIS ONCE SLEEPY FISHING VILLAGE HAS BEEN CATAPULTED from obscurity to become one of Costa Rica's most popular beach resorts, offering a rare sophistication and a handy base for exploring the adjacent Parque Nacional Marino Las Baulas and the wildlife-rich ecosystems adjoining.

Refugio Nacional de Vida Silvestre Tamarindo

🅰 130 B4
✉ Tamarindo
☎ 296-7074
🕐 Call for details
💲 $$

Sunset is the only real reason to stash the surfboard at Tamarindo.

Tamarindo, which is named for the tamarind trees backing the beach, looks west over a deep bay and the long silver sweep of Playa Grande, which is separated from Tamarindo by the Río Matapalo unfurling majestically to the northeast. The beach is lackluster—pebbly, of dark gray sand, and studded with rocks—though tide pools offer interest at low tide. **Isla Capitán** beckons a short distance offshore, and pelicans swoop down to perch on fishing boats tethered at anchor.

Surfers come for the waves that barrel onto the beach. Several local tour operators run surf trips to more remote spots, including **Playa Langosta,** an unspoiled white-sand beach that extends southward from the estuary of the Río San Francisco, to the south of Tamarindo. Various marine turtles, including leatherbacks, come ashore to nest in peace, protected by the national park service. And the tidal waters of the river feed mangroves that support a slew of other birds and beasts.

Tamarindo's greatest natural appeal is the **Refugio Nacional de Vida Silvestre Tamarindo,** protecting 1,000 acres (400 ha) of mangrove-riddled wetlands and dry forests at the estuary of the Río Matapalo, which extends inland from Parque Nacional Marino Las Baulas. Monkeys can sometimes be seen cavorting on the estuarine sands at the tip of Playa Grande. Crocodiles lurk in the dark brackish waters. Waterfowl abound. And ocelots, deer, and several other endangered species have reappeared in recent years. You can hire canoes or take organized boat excursions arranged in Tamarindo village.

Tamarindo's growing popularity has spawned a profusion of upscale hotels, restaurants, and chic cafés under the aegis of European and North American proprietors who have imbued the resort with a unique savoir faire. ■

Refugio Nacional
de Vida Silvestre
Ostional

✉ 3 miles W of
    Nosara
☎ 682-0410
$ $$

Refugio Nacional de Vida Silvestre Ostional

AROUND OSTIONAL THERE ARE ALMOST ALWAYS TURTLES in the water, particularly during the July to December nesting season, when battalions of helmeted turtles storm ashore in an astonishing example of synchronized reproduction.

important turtle hatcheries. The Ridley, known as the *lora*, has hit on a clever idea to ensure its survival…an occurrence known locally as an *arribada* (see p. 147). Playa Ostional is one of two arribada sites in Costa Rica and nine worldwide.

During full moon periods, tens of thousands of turtles congregate offshore then surge ashore like armored battalions. Each arribada can occupy an entire week as wave after wave of turtles come ashore: often as many as 150,000! Stragglers come ashore at other times of year, as do leatherbacks between October and January.

Visitors must report to the **ranger station** or the **turtle cooperative** *(tel 682-0410)* in the village center. You can visit the University of Costa Rica's **Sea Turtle research station** *(tel 682-0267)* by arrangement.

Southward Playa Ostional melds into Playa Nosara, which had its first arribada in 1997. The recovery of the population at Playa Ostional is such that overpopulation has resulted in spill-over onto adjacent beaches. Both these beaches are backed by steep forest-clad hills that are good for hiking. The **Río Montaña** and **Río Nosara** tumble down from the hills and snake across the coastal plain, forming a tangled estuary of mangroves and forests full of playacting monkeys, coatis, iguanas, and more than 190 species of birds including parrots. You can take several boat trips locally.

The Nosara beaches, with Playa Ostional in the background

This 613-acre (248 ha) reserve protects three critically important nest sites for olive Ridley turtles—Playa Ostional, Playa Nosara, and Playa Guiones—extending along 9 miles (15 km) of shoreline between **Punta India** and **Punta Guiones.** The refuge centers on the coastal hamlet of **Ostional** midway down a gray-sand beach that is one of the world's most

NOSARA

The Río Nosara is hemmed by a craggy headland, **Punta Nosara** in whose lee a cove with a blowhole and cave full of bats lies cupped by **Punta Pelada.** Punta Pelada offers stupendous views over **Playa Guiones,** a wide coral-colored beach arcing 2 miles (3.2 km) south. Tidal pools tempt you to wade the knee-deep shallows, and rollers crash ashore, tempting the many surfers.

Behind Playa Guiones is Beaches of Nosara, a residential area for North Americans and Europeans, which extends up into the Fila Hormigosa mountains. A few cafés and small hotels, and the **Nosara Yoga Institute** *(tel 682-0072)* nestle amid the foliage, connected by a maze of dirt roads. Howler monkeys abound and are often seen down by the beach, scaring tourists with their stentorian roars.

The road connecting Nosara to the town of Nicoya and Highway 21 is often impassable. An airstrip is located in the middle of the main village, **Bocas de Nosara,** an attractive rustic hamlet redolent of campesino life. It is on the south bank of the Río Nosara, 3 miles (4.8 km) inland of Playa Guiones. ■

Loras (olive Ridleys) come and go on a beach littered with turtle eggs.

Making good on the *arribadas*

As part of a plan designed to help save the Ridley, the residents of Ostional hold a unique license to harvest the turtles' eggs and sell them. Because so many turtles pack the beach during the *arribada* (or egg-laying) season, eggs laid on the first few nights are often destroyed by turtles on subsequent nights; at the same time, incubating eggs are often dug up and destroyed when another *arribada* occurs before the first batch has hatched. To make matters even worse, poaching by locals was threatening to reduce the already severely stressed Ridley population beyond the point of no return.

In 1987 the government of Costa Rica approved a plan to permit residents to harvest a quota of eggs—those that would likely be destroyed anyway—during the first 36 hours of each *arribada*. By removing these eggs, bacterial infections have been reduced and significantly more eggs are hatching. The local community has benefited from the new income, fostering support for conservation, while the presence on the market of eggs bearing the stamp of approval has undercut the market for eggs poached from other beaches. ■

Sámara to Malpaís by four-wheel drive

There is no shortage of adventure in Costa Rica, where one of the best to be had is this 57-mile (91 km) drive along the rugged southwestern shore of Nicoya. You will need a sturdy four-wheel drive vehicle and an Indiana Jones spirit to tackle the rough dirt track that turns travel into a minor expedition, especially in wet season when swollen rivers can add to the adrenaline rush.

This rutted dirt road clambers over mountainous headlands and down to hidden beaches passing forlorn fishing villages and farming communities separated by long stretches of jungle-green shoreline. There are no road signs and many deceptive forks. Fill up before setting off: there are no gas stations. Don't attempt this drive late in the day.

Begin your journey in **Sámara ❶**, reached from Nicoya township via Highway 150, a well-paved road. This off-beat funky fishing hamlet and resort is popular with budget-conscious European travelers and young ticos. It has gained a few upscale touches of late but nonetheless retains its slightly raffish, impecunious charm, assisted by vultures hopping about the sand-blown unpaved streets. Sámara is set in a deep basin and faces onto a handsome horseshoe bay where pelicans dive for fish and surf rolls in, bringing the surf-crowd to town.

Immediately south of town, the dirt road narrows and begins to dip and rise before spilling you onto **Playa Carrillo ❷**, a sliver of white sand with an eponymous fishing hamlet—a base for sportfishing sorties—tucked into the cove at the southern end of the beach. Further beaches lie hidden along the shore as the road runs inland, parallel to the coast, deteriorating all the while. Leatherback and Ridley turtles nest all along the jungle shore, including at **Playa Islita ❸**, beyond which the track begins a stiff climb that would challenge a goat. The hilltop **Hotel Punta Islita** (see p. 250), makes a perfect break-point thanks to its sublime decor and the magnificent vistas to be enjoyed from the bar and excellent restaurant. It has a private beach and offers a variety of activities, including horseback riding.

You then spiral down to the hamlet of **Islita ❹** and ascend again over **Punta Barranquilla**, with the narrow dirt road clinging magically to the mountainside. From above, the road seems to descend into oblivion but disgorges you at **Playa Corazalito ❺**. Farther south come **Playa Bejuco ❻** and **Playa Coyote ❼**, both good for turtle spotting, with the road running inland parallel to a shore backed by thick wetland swamp teeming with wildlife. You will pass through the hamlets of **Quebrada Seca, Pueblo Nuevo,** and **Jabilla,** to the crossroads of **San Francisco de Coyote ❽** where the going begins to get tricky. Unpaved Highway 162 links San Francisco to Highway 21, and continues southwest along the **Río Jabillo,** which you must ford: the road is subject to flooding, but as long as you can resist being carried off into the mangroves, you will get through. The river winds through mangroves that form a haven for egrets, snakes, turtles, and other wildlife. Don't be surprised to see a crocodile padding across the road.

After twisting for 4 miles (6.4 km), turn right at the Y-fork beside the sugarcane field. This will bring you to the **Salon La Perla India ❾**, at a road junction. Whether you continue straight or turn left, you will have to ford the **Río Bongo,** a seemingly shallow crossing that can make your pulse quicken. By keeping straight, you will emerge near **Playa Bongo ❿** , where at low tide (and *only* at low tide!) you can run along the beach with not another soul for miles—just you and the bellows of howler monkeys, the screeching of toucans and parrots, and the crashing of surf

Proud angler with dolphin fish

See area map pp. 130–131
Sámara
57 miles (91 km)
4 hours (one way)
Malpaís

NOT TO BE MISSED
- Playa Carrillo
- Playa Coyote
- Playa Bongo

Corozalito · Quebrada Seca · Bejuco
5 Playa Corozalito · Pueblo Nuevo · **6** Playa Bejuco
Jabilla · **8** San Francisco de Coyote
7 Playa Coyote · Puerto Coyote · Salon La Perla India
Punta Coyote · Caletas · Playa Caletas · **9**
Playa Bongo · **10** · Bajos de Arío
Playa Arío · Arío · **12** Betel
Playa Manzanillo · **11** Manzanillo · Cóbano
Punta Pochote · Santiago
Playa Santa Teresa · Santa Teresa
Malpaís · **13**
Cabo Blanco

Surf and turf, Playa Hermosa

Playa Manzanillo

as the track skirts the shore. After 3 miles (5 km) you will hit the main coast road again at the fishing hamlet of **Manzanillo** ⑪. A left turn at Salon La Perla India leads across the Río Bongo and from there to the **Río Arío,** which is hemmed in by steep-sided embankments—no problem by day, but the egress is 100 yards (90 m) upriver and impossible to detect at night. If you hit a log, *do not* step out—it could well be a crocodile! Beyond the river, you will arrive at the hamlet of **Betel** ⑫. Turn right. After 1.5 miles (2.5 km) you will meet the shore at Manzanillo.

The rough-and-ready track claws over **Punta Pochote** and follows surf-washed **Playa Santa Teresa.** In wet season, or after a good downpour, the mud can be deep. Surf pounds the beaches that limn the jungle-green shore, drawing surfers. Rustic hotels and surf camps announce your arrival in the off-beat surfers' resort of **Malpaís** ⑬, where you can pick up the paved road that links to Highway 160. ∎

The eastern shore

Refugio Nacional de Vida Silvestre Curú

www.curu.org

🅼 131 E2

✉ Hwy. 160, 2 miles S of Paquera

☎ 661-2392

🕐 By appointment

💲 $

NICOYA'S SERRATED EASTERN SHORE RUNS SOUTHWEST like a great saw, deeply indented with swampy coves and beach-lined bays in the lee of sheer cliffs. Tropical dry deciduous forest merges into moister jungle replete with wildlife, protected in several prime retreats including Costa Rica's most exquisite island.

From **Paquera,** Highway 160 writhes over rugged headlands. The road is mostly unpaved and badly deteriorated and, in some sections, becomes a washboard that shakes your bones loose. Grand coastal vistas make amends for this. The largest indentation is **Bahía Ballena,** named for the whales that sometimes come into the bay.

Travelers can choose from several key resort hotels around **Tambor,** a small fishing village. Caimans and waterfowl are among the wildlife to be seen in the mangrove swamps to the northeast at the estuary of the **Río Pánica.** The endearing **Tango Mar hotel,** 3 miles (4.8 km) south of Tambor (see p. 250), offers a nine-hole golf course, and sits over its own splendid beach. Inland, the **Profelis Wildcat Center** breeds and rehabilitates wild cats for reintroduction into their natural habitats. Visitors are welcome; call for times.

Highway 160 runs to **Cóbano,** a crossroads gateway to Malpaís (see p. 149) and to Reserva Natural Absoluta Cabo Blanco (see p. 152). It is reached via **Montezuma,** a quintessential laid-back retreat with superb coral-colored beaches that feature both rocky outcrops and fascinating tidal pools. The village has a reputation for attracting New Age types with its inexpensive accommodations and health-food cafés. A local citizens' association tends the hamlet conscientiously. You can cool off in the waterfalls that cascade down from the forest-clad hills where monkeys cavort in open view.

The dusty coast road continues west to the hamlet of **Cabuya,** which provides access to Cabo Blanco. At low tide you can cross the causeway to **Isla Muertos** ("Isle of the Dead") which locals continue to use as a cemetery. The land has served as such since pre-Columbian times.

Beach volleyball is the thong to do on Isla Tortuga.

Located between Cóbano and Montezuma, the **Montezuma Canopy Tour** *(tel 642-0808)* lets you whiz through the treetops full of wildlife.

REFUGIO NACIONAL DE VIDA SILVESTRE CURÚ

Tucked within the pleated shore of Golfo Curú, this 208-acre (84 ha) jewel forms the nucleus of a 3,000-acre (1,214 ha) private cattle hacienda. Two-thirds of the hacienda is smothered in primary forest that extends along 3 miles (4.8 km) of shore and into the hills behind. Its Lilliputian scale notwithstanding, Curú's habitats range from mangrove swamps along the banks of the Río Curú to deciduous forest atop the hills. You can reliably expect to see caimans, and howler and capuchin monkeys. Sloths, shy agoutis, ocelots, pumas, endangered spider monkeys, and white-tailed deer are also present, along with more than 150 species of birds. Both hawksbill and olive Ridley turtles consider the beaches **Playa Curú, Playa Colorado,** and **Playa Quesara** clean

enough to lay eggs. (Visits are made with prior arrangements.)

ISLA TORTUGA

This emerald jewel in a sea of aquamarine is everything you hope a tropical isle will be—white-rimmed, shaded by tousled palms, lapped by ripples washing lazily onto the beach. Tortuga, 2 miles (3.2 km) offshore of Curú, is all this and more. The 770-acre (312 ha) isle rises steeply from the shore, with trails into the forested hills.

This idyll draws day-trippers on cruise tours from Puntarenas, who come to play volleyball, snorkel, and paddle kayaks, glass-bottom boats, and water-bicycles. Others flock simply to laze in a hammock and soak up the sun with a *coco loco* (rum, coconut milk, and coconut liqueur served in a husk) in hand. Calypso Cruises (see p. 262) was the company that pioneered the cruises and they still lead the way, whisking guests from Puntarenas aboard a state-of-the-art catamaran *Manta Ray.* Weekends, which get crowded, are best avoided. ∎

White sands and jade waters draw day-cruise boats to anchor at Isla Tortuga.

Profelis Wildcat Center
www.seibermarco.de/ profelis

🅜 131 E2

✉ San Rafael de Paquera, 5 miles NW of Paquera

☎ 641-0644

🕐 Mon.–Fri. by appointment

💲 $$

Reserva Natural Absoluta
Cabo Blanco

Reserva Natural Absoluta Cabo Blanco

✉ 10 miles SW of Cobano

☎ 642-0093

⊕ Closed Mon.–Tues.

💲 $

DANGLING OFF THE TIP OF NICOYA, THIS 2,896-ACRE (1,172 ha) reserve lies at the boundary between tropical dry and tropical wet ecosystems and is known for its rich biodiversity, including Pacific tropical lowland forest unique to southwest Nicoya. For hardy hikers (with a trail guide and plenty of water) the rewards are enriching.

Pelican wings homeward at Cabo Blanco.

The reserve wraps around the southwestern shores of Nicoya, protecting precious forests that drape mountainous shoulders. It was here, in 1963, that Costa Rica's national park system was born—the culmination of a remarkable dedication shown by Olof Wessberg, a Swedish immigrant who arrived to find the lush wilderness under siege. Ultimately, this ceaseless campaigner paid with his life—murdered in 1975—for the wilderness he managed to save. A plaque at the **ranger station** situated at the end of the road 5 miles (8 km) west of Montezuma commemorates his work. From here a trail leads into the park.

Sendero Sueco is a stiff climb over steep ridges before dropping down to lonesome **Playa Cabo Blanco** and **Playa**

Balsita, separated by a great headland. The crushed-diamond beaches have tidal pools good for spotting sea urchins and sea stars. From Balsita, **Sendero El Barco** follows the coast west before climbing inland and looping north. Don't try walking the shoreline trail at other than low tide—you might get cut off! Rising out of the ocean about a mile (1.6 km) offshore is **Isla Cabo Blanco,** strung like a pearl off the southern tip. It gains its white hue from guano deposited by a large colony of brown boobies and other seabirds.

The park was initially off limits, but visitors have been permitted entry since 1989; the trail system remains limited, however, making most of the park inaccessible. Commonly seen species include anteaters, howler, capuchin, and spider monkeys, coatis, sloths, boa constrictors, and other snakes. With great fortune, tepezcuintles or agoutis might run across your path, chased by an ocelot or puma. Peccaries are also abundant and not to be trifled with. Sulfur-winged parakeets chatter in treetops that soar to 150 feet (45 m), and crested caracaras, elegant trogons, and herons are among the scores of other rainbow-hued birds.

The park is once again under threat, this time from too much visitation, and wildlife species have increasingly retreated to the park interior, bringing demands for further restrictions. ∎

A pencil-thin coastal strip walled by jungle-clad mountains cut by plunging rivers that spill to the surf-pounded shore, the Central Pacific offers adventure, fantastic wildlife, and a splendid choice of accommodations.

Central Pacific

White-faced capuchin monkey

Central Pacific

IT IS NOT HARD TO SEE WHY THE CENTRAL PACIFIC REGION HAS BECOME one of the country's most visited areas, attracting visitors seeking a medley of treats from easy-going immersions in nature to wild white-water rides on mountain rivers. A large percentage come specifically to visit Parque Nacional Manuel Antonio, a shining star in the park system, within walking distance of more than 60 fine hotels. Backed by kelly green mountains, the surf-washed beaches offer something for everyone, whether they are surfers in search of the ultimate wave or sybarites seeking a poolside retreat at Playa Jacó, Costa Rica's party-hearty resort town that is the yang to Manuel Antonio's yin.

GUANACASTE
p. 99

CENTRAL HIGHLANDS
p. 67

Tárcoles

PARQUE
NACIONAL
CARARA
667m
Cerro Bijagualito
Carara

Tárcoles

Quebrada
Ganado
Delicias

Punta Leona

Villa
Caletas
San Gabriel

239

Punta Conejo
Herradura
Gloria

Playa Herradura
I. Herradura
Jacó
Pacific Rainforest
Aerial Tram

Playa de Jacó
Pochotal
Tulin
Surubres
Palo Seco
Porvenir
Fila Chonta

Punta Guapinol
34

Playa Hermosa
Esterillos
Oeste
Esterillos
Este
Loma
Valle de Parrita
Rainmaker
Conservation
Project
Paso
Real

Punta Judas
Playa Esterillos Oeste
Playa
Esterillos
Este
Julieta
Parrita
Esquipulas

Playa
Palma
Playa
Palo Seco
Damas
Naranjito

Estero
Damas
Boca Vieja
Bijagual

Finca Naturales Wildlife Refuge
& Butterfly Garden
Quepos
Manuel Antonio
Rafiki Safari
Lodge

Punta Quepos
Playa Espadilla
Punta Catedral
PARQUE
NACIONAL
MANUEL
ANTONIO
Playa
Manuel Antonio

Playa
Savegre

A   B   C   D

0   20 kilometers
0   10 miles

4▷
3▷
2▷

Everything happens down on the coastal plain. To the north, rugged spurs of the Talamancas curl around the plain and crash to the coast, dramatically marking the transition from dry to wet life zones. South of Jacó the mountains recede and the plains open out, dominated by cattle farms and, further south, row upon row of sturdy palms grown for palm oil and centered on the town of Parrita. Still further southward, the plain is crimped by a range of coastal mountains—the Fila Costeña—that seem to rise straight up from the sea.

A single highway—Highway 34—runs inland parallel to the shore. It is maddeningly potholed and unpaved for long stretches, forging a dusty path through a string of tidy little plantation villages. It was as late as 1996 before the highway pushed beyond Punta

Uvita, providing a link with Golfo Dulce and the Inter-American Highway via the rugged, rain-forest-green Brunca Coast. Highway 24 is being widened and paved to become the new Inter-American Highway.

Lonesome gray-sand beaches stretch for miles in a long daisy chain, one after the other, separated by rugged headlands. Many beaches are hidden from the main highway by thick stands of forest. The wide-open coastline receives waves head-on and offers fantastic surfing, though swimming is dangerous everywhere due to strong rip tides.

Several beaches have long been popular with Josefinos who come here from the capital on weekends. Playa Herradura comes to mind. Today this once languid hamlet is the setting

Many beaches in the Central Pacific, such as this one at Manuel Antonio, are so deserted you may be surprised to find footprints.

of a new mega-development that will bring the region's first golf-course and finest marina. Nearby Jacó has traditionally served a budget-minded Canadian market, plus surfers drawn to the endless swells. The resort has gained a modicum of sophistication, as has Quepos, a sportfishing center that now boasts a lively restaurant and night scene. The forested mountains are popular for both hiking and horseback

riding—activities offered in mountain retreats such as Escaleras and the Rainmaker Conservation Project. The rivers that tumble out of the mountains provide enthralling white-water rafting. Below, the rivers meander lugubriously through swathes of mangroves and riparian forest that provide vital habitats for a Noah's Ark full of wildlife. Crocodiles are numerous, notably in the estuary of the Río Tárcoles. And Parque Nacional Carara and Parque Nacional Manuel Antonio offer even the least intrepid souls the opportunity of coming face to face with wildlife. Manuel Antonio even has a coral reef and beach. ■

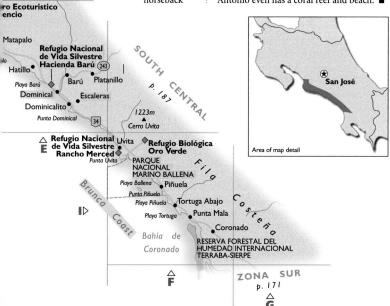

Groom with a view: White-faced capuchin monkeys are easy to spot in Parque Nacional Carara.

Parque Nacional Carara & Río Tárcoles

Parque Nacional Carara

🅰 154 B4

✉ Hwy. 34, 14 miles S of Orotina

☎ 383-9953 or 200-5023

💲 $

SMALL IT MAY BE, BUT CARARA IS ASTOUNDINGLY RICH. This seminally important national park lies at the meeting point of the dry and wet climatic zones, marking the shift from predominantly Mesoamerican to Amazonian influences. Carara—a Huetar Native American name meaning "crocodile"—protects the last major stand of transitional forest on the isthmus; representative species from both ecosystems abound within its 11,613 acres (4,700 ha). A broad river flows to a sweeping mangrove and wetland system that is one of the nation's largest troves of birdlife.

CARARA

Easily reached from San José, a one-hour drive away, Carara shrouds the westernmost foothills of the Talamancas and owes its existence in part to the stewardship of the Cervantes family, who protected the lush mountain watershed on their huge cattle-ranch, Finca La Coyola, before handing it to the National Parks Service in 1977.

The profusion of tree species belies Carara's scale. Hardwoods soar over the evergreen forests that cloak **Cerro Bijagualito** (2,188 feet, 667 m). Access is via a mile-long (1.6 km) loop trail—**Sendero Las Araceas**—from the entrance and **Quebrada Bonita ranger station** beside Highway 34, 2 miles (3.2 km) south of the **Río Tárcoles,** which forms the reserve's northern boundary. A second trail—**Sendero Sura**—begins just south of the bridge over the Río Tárcoles and follows the course of the river inland for 3 miles (4.8 km). The terrain is relatively flat, making access easy for everyone.

You are almost assured of seeing capuchin monkeys. Endangered spider monkeys are also present, plus howler monkeys, coatis, peccaries, great anteaters, ocelots, and in moister sections, poison-arrow frogs hopping about on the dank forest floor, secure in their Day-Glo liveries. Birding is especially rewarding. The riverbanks are good places to spot kingfishers. Parrots abound. And toucans are everywhere. So are their cousins the fiery-billed aracari. The most colorful denizen, and reason enough to visit, is the endangered scarlet macaw. Around 40 pairs breed in Carara, where their nests are guarded against poachers. Time your arrival for dawn or dusk and you can see the flock migrating between Carara's tropical wet forest interior and the mangrove forest at the mouth of the Río Tárcoles, where they roost.

Numerous archaeological sites have been excavated though none are open to visitors. To minimize human impact, visitation is limited to 60 people at one time, and to a small lowland section of the park. Insects abound, so bring repellent. Carara's weather is seasonal: March and April are driest. It pays to hire a naturalist guide through companies in San José.

RÍO TÁRCOLES

Highway 34 crosses the **Río Tárcoles,** where crocodiles are almost always present, basking motionless as logs on the banks. You have a grandstand view from the bridge on the main highway. Close-up views of these monsters are easily arranged at the funky fishing village of **Tárcoles,** where local guides lead "crocodile safaris." Dozens of the reptiles gather near the mangrove-lined river mouth, and you may even see one or more of these awesome beasts being hand-fed by your guide.

The estuarine mangroves also form one of the richest repositories of avian fauna in Central America. More than 400 species have been recorded—an astonishing number that includes roseate spoonbills, a significant breeding population of scarlet macaws, and boat-billed herons, named for their broad keel-shaped beaks. ■

What a croc!

Despite their rather fearsome reputation, crocodiles are good parents. Female crocs build nests of compost above the high-water mark, in which they lay 30 to 70 eggs. They tend their nests assiduously; then, when they hear the first peeping squeaks of hatchlings, they carefully dig open the nests and take the little ones into their mouths. The male crocodile helps guard the nursery. ■

Fishing boats on the shores of the beach at Jacó. This is Costa Rica's most developed resort area.

Jacó

THE NATION'S MOST POPULAR RESORT HAS BEEN DRAWING visitors for two decades. Though its own appeal seems limited, its proximity to San José assures a regular local clientele. Jacó also remains steadfastly popular with Canadian charter tourists—so much so, in fact, that the maple-leaf flag flutters above the town.

Pura Vida Botanical Garden
- 154 B4
- 3 miles E of Táracoles
- 200-5040
- $$$

Pacific Rainforest Aerial Tram
www.rainforesttram.com
- 154 B4
- 2.5 miles E of Jacó
- 257-5961
- $$$$

Jacó, 9 miles (15 km) south of Parque Nacional Carara, remains Costa Rica's most developed retreat, and scores of hotels, international restaurants, surf shops, and travel services line the sole drag, which runs parallel to Highway 34. Jacó's unpretentious character appeals to party-hearty Josefinos, who flock on weekends and holidays, and to the young, carefree surf crowd that lend the town an irrepressibly off-beat edge. Slowly but surely it is gaining in sophistication however, helped along by the recent opening of the deluxe Los Sueños Marriott Ocean & Golf Resort (see p. 252) north of town at Playa Herradura and by the presence of Villa Caletas (see p. 170), a stunning cliff-top resort hotel featuring fine dining and classical concerts.

Flanked by headlands, the palm-fringed beach of gray sand extends for 2 miles (3.2 km). Tidal pools beneath the headlands can be tempting, but beware of the strong riptides. Try horseback riding on the beach, or arrange an excursion with a tour company. Offshore, **Isla Herradura** is an important nesting site for seabirds.

Pura Vida Botanical Garden, in the mountains outside town, has manicured self-guided trails; its riotous colors and scents draw birds in profusion.

To view wildlife amid native forest, take a ride on the **Pacific Rainforest Aerial Tram,** which leisurely ascends into the coastal mountains, offering a chance for eye-level encounters with monkeys and other canopy dwellers. ∎

Lonesome beaches

THE LONG, LINEAR COAST SOUTH OF JACÓ IS STRUNG WITH a necklace of surf-pounded beaches that are divided by estuaries where silt-laden rivers snake through swamps and mangrove. Hardly noticed by the tourist industry, these beaches offer a rare chance to play Robinson Crusoe.

At low tide, when the sea recedes up to 200 yards (180 m), the sparkling sands are ideal for long, solitary walks.

South of Jacó, Highway 34 crests a steep headland—**Punta Guapinol**—where you have your first magnificent view of the beaches, beginning with **Playa Hermosa** rolling southward for 6 miles (9.6 km) like a ribbon of silver lamé, with tiny surfers like ants rolling in on the waves. Don't get too close to the cliff edge, as it is unstable in places. An international surfing championship is held here annually. The beach has its share of budget accommodations catering to the laid-back surf crowd, as well as more upscale accommodations.

The central and southern parts of the beach are backed by a wetland area offering birders the splendid delight of viewing stilt-legged waders, kingfishers, parrots, and scores of other exotic species.

Punta Judas separates Playa Hermosa from **Playa Esterillos Oeste** and **Playa Esterillos Este,** three ruler-straight beaches backed by palms and thick tropical forest, and kept clean by pounding surf. Playa Esterillos Oeste is intriguing for the fossils that can be seen in the rocks at the northern end of the beach. Farther south are the **Río Palma** and **Río Parrita,** which feed the vast wetland systems that back **Playa Palma** and **Playa Palo Seco.**

So far relatively undiscovered by foreign tourists, the beaches draw Josefinos to a selection of rental cottages and simple cabanas that are built right onto the beach. But mainstream commercialism has so far managed to pass this stretch of coast by. ■

Quepos

QUEPOS IS KNOWN AS A SPORTFISHING CENTER WHOSE FOR-
tunes were boosted by Parque Nacional Manuel Antonio (see pp.
162–163), 4 miles (6.4 km) away. It is a service-and-entertainment center to the hotels that line the hilly road between the town and the park.

Quepos
🅰 155 D3
**Visitor
information**
☎ 643-1000 or
643-3010

Quepos is coddled by forested hills
and nestles at the foot of a bay 2
miles (3.2 km) southwest of Highway 34. In the 1930s, banana plantations were established and
Quepos became a key shipping
port. Alas, a banana blight swept
through the plantations during the
1950s, and the Standard Fruit
Company switched its interest to
African palms. Years later, an earthquake that struck Quepos on
November 22, 2004, and caused
some considerable damage.

Today, Quepos's fortunes rest
squarely on tourism. Small hotels,
hip restaurants, and nightclubs
have proliferated as the result of
a recent tourist boom. The town
hosts a Carnival each February
that attracts visitors.

The compact town center melds
northward into the fishing village
of **Boca Vieja,** a ramshackle old
assemblage of stilt-legged wooden
houses perched rather precariously
over the dun-colored waters of the
mangrove-lined **Estero Boca
Vieja.** More handsome clapboard
homes lie hidden in the hills south
of town, where the Standard Fruit
Company once had its residential
compound. Do not swim off the
gray-sand beach that fronts the
town; as a result of a local sewage
problem, the bay is polluted.

Nearby is the **Río Naranjo,**
which spills down the flanks of the
Fila San Bosco mountains and
is popular for white-water rafting
excursions. Horseback rides are
available at several nearby estates.
But by far the biggest activity is
sportfishing—with marlin the main
lure in the December to April peak
season. Several outfitters berth their

facilities for such endangered animals as the tepezcuintle. Take the guided nocturnal tour along trails lit by ultraviolet lighting to show off the insects' markings, visible only to potential mates with ultraviolet vision.

DAMAS ESTUARY

This vast wetland system extends northwest of Quepos for 12 miles (19 km). It is fed by the **Río Palo Seco** and **Río Damas,** both of which wash large volumes of silt down from the mountains to make the estuary a Minotaur's maze of tangled, interconnected channels, some of which open into broad lagoons while others peter out in narrow cul-de-sacs.

Boat and sea-kayaking trips depart from **Damas wharf** for "mangrove safaris" (see p. 264). You are sure to see crocodiles and monkeys and countless wading birds. With luck you might spot raccoons and their native cousins, coatis. Mosquitoes whine in your ears: bring repellent. And watch for snakes.

Isla Damas pins the main estuary and is good for walks. Its attractions consist of a small zoo and a floating restaurant. ∎

sportfishing vessels here, and are available to take you out at short notice usually.

The **Finca Naturales Wildlife Refuge & Butterfly Garden,** south of Quepos on the road to Manuel Antonio, provides an immersion in lepitodera lore. This 30-acre (12 ha) "living laboratory of nature conservancy" features trails, plus netted flyways, butterfly exhibits, and reproduction

**Finca Naturales
Wildlife Refuge &
Butterfly Garden**
www.butterflygardens.co.cr
🅰 154 D3
✉ 2.5 miles S
    of Quepos
☎ 777-0973
🕐 Closed Sun.
💲 $$$

**Makeshift homes
are a landmark of
funky Boca Vieja.**

Breakers wash up
to the rain forest.

Parque Nacional
Manuel Antonio

**Parque Nacional
Manuel Antonio**

🅰 154 D2

✉ 4 miles S
of Quepos

☎ 777-0644

🕐 Closed Mon.

💲 $$

TUCKED INTO A RUGGED CRANNY MIDWAY DOWN THE
Pacific coast, pocket-size Parque Nacional Manuel Antonio embodies
many of the diverse attributes that visitors hope to see in Costa Rica.
The popular park offers white-sand beaches, a coral reef, and rain for-
est teeming with wildlife that loves to put on a song and dance.

The 1,685-acre (682 ha) park is set
on a blunt-nosed peninsula backed
by forested hills; it also includes the
waters of the Pacific on three sides.
The peninsula is in fact a tombolo:
a slender, low-slung sand spit con-
necting two larger sections of
land—in this case, a former island
called **Punta Catedral,** which
seems to hang on the map like a

pearl. You can hike to its summit
via a steep trail at the end of **Playa
Espadilla Sur,** a quarter-mile
(400 m) scimitar that forms the
west side of the tombolo and is one
of four white beaches in the park.
   On the east side, the smaller
Playa Manuel Antonio is the
prettiest of the bunch, curling
around its deep flask-shaped bay

like a shepherd's crook. A small coral reef a short distance offshore is perfect for snorkeling; dry season months are best, when water-clarity improves. There are plenty of tidal pools too, good for wading out into the crystal clear shallows to spot sea stars and crayfish. And Pacific Green and olive Ridley turtles come ashore to lay eggs. Pre-Columbian Native Americans captured them; you can still see traps hollowed into the rocks and exposed at low tide. The turtles swam in at high tide and got caught in the scalloped basins when, exhausted after their exertions ashore, they struggled back to sea with the receding tide.

The park entrance is 600 yards (550 m) east of Manuel Antonio hamlet, at the east end of Playa Espadilla. You will have to wade across the mouth of the **Río Camaronera;** a boatman will ferry you across at high tide. Wide, well-maintained trails perfect for wildlife viewing lead into tropical forest. Sightings of certain species are virtually guaranteed by following the easy *Sendero Perezoso* ("sloth trail"). Cheeky white-faced capuchin monkeys chatter within fingertip reach in the trees that shade the beaches (it is best not to get too close; they can be aggressive). Away from the shore you can see howler monkeys, iguanas, and sloths high up in the trees, while many a hiker reports seeing a coati scamper across their path. Toucans, parrots, and scarlet macaws are commonly seen.

A more adventurous hike along the Mirador Trail *(Sendero Mirador)* leads into the farther reaches, where with luck you might encounter spider monkeys; Manuel Antonio is home to a population of more than 350. The steep trail, which is muddy in wet season, leads to a *mirador* offering fabulous views over the park and out to sea.

The park has proved so popular in recent years that it has begun to feel the adverse effects of all those trampling feet. In 1997, a daily quota of visitors was introduced: no more than 600 are permitted.

THE ROAD TO MANUEL ANTONIO

Manuel Antonio's umbilical cord is a narrow serpentine highway that connects it to Quepos, some 4 miles (6.4 km) to the north. The forest-fringed road clambers over a steep headland and wriggles along the top of the ridge, offering teasing views best enjoyed from one of the scores of hotels and restaurants that command grandstand seats.

A **Fairchild C-123** airplane, formerly used by the CIA, stands by the road on top of a hill that is midway between Quepos and Manuel Antonio.

Dirt trails lead down through the forests that cascade into carefully secreted coves. The road drops down to the bustling hamlet of Manuel Antonio, which clings to the edge of **Playa Espadilla,** a popular hangout, and then dead-ends at the park entrance. ■

Zapped by sap

Poisonous manchineel trees *(Hippomane manicinella),* colloquially called "beach apple" or *manzanillo,* shade the beaches of Manuel Antonio. Make sure to avoid sitting underneath them; the sap is caustic. The fruits are poisonous, and simply touching the bark causes severe irritation. If you are camping, bear in mind not to burn the wood, which gives off a poisonous smoke. ■

Sportfishing

The waters off Costa Rica have far more fish than fishhooks, making the country one place from which you can return home with tales of the one that didn't get away. The angling on the Pacific coast differs markedly from that on the Caribbean; in each case, however, feisty game fish are guaranteed to give anglers a rod-bending fight to remember.

Every season you can be sure that at least one International Game Fishing Association (IFGA) record will be broken in Costa Rica. The nation holds the world record for sailfish and marlin catches in international tournament history. It has also posted more "grand slam" records—all three species of marlin and one or more sailfish caught the same day—than anywhere else in the world.

More than a dozen dedicated sportfishing lodges cater to serious anglers with package programs. Most are operated by North Americans and follow a similar regimen using top-rated boats and equipment plus skilled guides. Scores of smaller outfitters also offer half- and full-day sportfishing trips from beach resorts up and down the Pacific coast. Most operate a catch-and-release policy to ensure the continued health of the game fish population. Four people can expect to pay $250 to $400 for half a day fishing and $350 to $600 for a full day.

The Pacific
On the Pacific side, game fish run offshore year-round and snagging the big one comes really easy. In good years the big fish seem to be jostling for space and the Pacific Ocean seems to boil with marlin, tuna, and wahoo fighting to get a bite on your hook. Seasons vary, however. After a record run up to 1991, sportfishing slumped as the fish seemed to disappear—a response to the climatic change caused by El Niño. In 1996 they came back with a vengeance, with big marlin streaming through the Pacific waters like salmon following a mass spawning urge.

The big draw is the blue marlin—the "bull of the ocean." They are present year-round, though the big run begins in May, with June and July the prime months. Then, too, tuna school close to shore and the dorado begins to peak. In general, the fish move seasonally, with summer months offering the best catches in the Golfo de Papagayo, while winter months are best in southern waters centered on the Golfo Dulce. Playa Flamingo and Tamarindo, and Quepos and Golfito, respectively, are the main sportfishing centers. High winds during the winter in the Golfo de Papagayo make fishing dangerous, and many operators move their fleets south for the season.

The Caribbean and lowlands
The Caribbean side is different, with offshore fishing limited. Here anglers cast their light-tackle lures in river estuaries, backwater lagoons, and wide rivers that extend inland from Tortuguero and Barra del Colorado, the two sportfishing centers. The fish of choice is tarpon, a tempestuous "silver bullet" that can weigh up to 150 pounds (68 kg). Costa Rica, no surprise, is the world's premier site for tarpon, which puts up a fight like no other.

Large trophy-winning snook, a smaller yet aggressive adversary weighing up to 30 pounds (14 kg), can also wear you out. Costa Rica holds the all-tackle IGFA world record for this fish. They return from the Caribbean Sea to spawn in the calm river mouths from August to January, when anglers stand knee-deep in the estuaries, or in the surf where the best catches are reeled in. *Calba*, or smaller snook, also run in midwinter, providing good sport on lighter tackle. And in the ocean, large jacks and barracudas can be caught year-round. Both are voracious; barracuda is so rapacious that it will even go for a shoestring.

The granddaddy of the Caribbean rivers is the Río Colorado, fed by the Río San Juan, which can both be fished far inland from Tortuga Lodge (see p. 256) in Tortuguero, a fistful of lodges at Barra del Colorado, or aboard dedicated sportfishing houseboats that offer three- to seven-day packages (see p. 264). Inland, the waters of Lago Caño Negro also offer superb opportunities for tarpon and snook, while Laguna de Arenal is renowned for its *guapote* (rainbow bass). ∎

From dolphin fish (above) to tarpon (right),
snagging the big one often comes easy in
Costa Rica.

Dominical

WELL ON ITS WAY TO BECOMING THE PACIFIC COAST CAPI-
tal of cool, Dominical is synonymous with surfers and a laid-back
lifestyle. This former fishing village beside the estuary of the Río Barú
also makes an excellent jumping-off point for hiking and horseback
riding in the surrounding mountains.

Dominical

155 E2

Dominical's barefoot, casual dress
code appeals to vacationers seeking
a refuge that shuns all pretension.
The college crowd joins middle-
aged misfits with sun-bleached hair
and ankle beads, who together
make waves by day and party by
night at colorful bars and cafés run
by transplanted gringos.

The hamlet backs a 2-mile-long
(3.2 km) gray-sand beach that runs
south from the mouth of the **Río
Barú,** along whose banks hundreds

of roosting egrets gather at dusk.
You can walk along the beach to the
hamlet of **Dominicalito** beneath
the rugged headland of **Punta
Dominical.** Surfers rave about
Dominical's beach breaks, but the
riptides are a danger to swimmers.
Both whales and dolphins can
sometimes be seen from the shore.

Between Quepos and the village
of Dominical, a distance of some
30 miles (48 km), rugged ranges
push up hard against the coast and

the narrow Highway 34—the Costera Sur—is pinned between forest-festooned mountain and mangrove-lined shore. Highway 34 passes through long stretches of almost uninhabited forest, but has attractions for the adventurous: horseback riding at **Rancho Savegre** *(tel 777-0528);* surfing at **Playa Guapil** and at off-beat **Playa Matapalo.**

Inland, the mountains are renowned for their waterfalls, notably **Cataratas Nauyaca,** tumbling more than 200 feet (60 m). These falls are best approached from **Platanillo,** high above Dominical in the valley of the Río Barú. Be prepared for a vigorous hike. **Centro Ecoturistico El Silencio** *(tel 380-5581),* near Savegre, has a wildlife rescue center.

REFUGIO NACIONAL DE VIDA SILVESTRE BARÚ

This private reserve, on former farmland at Hacienda Báru, offers a smorgasbord of natural treats revealed on trails through cocoa plantation and pasture and into the thick of forest and mangrove backing a beautiful beach—**Playa Barú**—cleansed by surf that brings ashore hawksbill and olive Ridley turtles. Anteaters, iguanas, monkeys, ocelots, and even rare tayras and jaguarundis are among the mammal species to be seen. And the birding is fabulous, with more than 300 species from roseate spoonbills to anhingas. The local ecology is explained in exhibits at an **interpretive center.**

The property also features pre-Columbian archaeological sites, as well as a canopy tour and jungle tent camp. Kayaking and horseback rides are offered.

ESCALERAS

Escaleras ("staircase") refers to the mountain range that steps steeply inland of Dominicalito, accessed by dirt roads that clamber up from the main coast highway. Exuberantly forested, the mountains provide rewarding hiking and horseback riding along sometimes daunting trails. One leads to the **Pozo Azul** ("blue hole"), where you can take a shower in the chill waters of a thunderous cascade.

Escaleras is blessed with a variety of accommodations, each as distinct as a thumbprint—from the cozy rusticity of **Finca Brian y Emilia** *(cell tel 396-6206, by appointment),* which offers an immersion in a true campesino lifestyle, and **Bella Vista Lodge,** which resembles a rustic Western-style dude ranch, to luxurious villas with their own swimming pools inset like sparkling jewels in the green hillside. ∎

Refugio Nacional de Vida Silvestre Barú
www.haciendabaru.com
✉ Hwy. 34, 1 mile N of Dominical
☎ 787-0003
💲 Guided tours $$

A kinkajou's prehensile tail comes in handy for acrobatics.

Wild and undevel-
oped—so far—the
Brunca Coast is a
virgin beauty.

The Brunca coast

DEVELOPMENT IS STILL RELATIVELY NASCENT ON THE
Brunca coast, one of the last ocean stretches to be placed within easy
reach of tourists following the completion of the Costera Sur
Highway. Nonetheless, a prime wildlife refuge and a marine refuge
grant potentially thrilling encounters, while mountain farms offer
forays far from the madding crowd.

**Reserva Biológica
Oro Verde**
www.costarica-birding-
oroverde.com
🗺 155 F1
✉ 9 miles SE of
    Dominical
☎ 743-8072
💲 $$$ for horseback
    and birding tours

**Refugio Nacional
de Vida Silvestre
Rancho Merced**
🗺 155 F1
✉ 9 miles S of
    Dominical
☎ 823-5858
💲 $$ guided horse-
    back tours

The Brunca Coast, named for a
local Indian group, extends south
from **Punta Uvita,** 9 miles (15
km) south of Dominical, to the
mouth of the **Río Terraba** and
the **Bahía de Coronado.**
A range of mountains—the **Fila
Costeña**—runs parallel to the
thread-thin coastal plain. Pleated
in folds of velveteen foliage, the
mountains are good for hiking and
horseback rides at **Reserva
Biológica Oro Verde,** where the
Duarte family specializes in birding
tours of their forested farmstead.

Down by the shore, **Refugio
Nacional de Vida Silverstre
Rancho Merced,** situated on the
north side of Punta Uvita, protects
a vital mangrove ecosystem and
patches of primary forest on a

3,130-acre (1,267 ha) privately
owned cattle farm that offers horseback rides.

Highway 34—wide, fast, unpaved—hugs the shore south of
Punta Uvita, tracing a series of
lonesome, miles-long, palm-shaded
beaches. Sea kayaking is a popular
activity, with the caves on the south
side of **Punta Piñuela** a favorite
destination; note, however, that the
seas are rough and the journey is
not for the faint of heart.

The plain fans out to the south,
where the Río Terraba spills into
the ocean through a vast swampland—the **Delta del Terraba.**
This braided, labyrinthine delta
makes up Costa Rica's most extensive mangrove system, providing an
invaluable home for crocodiles,

caimans, and innumerable stilt-legged waders and waterfowl. You can explore this rich and redolent world by boat or kayak, easily arranged from any of the fistful of ecologically focused hotels hereabouts. **Isla Garza,** on the ocean side of the delta, is a kind of Gilligan's Island with camping facilities for lazy tourism.

PARQUE NACIONAL MARINO BALLENA

The 9 miles (15 km) of shoreline from Punta Uvita to Punta Piñuela is protected within Parque Nacional Marino Ballena (Ballena Marine National Park). The park forms a quadrant that extends 10 miles (16 km) out to sea, encompassing 11,120 acres (4,500 ha) of inshore ocean. It is named after the Pacific humpback whales that gather here at predictable times to mate and give birth. Bottlenose and common dolphins can be seen frolicking off-shore year-round; they weave their way through the bow waves of boats like ribbons of silver.

The nation's largest coral reef is found within the park; it fringes a small island that is connected to Punta Uvita by a tapering tombolo. The reef also extends in patches southward toward **Isla Ballena.** Between, rising from the sea like witches' fingers, are **Las Tres Hermanas** ("The Three Sisters"), rock formations atop which boobies, frigatebirds, and pelicans all maintain nesting sites.

The undersea world here is enthralling. Plentiful hard corals, sponges, and sea anemones sway to the rhythm of the ocean currents. Snorkeling and scuba diving are available from Piñuela, but snorkelers should beware the rough seas. At low tide, try wading in the tide pools at the tip of Punta Uvita. With good timing, you may even be blessed with the exhilarating sight of female marine turtles coming ashore to lay their eggs, notably at the namesake **Playa Tortuga** (September and October are the best months to visit). Both olive ridley and hawksbill turtles are a frequent sight.

Though this is a national park, camping is allowed. A small donation is suggested for both daily and overnight use. There is no centralized park entrance, but a ranger station is located in the small community of Bahía; boat tours to Ballena Island can be arranged from here. ∎

Parque Nacional Marino Ballena

- 155 F1
- ✉ 12 miles S of Dominical
- ☎ 735-5282 or 735-5440
- 💲 $ by donation

For the love of pod

You can depend on seeing humpback whales close to Costa Rica's shores. Two populations migrate from colder Californian (July–October) and Antarctic (December–March) waters to court and calve. These gentle giants reach lengths of 50 feet (15 m), weigh up to 40 tons, and wear their fingerprints on their tails; each animal has its own distinctive markings. Individuals sighted in Costa Rica have been seen as far north as Alaska. Watch for their explosive exhalations of breath. With luck, you may witness a Herculean leap called "breaching." ∎

The telltale fluke of a humpback

More places to visit in the Central Pacific

RAFIKI SAFARI LODGE
Inspired by the classic lodges of Africa, this thatched mountainside nature lodge overlooks the raging Río Savegre in the thickly forested upper Savegre valley. White-water rafting and kayaking are offered, as is horseback riding. In the dry season, visitors can cast for mojarra, snook, and other fighting fish. A 328-foot-long (100 m) water slide whisks you away into a freshwater pool like a log down a flume. Using techniques successfully developed in their homeland, the South African owners have initiated a tapir breeding and reintroduction program in the lodge's 700-acre (28,111 ha) rain forest reserve, accessed by trails.
www.rafikisafari.com   🅜 154 D3   ✉ 6 miles E of El Silencio, 12 miles E of Hwy. 34   ☎ 777-2250   🆂 $

RAINMAKER CONSERVATION PROJECT
This private 1,500-acre (600 ha) reserve in the soaring **Fila Chonta** range is a realm of lush forests. Part of the Quepos Biological Corridor, it is a vital link in a medley of contiguous forest reserves that make up a migratory pathway for wildlife that ranges as far afield as the Talamancas. Clambering up through four separate habitats, from lowland tropical moist forest to cloud forest at 5,600 feet (1,700 m), the reserve harbors a variety of wildlife. Trails lead to waterfalls and natural pools, good for an exhilarating dip, and to the **Damas Caves,** decorated with fanciful dripstone formations. Visitors with a head for heights can ascend into the treetops, where a series of wooden suspension bridges make up an aerial boardwalk, fantastic for eye-to-eye encounters with wildlife (this trip is not for timorous tourists!). Horseback rides are available, and a visitor center provides a good background to the reserve and its history.
www.rainmakercostarica.com   🅜 154 C3   ✉ E of Hwy. 34   ☎ 777-1250   🆂 $$$$

VILLA CALETAS
Built in the style of a Roman villa, this hotel stands out for eclectic appeal, even in a country brimming with unique hotels. Villa Caletas is an opulent, stunning place with two restaurants overlooking the Pacific and a spa. Guests can swim either in the infinity pool—equipped with its own tropical island and waterfall—or private beach not far from the hotel. There's also a Greek amphitheater carved into a cliff that seats 150.
www.hotelvillacaletas.com   🅜 154 A4   ✉ Hwy. 34, 4 miles N of Jacó   ☎ 637-0606 ■

Wildlife under siege

Despite Costa Rica's remarkable conservation record, illicit logging still occurs in protected areas, banana plantations are expanding toward national parks, homesteaders still practice slash-and-burn agriculture, and hotels and houses are built by the shore.

Parque Nacional Manuel Antonio protects a peninsula of tropical moist forest, but animals have traditionally moved in and out of the park. Construction has severed migratory corridors, effectively creating an island. Unable to interact and breed with groups outside the park, populations are declining.

In complex tropical ecosystems, the loss of a single species affects the whole ecology. The loss of a single patch of forest allows non-native species to take over, as when the forests of Guanacaste are burned and grasses come to dominate the land. Many species are found only in tiny niches, and thousands become extinct each year from habitat destruction.

Coral reefs are damaged by siltation and agri-chemicals washed out to sea, and shrimp fishermen trawl within the parks. The System of Marine Parks and Reserves (SIPREMA), which protects marine environments, warns that "fish, turtle, and seafaring bird migrations are decreasing in size and frequency."

The boom in ecotourism has helped to reverse the trend: Monitoring agencies are being given more teeth, and a development plan for sustainable tourism has been put in place. The profit potential from tourism is even encouraging landowners to safeguard their lands. ■

Abutting Panama at Costa Rica's remote southwest corner is Golfo Dulce, centerpiece of the Zona Sur (the southern zone). This wet and wild area is the proud possessor of a vast swath of rain forest.

Zona Sur

Elusive jaguar

Zona Sur

KNOWN FOR ITS LUSH FORESTS AND ABUNDANT WILDLIFE, THIS
rain-soaked southwestern quarter of the country offers a nether-reaches
appeal, epitomized by a remote national park protecting the largest
extant stand of primeval rain forest along the Pacific coast of Central America. The steep mountains and much of the
Península de Osa are sparsely inhabited. Numerous lonesome wilderness lodges, sportfishing lodges, and diving lodges cater to
travelers with an interest in nature.

This humid region has a lingering wet season,
typified by violent thunderstorms from
October to December. It forms a quadrangle
aligned northwest-southeast and hemmed
inland by the soaring Fila Costeña mountains,
along whose base runs the Inter-American
Highway (Highway 2), running ruler-straight
to the Panamanian border. To the northwest
lies a broad plain—the Valle de Diquis—
drained by rivers that flow north and braid the
mangrove estuaries of the Delta de Terrabas.
To the southeast is the Valle de Coto Colorado,
which is drained by an eponymous river and
its tributaries, which flow westward into the
shallow Golfo Dulce.

Banana plantations cover much of the two
major valleys and are the economic mainstay
of the somnolent towns of Palmar Norte,
Ciudad Neily, and Golfito. Golfito, the colorful
and somewhat forlorn capital of the region,
has a lassitude typical of tropical ports and
derives much of its income today from a duty-
free zone and sportfishing. Paso Canoas, at the
Panama border, is also a duty-free zone.

Costa Rica and Panama share the Península
de Burica, a pendulous piece of real estate
tapering into the Pacific like a crocodile's
snout at the very southernmost tip of the
country, with nothing but the blue expanse of
the Pacific beyond. Most of the peninsula is
protected as tribal land of the Burica Indians.
Many of the beaches here are prized nesting
sites for marine turtles. Whales frequent the
warm waters, and the open ocean and Golfo
Dulce draw anglers hooked on the desire to
snag blue marlin, dorado, tuna, wahoo, or any
of the other big game species that run here,
thick as sardines.

Hooking around the gulf to the north is
the Península de Osa, a rugged region still
mostly covered in primary rain forest, shining
and sweet-smelling. Wildlife viewing is some
of the best in Costa Rica, reaching its zenith in
Parque Nacional Corcovado, which resounds
to the grunts, roars, and chirrups of abundant
wildlife. Scarlet macaws are particularly

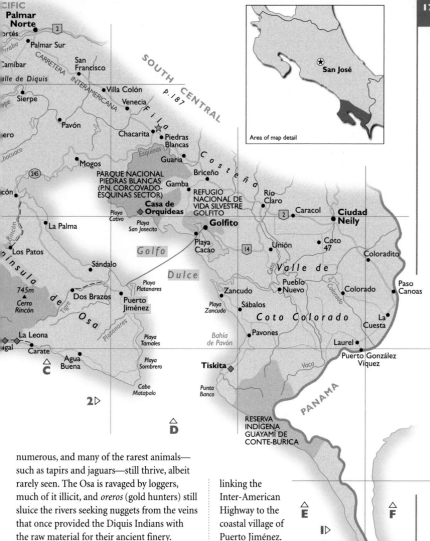

CIFIC
**Palmar
Norte**
ortés
Palmar Sur
amíbar
San
Francisco
lle de Diquis
Villa Colón
SOUTH
CENTRAL
p. 187
Sierpe
Venecia
Pavón
Chacarita
Piedras
Blancas
Mogos
Guaria
Briceño
Fila
Costeña
PARQUE NACIONAL
PIEDRAS BLANCAS
(P.N. CORCOVADO-
ESQUINAS SECTOR)
Gamba
REFUGIO
NACIONAL DE
VIDA SILVESTRE
GOLFITO
Río
Claro
Caracol
**Ciudad
Neily**
La Palma
Casa de
◆Orquideas
Playa
Cativo
Golfito
Unión
Coto
47
Coloradito
Los Patos
Playa
San Josecito
Golfo
Playa
Cacao
Paso
Canoas
Sándalo
Dulce
Pueblo
Nuevo
Colorado
745m
Cerro
Rincón
Dos Brazos
Puerto
Jiménez
Playa
Platanares
Zancudo
Sábalos
Coto Colorado
La
Cuesta
La Leona
Platanares
Playa
Zancudo
Pavones
Laurel
igal
Carate
Agua
Buena
Playa
Tamales
Bahía
de Pavón
Puerto González
Víquez
C
Playa
Sombrero
Tiskita◆
Cabo
Matapalo
Punta
Banco
PANAMA
2▷
D
RESERVA
INDÍGENA
GUAYAMÍ DE
CONTE-BURICA

San José
Area of map detail

E
F
I▷
Península
Burica

numerous, and many of the rarest animals—
such as tapirs and jaguars—still thrive, albeit
rarely seen. The Osa is ravaged by loggers,
much of it illicit, and *oreros* (gold hunters) still
sluice the rivers seeking nuggets from the veins
that once provided the Diquis Indians with
the raw material for their ancient finery.

The legacy of pre-Columbian culture can
be seen in the many *bolas,* perfectly spherical
granite rocks found in the ground only here.
Uninhabited Isla del Caño, studding the
Pacific about 10 miles (16 km) due west of
Osa, is a major source and was once a sacred
burial ground. Scuba diving is also highly
rated, notably at Isla del Coco, 300 miles (480
km) due south, where you can expect one-on-
one meetings with manta rays, whale sharks,
and schooling hammerheads. Scuba diving is
popular out of Bahía Drake, a rustic hamlet on
the Osa's hard-to-reach western shore. The
Osa's eastern shore is accessible via a road

linking the
Inter-American
Highway to the
coastal village of
Puerto Jiménez.
Corcovado
Conservation Area
links reserves and
protected areas, such
as wetlands supporting
crocodiles and waterfowl,
which you can see on forays
into the deltas of the Río Coto and
Río Terrabas. Several reserves occupy a small
mountain range separated from the Fila
Costeña by the valley of the Río Esquinas,
which links the Valle de Diquis and Valle de
Coto Colorado, forming the connecting piece
in the regional mosaic. ■

The rugged
Península de Osa
demands much
of hikers.

Península de Osa &
Isla del Caño

ACCLAIMED FOR ITS ASTONISHING BIODIVERSITY, THE
Península de Osa is swaddled in the largest expanse of tropical rain
forest along the Pacific coast of the isthmus. Beach lovers can choose
from a panoply of endearing beaches, where the surfing is fabulous
and a bevy of top-ranked eco-lodges belie the "final frontier" feel.

**Peninsula de Osa
& Isla del Caño**
🔼 172 & 173 A4,
B3/4, C2/3, D2/3

The Península de Osa receives more
than 200 inches (500 cm) of rain
annually, most falling from April
to December. Much of its jungle-
cloaked interior is banked within
Parque Nacional Corcovado
(see p. 182), created in the 1970s to
guard against the encroachment of
man. However, much of the Osa is
owned by logging companies which
still fell hardwoods. *Precaristas*
(squatters) continue homesteading
by clearing forest, and the rivers
that wash down from the interior
bear gold that in past decades has
brought would-be millionaires with
chain-saws and shovels in hand.

The former gold-mining villages
of **Los Patos** and **Dos Brazos
de Río Tigre** now cater to ecotourism, offering horseback riding
and guided hikes into Corcovado.

PUERTO JIMÉNEZ
Barely the size of a postage stamp,
Puerto Jiménez, on the east side
of the Osa and reached from the
Inter-American Highway via
Carretera 245, is the Osa's sole
town. It attracts the college and
counterculture crowd, and active
travelers seeking sea kayaking,
surfing, and other adventures. The
town clings proudly to the memory
of a colorful past based on the
antics of prospectors (not to mention of prostitutes who charged
by the ounce). Beside the airstrip is
the administrative office for Parque
Nacional Corcovado.

A dun-colored beach offers views across the gulf. Eastward, in the mangrove estuary of the **Río Platanares,** crocodiles and caimans cool off in brackish waters, white-faced monkeys cavort in the branches, and scarlet macaws fly overhead. Beyond is **Playa Platanares,** its white beach a major nesting site for turtles.

NORTHWEST SHORE
On Osa's remote northwest side, and popular with yachters, is deep-scalloped, palm-fringed **Bahía Drake** (Drake Bay). At **Agujitas,** local women stitch colorful molas in reverse-stitched appliqué. The **Original Canopy Tour** (tel 257-5149, $$) offers a treetop adventure by suspended walkway and exhilarating zipline rappel to the ground.

Getting to Bahía Drake is half the fun—it is a two-hour boat-trip down the Río Sierpe. Although a dirt road now links Agujitas with Rincón, Bahía Drake may strike you as being much the same as the day in March 1579 when Sir Francis Drake careened (deliberately beached) his *Golden Hind* here. Running water, for example, still means a boy with a bucket, although telephones and electricity arrived for the millennium.

To the south is **Río Agujitas,** flowing down a canyon good for kayaking. Whale-watching trips offered by hotels and tour operators take visitors to see the humpback whales. Hikers can sally forth to Parque Nacional Corcovado, 8 miles (13 km) via a coastal trail and pearly beaches washed by warm waters (but beware of riptides!).

Commanding the jungle-green hillsides above **Playa Caletas** is the 1,235-acre (500 ha) **Refugio Nacional de Vida Silvestre Punta Río Claro,** which abuts Corcovado and protects an array of wildlife. Scarlet macaws squawk noisily, as do toucans, parrots, and monkeys. Self-guided trails provide access to this pristine world. Nearby, **Reserva Biológica Campanario** offers simple accommodations and a field station where ex-Peace Corps volunteers now lead treks.

RESERVA BIOLÓGICA ISLA DEL CAÑO
Isla del Caño hovers tantalizingly on the horizon. It is a 740-acre (300 ha) expanse 10 miles (16 km) west of Osa. Day excursions (overnight stays are not permitted) are offered by local lodges. It was a sacred burial site for pre-Columbian Indians, and many archaeological sites and bolas have been excavated. These can be seen beside forest trails. Olive Ridley turtles swim in over the coral reefs to nest on coral-sand beaches. Snorkeling is enthralling and whales and dolphins gather in the warm waters farther out. ∎

Refugio Nacional de Vida Silvestre Punta Río Claro
www.puntamarenco.com
🗺 172 B4
✉ 5 miles S of Bahía Drake
☎ 222-3305 or 735-5282
💲 $$

Reserva Biológica Campanario
www.campanario.org
🗺 172 B3
✉ 8 miles S of Bahía Drake
☎ 258-5778
💲 $$

The largest population of scarlet macaws in Costa Rica is protected by the peninsula.

Gold!
The Diquis Indians found flecks of gold in the streams of the Osa, which they melted down to create their fine pre-Columbian jewelry. Spanish *conquistadores* searched in vain for the fabled gold mines of Veragua. In the 1980s, when the United Fruit Co. pulled out of Zona Sur, unemployed workers poured into Corcovado to tear down the trees and rip up the soil, destroying countless acres in a fit of collective gold fever. Their ousting from the park in 1986 was violent. A few *oreros* (prospectors) still work the streams, questing for that eternally elusive nugget that will land them on Easy Street. ∎

A drive along the Osa

A single road—Highway 245—probes the peninsula and snakes along the western shore of the Golfo Dulce, curls around Cabo Matapalo, and peters out at Carate, midway along the southern coast. It's only 73 miles (117 km) from the Inter-American Highway to Carate, but don't let that distance mislead you. Although the road is paved and in relatively good condition for the first third of the trip, conditions deteriorate thereafter; beyond Puerto Jiménez, the journey becomes an adventure. You will need a four-wheel drive vehicle to make a fun trip of what could otherwise be an ordeal.

Highway 245 begins at **Chacarita ❶**, a trucker's stop at the junction with the Inter-American Highway. From here the well-paved road sweeps southwest, undulating like a roller-coaster, with giant hardwoods—mahogany, strangler figs, and kapok—framing your passage in shades of lustrous green. After 10 miles (16 km) you get your first dramatic view of the sea. You will pass cattle ranches freshly hewn from the lush green forest, and huge logging trucks may thunder past in the other direction, hauling loads of precious hardwoods. After 25 miles (40 km) you arrive at the hamlet of **Rincón ❷**, where the paved road gives out. Here the views open up like fanciful Hollywood creations, with an endless vista sweeping eastward across the length of the Golfo Dulce all the way down to Panama and southward across the immensity of the Península de Osa, swollen with billowing greenery like a violent sea.

The road, now dusty, corrugated, and badly potholed, drops down to **La Palma ❸**, 7 miles (11 km) south of Rincón. Turn left at the T-junction for Puerto Jiménez, 18 miles (29 km) southeast. The road parallels the shore inland, offering occasional tantalizing glimpses north toward the Fila Golfito mountains. Just before Puerto Jiménez, you might detour through the valley of the Río Tigre to the community of **Dos Brazos,** where the former gold-mining community operates a cooperative that leads gold-panning tours.

If you are low on gas, you should fill your tank up at **Puerto Jiménez ❹** as there is none to be had farther along. The road is mostly level for the 10 miles (16 km) to **Cabo Matapalo,** the snub-nosed southeasterly tip of Osa. Your route is lined with ranches on one side and numerous handsome beaches on the other, notably **Playa Tamales** and

> ⓜ See area map pp. 172–173
> ► Chacarita
> ⬌ 73 miles (117 km)
> ⊙ 3 hours (one way)
> ► Parque Nacional Corcovado
>
> **NOT TO BE MISSED**
> - Dos Brazos
> - Cabo Matapalo
> - Lapa Ríos
> - Corcovado Lodge Tent Camp

Playa Sombrero, beloved of surfers for the terrific swells that peak in mid-summer. For the best view around, stop in at **Lapa Ríos ❺** (see p. 253), a cliff-top eco-lodge surrounded by greenery, with a soaring *mirador*, or lookout tower, with spectacular views over the coastline and, inland, a 1,000-acre (400 ha) private rain-forest reserve accessed by trails.

From here, the going begins to get fun. You will ford a few streams (the mightier flows that used to set your heart racing—particularly after torrential rains—are now bridged), and in places the gradient grows acute enough to challenge a goat. In really wet weather you will need a low gear to call on as you walk your vehicle up and over hills that can have you slithering back two feet for every three that you gain. In some places the foliage closes in on the road, brushing against you. Signs of human habitation gradually peter out and you begin to feel that you are all alone in the world. But no: 27 miles (44 km) from Puerto Jiménez you arrive at **Carate ❻,** where the road comes to a stop beside an airstrip by a brown-sand beach that stretches endlessly westward, and is backed by the teeming jungle of Parque Nacional Corcovado.

RESERVA FORESTAL GOLFO DULCE

START

Chacarita ❶ Piedras Blancas

Esquinas

Mogos

Punta Islotes

245

Bahía Rincón

Punta Estrella

❷ Rincón

Puerto Escondido

❸ La Palma

Barrigones

Rincón

Agujas

Lajitas

PENÍNSULA

Dos Brazos

Tigre

745m ▲ Cerro Rincón

DE OSA

PARQUE NACIONAL CORCOVADO

Fila Golfito

Golfo Dulce

Puerto Jiménez ❹ Playa Platanares

The tranquil beach at Puerto Jiménez

PARQUE NACIONAL CORCOVADO ❼

Corcovado Lodge Tent Camp

Carate

Playa Carate ❻

RESERVA FORESTAL GOLFO DULCE

Agua Buena

326m ▲ Cerro Osa

Lapa Ríos ❺

Punta Tigre

Playa Tamales

Playa Sombrero

Cabo Matapalo

0 ————— 10 kilometers
0 ————— 6 miles

Lapa Rios—a room with a view

Plan in advance and book a canopy tour at **Corcovado Lodge Tent Camp** (see p. 253) on the edge of **Parque Nacional Corcovado ❼**, one mile (1.6 km) west of Carate. You can drive along the beach at low tide, but don't get stuck on the way back! A tree house 90 feet (27 m) high offers a monkey's-eye view of the rain-forest canopy. Scarlet macaws fly past as guests move between the treetops in a bosun's chair—a fitting finale to an adventure drive. ■

Río Sierpe & the
Valle de Diquis

GREEN MELDS WITH GREEN AS EMERALD BANANAS FLOW into the sea-green of mangroves across the slate-smooth Valle de Diquis. The birding is fabulous along the banks of the Río Sierpe and Delta del Terraba.

Río Sierpe & the Valle de Diquis
172-73 C4/5

At the north end of the Valle de Diquis is the broad **Río Terraba,** which flows down from the Valle de El General and pours out of a canyon to begin its meandering route to the sea through a vast mangrove system. **Palmar,** the only town of significance, spans the banks of the silt-laden river. The sleepy settlement has a significant population of Chinese who dominate the restaurant trade. In a grassy plaza on the south side of town is a sight worth seeing: an old steam locomotive and, next to it, a pre-Columbian bola.

The town relies on the fortunes of the local banana economy, and the land south of the river is swathed in plantations of tousle-topped bananas penetrated by a gridwork of dirt service roads that after 9 miles (15 km) will deposit

A stone *bola*, legacy of the ancient Diquis culture (A.D. 400–1400).

you in the funky riverside hamlet of **Sierpe.** The village sits on a great loop of the **Río Sierpe.** It is surrounded by swamps and *manglares* (mangroves) that form the **Reserva Forestal del Humedad Internacional Terraba-Sierpe,** which runs along the 25-mile shoreline between the mouths of the Sierpe and Terraba rivers. The waterways form a convoluted lacework opening up into a series of wide tidal *esteros* (estuaries) and isles. Sierpe offers a fistful of off-beat nature lodges, including the tiny Italian-run **Veragua River House** (see p. 254)—a little piece of Tuscany amid the swamps. Dugout canoes and motor boats depart Sierpe's small dock on forays sure to provide close-up encounters with crocodiles, caimans, and scores of exotic bird species. ∎

Bolas

Pre-Columbian *bolas*—man-made granite balls with the perfect sphericity of glass beads—litter the Zona Sur, where they lie deep in luxuriant undergrowth. They measure from a few inches to 10 feet (3 m) wide and weigh up to 15 tons. Some are found singly; others occur in groups of 20 or more. Were they religious totems? No one knows. How were they made? No one seems to know that either—though one plausible theory suggests that boulders were tumbled like ball bearings at the base of mighty waterfalls. ∎

Life in the lowland rain forest

The lushest environments on Earth, lowland rain forests teem with animal life. Of the world's estimated five million plant and animal species, as many as two-thirds inhabit this sodden world of throttling green, each species interdependent on other species in a complex web.

Within the dense lowland rain forest the air is cool and dank and underwater green, heavy with a silence that seems to ignore the crushing intensity of the sun dancing on the forest canopy, which from above looks like a vast vegetal ocean of green. What first appears to be silence and stillness is neither silent nor still. Unseen creatures are on the move. The forest is alive with liquid, musical calls and the whistles, squawks, and raucous screeches of parrots squabbling among the high branches. Peccaries

This baby spider monkey has a good chance of survival in the rain forest.

and jaguars roam unseen in the cobalt shadows, while bats roost in the towering grottos of hollow trees. A brilliant blue tanager flashes by, its short stubby wings especially adapted for fighter-jet maneuvers between densely packed branches, followed by an enormous turquoise morpho butterfly which floats by like a flashing neon sign. High in the canopy, silhouettes move slowly in the subaqueous shadows. Perhaps a band of spider monkeys swinging hand over hand, foraging for fruiting trees while eagles soar high above the canopy, hoping to snatch up an iguana innocently crawling along a branch.

At first glance, the overwhelming riot of greenery might suggest that the rain forest is a place of disorganized chaos. In fact, it has a well-evolved structure. Although difficult to appreciate from the ground, the rain forest is

actually built up of layer upon layer of overlapping habitats, like a Russian doll, each with its own characteristic amalgam of flora and fauna interrelated in a unique dynamic. As biologist Paul W. Richards, the father of modern rain forest science, has noted: "Tall trees, short trees, vines and epiphytes each have a specific role in the general scheme of things. And animal life in turn is well fitted into the overall architecture of the rain forest. In the jungle, in short, there is a place for everything—and everything remains pretty much in its place."

The abundance is truly prodigious, and the overwhelming majority of species are far smaller and far less noticeable than the species most of us recognize easily. Insects—in particular beetles and ants—predominate. A single tree can harbor more than 10,000 beetle species, including dozens of species of scarab beetles that look as if they are made of platinum, silver, or gold. The relative paucity of undergrowth in lowland rain forests is such that by far the greatest diversity and concentration—some 90 percent fauna—exists unseen in the treetops. The forest floor is a relatively stagnant world by comparison. The sunlit canopy is a factory of fecundity teeming with animals, birds, and insects—most species being unique to their lofty realm. This universe of the canopy is a final frontier of scientific research, one of the last outposts of relative obscurity, what the 19th-century naturalist William Beebe described as an "undiscovered continent." Only in recent years have scientists begun to study life in these cathedral-like vaults—an experience now made easy for lay visitors with the range of canopy tours by suspended walkways or in harnesses such as bosun's chairs.

Countless animal species spend their entire lives in the canopy and have evolved to avoid the need to come down to the ground. Humus accumulates so thickly on high branches that subspecies of arboreal earthworms have evolved, while arboreal snakes have developed who can stiffen their elongated bodies to bridge gaps between trees. Many mammal species have also adapted for climbing and leaping: The spider monkey's muscular tail, which can support the animal's whole weight, has a sensitive fingertip-like pad that makes it good for grasping. And tail-less sloths move lethargically from branch to branch using hooked claws perfectly adapted for a life in the trees. Frogs, mice, scorpions, even a species of crab, are among the many terrestrial creatures that have adapted to a life in the treetops.

Although it may not be obvious, animals tend to move between known and well-worn routes through the canopy, rather like traffic streaming along major highways. Where howler monkeys and anteaters might pass by day, a kinkajou makes nightly forays, followed perhaps by a chocolate brown tayra prowling silently, with its teeth bared in a toothy grimace. Well-camouflaged snakes such as the green tree viper lie patiently in wait for prey such as opossums or mice scampering by, oblivious to their potential fate.

Ironically, the voluptuousness of this fecund realm is not derived from the soil, which is nutritionally barren. Whereas in deciduous forests, leaves drop simultaneously, accumulate, and build up a rich layer of humus, leaf fall in tropical forests occurs throughout the year. The individual leaves that drop decompose quickly as a result of the constant heat and daily rains, so that their nutrients are swiftly reabsorbed into the canopy without allowing any build-up in the soil. Over millions of years, tropical soils have been leached so efficiently that only aluminum and iron oxides remain in quantity. Tinged rust-red, this earth is acidic, further adding to the destruction of nutrients. Homesteaders convinced of the richness of tropical soils are swiftly brought down to earth. Within two or three years, the land they clear and plant for farming is usually left sterile. ■

LOWLAND RAIN FOREST

A harpy eagle perches in the treetops, its sharp eyes searching for prey below.

Spider monkeys live among canopy plants that enfold the boughs of the forest ceiling.

Relatively sparse foliage at lower levels lets the tanager and the tayra move freely.

Tapirs roam the light-starved forest floor.

Macaw soars over the emergent layer, where scattered giants top the canopy.

Toucans and howler monkeys live high in the canopy.

Branching out at low level, under-story trees form a sub-canopy.

A katydid and a mantis rest in the thin leaf litter.

Parque Nacional Corcovado

🅰 172 B/C 3

✉ 30 miles SW of Puerto Jiménez

☎ 735-5036 or 735-5282

💲 $$

Parque Nacional Corcovado

THIS CROWN-JEWEL OF RAIN FOREST BIOLOGY FORMS A mini-Amazon whose appeals are worth the discomforts of sodden humidity and rains—up to 25 feet (8 m) per year at higher elevations. In the tropics, water (and lots of it) spells life. From crocodiles in the marshy wetlands to sleek jaguars on the prowl, Corcovado has earned a reputation for some of the nation's best wildlife viewing.

Corcovado was established in 1975 to protect 103,259 acres (41,787 ha) of tropical rain forest in addition to seven other distinct habitats, which include rare jolillo palm forest, mangrove swamps, and even areas of montane forest on the upper slopes of **Cerro Rincón** (2,444 feet, 745 m).

You can enter the park either from the northwest via the **San Pedrillo** ranger station; from the northeast via the **Los Patos** ranger station; or from the southeast via the **La Leona** ranger station. The park headquarters is at **Sirena,** in the heart of the park. Basic dorm rooms are available at Sirena, and you can camp at any of the stations. Alternatively, you can easily visit the park from any of a half dozen or so eco-lodges that fringe the shore just outside the park boundaries.

Raucous keel-billed toucans are common in Corcovado.

A WELTER OF WILDLIFE

This lush ecological Eden boasts wildlife in astonishing abundance. Around one-tenth of all mammal species in the Americas live in the park. You are certain to see howler and capuchin monkeys, and possibly even endangered squirrel monkeys. Anteaters are common, as are peccaries and tapirs. One of the best places for viewing tapirs is **Laguna Corcovado,** where the timid and strange-looking creatures commonly come to drink at dawn and dusk. After dark you can watch fishing bats swooping down to pluck fish on the wing from the water. And Corcovado is one of the few places in the country where sightings of jaguars and other big cats are common. These cats also hang out around the lagoon, in wait for tasty tidbits, as do large, fast, and toothy crocodiles.

Corcovado's forests vibrate with the squawking and chirrups of countless birds. Of the more than 400 bird species, 20 are endemic—found only here. Egrets, herons, and ibises pick among the sedge wetlands, where jacanas can be seen walking across water, tiptoeing across the lily-pads by using the ultra-wide span of their toes to disperse their weight. Even the harpy eagle, recently considered locally extinct, has been seen with increasing frequency. And nowhere else in Central America has such a large population of scarlet macaws—about 1,200 birds. You are sure to see them feeding on almond trees as you walk along the beach, or flying overhead in pairs, male and female, squawking to their mates.

There are in excess of 115 reptile species, including poison-arrow frogs that hop about the jungle floor like enameled porcelain figurines. You may even spot the diminutive red-eyed tree frog or a species with transparent skin, appropriately called the glass frog. Do not be surprised to come across female marine turtles as you walk along the miles of beaches: Hawksbills, leatherbacks, olive Ridleys, and Pacific greens all lay their eggs above the high-water mark.

HIKING

The only way to see Corcovado is on foot, exploring along poorly maintained footpaths, and there is no place in Costa Rica that will more richly reward the investment thus spent. You do not need to venture far to get close to the magnificent wildlife. You will need good walking shoes, as the trails are muddy and at times you will have to ford streams and rivers; arm yourself with the Instituto Geográfica Nacional (see p. 257) 1:50,000 map, as trails are poorly marked. You can go it alone, or hire guides in Puerto Jiménez. Bring bug spray, and water to stave off dehydration. Watch out for poisonous snakes, not the least fer-de-lances, pit vipers with yellow-brown backs and pink bellies, at least six feet long, and whose bite can be fatal in minutes.

The 24-mile-long (39 km) main trail from La Leona to San Pedrillo follows the beaches for much of its length. Allow two days for this hike, with time for a side trip to Laguna Corcovado from Sirena, 9 miles (15 km) northwest of La Leona. As a special treat, cool off beneath **Catarata La Llorona,** midway between Sirena and San Pedrillo which plunges 100 feet (30 m) onto the beach. You can also hike from Los Patos to Sirena (13 miles, 21 km). There are rivers that must be waded on all trails, and these should be tackled at low tide, not the least to avoid any entanglements with crocodiles. ■

Golfito & the Golfo Dulce

THE ERSTWHILE "BANANA CAPITAL" GOLFITO, CAPITAL OF
Zona Sur, is long on authentic character. It makes a perfect base for
sportfishing in the gulf, hiking in nearby rain forests, boating along
the mangrove-lined shores, and snorkeling at remote beaches where
both surfers and marine turtles come ashore.

Golfito
🅜 173 D3
**Visitor
information**
☎ 775-1614

GOLFITO

Golfito is connected to the Inter-
American Highway, 16 miles (26
km) away, by Highway 14, which
dead-ends in town. The town itself
sprawls along 5 miles (8 km) of
shoreline paralleled inland by steep
jungle-clad mountains. Its sultry
setting midway down the east shore
of Golfo Dulce is a bust for the
weather, as the hills enclosing the
gulf preclude breezes from reaching
Golfito, which stews.

The town was born in 1938,
when the United Fruit Company
established its plantations nearby
and built the town from scratch in a
unique plantation style. Golfito
swiftly became the main banana
shipping port in Costa Rica. World
War II injected new vigor when the
U.S. military arrived. The good

times ended abruptly in 1985 when
"Big Fruit" pulled out. To offset the
decline, the government created a
duty-free zone where Costa Ricans
can purchase 500 dollars-worth of
goods every six months. The many
basic hotels here cater to this itiner-
ant trade. A considerable expatriate
population in Golfito includes a
good number of yachters who
arrived and succumbed to a spell
from which they have never
escaped. Others have washed up in
more ways than one.

The **Pueblo Civil,** to the east,
is a bedraggled section where the
main bars and services are located.
Highway 14 meanders north past
the Muelle de Golfito banana-
loading dock and into the tranquil
Zona Americana, the former
administrative center of the United

Fruit Company, with charming, gaily-painted two-story clapboard houses atop stilts. The airstrip and duty-free shopping compound—the *depósito libre*—are here.

A stiff hike uphill leads to the **Refugio Nacional de Vida Silvestre Golfito,** which protects 3,235 acres (1,310 ha) of forested hills boasting all four species of monkeys plus scarlet macaws, among other magnificent critters. Water-taxis depart from Muelle de Golfito for **Playa Cacao,** a 10-minute trip to a small beach with idyllic views across the bay.

AROUND THE GULF

North of Golfito, steep mountains flank the gulf shores and emerald forests spill down to lonesome brown-sand beaches—**Playa Cativo, Punta Encantado,** and **Playa San Josecito**—where a series of eco-lodges offer hiking, horseback riding, snorkeling and kayaking. Water-taxis will whisk you to your desired spot from Golfito. Worth a visit is the **Casa de Orquídeas,** at Playa San Josecito. Here, guided tours lead through a botanical *Fantasia* of orchids and ornamentals collated over two decades.

Mountains comprise the **Esquinas** part of Parque Nacional Corcovado, a park that embraces **Parque Nacional Piedras Blancas;** funded by the Austrian government, it's also called "Rain Forest of the Austrians." The **Esquinas Rainforest Lodge** *(tel 775-0901),* run as a local cooperative, offers guided nature hikes.

A 10-mile (16 km) water-taxi trip east from Golfito, (44 miles, 71 km by road) lands at **Zancudo,** a charmingly funky hamlet—popular as a sportfishing center—sprawling along a sand spit that separates the **Coto Swamps** from the sea. You can explore mangrove and wetland ecosystems by kayak or on guided boat excursions (see p. 264)—a chance to shoot river otters and crocodiles with your camera.

A dusty track leads south from Zancudo to the fishing community of **Pavones,** legendary for what is ostensibly the longest surf ride in the world. Rocky outcrops puncture the dramatic shore, where marine turtles also pop up out of the surf, mainly from August to December. The road dead-ends at **Punta Banco,** 5 miles (8 km) south of Pavones, at the gateway to the **Reserva Indígena Guaymí de Conte-Burica** *(closed to the public)* and the **Península de Burica.**

Call in at **Tiskita Lodge** (see p. 253), a fruit farm with a rustic nature lodge set on a mountain ridge caressed by breezes. The farm is backed by a private 370-acre (150 ha) swatch of rain forest that awaits exploration along well-maintained trails that lead to waterfalls and plunge pools. The birding is stupendous, assisted by a booklet for self-guided tours. ■

Refugio Nacional de Vida Silvestre Golfito
- 🗺 173 D3
- ✉ 0.5 mile E of Golfito
- ☎ 789-9092
- 💲 $$

Casa de Orquídeas
- 🗺 173 D3
- ✉ Playa San Josecito
- ☎ 775-0353
- 🕐 Guided tours Sun.–Thurs.
- 💲 $$ guided tour

Parque Nacional Piedras Blancas
- 🗺 173 D3
- ✉ Within the Esquinas sector of Parque Nacional Corcovado
- ☎ 775-0901
- 💲 $$$ guided tour

Oil palm seeds await transport to market.

Isla del Coco

Isla del Coco
🔼 172 A4
Visitor information
www.sinac.go.cr
☎ 223-6963 (MINAE)

FOR ANYONE WITH THE TIME AND RESOURCES, ISLA DEL Coco will make a memorable high point of a Costa Rica visit. This island, a geographic oddity 300 miles (480 km) southwest of Costa Rica, receives only a fistful of visitors. Yet it is the nation's prime dive spot—not to mention one of its most important seabird rookeries and a repository for endemic bird species.

Geographically part of the Cocos volcanic chain that extends south to the Galapagos islands, this sodden island is wed to Costa Rica by a purely political link. The youthful 20-square-mile (52 sq km) island pierces the Pacific and reaches 2,080 feet (634 m) atop **Cerro Iglesias.** Relatively young, it owes its genesis to a hot-spot...a point in the seabed where molten magma has welled up from deep within the

earth's bowels, giving birth to a chain of submarine volcanoes as the Pacific plate has slowly moved over it (see p. 118).

Feral pigs are the only mammal species, but Isla del Coco shares several bird species with its southerly cousins: a subspecies of Galapagos finch plus blue- and red-footed boobies. Endemic species include the Cocos Island Cuckoo

A male frigate-bird inflates his credentials as a mate, hoping to lure a female flying overhead.

and Cocos flycatcher. Frigate birds find the steep bushy cliffs perfect launch pads, and the beautiful snowy white tern, locally called the Holy Spirit bird *(espiritú santu)* soars overhead, its tail feathers trailing behind, like feather boas.

Isla del Coco is a UNESCO World Heritage site. Traipsing the island is by permit only, although yachters call in, as do scuba divers operating from live-aboard dive vessels (see p. 264), which provide the only transport to the island. The diving here is daunting—and exhilarating. Swirling currents stir up nutrients upon which fishes thrive, drawing hammerhead and white-tipped sharks in abundance. The thrill of diving amid schooling hammerheads is one of the island's greatest draws. Encounters with harmless whale sharks and giant manta rays are also common. And inshore snorkeling amid the coral reefs reveals a world more beautiful than a casket of gems.

Following its discovery in 1526, the island became a popular stop-over for pirates and other mariners. Many a pirate supposedly buried his treasure here. Scores of expeditions have scoured the island to no avail. Hefty fees are now charged by the Ministry of Natural Resources, which leases the island to treasure hunters. At **Bahía Chatham,** the main anchorage, you can see the etchings of sailors from centuries past carved into the face of the cliff. This is the only secure anchorage. ∎

E xtreme in contrasts of valley and mountain, this area invites visitors to experience the serenity of a superb botanical garden, the thrill of premier white-water rafting, the achievement of climbing the country's highest peak.

South Central

Guaria morada, the national flower of Costa Rica

South Central

THIS REGION ENCOMPASSES THE NATION'S MOST RUGGED TERRAIN. MUCH of it is part of the Talamanca massif, whose igneous and sedimentary rocks (many lifted up from the ocean bed) underlie a rugged landscape of forest and, higher up, wind-scoured alpine grasslands. Few people live in these gargantuan ranges, and much of the area remains unexplored.

Most of the vast massif is enshrined as Parque Internacional La Amistad; shared with neighboring Panama, the park covers a whopping 479,000 acres (193,929 ha) and encompasses numerous indigenous reserves, biological reserves, and Parque Nacional Chirripó. A network of trails crisscrosses the range, tempting intrepid adventurers to pioneer pathways that are trodden by few. Unique wildlife encounters—jaguars and tapirs, anyone?—are possible.

The Talamancas loom over two fertile valleys that spread along its feet and are sandwiched between the Talamancas and the Fila Costeña coastal range, to the west. The most important is the Valle de El General, a narrow strip of land some 60 miles (96 km) long by 20 miles (32 km) wide drained by the Río General, which is fed by rivers that thunder down from the mountain massif and provides some of the heartiest white-water rafting in the country. To the south are the Río Coto Brus and its tributaries, which drain a short, eponymous valley. The two rivers merge to form the Río Terraba, which funnels westward through the Fila Costeña via a steep gorge, linking the South Central region with Golfo Dulce.

The steepled Talamancas reach 12,530 feet (3,819 m) atop Cerro Chirripó, whose summit is usually hidden from view by clouds whipped up by a whistling wind that brings torrential rains from the Caribbean. While the uplands are rain-lashed, the twin mountain ranges shelter the valleys from rain-bearing winds so that the vales bask in a balmy Mediterranean climate. This, combined with the richness of alluvial soils washed down from the mountains, lends the Valle de El General great importance as a bread basket for the nation. The sun shines benevolently upon pineapple plantations and other fruit fields that smother much of the valley, while the steep flanks of the Valle de Coto Brus are adorned with shiny, dark green coffee bushes.

Despite its agricultural vitality, the region developed only late in colonial history and remained sparsely settled until the arrival of the Inter-American Highway in the late 1950s. Before this, the poor farmers of the region had to haul their produce to market in Cartago and San José over the dauntingly sheer and inhospitable Cerro de la Muerte. Today the two-lane highway spirals dizzyingly down from Cerro de la Muerte to the regional capital of San Isidro, an agricultural center at the head of the Valle de El General. Nearby San Gerardo de Rivas nestles high in the valley of the Río Chirripó and makes an exceptional base for spotting quetzals, for trout-fishing, and for soothing soaks in hot springs best appreciated after a vigorous hike to the top of Chirripó. The only other town of consequence—San Vito—sits on the northern flanks of the Fila Costeña, at the head of the Valle de Coto Brus, and is unusual for its

pervasive
Italian heritage.

The region is also
the heartland of indigenous
culture. Here, in the fastness of
mountain valleys, members of the
Boruca and Guaymís tribes live secluded
lives on territory held in trust as indigenous
land. Several reserves are beginning to open to
tourism. The inaccessibility of much of this
region is one of its appeals. ∎

The route to San Isidro

San Isidro
- 188 B3

Visitor information
- 770-9393

Centro Biológico Las Quebradas
- 188 B4
- 1.5 miles N of Quebradas
- 771-4131
- Closed Mon.
- $$

Los Cusingos Neotropical Bird Sanctuary
www.cct.or.cr
- 188 B3
- Quizarrá de Pérez Zeledón
- 200-5472
- Reservation required
- $$$

TOURISM HAS BYPASSED THIS PEACEFUL VALLEY, DESPITE the fact that the all-important town of San Isidro is a gateway to Parque Nacional Chirripó—set in a vale popular with rafters, hikers, and birders. The Valle de El General is devoted to agriculture, mainly fruit plantations and flower farms raising tropical plants for export.

The descent into the valley from San José via the Cerro de la Muerte is a head-spinner, as the narrow Inter-American Highway (Highway 2) spirals down more than 9,000 feet (2,745 m) in 20 miles (32 km). On clear days views are sublime, with the valley spilling away below, green and flat as a billiard table.

The **Centro Biológico Las Quebradas,** at the base of Cerro de la Muerte, is a good place to spot quetzals. Accessed by a turnoff north of San Isidro, east of the Inter-American Highway, it has 5,930 acres (2,400 ha) of primary forest, including cloud forest at higher reaches. Trails are difficult.

A cliff-top statue of Christ floats over the highway one mile (1.6 km) north of the roadside community of **San Rafael,** at Km 104.

SAN ISIDRO

The main market and center for the region is this unprepossessing town, known by its municipal name of Pérez Zeledón. The town comes alive during its Fiesta Cívica in late January when farmers and their families thrill to the rodeos and mariachis; and on May 15, when *boyeros* (oxcart drivers) celebrate with a colorful parade highlighting an entire month given to honoring San Isidro, patron saint of farmers.

The town offers few attractions and its primary role is as a service center for fuel and as the gateway to Dominical and the Central Pacific, and to Parque Nacional Chirripó. Nonetheless, the concrete cathedral in modernist style, one block east of the modest **plaza** at Calle Central and Avenida 0, is worth a peek for the stained glass windows, and the meager **Regional Museum and Cultural Center Pérez Zeledón** *(tel 771-5273),* on Calle 2 between Avenida 0 and 1, offers a glimpse into campesino culture and that of the indigenous peoples.

THE VALLEY

South of San Isidro, the aroma of *piñas* (pineapples) tangs the warm air. Soon you are surrounded by fields of pineapples in tidy rows rolling to meet the horizon. The vast commercial enterprise is centered on **Buenos Aires,** 40 miles (64 km) south of San Isidro. You can hike into Parque Internacional La Amistad from here. To peek inside the canned world of pineapples, call in at the **Pindeco processing factory** *(tel 730-2053)* for guided tours.

On the western bank of the Río Peñas Blancas, near Santa Elena, between San Isidro and Buenos Aires, is **Los Cusingos Neotropical Bird Sanctuary,** a fabulous place for birding. Situated on the lower slopes of the Talamancas, this 350-acre (142 ha) reserve was for many years the home and research site of the late Alexander Skutch, coauthor (with Gary Stiles) of *Birds of Costa Rica.* Today, the Tropical Science Center manages Los Cusingos—named after a small, orange-billed toucan *(Pteroglossus frantzii)*—for ecological tourism and bird observation. Trails go past Indian petroglyphs. ∎

Opposite: A blue-crowned mot-mot pauses for lunch at Los Cusingos Neotropical Bird Sanctuary.

Clouds swirl hauntingly among the mid-elevation forests.

A walk in the clouds

Cerro Chirripó (12,530 feet, 3,819 m) lures intrepid hikers seeking the satisfaction of hiking to the top of Central America's highest peak. This non-technical ascent demands no more of you than stamina, determination, good hiking shoes, and a sleeping bag to guard against the cold during an overnight stop at cloud-hung heights.

The peak crowns a 123,920-acre (50,150 ha) national park that is a high-mountain refuge of pristine and rugged splendor. When hiking this forbidding terrain, it's easy to appreciate why pre-Columbian Indians believed the mountain was sacred (its summit was closed to all but the social elite). Today, you'll be happy to hear, mortals are no longer sacrificed for tramping hallowed ground. The park remains a sanctum of a different sort: Endangered wildlife—including tapirs and jaguars—are numerous. A side trek to the Savannah of the Lions gives you a good chance of spotting pumas. And because you ascend through three distinct life zones, the birding is excellent.

Before setting off, call in at **park headquarters** in the hamlet of **Canaan ❶,** one mile (1.6 km) south of San Gerardo, to pick up a copy of the "Visitors' Guide" and trail map; inquire here about hiring an *arriero* (guide/ porter, *$$$ per day*). No camping is

permitted, but you can cook at a refuge hut. The ascent covers 7,500 feet (3,035 m), so dress to foil the rain and the wind. The National Park Service *(tel 283-8004 or 771-4836)* limits visitors to no more than 60 people on the trail at one time. Hikers must register for three-day stints in the park, so book ahead; payment should be made at the ranger station in Canaan *($$ entrance, plus $$ per night).*

THE TREK

Begin your two- or three-day round-trip trek at **San Gerardo de Rivas ❷,** from where the 9-mile (15 km) *Sendero Termometro* is well marked. Begin at dawn, as the first day's haul takes six to twelve hours depending on the weather and personal fitness. Rains frequently deluge the mountain in afternoons.

From here, follow the dirt road east. Keep right at each of two Y-forks, bringing you to a fence signed "*Sendero al Cerro Chirripó.*" The

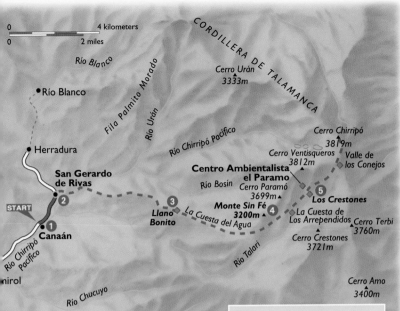

See area map pp. 188–189

San Gerardo de Rivas

11.5 miles (18.4 km)

2-3 days (1 night on mountain)

The summit

NOT TO BE MISSED
- Canaan ranger station
- Monte Sin Fé
- *albergue*
- Los Crestones
- Valle de los Conejos

track crosses mostly open pasture, good for birding. After one mile (1.6 km) you will reach the official trail, also signed. The trail becomes steeper (notably so beyond the **Llano Bonito** ③ marker) and you begin a tough uphill climb along the **La Cuesta del Agua** that will have you puffing as you ascend through lush forest. You can fill up on water (which you should boil or treat with chlorine tablets) from the trail-side stream. After about two hours on this "staircase" you will crest at **Monte Sin Fé** ④ (Mountain Without Faith), where you can rest and listen to the sounds of the forest: the stentorian calls of howler monkeys, the trillings of trogons and toucanets, and the whistling of the wind in the pines. A wooden shelter—*refugio natural*—marks the halfway point.

Mists swirl overhead as you enter the cloud forest at 7,500 feet (2,300 m)—it is a haunting world of gnarly trees festooned with epiphytes and dripping with Old Man's Beard. The 2-mile (3.2 km) ascent through this spectral landscape is known as **La Cuesta de los Arrepentidos** (Repentant's Hill), ending in the salvation of an *albergue* (hostel, *tel 777–8040*) beside the **Río Talari** in the saddle between **Cerro Crestones** and **Cerro Paramó**. The hut sits beneath unusual rock formations called **Los Crestones** ⑤.

After a chill night at Centro Ambientalista El Páramo (bring a warm sleeping bag), you should be back on the trail at dawn to beat the fogs that shroud the peak by mid-morning. The 3-mile (4.8 km) hike leads past waterfalls and through the **Valle de los Conejos** (Valley of the Rabbits), named for an abundance of furry critters. You are now amid alpine grasslands called *páramo*. After about 90 minutes you will reach the summit upon which, with luck, the sun will shine and you can enjoy the views. The peak is surrounded by lakes good for an invigorating dip.

Expect the clouds to appear soon, and the wind to whip around the summit—time to head back to San Gerardo, to make it by late-afternoon. Or you can explore summit trails, and extend your stay on the mountain. ■

**A tamandua
anteater**

Valle de Chirripó

DUE EAST OF SAN ISIDRO, A DEEP VALLEY CLEAVES THE
Talamancas; the rock-strewn Río Chirripó tumbles between its steep
flanks. The valley is popular with fly-fishermen, white-water enthusiasts, and birders on the trail of quetzals.

Valle de Chirripó
🗺 188 B4

**Chirripó
Cloudbridge
Reserve**
www.cloudbridge.org
🗺 188 B4
✉ I mile E of San
   Gerardo de Rivas
☎ 771-1866
💲 By donation

Several sites of interest line the
paved road that leads through the
valley, whose deep seclusion fosters
a balmy microclimate perfect for
growing fruits: you can buy apples,
citrus, peaches, and other treats
from stalls along the route.

Four miles (6.4 km) into the
valley is **Rivas,** a rustic hamlet and
setting for **Rancho La Botija** *(tel
770-2146, closed Mon., $),* a farm

famous for its traditional hand-
operated *trapiche* (sugarcane press)
and a boulder etched with pre-
Columbian petroglyphs. Its
restaurant is charming and visitors
can enjoy horseback rides and dips
in the swimming pool.

Beyond Rivas, the paving gives
way and the dirt road narrows and
scrambles tenuously into the upper
reaches of the valley.

wild and effervescent as champagne in the lee of the Talamancas. The aroma of pine trees and log fires scents the crystal-clear air. The nearby hamlet of **Canaan,** immediately south, is headquarters for Parque Nacional Chirripó. Together these villages offer a selection of rustic *albergues* (hostels), including the **Albergue Montaña El Pelícano** *(tel 390-4194)*. Set on a small coffee farm, this hostel includes the **Museo El Pelicano,** whose owner—Rafael Elizondo Basulto—crafts sculptures from wood and stone. A "marathon" race from San Gerardo to the top of Costa Rica's highest mountain is held each February for local runners; the winner completes the contest in a matter of hours.

A dirt road leads northwest from Canaan and follows the **Río Blanco** to the trail for **Aguas Termales**—hot springs—which you can reach via a 20-minute uphill trail.

Chirripó Cloudbridge Reserve, at the end of the dirt road east of San Gerardo, offers forest hikes on the mid-level slopes of Chirripó. This 430-acre (174 ha) private reforestation project has trails and guides. Don't be surprised to see spider monkeys and tayra here; they're common, and so are birds such as the black guan and emerald toucanet. ■

AROUND SAN GERARDO DE RIVAS

About 14 miles (23 km) east of San Isidro is an alpine village poised above the Río Chirripó, which runs

The dirt road and rickety buildings of San Gerardo de Rivas are typical of many small Costa Rica towns.

White-water rafting

C osta Rica is a white-water paradise, and rafting is a popular outdoor activity. As you plunge like a log down a flume through a no-man's land of dark, brooding rain forest, rafting provides the ultimate combination of thrills and natural beauty. Below the mountains, the rivers settle down, flowing for mile after mile in solitude and peace. The country's combination of high mountains and plentiful rain produces scores of runnable rivers—enough to keep even experienced rafters occupied for weeks.

The country boasts some of the most diverse and spectacular river runs on the continent. Depending on the river chosen, you'll pass through several life zones as you tumble through canyons overhung with tropical foliage. You are sure to find something that appeals to you. Travelers have gotten more adventurous in their demands, taking up paddles with gusto; river trips are now also available for the physically challenged.

Whatever the time of year, you'll find a river trip being offered. Major rivers such as the Pacuare, the Reventazón, and the Corobicí are run year-round. Others are seasonal, depending on water levels. In general, the best times are May to June and September to October, when water levels are high and the rainy season serves up more potent excitement. Trips vary from half-day to four- and five-day trips. The Río General and the Río Chirripó—two mammoth rivers that tumble out of the Talamancas and cascade through great gorges—are often compared with California's Tuolomne and Idaho's Middle Fork of the Salmon.

The Río Reventazón is the intoxicating Dom Perignon of white water, a river that will have you laughing with sheer delight. It and the adjacent Río Pacuare are considered the quintessential rivers on which to experience an immersion in the rain-forest environment. Both rivers pour down through mountain gorges and spill onto the Caribbean plains. Monkeys and toucans screech in the canopies en route, and there are waterfalls and tranquil stretches that allow quiet contemplation of

nature. In the crisp mountain air and bright sunlight, the white water literally sparkles.

In Guanacaste, the lazy Río Corobicí offers an entirely different experience, perfect for children. This short, relatively calm river flows through a dry forest environment. Its waters—controlled by dam and released year-round—draw to its banks all manner of wildlife, from howler monkeys and giant iguanas to herons and snakes.

Rivers are rated from Class I (flat water, considered a "float" trip) to Class V (high

waves, deemed suitable for experts only). No prior experience is necessary for Class I to III runs; some companies accept beginners on Class IV runs as well. Life vests and helmets are mandatory, but the tour operator will supply all equipment (plus expert guidance). The industry was established by North American experts and is operated to strict professional standards. More than a score of established companies operate rafting trips under the watchful eye of government regulators. Most companies offer paddle trips where you and your raft-mates do the work of powering through a rock-pocked slalom course while your guide controls things from the rear.

On some rivers, all you need to wear is a swimsuit, a T-shirt, and river sandals or sneakers that you don't mind getting wet. Expect to get drenched on Class III to V rivers—that's half the fun! A wet suit is recommended for the upper reaches of such high-mountain rivers as the Río General and Río Chirripó. Remember to take plenty of sunscreen—you'll be out in the sun all day—as well as a set of dry clothes and shoes to change into at float's end. On overnight trips you will sleep in tents or jungle lodges, where the day's rafting guides often rematerialize as the evening's chefs. ■

A wet and wild moment on the Río Pacuare

Parque Internacional La Amistad

BEYOND THE PALE OF HUMAN INCURSION, THE VAST Talamanca massif is a last frontier for tourism. Here Costa Rica's wildest terrain has been enshrined for posterity in a mammoth park that the country shares with its southern neighbor, Panama.

A quetzal feeds its chick.

Parque Internacional La Amistad
www.sinac.go.cr
⚠ 188–189
☎ 771-3155 or 771-4836
$ $$

Durika Biological Reserve
www.durika.org
⚠ 189 D3
✉ 13 miles NE of Buenos Aires
☎ 730-0657

The 479,200-acre (193,920 ha) park, the nation's largest, girdles the Talamancas, a great tectonic massif thrust from the ocean over several million years and twisted into a number of ranges. Unlike the northern mountain ranges, the Talamancas are not volcanic, but are composed of sedimentary rock and igneous intrusions. Rising with a heart-aching loveliness, these mountains span a width of 50 miles (80 km) and take up a fifth of the national territory.

La Amistad, which extends south into Panama, begins at barely 450 feet (137 m) above sea level along the southern Caribbean shore and rises to the dizzying heights of Cerro Chirripó. The park spans eight of Costa Rica's twelve life zones, encompasses other national parks, and shelters the largest repository of animals, birds, and tropical forest in the nation. On the Caribbean slopes, La Amistad protects the largest area of montane rain forest in Central America, rising above 3,500 feet (1,060 m) to a prodigious expanse of cloud forest—home to the largest concentrations of quetzals in the country. The mountain fastness is a last refuge for several endangered species. Tapirs thrive in isolation, as do pumas and jaguars and most other large mammals. And harpy eagles, locally extinct elsewhere in Costa Rica, still soar above the southern Talamancas.

Hiking is a true adventure but should only be undertaken with adequate preparation. The park has scant facilities but the headquarters in San Isidro provides information, as does CONAI, the office of indigenous affairs at **Ujarras,** 7 miles (11 km) northwest of Buenos Aires. An arduous trail across the mountains begins at Ujarras and ends in the Reserva Biológica Hitoy-Cerere. A local guide is a prerequisite for a trans-Talamanca journey, and travelers intending to make the crossing must register in advance with CONAI. The park headquarters can provide a list of ranger stations from where you can

Native American reserves

The Spanish occupation proved devastating to indigenous cultures, which retreated to valleys where their descendants still live.

Each tribe has its own territory. The most accessible reserves can be reached by 4WD vehicles over trails. Parts of La Amistad, for example, rarely see outsiders.

Traditional beliefs and customs, based on a way of life that few remember, exist in remote regions. Tourism is being promoted. No permit is needed for Boruca, where a museum describes local culture. Visitors can see women weaving traditional cloth and men carving balsa-wood masks and gourds. ■

hike into the park. There are few facilities, although the **Estación Altamira** *(tel 730-0846),* near Buenos Aires, has a small museum and camping facilities.

You do not have to be Indiana Jones, however, to probe the park. A good base for exploring is the homey **La Amistad Lodge** (see p. 254), within the Las Tablas Protective Zone abutting the southeastern border of the park and accessed by four-wheel drive. Its 40 miles (64 km) of trails lead to two basic high-mountain camps at a 6,000-foot (1,830 m) elevation.

At **Durika Biological Reserve,** a farm and reforestation overseeing a 18,533-acre (7,500 ha) private reserve, you can assist the local community in their efforts to conserve the land. ■

Fed by torrential rains, a stream rushes to join one of the mighty rivers of La Amistad.

A drive around Valle de Coto Brus

Superbly scenic yet forsaken by tourists, the Valle de Coto Brus carves a deep gorge between the Talamancas and Fila Costeña. Highway 237 runs the length of the valley along the flank of coastal mountains, offering elevated vistas over the vale; in the distance, the southern peaks of the Talamancas rise grandly to mauve-colored, cloud-shrouded heights.

Cattle driven along a rural road create gridlock, Costa Rica-style.

Your journey begins at the community of **Paso Real ❶,** at the eastern end of the Valle de El General, where the Río General and Río Coto Brus merge to form the **Río Terraba,** which flows south and carves a deep gorge in the Fila Costeña. About half a mile (0.8 km) south of Paso Real, turn off the Inter-American Highway and span the wide Río Terraba by a bridge that has replaced the old ferry, taking the fun out of the crossing. The wiry bare-chested ferrymen who operated the motor looked, thought local ecologist Gail Hewson de Gómez, "as if they were born in the reeds with the crocodiles" (which once waited for scraps thrown from the ferry).

Highway 237, intermittently paved, runs east from here along the valley floor. The soaring peak of **Cerro Kamuk** (11,660 feet, 3,554 m) reaches to the sky in the northeast, shadowing the valley, which is grazed by hardy humpbacked cattle. You will pass the signed

turnoff for **Estación Tres Colinas ❷,** 17 miles (27 km) via dirt road. Nearby is Helechales, one of several ranger stations for Parque Internacional La Amistad. And at **Jabillo ❸,** 8 miles (13 km) farther, you pass the turnoff for the regional center of **Coto Brus** hunkering in the valley bottom. The road has now risen above the valley and sidles east along the ridge crest of the **Fila Guacimo,** giving you a grandstand view.

The local climate is favorable to coffee, and glossy green bushes brighten the hillsides, stippled in tree-shaded rows like endless folds of green silk—a delicate counterpoint to **Cerro Echandi** (10,374 feet, 3,162 m), a hulking mass veiled in forest and cloud.

About 30 miles (48 km) southeast of Paso Real, the road coils steeply up towards the regional capital of **San Vito ❹** (see p. 202). Follow the main road—Highway 16—south as it snakes uphill past coffee farms including **Finca Cántaros ❺** *(tel 773-3760, closed Mon.–Fri. high season, open by request low season, $),* where you should stop for a nature walk along trails through the 15-acre (6 ha) reserve and, sitting on benches beside **Laguna Julia,** delight in the herons, grebes, and other waterfowl feeding on fish and frogs. It also has a splendid fine art gallery and an educational center for local children.

Four miles (6.4 km) south of San Vito you will pass **Las Cruces Biological Station ❻** (see p. 202) and shortly thereafter you will crest the mountain ridge. The world seems to drop away in front of you, as you stare down over the Valle de Coto Colorado, the Golfo Dulce, and the emerald forested carpet of the Península de Osa beyond. The view inspires awe. Drive with utmost care as you descend the switchback that claws its way downhill to the town of **Ciudad Neily**—a drop of some 3,000 feet (915 m)—and the end of your scenic drive. ∎

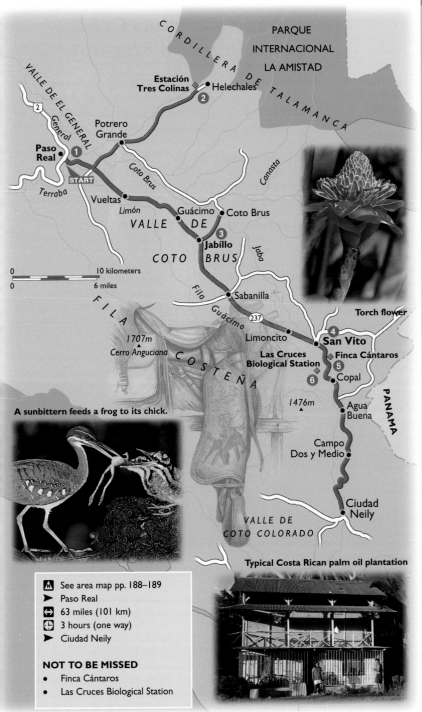

PARQUE
INTERNACIONAL
LA AMISTAD

CORDILLERA DE TALAMANCA

VALLE DE EL GENERAL

2

General

Estación
Tres Colinas ◆ ● Helechales
2

Potrero
Grande

Paso
Real ●
1

START

Coto Brus

Canasta

Vueltas
Limón

VALLE   DE

Guácimo ● ● Coto Brus

3

Jabíllo

COTO   BRUS

Jaba

Terraba

0   10 kilometers
0   6 miles

FILA

Sabanilla

237

Fila Guácimo

1707m
▲
Cerro Anguciana

COSTEÑA

Limoncito ●

Torch flower

4

San Vito

Las Cruces
Biological Station ◆ Finca Cántaros
5
6 ◆ ● Copal

1476m
▲

Agua
Buena ●

PANAMA

A sunbittern feeds a frog to its chick.

Campo
Dos y Medio ●

VALLE DE
COTO COLORADO

Ciudad
Neily

Typical Costa Rican palm oil plantation

⛰ See area map pp. 188–189
► Paso Real
↔ 63 miles (101 km)
⏱ 3 hours (one way)
► Ciudad Neily

NOT TO BE MISSED
● Finca Cántaros
● Las Cruces Biological Station

San Vito & Las Cruces
Biological Station

Las Cruces Biological Station & Wilson Botanical Garden
www.ots.ac.cr

🅰 189 E1

✉ 4 miles S of San Vito

☎ 773-4004 or 524-0628

💲 Garden entrance $$, guided tours from $$$$

THE REGIONAL CAPITAL OF SAN VITO IS A JUMPING-OFF point for Las Cruces—one of the world's leading research centers for the study of tropical biota. A bonus is its cultivated botanical garden, which ranks among the most complete in the tropical world.

Italian farmers founded the compact hill town of San Vito, at about 3,250 feet (990 m), in the mid-19th century. Unlike most Costa Rican towns, San Vito lacks a main plaza. The *plazuela* at the southern end of the main street contains an intriguing verdigris-covered statue of two children who symbolize Italian-Costa Rican brotherhood. You may see Indian women in colorful traditional clothing.

The tightly wrapped leaves of bromeliads act as cisterns, providing nutrients from trapped and decaying insects.

The lush forest, which is often veiled with the mists that nourish a profusion of bromeliads, epiphytes, and other air plants, is a veritable Garden of Eden in a region that has suffered significant deforestation. Birding is especially rewarding—more than 330 species have been recorded. And anteaters, armadillos, deer, kinkajous, monkeys, ocelots, sloths, and tayras are among the many large mammal species that visitors have a good chance of seeing while walking the miles of well-maintained trails.

The best time to visit is from mid-December through mid-April, when the persistent sopping rains diminish. The biological station offers a limited range of accommodations to nonscientific visitors by reservation (see p. 254).

WILSON BOTANICAL GARDENS

The real highlight of a visit to Las Cruces is this 25-acre (10 ha) garden laid out in 1963 under the genius inspiration of Brazilian gardener Roberto Burle-Marx (1909–1994) using a theme of gardens within a garden. Some 6 miles (10 km) of trails dip and rise through lily beds, heliconia groves, a fern grove, orchid grotto, and the world's largest collection of palms. Make sure that you call in at the green-houses, where spectacular assemblages of anthuriums, cacti, ferns, and other tropical plants together comprise a veritable hothouse *Fantasia*. ∎

LAS CRUCES BIOLOGICAL STATION

Las Cruces, situated a mere 4 miles (6.4 km) south of San Vito, protects a 583-acre (236 ha) reserve of montane tropical rain forest on a ridge of the **Fila Zapote** range of mountains. It is owned and run by the Organization for Tropical Studies (see p. 112), with whom you can arrange educational stays.

A billiard table on a grand scale, the Northern Lowlands comprise a watery world of lagoons, rivers, and rain forest—all of it superb for birding, fishing, and other adventures.

Northern Lowlands

Eyespots on the underside of a butterfly wing contrast with its iridescent surface.

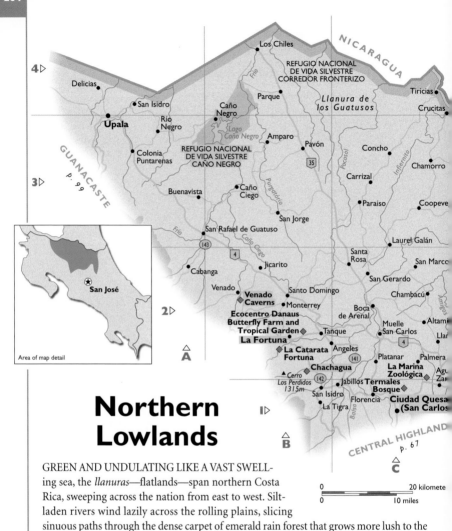

4▷

Los Chiles

NICARAGUA

Delicias

REFUGIO NACIONAL
DE VIDA SILVESTRE
CORREDOR FRONTERIZO

Tiricias

San Isidro

Parque

Llanura de
los Guatusos

Crucitas

Caño
Negro

Río
Negro

Upala

Lago
Caño Negro

Amparo

Pocosol

Concho

Chamorro

Infiernito

Colonia
Puntarenas

REFUGIO NACIONAL
DE VIDA SILVESTRE
CAÑO NEGRO

Pavón

35

Carrizal

3▷

GUANACASTE
p. 99

Buenavista

Caño
Ciego

Purgación

San Jorge

Paraiso

Coopeve

San Rafael de Guatuso

Laurel Galán

Frío

143

Caño Ciego

Santa
Rosa

San Marco

San José

4

Jicarito

Cabanga

San Gerardo

2▷

Venado

**Venado
Caverns**

Santo Domingo

Chambacú

Amigos

Monterrey

**Ecocentro Danaus
Butterfly Farm and
Tropical Garden**
La Fortuna

Boca
de Arenal

Muelle
San Carlos

Altam

Tanque

4

Llar

△
A

△
A

**La Catarata
Fortuna**

Angeles

141

Platanar

Palmera

Chachagua

**La Marina
Zoológica**

Agu
Za

▲Cerro
Los Perdidos
1315m

142

Jabillos

**Termales
Bosque**

Northern
Lowlands

San Isidro

Florencia

**Ciudad Quesa
(San Carlos**

I▷

La Tigra

Balsa

CENTRAL HIGHLAND
p. 67

△
B

△
C

Area of map detail

0   20 kilomete
0   10 miles

GREEN AND UNDULATING LIKE A VAST SWELL-
ing sea, the *llanuras*—flatlands—span northern Costa
Rica, sweeping across the nation from east to west. Silt-
laden rivers wind lazily across the rolling plains, slicing
sinuous paths through the dense carpet of emerald rain forest that grows more lush to the
east. The sparkling streams and rivers that rush down from the vaulting mountains leave
indelible impressions on those who venture into the Northern Lowlands.

The plains were formed by alluvial sediments
washing down over eons into the basin of
Lago de Nicaragua. Millions of years ago the
lake extended much further south; deposition
has since pushed its southern shore north. The
llanuras form an elongated triangle with the
Río San Juan—the Nicaraguan border—as its
northern perimeter, the Caribbean Lowlands
to the east as the right-angled side, and the
central cordillera or mountain range,

studded with volcanoes, for the hypotenuse.
The cordillera rises from the grasslands in tiers
of receding jungle, adding a note of physical
drama to an otherwise monotonously level
landscape. Volcán Arenal appears at its most
memorable viewed from the north. The plains
are divided into the Llanuras de los Guatusos
to the west and, to the east, the Llanura de San
Carlos. Dozens of rivers cascade from the
mountains and merge into the Río Frio, the

Río San Carlos, and the Río Sarapiquí; those watercourses in turn debouch into the Río San Juan, which then drains into the Caribbean Sea. In the west, rivers flow into a vast swamp lands that drains into Lago de Nicaragua.

Rivers were arteries for colonization during the 16th and 17th centuries and gained prominence two

Nicaraguan border in the wake of the recent cessation of decades of warfare. And much of the Llanuras de los Guatusos have been claimed in recent years for large-scale citrus operations.

The entire region remained isolated from mainstream Costa Rica until 1957, when Highway 126 finally linked Puerto Viejo to San José. Highway 4, which runs east-west along the base of the mountain range and links lowland settlements, is a more recent development and from it a Jacob's ladder of minor highways work their way between the range of volcanoes, tethering the lowlands to the highlands and to Guanacaste. A third highway runs north through the center of the region to the border town of Los Chiles, ground zero for cross-border subterfuge during the heady days of the Contra conflict. The regional capital and agricultural center of Ciudad Quesada is perched high above the flatlands, on the northern flanks of Volcán Platanar. The main tourist center is Fortuna, gateway to Tabacón Hot Springs and Parque Nacional Arenal.

Despite its east-west expanse, climactically the Northern Lowlands lie fully within the aegis of the Caribbean. Visitors should be prepared for hot and humid weather and the relatively ill-defined seasonal differences. Much of the region is prone to floods during the prolonged rainy season (May to January), drawing in migratory waterfowl in astonishing numbers. As elsewhere in Costa Rica, nature lovers can find their nirvanas. Caño Negro is a vast wetland ecosystem and a prime choice for birding, for viewing crocodiles, and also for tackling feisty tarpon and other game fish. Several private reserves protect huge swathes of montane rain forest on the lower slopes of the cordilleras. There is always something for everyone: Selva Verde, for example, is laced with boardwalks and well-maintained trails on the flatlands, while nearby Rara Avis offers a more rugged option with trails leading up the rain-soaked mountain slopes. Several butterfly farms, a small zoo, and a crocodile farm also guarantee close-up encounters of the first kind with a variety of wildlife. There are caverns to explore at Venado. Mineral hot springs provide soothing soaks. And a well-equipped sports complex and two spa retreats provide therapeutic treatments. ■

centuries ago during the early coffee boom, when a trail was cut from Heredia, in the highlands, to today's Puerto Viejo de Sarapiquí, and the Río Sarapiquí became the major highway to the Caribbean Sea. Colonization, however, came late to the region, which remained virtually unsettled until the middle of this century. Throughout the mid-20th century, the Costa Rican government encouraged homesteading for cattle (subsidized by the World Bank). The rain forest echoed with the sound of axes and chainsaws. At the same time, large-scale banana plantations began to encroach from the east. Precious hardwoods continue to fall as homesteaders and logging companies nibble at the remnants of rain forests close to the

Llanura de San Carlos

THIS BROAD PLAIN, DRAINED BY THE SAN CARLOS, SUCIO, and Sarapiquí rivers, is a patchwork of banana plantations and rain forests; the latter sweep down the northern flanks of Barva and Cacho Negro volcanoes and extend north in billowy green waves to the Río San Juan. The lush rain forests and riverbanks provide birding non-pareil—including a unique opportunity to spot the endangered green macaw (*Lapa verde buffon*).

One of the distinctive attractions in the region is **Rara Avis,** a private reserve that protects 3,163 acres (1,280 ha) of remote montane rain forest abutting Parque Nacional Braulio Carrillo (see p. 85), on the eastern flank of Volcán Cacho Negro. The rain forest is fed by an overwhelming 200 inches (500 cm) of rainfall annually, which means that visitors are sure to be deluged on almost any day. Rara Avis was created as an experiment to explore ways that income could be derived from harvesting the rain forest ecosystem without felling trees—through sales of ornamental epiphytes and orchids, fruit seeds and saplings, and a variety of other commercially valuable products. The complex includes a biological research station. Rara Avis is also famous as the site for Dr. Donald Perry's pioneering canopy research, described in his biographical *Life Above the Jungle Floor* (1986). The economic mainstay of Rara Avis, however, is ecotourism.

Visitors can don waterproof boots to tramp the miles of trails, which range from easy to arduous. You can also explore a butterfly farm and an orchid garden. And treetop platforms permit visitors eye-to-eye views with monkeys and other canopy species; one platform overlooks a thunderous waterfall—one of dozens that spill through the forest, forming invigorating swimming pools at their base. Your exploration is sure to lead to some thrilling wildlife encounters: Close-up sightings of monkeys, sloths, and toucans are virtually guaranteed, and the reserve is prowled by big cats such as jaguars, jaguarundis, and ocelots. That rustling in the undergrowth could turn out to be a brocket deer or a tapir foraging in the deep recesses of the forest. Poison-arrow frogs, brightly liveried, are easy to spy among the leaf litter. The 390-plus species of birds include endangered green macaws and umbrella birds.

The reserve's remoteness and inaccessibility make day visits impossible. Rustic lodges provide accommodations. Rara Avis is 9 miles (15 km) west of **Las Horquetas,** a tiny farming community beside Highway 4, and is reached by an arduous and muddy clamber up the steep, rain-soaked slopes on a rutted dirt road.

Nearby, **Heliconia Island** is ablaze with heliconia and ginger blooming in riotous color. Manicured to near perfection, this 5-acre (2 ha) garden—the creation of American naturalist Tim Ryan—displays more than 80 species of heliconia from around the world, as well as scores of bamboo, orchid,

and other species. Birding is stupendous; the air thrums with the buzzing wings of hummers. For an unusual experience, request a nighttime tour.

PUERTO VIEJO DE SARAPIQUÍ

Puerto Viejo, the only town of note in the region, huddles at the confluence of the Río Puerto Viejo and Río Sarapiquí, at the foot of the Cordillera Central, whose eastern slopes bear the brunt of damp air masses moving in from the Caribbean. Puerto Viejo long ago relinquished its former importance as the country's main shipping port for coffee brought down from the Meseta Central by mule.

Puerto Viejo makes its living serving banana plantations, which unfurl eastward mile after mile. It also caters to ecotourism. Several lodges take advantage of the superb nature viewing. **El Gavilán** (see p. 265), on the south bank of the Río Sarapiquí, offers guided hikes and horseback rides along trails that probe its 450 acres (182 ha) of primary rain forest.

The stupendous variety of wildlife can also be seen on boat rides that put out from the *muelle* (dock) at the eastern end of town. Water-taxis ply the Ríos Sarapiquí and San Juan as far as Barra del Colorado, and you can charter motorized canoes and canopied tour boats with Oasis Nature Tours *(tel 766-6108, $$$ per hour per person).* Expect to see caimans, monkeys, sloths, and even crocodiles as you cruise along the wide, sluggish waterways. Take a pair of binoculars and plenty of clothing you can wear in wet weather.

The quickest way to reach Puerto Viejo from San José is via Highway 4, which branches north from the Guápiles Highway (Highway 32) at **Santa Clara.** An

Rara Avis
www.rara-avis.com
🅰 205 E1
✉ 9 miles SW of Las Horquetas
☎ 764-3131
🅂 $$$$ guided hikes including canopy tour

Leaf-cutter ants tote cargo to their nests, where it will be mulched into fertilizer.

Cámara de Turismo de Sarapiquí
☎ 761-1579

Heliconia Island
www.heliconiaisland.com
🅰 205 E1
✉ 3 miles N of Horquetas
☎ 762-0520
🅂 $$$

A cruise on a canopied boat up the Río Sarapiquí is a great way to view nature.

La Selva Biological Station
www.ots.ac.cr
⬆ 205 E2
✉ 2 miles S of Puerto Viejo
☎ 766-6565
$ Guided hikes from $$$$

Centro Neotrópico Sarapiquís
www.sarapiquis.org
⬆ 205 D2
✉ 1 mile N of La Virgen
☎ 761-1004
$ $$

alternate, more scenic route is via Highway 126, which crawls down the western flanks of Volcán Barva and touches the lowlands at the hamlet of **La Virgen.** Here you might stop for refreshments at **Rancho Leona** (see p. 259), where North American transplant Ken Upcraft welcomes visitors to his stained-glass studio. Ken offers accommodations, as well as white-water kayaking trips on nearby rivers and hiking into Parque Nacional Braulio Carrillo.

Nearby, the **Centro Neo-trópico SarapiquíS,** on the banks of the Sarapiquí River, draws visitors for its medley of fascinating attractions. Among them is the state-of-the-art **Museo de Cultura Indígena,** celebrating the still extant indigenous cultures of Costa Rica and featuring an impressive collection of artifacts, masks, decorations, and shamanic objects. An auditorium has a revolving documentary. This eco-logical center is also an archaeologi-cal site featuring a pre-Columbian burial field and a reconstruction of an Indian village. And it serves as an experimental farm with fruit orchard and botanical garden dis-playing a vivid palette of native species. A lush contemporary hotel at its heart offers fine dining. Trails lead into 330-acre (133 ha) **Tirimbina Biological Reserve,** where a suspended canopy walkway gets you up-close to monkeys that cavort in the treetops.

LA SELVA BIOLOGICAL STATION
This research center, immediately south of Puerto Viejo, occupies land abutting the northern reaches of Parque Nacional Braulio Carrillo. It is owned and operated by the Organization for Tropical Studies (see p. 112), an international body made up of 50 or so universities that share research facilities. These con-sist of laboratories, an arboretum with more than 1,000 tree species, and experimental lots surrounded by 3,700 acres (1,500 ha) of virginal premontane rain forest.

La Selva averages a hefty 160

Freshwater sharks?

The presence of sharks in Lake Nicaragua has baffled both casual observers and scientists for centuries. This freshwater lake is linked to the Caribbean by the 106-mile-long (170 km) Río San Juan, whose rapids were thought a suffi-cient barrier to the passage of sharks. Early scientists believed that the lake was once part of the Pa-cific Ocean, and that its sharks had adapted to freshwater. In fact, the lake was formed by tectonic subsi-dence and was never part of a sea. Sharks are a euryhaline species, able to tolerate both fresh and salty water; electronic tagging has shown that they migrate between Lake Nicaragua and the Caribbean Sea via the rapids. ■

inches (400 cm) of rainfall per year;
rare is the day when no rain falls.
Boardwalks provide for easy hiking
close to the educational center, but
most of the 38 miles (61 km) of
trails can be muddy going
(February and March are the driest
months). Guided hikes are offered
twice daily for call-in visitors, by
reservation only. More than 420 bird
species have been recorded, as have
more than half of all butterfly species in Costa Rica and two-thirds of
the nation's mammal species (not to
mention 55 of its 162 species of
snakes, for which hikers should keep
a wary eye).

SELVA VERDE

This private reserve, at Chilamate,
4 miles (6.4 km) west of Puerto
Viejo, protects 475 acres (192 ha) of
lowland rain forest bordering the
northwestern extent of Parque
Nacional Braulio Carrillo. Miles of
trails and boardwalks penetrate the
dark forests, where snakes and
poison-arrow frogs abound.

Bird cries explode like gunshots
in the murky stillness. Blue-and-
gold tanagers, jacamars, motmots,
parrots, and toucans are numerous
and are most easily identified in the
company of a trained naturalist
guide. Noisy flocks of oropendolas
with long tails the color of daffodils
are particularly numerous.

Selva Verde has a butterfly
garden within a netted enclosure
that visitors can enter to gain a
close-up familiarity with the
goings-on of lepidoptera. Selva
Verde also has canoe and horseback
trips, plus nice accommodations. ■

**Suction-cup pads
on its feet help
the red-eyed tree
frog hop to it.**

Selva Verde
www.selvaverde.com
🄰 205 D2
✉ 6 miles W of
    Puerto Viejo
☎ 766-6800
💲 $$$ (guided hikes),
    $$ (butterfly
    garden)

Snakes

Snakes—*culebras* or *serpientes*—are a fact of life in Costa Rica, which is home to 162 species. These ubiquitous creatures—much maligned, little understood—are found in every one of the country's environments. The majority, being nocturnal, are rarely seen.

Many species are painted in exquisite colors and patterns, with a beauty that belies their fearsome reputations. In fact, only 22 species are venomous, of which nine are potentially fatal to humans (excepting the coral snakes, which produce a unique venom, the species all produce the same venom, which varies only in degree of toxicity). While most species are camouflaged in greens and browns the better to catch passing prey, many species—such as the coral snakes—boast gaudy colors meant to advertise their highly venomous nature.

Snakes range in size from diminutive species such as the foot-long (30 cm), pencil-thin bright green vine snake *(bejuquillo)*, with its beaked nose, to the 10-foot (3 m) boa constrictor *(boa)*, which coils around its prey and squeezes it to death. The boa, which gives birth to live young, is normally benign and retiring, but will strike if you approach too closely; though they are non-venomous, their fangs can inflict a nasty bite.

Some species are highly localized, such as the *cascabel,* the sole tropical species of rattle-snake (a member of the viper family) found only in Guanacaste. It rarely uses its rattle and produces an unusually toxic venom. Vipers include the highly venomous eyelash or palm viper *(bocaracá).* This exotically colored Day-Glo green or yellow arboreal snake lies in sensuous coils on branches, where it can keep a keen eye for passing prey. The much-feared bushmaster *(matabuey)* is a giant among the poisonous snakes and highly aggressive—it has even been known to chase people. The bushmaster is restricted to densely forested mountain terrain. Its equally lethal cousin, the terrestrial fer-de-lance—colloquially called the *terciopelo* ("velvet")—is far more ubiquitous

and accounts for four-fifths of snake bites in Costa Rica, as well as most fatalities. Rather than slink away at the approach of humans, the fer-de-lance holds its ground and will strike with little provocation. Although found in every major life zone, it prefers wet habitats; it is prevalent in tall grassland and along riverbanks in drier regions. Amazingly, even the fer-de-lance has something to fear in Costa Rica: *Clelia clelia,* an arboreal snake that feeds on small reptiles, preys on juvenile fer-de-lances.

Vipers are mostly nocturnal. They hunt with the aid of a sensory device located in a pit, or depression, between the nostril and eye. The device detects infrared radiation and is so sensitive that it can sense a rise in temperature of three hundredths of a degree Centigrade per yard, which indicates the presence of warm-blooded prey. This serpentine infrared sensor can also tell the direction of a heat source in pitch darkness, allowing the pit viper to close in unseen until within striking range of its victim. Pit vipers are the most evolved snake of all; like mammals, they nourish their unborn young through placental membranes. Uniquely, they even guard their young.

Costa Rica also has four species of coral snakes, identified by their bands of carmine red, white or yellow, and black. If threatened, they typically flatten their backs and perform a balletic dance meant to intimidate aggressors. One non-venomous snake, the false coral snake, mimics these markings but is easily identified: Its rings are in the reverse order. Pelagic sea snakes—black backed and yellow bellied—are distant relatives of the coral snake; they are common off the Pacific shore, where they use their spatula-like tails to sidle through the warm water.

One commonly seen species is the chunk-headed snake, an extraordinarily slender snake that has evolved to forage for prey on thin branches (its I-beam shape is ideal for bridging gaps between branches). It hides in bro-meliads, then ambushes lizards and frogs. ■

Above: A huge head and exquisite markings are dead giveaways of the boa.

Below: The fer-de-lance has dappled gray-brown skin—perfect camouflage for lying in wait amid decaying leaf litter.

Above: The banded coral snake, highly venomous, has a stunted head and stubby tail.

Opposite, top: Scales overhanging its eyes betray the highly venomous eyelash viper.

Around Ciudad Quesada

Ciudad Quesada
🅰 204 C1
Visitor information
✉ Calle Central & 1
☎ 479-9106
🕐 Closed Sun.

**La Marina
Zoológica**
🅰 204 C2
✉ 8 miles E of
Ciudad Quesada
☎ 474-2100
💲 $

**Termales del
Bosque**
✉ Aguas Zarcas
☎ 474-4740
💲 $$. Canopy tour:
$$$$$.

**Tapirs can often
be seen drinking
from lakes at dusk
in many parts of
Costa Rica.**

THE CAPITAL OF THE REGION IS NOT ACTUALLY IN THE
Northern Lowlands; instead, it perches loftily at 2,145 feet (654 m) on
the slopes of the Cordillera Tilarán, while the *llanuras* (lowlands)
unfurl majestically below. The town is a vital link to both lowlands.

The bustling market town, which
slopes sharply northward and is
known colloquially as San Carlos,
is surrounded by emerald-green
pastures munched by brown Swiss
cattle and black-and-white Hol-
steins. Saddlemakers' shops—*tala-
barterias*—are a curiosity as you
browse the town center, laid out in
a grid around a tree-shaded square.
If possible, time your visit for April,
when a **Fería del Ganado** (cattle
fair) is held. The main office for
Catuzón, the Cámara de Turismo
de Zona Norte, has literature and
helpful guides; it is on Calle Central
at the south end of town.

From the main plaza, Highway
140 sidles down the northern flank
of Volcán Platanar, from which
gush forth thermal waters. At
Termales del Bosque visitors
can bathe in the mineral springs
after hiking or horseback riding
through lush forest, or after joining
monkeys and sloths in the treetops
on a canopy tour. Spa treatments
are offered at **Thermae Spa**
(Hotel El Tucano, tel 460-6000),
which enjoys a splendid setting
beside a ravine of steaming springs.

The road descends to **Aguas
Zarcas,** setting for **La Marina
Zoológica,** a private zoo caring
for orphaned and confiscated birds
and animals, including dozens of
monkeys and such treasures as
tapirs, jaguars, and a Bengal tiger.
Travelers with an interest in pre-
Columbian archaeology can visit
Ciudad Cutris, where the much
deteriorated ruins of an ancient set-
tlement emerge through the en-
veloping foliage. You will need a
four-wheel drive vehicle to reach
this site. ■

Around La Fortuna

THE PROSPEROUS TOURIST CENTER OF LA FORTUNA DE SAN Carlos nestles against the Cordillera de Tilarán in the lee of smoldering Volcán Arenal, which towers over the town to the west. La Fortuna is the main gateway to the volcano, enshrined within Parque Nacional Arenal, which is the primary draw for tourists. The attention has fostered a blossoming of local ecotour attractions.

Volcán Arenal looms over the sign-happy town of La Fortuna.

La Fortuna
△ 204 B2
Visitor information
☎ 460-9998

The compact town of **La Fortuna** is bustling with travelers hoping to watch a volcano explode, a feat that Volcán Arenal—4 miles (6.4 km) west of town—obligingly performs regularly. At night pyrotechnics light up the ink-black sky. There's no shortage of accommodations to cater to the constant traffic. One rustic option, Albergue Ecoturística La Catarata, features the **Zoo Tepescuintle** *(tel 479-9522, $),* named for the dark brown and white-speckled dog-size rodents,

also called *agoutis,* that in the wild are endangered. Here, a farmers' cooperative raises agoutis for release to the wild. There is a small orchid garden, and a small butterfly garden allows visitors to wander freely beneath a netted enclosure.

Highway 142 runs through town and continues toward the volcano (see p. 116) and Tabacón Hot Springs Resort. En route you will pass **Jungla y Senderos Los Lagos** *(tel 479-8000),* a private reserve with trails into a 1,200-acre (485 ha) swath of premontane rain forest at the foot of Arenal; visitors can hike or ride horses. Crocodiles and caimans slosh about in a series of man-made lakes. A water-slide augers down to a large swimming pool popular on weekends. Set in landscaped gardens, **Baldi Termae Spa** *(tel 479-9652)* nearby has soothing, hot mineral baths; one has a swim-up bar.

Despite the tourist boom, Fortuna still serves as a regional agricultural center and retains its strong ties to the local beef cattle economy. *Sabaneros* (cowboys) with lassoes and machetes are a local feature. Horseback riding is popular, and several tour operators, such as Desafio Adventures (see p. 265), offer rides as far as Monteverde, atop the Cordillera de Tilarán. The most popular ride is to the **Catarata La Fortuna,** one mile (1.6 km) south of Highway 142, 3 miles (4.8 km) southeast of town. After dismounting, you can follow a narrow trail and steep staircase downhill to a waterfall, which has pools good for bathing. Intrepid travelers can also hike the steep and rain-soaked flanks of **Cerro Los Perdidos** (4,314 feet, 1,315 m) and ascend into the Reserva Biológica del Bosque Nuboso de Monteverde (see p. 110) and the Bosque Eterno de los Niños (see p. 111).

Tour operators in town also offer a wealth of local adventure travels—everything from mountain biking, kayaking and floating on the **Río Peñas Blancas,** fishing on Laguna de Arenal, and spelunking at Venado Caverns (see p. 216) to bungee jumping from a bridge over the Río Peñas Blancas at San Isidro.

CHACHAGUA

This private reserve protects a 124-acre (50 ha) swatch of montane rain forest that melds into the Bosque Eterno de los Niños at the base of the Cordillera de Tilarán. Naturalist guides lead hikes in search of birds and wildlife, such as the large populations of poison-arrow frogs, ocelots, toucans, and howler and white-faced monkeys. The facility is centered around a working cattle hacienda where visitors can watch cowboys ride bulls bareback. A stream bubbles down through the property, where guests are accommodated in rustic cabins at the edge of the forest.

It is best to use a four-wheel drive vehicle to negotiate the dirt road that leads to the hacienda. ∎

Chachagua
www.chachaguarain
foresthotel.com
🅰 204 B2
✉ Hwy. 142, 6 miles
E of Fortuna
☎ 239-1164
💲 $$

Refugio Nacional de Vida Silvestre Caño Negro

THIS 24,633-ACRE (9,968 HA) RESERVE IS A WATER WORLD OF swampy bayous. At its heart is a vast lake, which draws migratory waterfowl in such numbers that their rushing wings may be mistaken for the muffled roar of a distant jet aircraft. The waters also teem with plump, olive-green crocodiles, grown fat on the local fish.

The vast swamp lands occupies a large basin. **Lago Caño Negro,** at its heart, is filled by the **Río Frío** and other rivers that wash down from the Cordillera de Tilarán. In May the lake begins to swell, and vast lagoons form in the basin. Thousands of waterbirds then flock here: anhingas, cormorants, ducks, egrets, grackles, and grebes, as well as ibis, wood storks, and roseate spoonbills ladling the black waters with their long, spatulate bills. In the relatively short dry season from February to April, many of the lagoons dry out; the lake shrinks, and a large proportion of the waterfowl departs for other climes.

Jaguars, ocelots, deer, tapirs, monkeys, sloths, and other large mammals inhabit the vast carpets of sedge and jolillo palm groves. Caimans are abundant, as are freshwater turtles. Pugnacious crocodiles the size of Peterbilt trucks can be seen sunning in saurian splendor on the banks of muddy sloughs.

Caño Negro is an angler's dream, with tarpon the ultimate prize during fishing season (July to March, licenses required). Fishing trips and boat tours leave from the small border town of **Los Chiles,** about 60 miles (96 km) northwest of Ciudad Quesada, on the banks of the Río Frío. Canopied boats make the 16-mile (25 km) journey to **Caño Negro.** Boat trips also depart the hamlet of Caño Negro, on the western shore of the lake. ■

Refugio Nacional de Vida Silvestre Caño Negro
- 🅰 204 B3/4
- ✉ Off Hwy. 35, 40 miles NW of Ciudad Quesada
- ☎ 661-8464 or 460-6484
- 💲 $

More places to visit in the Northern Lowlands

ECOCENTRO DANAUAS BUTTERFLY FARM & TROPICAL GARDEN

This ecocenter is wonderful collection of tropical foliage, much of it part of a refor-estation program for native species. Highlighting the "farm" is a netted butterfly garden where you can walk amid butterflies. A *ranario* (frog garden) displays poison-arrow frogs and red-eyed tree frogs, and a *serpentario* provides a close-up look at eye-lash vipers and other exotic snakes. 🄰 204 B2 ✉ 2 miles E of La Fortuna ☎ 460-8005 💲 $

The Venado Caverns near Venado were unknown until 1945, when a farmer fell into the entryway.

HACIENDA POZO AZUL

Horseback rides are a specialty at this work-ing cattle ranch, and so are white-water trips on the Río Sarapiquí, rappelling in the river canyon, and mountain biking. A zipline canopy tour will whisk you through the rain forest treetops. Guests can stay in a riverside tent camp, or at the Magsasay Lodge on the border of Parque Nacional Braulio Carrillo. www.haciendapozoazul.com 🄰 205 D2 ✉ La Virgen de Sarapiquí ☎ 761-1360 🕐 Guided tours 💲 $$$

LAGUNA DEL LAGARTO

This private reserve (four-wheel drive access only) protects 1,200 acres (485 ha) of virgin rain forest and crocodile-rich swamps near the confluence of the Ríos San Carlos and San Juan. The forests abound in wildlife, including a plentiful supply of poison-arrow frogs red as bright lipstick and blue as the morning sky. Visitors can see two-toed sloths, which spend most of their lives hanging upside down, and crocodiles. The nature lodge overlooks the Río San Carlos, which is good for exploring by canoe or on canopied boat trips. www.adventure-costarica.com/laguna-del-lagarto 🄰 205 D3 ✉ 28 miles NE of Aguas Zarcas ☎ 289-8163 🕐 Guided tours 💲 $$

REFUGIO NACIONAL DE VIDA SILVESTRE CORREDOR FRONTERIZO

Stretching the width of the country, the slen-der 230-square-mile (59,570 ha) wildlife refuge guards the forests along the Nicaraguan border. Much of the refuge fringes the broad Río San Juan, which can be explored by boat from the community of Boca San Carlos; at El Castillo, 25 miles (40 km) upstream, the Fortaleza de la Immaculada Concepción has been restored and has a museum on colonial history. Wildlife viewing along the banks is terrific. ✉ Bahía Salinas to Punta Castillo ☎ 283-8004 💲 $$ Nicaraguan border fee

VENADO CAVERNS

These limestone caverns extend for almost 2 miles (3.2 km) beneath the foothills of the Cordillera de Tilarán. They are filled with underground streams, as well as stalactites and stalagmites in fascinating formations. Bats roost on the ceiling, transparent frogs hop about underfoot, and a blind species of fish swims in streams. Guides lead two-hour tours. Safety helmets and flashlights are pro-vided. (Bring waterproof footwear.) The cav-erns are on the Solis family farm one mile (1.6 km) south of Venado, about 22 miles (35 km) northwest of La Fortuna. 🄰 204 B2 ✉ 5 miles S of Jicarito on Hwy. 4 ☎ 479-9191 💲 $ ■

The slender Caribbean coast is lined by beaches washed by pounding waves and beloved by marine turtles and surfers. A coral reef, superb fishing, wildlife refuges, and a unique culture all add to the offbeat appeal.

The Caribbean

The Caribbean coast has a culture distinct from that of the rest of Costa Rica.

The Caribbean

RUNNING 125 MILES (193 KM) RULER-STRAIGHT BETWEEN THE NICARAGUAN and Panamanian borders, Costa Rica's palm-fringed, surf-pounded Caribbean coast is as wild as the nation's towering interior. Primeval rain forest spreads inland from the sandy littoral, melding into swampy lagoons to the north and rising into the spiraling, cloud-draped heights of the Talamancas to the south. The entire coast, lying within Limón province, varies little in its hot, humid climate: Rain cascades in all months but peaks from May to August and December to January; then storms rush in, bowing down the palms and turning dirt roads into impassable quagmires. When the sun shines, the beaches glisten invitingly, surfers take to the waves, and the wildlife—never far away—bursts into song and dance.

The region is linked to the rest of the country by Highway 32, the Guápiles Highway, an arrow-shot road linking San José with the former banana port of Puerto Limón, which lends its name to the province that encompasses the Caribbean north to south. This funky terminus of the now defunct Atlantic Railroad idles with a languor typical of down-at-heel tropical ports, except during Carnival when it explodes briefly to life.

North of Limón, long, lonesome gray-sand beaches limn the wave-washed shore. The rain-sodden hinterland (rains increase northward along the Caribbean) is a watery world backed by a broad alluvial plain—the Llanura de Tortuguero and Llanura de Santa Clara—that extends far inland, smothered in banana plantations and rain forest culminating to the northeast in the lush, wildlife-rich world of Parque Nacional Tortuguero and Refugio Nacional de Vida Silvestre Barra del Colorado. These two pristine environments form a haven of limpid lagoons fed by the murky waters of the Río San Juan and Río Colorado, providing anglers with world-class fishing for tarpon and snook. Numerous lodges cater to fishing enthusiasts and to nature lovers keen to spy the crocodiles, river otters, and manatees that inhabit the sloughs. The birding is equally fabulous. Motorboat tours give visitors the chance to glimpse a wealth of arboreal and terrestrial mammals. So vast and impenetrable is the dense jungle swampland that Tortuguero and

Barra can still only be reached by river or air.

South of Limón, the alluvial plain tapers sharply as the Talamanca mountains crowd up to the shore. The steep slopes, veined in violet shadow, are deluged in year-round rains that nourish the virtually impenetrable montane rain forest. Reserva Biológica Hitoy-Cerere, albeit dauntingly rugged, is the most accessible of the belt of reserves that includes indigenous reserves tucked into valleys deep in the mountains.

A coral reef is a highlight at Parque Nacional Cahuita, giving snorkelers and scuba divers a rare opportunity to mingle with reef fish streaming in rainbows through dazzling aquamarine waters, shimmering like silk in the sunlight. The offbeat villages of Cahuita and Puerto Viejo draw surfers and other travelers who seek to shun pretensions. South of Puerto Viejo, the broad valley of the Río Sixaola opens inland, swathed in banana plantations and a portal to the indigenous reserves. This southern zone is known as *Talamanca*, a Native American word that refers to the slaughter of turtles. Marine turtles still nest at beaches up and down the coast: Tortuguero is the prime nesting site in the Caribbean for green turtles, and hawksbill and leatherback turtles come ashore in great numbers here and at swampy Refugio Nacional de Vida Silvestre Gandoca-Manzanillo, which extends to the Panamanian border.

Hernán Cortés, who mapped the region in 1522, recorded trade between local Indians and Aztecs from Mexico. Although cacao was an important export crop in the 18th century, shipped from the now defunct port of Matina, the inhospitable Caribbean coast was largely given short shrift by Spanish colonists, and pirates and illicit traders filled the void. The region thus evolved apart from the rest of the nation. Its isolation ended in the 1880s, when the Atlantic Railroad was built and Puerto Limón was developed as the chief port for coffee exports. The era saw the arrival of Jamaican laborers, who stayed to work the banana fields that were planted at the turn of the century.

Approximately 50 percent of the population today is of West Indian extraction. The irresistible, syncopated beat of reggae and the highly spiced cuisine hint at how much more enduring their presence has been.

The Caribbean region is culturally distinct; its offbeat mood is uniquely charming, leaning a recent en-vogue cachet to the region. The area's enfeebled economy is inextricably linked to the vicissitudes of the banana trade, an industry that was almost wiped out by a blight in the 1930s. Helping to overcome this dependency, tourism is now the economic mainstay of the region; accommodations from budget mountain retreats to chic cottages by the shore cater to this upsurge in popularity. ■

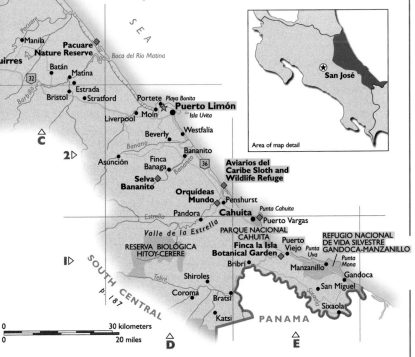

Llanura de Santa Clara

THESE UNDULATING ALLUVIAL PLAINS EXTEND EASTWARD from the foot of Volcán Irazú, forming a vast green sea of banana plantations that meld into swamplands—which, in turn, push up to the ocean. The plains are walled to the south by the steep slopes of Irazú and Turrialba volcanoes and, farther east, by the soaring Talamancas. Highway 32 runs along the base of this mountain chain, hopscotching scores of rivers that cascade from the high peaks above.

Bosque Lluvioso
www.bosque-u.com
🔺 218 B3
✉ 2 miles S of Hwy. 32 from Km 56, 4 miles W of Guápiles
☎ 232-3253
💲 $$

The three main towns along Highway 32—**Guápiles, Guácimo, and Siquirres**—are service centers for the vast Río Frío banana region that dominates the western plains, accessed by a labyrinth of dirt roads that extend to the very border of Parque Nacional Tortuguero. The towns are rather dirty, disheveled affairs—unappealing in themselves but offering attractions of note in their hinterlands. For example, one of Costa Rica's most acclaimed artists, North American Patricia Erickson, has a studio—**Gallery at Home** *(tel 710-1958, by appointment)*—4 miles (6.4 km) west of Guápiles, in her house beside the Río Blanco. Her husband, Brian,

makes and sells bamboo furniture.

A fistful of small private reserves are easily accessed from Highway 32. All protect precious premontane rain forest on the flanks of Volcán Irazú and Volcán Turrialba, and share in common a wealth of wildlife—coatimundis, howler and white-faced monkeys, ocelots, sloths, snakes, and exotically adorned birds such as aracarias, hummingbirds, motmots, oropendolas, and toucans are all commonly seen. Poison-arrow frogs—gaudily painted as porcelain figures—are profuse upon the damp forest floor and are easily spotted hopping about.

Half a mile south of Gallery at

Home and offering an effortless entrée to the rain forest is the small **Casa Río Blanco Rainforest Reserve** *(tel 382-9057)*, where charming cabins look directly over the forest canopy atop the banks of the **Río Blanco;** and **Bosque Lluvioso,** a scientific research facility protecting 420 acres (170 ha) of virgin forest, offers an even broader experience. You can see all the familiar species on self-guided hikes along manicured trails posted with educational boards (a booklet is also available). One trail leads to a lagoon; another to herbal and orchid gardens. Poison-dart frogs are particularly numerous, hopping about underfoot, secure in their brilliant liveries. A zipline gives a fleeting bird's-eye canopy experience, and there is a small zoo and exhibits on indigenous culture.

Jardín Botánico Las Cusingas, straddling the Río Santa Clara, also offers trails, hikes, and horseback rides into tropical montane rain forest, but it is better known for its botanical research and its vast gardens of ornamentals, raised for export. It has a visitors center, plus trails into the rain forest. Guided tours add immeasurably to the experience and enhance the chances of viewing wildlife.

Travelers with a keen interest in flowers should head north from Guácimo to **Costa Flores** *(tel 716-5047)*, claiming to be the largest flower farm in the world, with 300 acres (120 ha) of floral beds! Visitors are welcome at **EARTH,** a university dedicated to tropical agricultural sciences and preserving a 990-acre (400 ha) swatch of lowland rain forest. ■

Jardín Botánico Las Cusingas
- 218 A3
- 2.5 miles S of Hwy. 32, 1 mile E of Guápiles
- ☎ 382-5805
- $ $

EARTH
www.earth.ac.cr
- 218 B3
- 800 yards E of Guácimo
- ☎ 713-0000
- $ $$$$$ guided tours

Top bananas

The Llanuras de Santa Clara are awash with plantations that push up against the borders of Parque Nacional Tortuguero and Refugio Nacional de Vida Silvestre Barra del Colorado. Costa Rica is the world's second largest banana producer; it exported 1.723 million tons in 2003 (down from 2.03 million in 1999). Around 123,500 acres (50,000 ha) are planted, mostly in the Caribbean. U.S.-based Standard Fruit Company is the major producer. The monoculture that has resulted is blamed for many of the region's ecological ills, including the felling of rain forest for new plantations. Fertilizers washing downstream have caused water hyacinths and reeds to blossom, filling in habitats and channels, while silt washing out to sea has destroyed much of the offshore coral reefs. Pesticides such as DBCP, banned in North America, have poisoned plantation workers, and plastic bags used to protect fruit stems routinely wash out to sea, where marine turtles mistake them for jellyfish and choke. In a bid to secure an Eco-OK seal of approval, Costa Rica's banana industry is adapting more ecologically responsible methods; you might say it's turning green. ■

Women sort bananas, which are segregated by shape and the condition of their skin.

Refugio Nacional de Vida Silvestre Barra del Colorado

RÍO SAN JUAN FORMS THE BORDER WITH NICARAGUA. BEtween it and Laguna de Tortuguero lie 225,365 acres (91,200 ha) of swampland and rain forest teeming with exotic wildlife. The labyrinthine lagoons and rivers boil with tarpon, snook, and antediluvian garfish, making the refuge the premier sportfishing center in Costa Rica.

Refugio Nacional de Vida Silvestre Barra del Colorado

- 218 B4
- 40 miles N of Guápiles
- 771-1201
- $$

The rivers move sluggishly, depositing vast amounts of silt that shift the watercourses yearly in a mosaic of deltas. Endless green rain forest fills the horizon; the forests are gnawed at by loggers, and banana plantations push up against the park's southern borders. The soggy lowlands are pimpled by small hillocks and bordered to the west by 1,096-foot-high (334 m) hills, the **Lomas de Sierpe.**

Swampy sloughs meander from lagoon to lagoon. Most backwaters are inaccessible; here manatees breed in relative isolation. Jabiru storks, orpendolas and green macaws are among the numerous intriguing bird species. Crocodiles bask on mud banks. And caimans, monkeys, sloths, river otters, and terrapins are sure-bet sightings.

The tumble-down village of **Barra del Colorado**—served by an airstrip—straddles the **Río Colorado,** a branch of the Río San Juan. Anglers set out from sportfishing lodges for colossal fights with record-beating tarpon and snook. The **Caño de Penitencia,** clogged by silt and water hyacinths, links Barra to Tortuguero (see p. 224).

All along the riverbanks are dilapidated shacks on stilts. The river is entirely within Nicaraguan territory; you will need a passport and be prepared to pay a fee. ∎

Parque Nacional Tortuguero

THIS 47,000-ACRE (19,000 HA) PARK ENCOMPASSES DIVERSE wetlands penetrating inland for 9 miles (15 km), a 14-mile-long (23 km) section of shoreline that is the Caribbean's premier nesting site for green turtles, and ocean waters that stretch 18 miles (29 km) offshore. Tortuguero is also astonishingly rich in wildlife. No wonder, then, that it is one of the nation's most popular parks.

Parque Nacional Tortuguero
- 219 B/C4
- 10 miles NE of Zancudo
- 710-2929 or 709-8086
- $$

Natural History Visitor's Center
- 219 C4
- Tortuguero
- 711-0680
- $

This remote park is pinned by the funky hamlet of **Tortuguero,** sprawling along a 4-mile-long (6.4 km) sandy peninsula between a lagoon and the sea. At the northern end of the promontory, aircraft swoop down to the grass strip, from where boats ferry travelers to lodges or to the isolated village, which offers budget accommodations, canoes and guides for hire. A trail leads north from **Tortuga Lodge** (see p. 256), a prominent nature and sportfishing lodge, one mile (1.6 km) from **Cerro Tortuguero,** a 360-foot (110 m) hummock with views over the park.

The park, which is deluged by up to 200 inches (500 cm) of rain a year and comprises coastal rain forest and several distinct wetland ecosystems, is cut by a maze of waterways that guarantee superb wildlife viewing. You are not likely to spot jaguars, tapirs, or any of the other endangered mammal species that inhabit the park. But visitors can reliably expect to see monkeys galore, giant iguanas, and mothridden sloths moving languidly among the high branches, while aracarias, oropendolas, parrots, and toucans are among the most commonly seen of Tortuguero's 300 bird species, which include rare green macaws. Caimans and river otters rarely prove elusive as you cruise the canals. And giant fishing bats can be seen at night, scooping up fish with their talons.

A well-timed visit may coincide with the arrival of hawksbill, leatherback, or green turtles, which come ashore to lay eggs between February and October. Tortuguero is the primary green turtle hatchery in the Caribbean. Although some community members still profit from the illegal harvest of eggs and turtles, a conservation ethic is seeping into the local mentality. Guides from a local cooperative escort nocturnal hikes on the beach *($)*, which is otherwise off-limits after 6 p.m. (only 350 people are permitted nightly). To learn more, call in at the **John H. Phipps Biological Station,** north of the village, where a **Natural History Visitor's Center** has exhibits. The **Cuatro Esquinas ranger station** is south of the village. ∎

Not-so-tiny bubbles

Endangered manatees inhabit lagoons in the remote western parts of the park. This herbivorous, heavily wrinkled mammal resembles a tuskless walrus with a spatulate tail. It grows to 12 feet (3.7 m) in length and can weigh a ton. It spends most of its time submerged, foraging on water hyacinths and other aquatic fodder that produce flatulence. Bubbles rising to the surface of the water are therefore a good indication that a healthy manatee is expressing itself below. ∎

A ride on the Canal de Tortuguero

Until the 1960s, travel along the Caribbean seaboard was virtually impossible. Rough waves and the lack of bays precluded safe passage and anchorage, while the vast swamplands that extend far inland thwarted the construction of roads. Then, during the Trejos administration (1966–70), a canal was dredged parallel to the shore, linking the remote hamlets of Barra del Colorado and Tortuguero with the port of Moín and Puerto Limón. Today a journey along the Tortuguero Canal is one of Costa Rica's most rewarding journeys—thrilling, too, as your boatman canes your craft with the throttle wide open.

The narrow, 70-mile-long (113 km) Canal de Tortuguero links the various lagoons and major rivers along the northern Caribbean plains and runs a few hundred yards inland of the surf-pounded shore. The canal is a liquid highway of commerce and the rhythmic throbbing of weary engines is its mantra. Most of the lodges at Tortuguero and Barra provide their own speedy watercraft for guests opting for the slow, scenic route. Watch for *cayucos*—motorized dugout canoes carved from a single log and traditionally used for ferrying bananas and other agricultural produce—and public water-taxis, usually fast-paced *lanchas*. These small river boats are not built for comfort; a waterproof poncho is recommended. (Bear in mind also that this boat ride can be done in either direction.)

It is a three-and-a-half-hour trip from **Moín ❶**, 3 miles (4.8 km) north of Limón. Private boats leave from the JAPDEVA dock *(tel 758-1106, $$$$$ round-trip)*. Within minutes you are enveloped in the deepest verdure, with patches of rain forest towering over the river. Egrets and numerous other stilt-legged waders stalk the grassy banks in search of tasty tidbits while kingfishers skim like low-level jet fighters over black waters.

Twelve miles (19 km) from Moín, the canal opens into the **Boca del Río Matina ❷**, a broad estuary whose sluggish river deposits silt from the mountains; the tides spin this into long, brown-sand beaches. Female green, hawksbill, and leatherback turtles favor these warm sands for their nests, as well as at Playa Barra de Matina, where 4 miles (6.4 km) of shoreline backing the beach are protected within the **Pacuare Nature Reserve ❸** *(tel 233-0451)*, where scientists conduct turtle research; trails run parallel to the beach and to an inland lagoon amid rain forest.

Public water-taxis depart for Tortuguero from Caño Blanco Marina *(reservations tel 259-8217, $$)*, at **Barra del Matina Sur,** 2 miles (3 km) upriver.

In all these miles there are no settlements to speak of, although occasionally you will pass a ramshackle hut made of wood and bamboo, raised on stilts to guard against flooding and snakes. The *cimaronnes* (literally, "wild ones" in reference to people of mixed-blood) who live along the riverbank subsist on fishing, the sale of bananas, and cattle that graze in clearings cut from the grasslands and sedge.

The canal opens into the wide estuary of the **Río Parismina ❹** a popular location for sportfishing, particularly during the spring run of tarpon, which can be hauled in from the surf; and for snook, notably mid-August through November. Three sportfishing lodges cater to anglers. The silt that the river brings often clogs the canal—do not be surprised if your boat grounds. Beyond the river, the canal penetrates **Parque Nacional Tortuguero** (see p. 223), indicated by a sign beside the **Jaloba ❺** ranger station. No fee is charged for passage via the canal.

Northward, the overriding sense is of swamp and jungle. In places the rain-forest canopy merges overhead, forming dark glades that explode with the roar of howler monkeys. Great stands of bamboo rise in feathery, heraldic clusters. Freshwater turtles and small caimans sunning themselves on logs will plop into the waters as you putter past. Toucans are noisy and numerous. And with good luck, you might even spot an endangered green macaw flying overhead.

After 49 miles (79 km) you will arrive at the village of **Tortuguero ❻**, facing a broad lagoon that opens northward to the azure waters of the Caribbean. Most passengers end their journey at Tortuguero.

South of the village, the canal cuts inland and zigzags through the wetlands of **Refugio Nacional de Vida Silvestre Barra del Colorado** ⑦ (see p. 222). Playful river otters are often seen along this 21-mile-long (34 km) section that slices through the aquatic wilderness, where raffia palms hang over the waters. Farther north, water hyacinths clog the channel. Eventually you come to a broad reach near the mouth of the **Río Colorado,** where crocodiles bask on the mudflats of the wide, soupy river.

Three and a half hours from Moín, the village of **Barra del Colorado** ⑧ marks the end of your journey. ∎

🅐 See area map pp. 218–219
▶ Moín
⇄ 70 miles (112 km)
🕐 3.5 hours (2 hours in opposite direction)
▶ Barra del Colorado

NOT TO BE MISSED
- Parque Nacional Tortuguero
- Refugio Nacional de Vida Silvestre Barra del Colorado

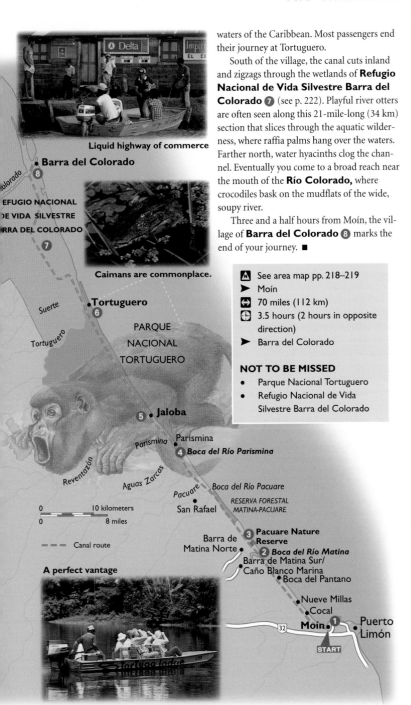

Liquid highway of commerce

Caimans are commonplace.

A perfect vantage

Barra del Colorado
⑧

EFUGIO NACIONAL
DE VIDA SILVESTRE
RRA DEL COLORADO
⑦

Suerte

Tortuguero
⑥

Tortuguero

PARQUE
NACIONAL
TORTUGUERO

⑤ Jaloba

Parismina
Parismina
④ Boca del Río Parismina

Reventazón

Aguas Zarcas

Pacuare
San Rafael

Boca del Río Pacuare
RESERVA FORESTAL
MATINA-PACUARE

③ Pacuare Nature Reserve
Barra de Matina Norte
② Boca del Río Matina
Barra de Matina Sur/
Caño Blanco Marina
Boca del Pantano

Nueve Millas
Cocal
Moín
Puerto Limón
32
START

0   10 kilometers
0   8 miles

- - - Canal route

Puerto Limón

PUERTO LIMÓN IS A SULTRY PORT TOWN THAT IS MORE A place to pass through rather than linger in. The only town along the Caribbean coast, Limón is the main service center for the eponymous region and is the country's main commercial port; it is also the gateway to both Tortuguero and Cahuita national parks. The many sailors' bars attract a colorful clique of hookers and unsavory characters; fittingly, vultures hop down the streets with leisurely sovereignty. Still, if you look hard enough, there are attractions.

The port evolved as a center for the export of precious hardwoods and, later, during the early colonial epoch, cacao, but soon fell beyond the pale of Spanish authority and emerged as a refuge for buccaneers and pirates scouring the Spanish Main. Its real genesis came in the late 19th century, when the Atlantic railroad was built and suddenly Puerto Limón blossomed with the banana trade. When blights scythed through the plantations from the 1930s onwards, the port suffered a decline from which it has only recently begun to recover. The city fathers have pulled the city up by its bootstraps in recent years. Cruise ships now arrive at the new port facility. And the streets are well paved—thereby making them unusual in Costa Rica.

Despite its somewhat forlorn aspect, the city boasts some fine clapboard colonial buildings adorned with filigreed ironwork balconies, and the avenues are lined with tall palms and mango trees that cast great pools of shade. The most appealing building is the **town hall**, or *alcadia*, on the north side of the town plaza, **Parque Vargas,** which lies at the east end of Avenida 1. At its heart is a small bandstand surrounded by promenades shaded by tousled palms and by vine-draped strangler fig trees. Note the bronze busts of Columbus and his son Fernando on the northeast corner. They were dedicated in

1992 in celebration of the five-hundredth anniversary of the Genoese explorer's landing in Mesoamerica. Facing it is an exquisite mural paying homage to Columbus, pre-Columbian Indians, and the immigrant workers who put down roots locally.

An uninspired boulevard on the seafront overlooks a coral reef thrust from the sea on April 22, 1991 by an earthquake that razed several buildings and compounded the city's ill fortunes. The small isle of **La Uvita** lies 800 yards (730 m) offshore. It was here on September 18, 1502 that Christopher Columbus anchored and became the first European to set foot ashore on the land he called *La Huerta*—the garden. You can hire a boat at the dock for trips out to the craggy island, which is pitted with caves.

The bustling, enclosed market that lies at the town's core is also worth a perusal for its colorful fishmongers, butchers, and artisans' stalls tucked into narrow alleys. The streets surrounding the plaza are lined with venerable wooden structures graced by filigreed iron balconies. Many restaurants and other businesses are run by Chinese, the offspring of indentured laborers who arrived to work on the Atlantic Railroad, then stayed on and stitched their own little patch of culture onto the quilt of the city. The community has its own cemetery—**La Colonia China**—on

Tour boats ply the waterways near Puerto Limón.

Puerto Limón
🅰 219 D2
Visitor information
☎ 758-1906

Museo Ethnohistórico
✉ Aves. 1 & 2
☎ 255-3051
🕓 Closed weekends
💲 $

Highway 32 west of town.

North of town, surfers ride the waves that wash onto Portrete and the appealing **Playa Bonita,** the latter boasting a handsome beach that is excellent for sunning with occasional breaks for ceviche and grilled fish (washed down, of course, by homemade cashew wine) from thatch-roofed ranchitas where you can eat with your feet almost in the water. ∎

Carnival

When Día de las Culturas (aka Carnival) comes around in mid-October, Limón explodes in a bacchanal in which the *Limoneses* let down their hair and succumb to a promiscuous delirium. Rum, beer, and guaro (the local grog of fermented sugarcane) flow freely. As many as 100,000 ticos come to witness (and participate in) costume parades, beauty contests, and general revelry. ∎

Costa Ricans throw their conservative side to the wind during Carnival.

Valle de la Estrella & Aviaros del Caribe

Aviarios del Caribe Sloth & Wildlife Refuge
www.ogphoto.com/aviarios
🏔 219 D2
✉ Hwy. 36, 17 miles
S of Puerto Limón
☎ 750-0775
💲 $$$$

Reserva Biológica Hitoy-Cerere
www.sinac.go.cr
🏔 219 D1
✉ Off Hwy. 36, about 15 miles W of Penshurst
☎ 798-3170
💲 $

Selva Bananito
www.selvabananito.com
🏔 219 D2
✉ 9 miles W of Bananito
☎ 253-8118
💲 $

SHADED BY COCONUT PALMS, A STRING OF BROWN-SAND beaches leads the eye south from Limón. Highway 26 hugs the shore and makes brief forays inland, seeking narrow necks by which to cross the wide rivers—the Ríos Bananao, Bananito, and Estrella—that flood down from the Talamancas and seasonally inundate the narrow coastal plain and broad valleys.

Twelve miles (19 km) south of Limón, the road meets the mouth of the wide **Río Estrella,** where lagoons and channels abound with wildlife, including flocks of cattle egrets. The wetlands extend north along the shore to the **Aviarios del Caribe Sloth & Wildlife Refuge,** a private wildlife sanctuary protecting 186 acres (75 ha) of marshes—a haven for caimans, river otters, and turtles—where visitors can take boardwalk hikes or paddle canoes. The reserve trills to the calls of birdlife, and serves as a refuge for orphaned and confiscated sloths.

Half a mile (0.8 km) south of the river, at **Penshurst,** a side road snakes inland into the Valle de la Estrella. **Orquídeas Mundo** *(tel 750-0789, $),* "world of orchids," 600 yards (550 m) inland, raises hundreds of species of orchid. Guided hikes are offered into the nearby forest. Upriver, the valley opens out into a wide alluvial basin carpeted with banana plantations and crisscrossed with dirt roads serving the various processing and packing plants.

The rugged Talamancas soar westward, clad in some of the densest montane rain forest in the isthmus. Some 22,363 acres (9,050 ha) is protected within **Reserva Biológica Hitoy-Cerere,** an undeveloped reserve accessed by four-wheel drive and deluged by 20 feet (6 m) of rain a year. Trails from the ranger station follow the valley of the Río Hitoy-Cerere to cascades, and across the mountains into the Valle de El General.

To the north of Hitoy-Cerere is **Selva Bananito,** a 2,350-acre (950 ha) cattle ranch and reserve with rustic cabins and a nature lodge in premontane rain forest, accessed by horseback or hiking trails. To reach it by road, you will need a four-wheel drive vehicle. ■

Cahuita

COLORFUL CAHUITA PRESENTS A TASTE OF ZESTY CREOLE culture and a laid-back lifestyle that draws a young, hip, unpretentious crowd keen to let down its hair. The rustic hamlet, gateway to Parque Nacional Cahuita, offers fine beaches, accommodations, some of the best regional cuisine in the country, and activities that range from horseback riding to scuba diving and glass-bottom boat tours.

A horseback ride along Playa Negra is an exciting way to explore Cahuita.

The southern Caribbean was neglected for a long time—a regional backwater shunned by the national government. This area survived by fishing and by growing cacao, but the latter industry was destroyed by the *Monilia* fungus two decades ago at about the same time Highway 36 arrived, linking the region to the rest of the nation. Today, Cahuita, the most colorful village, boasts a new spring in its step thanks to its unabashedly earthy charm.

The main village, approached via a palm-lined boulevard, has no central plaza, merely two dirt roads parallel to the coast, with four dirt roads in between. The main street ends eastward at **Kelly Creek** and the entrance to Parque Nacional Cahuita, with a coral-colored beach curling into the hazy beyond. North of the village, dozens of simple accommodations and eateries line a black sand beach—**Playa Negra**—sweeping north in a palm-shaded scimitar. Be cautious when swimming, due to riptides.

Cahuita—named from *cawi,* the Native American word for the mahogany used to make dugout canoes—is the most African of settlements along the coast; the spicy regional cuisine, the dialect, and the musical influences reflect long-standing links with Jamaica. Rastafarians are numerous, dressed in their trademark clothing of red, yellow, black, and green. Reggae riffs mingle with the surf, while the pungency of *ganja* (marijuana) hangs in the salt air. Locals pick up the beat each October, when a five-day Carnival prompts the Caribbeans to whirl and gyrate in the dusty streets, creating a kaleidoscope spinning to the rhythm.

The relaxed ways can lure visitors into a false sense of security. Cahuita has earned a negative reputation, combated recently by heightened community policing. ■

Cahuita
219 E1

Camara de Turismo del Cahuita
☎ 755-0017

A surfer gets a taste of La Salsa Brava, Puerto Viejo's renowned waves.

Parque Nacional Cahuita

THIS 2,711-ACRE (1,097 HA) PARK ENVELOPS A PROMON-tory—Punta Cahuita—clad with rain forests, where beaches curl away north and south around topaz-blue bays. A coral reef covers 600 acres (242 ha) and extends around Punta Cahuita to Punta Vargas.

Parque Nacional Cahuita
- 219 E1
- S of Cahuita village
- 755-0461
- $$

A 4-mile-long (6.4 km) trail traces the shoreline and links the **Kelly Creek ranger station** with the Vargas ranger station about one mile (1.6 km) south of Punta Vargas and midway down the park. You must be prepared to wade the shallow **Río Perozoso,** just west of Punta Cahuita. Much of the wildlife that inhabits the jungle-green shore can be experienced without leaving the beach. Bands of inquisitive white-faced monkeys often scamper about in the tree-tops; coatis, iguanas, and raccoons poke their noses onto the sands; and the barking of howler monkeys echoes from within the dark forest bowels. Agoutis, anteaters, and armadillos are among the other species to be seen while hiking—watch for snakes underfoot, and for harmless caimans cooling off in the lagoons and watercourses. Birdlife is also prolific, including green ibises, herons, toucans, garrulous parrots, and scarlet macaws, magnificent in their imperial cloaks of blue, red, and yellow, which flock seasonally (December to March).

Marine turtles—hawksbills, greens and leatherbacks—nest on the long, sweeping beach south of Punta Vargas, where waves help bring them in at high tide and the tidal pools are good on the ebb.

More than 125 species of fish, including blue parrot fish, gambol amid the hard and soft corals. The wreck of a slave ship with cannons and manacles in 20 feet (6 m) of water is an added highlight. Water clarity and reef ecology suffers from silt washing down from the banana plantations (February to April is best for viewing the reef). ■

Puerto Viejo

PUERTO VIEJO, THE CARIBBEAN COAST'S SURFING CAPITAL, emits a centripetal pull on counterculture vacationers; it is Costa Rica's mecca of the offbeat. The infamous Salsa Brava wave, legendary in surfing lore, pumps ashore in front of restaurants that bear an international imprimatur. It all results in a hamlet spiced with a cosmopolitanism that belies its otherwise funky flavor.

Finca la Isla Botanical Garden
- 🗺 219 E1
- ✉ 800 yards W of Puerto Viejo
- ☎ 750-0046
- 🕐 Closed weekends
- 💲 $ ($ guided tour)

Vultures hop about the muddy, unpaved streets of the village, which lies 2 miles (3.2 km) east of Highway 36 and 8 miles (13 km) south of Cahuita at the southern end of a black-sand beach—**Playa Negra**—that ends at an indistinct promontory called **Punta Pirikiki** in the lee of a steep coastal range. The area's traditional Creole culture mixes the local Bribrí Native American culture with black traditions. The Native American heritage is strong; guided trips into adjacent indigenous reserves are a popular activity for visitors. The **Asociación Talamanca de Ecoturismo y Conservación** (ATEC, see p. 265) acts as the local information bureau and arranges visits to the Bribrí, Cabecar, and KeKöLdi reserves. Snorkeling and diving, plus dolphin-viewing excursions, are offered by **River Runner Divers** *(tel 750-0480)*, as are horseback trips at **Don Antonio's Stables** *(tel 750-0342)*, one mile (0.8 km) south of the village.

The sole site of attraction around Puerto Viejo is the **Finca la Isla Botanical Garden,** which spans 12 acres (5 ha) of rain forest and expansive gardens where exotic fruits, ornamental plants, and spices are grown. A self-guided booklet explains the trails into the forest, where monkeys, sloths, and snakes abound. Poison-arrow frogs make their homes in the bromeliad gardens—a tough-to top photo op.

South of Punta Pirikiki are lonesome, glistening beaches—**Playa**

Cocles, Playa Chiquita, Playa Manzanillo—strung between rocky headlands extending 6 miles (9.6 km) south to Refugio Nacional de Vida Silvestre Gandoca-Manzanillo (see p. 232) and to Panama beyond. About sixty hostelries, from funky to chic, line the road; most are run by North American

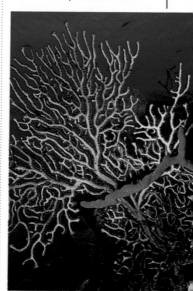

transplants and other foreigners who have moved here.

At night Puerto Viejo comes into its own, and ticos flock from far afield for the hip-hopping discos. The iconoclastic, hedonistic streak is exemplified by the many Stellas come to get their groove back with dreadlocked gigolos locally dubbed "rent-a-Rastas." ■

Right: Sea-fan coral sways in the warm-water currents of the Caribbean coast.

Refugio Nacional de Vida Silvestre Gandoca-Manzanillo

Refugio Nacional de Vida Silvestre Gandoca-Manzanillo

🅰 219 E1

✉ 12 miles E of Puerto Viejo

☎ 754-2133

💲 $

THIS REMOTE JEWEL EXTENDS FROM PUNTA UVA, 3 MILES (4.8 km) south of Puerto Viejo, to the Río Sixaola, forming the border with Panama. The refuge (a prime turtle sanctuary) combines lush lowland rain forest with a coral reef and an amalgam of wetland habitats where visitors may spot manatees, crocodiles, and even an endemic species of freshwater dolphin. With more than 360 bird species on hand, don't rule out a sighting of the rare harpy eagle.

The 23,348-acre (9,450 ha) refuge protects an invaluable mangrove system—the only one along Costa Rica's Caribbean coast—as well as the nation's only remaining orey swamp and two equally rare jolillo palm swamps where tapirs can find safe haven in watery sloughs. These labyrinthine mangroves extend along the estuary of the **Río Gandoca** and the **Gandoca Lagoon,** where they provide a breeding place for sealife, including tarpon.

You might catch a glimpse of endangered manatees and rare pink-skinned estuarine dolphins—the *tucuxí*—as they come to the surface, snuffling and snorting, to breathe. The endemic *tucuxí* can also be seen swimming in the mouth of the **Río Sixaola;** these dolphins are found in coastal lagoons as far north as Nicaragua.

The wetlands back a supremely beautiful palm-lined beach—**Playa Gandoca**—made of brown sand that four species of marine turtles consider a perfect place to deposit their precious eggs. To safeguard their cargoes, the sanctuary encompasses more than 10,961 acres (4,435 ha) of sea, which also enshrine a live coral reef. If you would like to help preserve this area, the **Marine Turtle Conservation Project** (see p. 265) welcomes volunteers.

Access is from the hamlets of **Manzanillo** or **Gandoca,** which are linked by a trail that skirts Gandoca Lagoon inland and provides fantastic wildlife viewing along the way. Another trail follows the coast to via **Punta Mona** ("Monkey Point"). Scuba diving and kayaking are available here.

Between Punta Uva and Manzanillo, the 8,765-acre (3,547 ha) **KeKöLdi Indian Reserve** meets the shore. Much of the reserve lies within the Gandoca-Manzanillo refuge; this safeguards the lands of the Bribrí and Cabecar tribes, which are exploring ecotourism and experimental income sources such as an **iguana farm.** Visits can be arranged in Puerto Viejo and Manzanillo through ATEC (see p. 265), as well as with ASACODE *(tel 751-2661);* the latter is a campesino association that operates an ecotourism project at **San Miguel,** located in the heart of the rain forest that smothers the hills inland. Here water buffalo have replaced tractors, while selective logging by community members has replaced destructive clearing of entire stands of precious hardwoods. Counter-culture types might enjoy a stay at **Punta Mona Center,** a community that practices and teaches about restorative agriculture. ∎

Travelwise

Costa Rica's roads can
require nerves of steel.

TRAVELWISE INFORMATION

PLANNING YOUR TRIP

WHEN TO GO

Time your visit according to where you wish to visit, as the country's climate varies by region. In general, dry season (verano, or summer) is Nov.–April, and wet season (invierno, or winter, called "green season" by the tourist board) is May–Oct.

The Central Highlands enjoy a year-round springlike climate, with clear skies and warm weather. The wet season means clear mornings and afternoon showers, although prolonged rain is possible. Upper mountain slopes have alpine climates, with persistent fog and high winds.

Guanacaste sizzles during the dry season, when temperatures soar. Trees explode into bloom and stiff northwesterly winds whip the Pacific—fun for surfers but putting a damper on fishing.

Rainfall increases progressively southward in Nicoya and along the Pacific coast. Golfo Dulce and the Osa Peninsula have torrential rainfall throughout the year, although clear skies are also frequent. Be prepared for stifling humidity. The same is true year-round, of the Northern Highlands and Caribbean coast, where rainfall increases northward (almost 200 inches—500 cm—annually in the Barra del Colorado and Tortuguero regions). January through April are the driest months, although heavy rain can fall at any time.

Most tourists visit in the dry season, when the more popular hotels may be booked solid. In green season, many hotels and car rental agencies drop their rates. This is a good time to visit, as many national parks and attractions are less crowded and the foliage is at its best.

WHAT TO TAKE

Costa Rica has a tropical climate so dress accordingly. Expect hot days with warm evenings, except mountain areas where nights can be chilly. On higher slopes, cold winds bring fog and driving rain, so wind- and rainproof gear is essential. A sweater is useful, and a poncho works well against downpours in lowland areas. Loose-fitting cotton shorts and T-shirts are fine, as are quick-drying, wash-and-wear cotton-polyesters. Avoid tight-fitting clothes (which promote fungal growth in the hot, humid climate), and bright colors (if you want to get close to wildlife). Informal wear is fine almost everywhere, but you might want a more elegant outfit for smarter restaurants in San José.

You'll want a comfortable pair of shoes for hiking, but be prepared to get them wet … pack a spare pair.

You will need insect repellent, particularly for wilderness excursions. Mosquitoes and other biting insects can be ferocious, although they are not such a problem in the highlands.

Do not underestimate the strength of the tropical sun. Sunglasses are important, and sunscreen is mandatory, even for brief periods outdoors. A hat or cap will keep you cooler in the tropical sun.

BEFORE YOU GO

CUSTOMS

Check with customs before bringing culture orchids and plants in sealed vials into the U.S. For details contact the U.S. Customs Service, 1300 Pennsylvania Ave., NW, Washington, D.C. 20229, tel 202/354-1000.

PASSPORTS

A passport is mandatory for entry into Costa Rica. U.S. citizens do not need a visa to visit Costa Rica if traveling as tourists with a U.S. passport valid for at least 30 days, and if they will be staying for no more than 90 days.

If traveling with children under 18, remember that they become subject to local child welfare laws after 90 days, and you must request permission to take them out of the country. Contact the National Child Protection Agency (Patronato Nacional de Infancia), Calle 10 and Calle 13, San José, tel 256-7328.

HOW TO GET TO COSTA RICA

BY AIR

The majority of flights arrive at Juan Santamaría International Airport, tel 437-2400, 11 miles (18 km) west of San José. An increasing number of flights arrive at Daniel Oduber International Airport, tel 668-1010, 8 miles (13 km) west of Liberia, the provincial capital of Guanacaste.

The national carrier, Taca (tel 800/400-8222, www.taca.com), serves more than 25 destinations throughout the Americas, including several in North America.

The following U.S. airlines offer regular flights to Costa Rica: American Airlines (tel 800/433-7300, www.aa.com), Continental Airlines (tel 800/231-0856, www.continental.com), United Airlines (tel 800/241-6522, www.united.com), and Delta (tel 800/221-1212, www.delta.com)

Several charter airlines from from major cities in the United States and Canada cities offer flights to and from Costa Rica.

BY CAR

The 2,000-mile (3,220 km) trip from the U.S.–Mexican border takes around two weeks. Preparation, and a four-wheel drive vehicle, are essential. Arrange all documentation in advance and check insurance. For advice, contact: **Sanborn's**, tel 800/222-0158, www.sanborninsurance.com.

GROUP TOURS

Around one-third of travelers to Costa Rica choose a packaged tour. Most such tours are nature related, though sightseeing tours are also available. Contact the Institute of Costa Rican Tourism (ICT; see p. 238) for a list of recommended tour companies. Or try CANATUR (see p. 239).

GETTING AROUND

BY AIR

Major destinations are linked to each other, to Juan Santamaría International Airport and to Tobias Bolaños domestic airport, tel 232-2820.

Two domestic carriers serve regional airstrips with a network of scheduled flights. Both use 20- to 35-passenger aircraft. **SANSA**, tel 221-9414, www.flysansa.com. A government-subsidized airline operating from Juan Santamaría International Airport. **NatureAir**, tel 299-6000, or 800/235-9272 in North America, www.natureair.com. Operates from Tobias Bolaños airport and offers a more flexible and reliable service.

Families and groups can charter small airplanes to airstrips throughout Costa Rica.

BY BUS

There is no national network. Dozens of private companies offer fast (directo) and slower (normal or corriente) service. Trips should cost less than $10. Standards vary, with comfortable, modern buses on major routes. Rural areas are often served by retired U.S. school buses. Some lines sell tickets in advance; on others you pay when boarding. Be prepared for crowded conditions, avoid travel on weekends, and guard against pickpockets and luggage theft.

Two shuttle bus services can take you almost anywhere in Costa Rica, with fares starting at around U.S.$21.
Interbus, tel 283-5573, fax 283-7655, www.interbuslineonline.com serves Cahuita, Fortuna, Manuel Antonio, Tamarindo, and other major destinations.
Grayline Fantasy Bus, tel 220-2126, www.graylinecostarica .com. Transfers between major tourist destinations.

Several bus companies also operate regular service from San José to destinations throughout Central America. Fares are cheap, but trips are time-consuming. San José's bus terminals are widely spread throughout the district called "Coca Cola." It is a high-crime area; caution is advised. The bus lines in Costa Rica are privately operated by a myriad of companies, so determining route information can be difficult. There is no central information source.

Bus fares are extremely low— from around 70–90 colones (18–23 cents) to travel from the suburbs to central San José, to U.S.$3–10 for cross-country trips.

CAR RENTAL

To rent a car, you should be over 21, hold a passport and a valid driver's license (a U.S. license is fine) that has been held for at least one year. You will also need a credit card and have to leave a hefty deposit (about $500). Beware additional charges that might appear on your bill when you return the car or get your credit card statement. Check that the rental includes unlimited mileage. Insurance is mandatory, and most rental companies, including U.S. franchises, refuse to honor insurance issued abroad. Rates vary from about $38 daily for the smallest vehicles, and $50 for mid-size cars, to between $60 and $90 for four-wheel drive vehicles (recommended, as the road network is in appalling shape). For off-road exploration, a rugged vehicle is essential.

In addition to Europcar, a reputable local company, most major international car rental companies are represented:
Avis, tel 232-9922, www.avis .com.cr
Budget, tel 255-4750, www.budget.co.cr
Dollar, tel 257-1585, www.dollarcostarica.com
Hertz, tel 221-18181, www.hertz.com
Europcar, tel 257-1158, www.europcar.co.cr
These agencies provide 24-hour breakdown assistance, but this can take hours to reach you in outlying areas.

Roads throughout the country are poor, with only 14 percent of the 18,000-mile (29,000 km) highway network paved. In the wet season many roads are quagmires, while Nicoya and Guanacaste are thick with dust during the dry season. Many tico (Costa Rican) drivers are inconsiderate and reckless— there is a high auto fatality rate. Drive slowly and be on your guard. Stray cattle, pedestrians in the road, and potholes are additional hazards.

PRACTICAL ADVICE

COMMUNICATIONS

MAIL
It costs 105 colones (about 22 cents) to mail a postcard to North America, 125 (26 cents) to Europe; and from 120 colones for a letter to North America, 140 (29 cents) to Europe. Never mail anything of value as theft is endemic within the postal service. Allow two weeks for air mail between Costa Rica and North America.

Most mail is delivered to shared postal boxes (apartados, abbreviated Apdo.). Most major settlements have a post office, usually open Monday to Friday, 7 a.m. to 6 p.m., and Saturday 7 a.m. to noon. In smaller towns, the Correo may close as early as 4:30, and not be open on Saturdays. Many gift stores and hotels sell postage stamps.

Private express mail services, such as DHL (tel 800/225-345, www.dhl.co.cr) and Federal Express (tel 800/052-1090, www.fedex.com/cr), offer faster and more reliable services.

TELEPHONES
In remote areas public phones are usually located at the local pulpería (grocery store and bar). Service is generally efficient, but public phones are more complicated to use than those in North America. Have a stack of coins ready: They do not accept credit and calling cards. Calls to the U.S. start at 65 cents per minute. Prepaid phone cards—look for the Viajera Internacional 199 symbol—valued from $2 to $10 for international direct-dial calls—are sold nationwide. Insert the card into the phone, and the cost of your call is deducted. USA-Direct phones link you to an AT&T operator. You can also dial direct to U.S. operators:
AT&T, tel 164 or 0800/011-4114
MCI, tel 162 or 0800/012-2222
Sprint, tel 163 or 0800/013-0123
Canada, tel 161 or 0800/015-0161.
U.K., tel 167 or 0800/044-1044.

Hotels often charge a high fee for calls from in-room phones.

For direct-dial international calls, dial 00 then the country code and area code, then the number. For information, dial 113. Dial 116 for assistance in placing international calls, or to call collect.

Calling from the U.S., dial 011 plus Costa Rica's country code 506. There are no area codes.

E-MAIL
Internet cafés are available throughout Costa Rica. Rates vary from about 350–900 colones (75 cents–$1.90) per hour, depending on venue.

CONVERSIONS

Costa Rica uses the metric system of measurement. Useful conversions are:

1 mile = 1.61 kilometers
1 kilometer = 0.62 miles
1 meter = 39.37 inches
1 liter = 0.277 U.S. gallons
10 liters = 2.8 U.S. gallons
1 U.S. gallon = 3.61 liters
1 kilogram = 2.2 pounds
1 pound = 0.45 kilograms

Weather reports use Celsius. To convert quickly (but roughly!) from Fahrenheit to Celsius, subtract 30 and divide by two. From Celsius to Fahrenheit, multiply by two and add 30.

0°C   = 32°F
10°C   = 50°F
30°C   = 86°F
100°C   = 212°F

ETIQUETTE & CUSTOMS

Costa Rican society is more formal than most. Ticos rarely address individuals by their first names without an invitation to do so. They are class conscious, with campesinos (peasant farmers) and the urban working classes deferring to people considered of a higher status. Black visitors may experience some aloofness. Costa Ricans use the formal "usted" for "you," while the informal "tu" is reserved for intimates. You may also hear the term "vos" used instead of "tu." They respect professional titles and use them when addressing title-holders, such as engineers (e.g. Ingeniero Rodríguez) and

architects (Arquitecto García).

Adults are addressed as Señor (Mr.), Señora (Mrs.), or Señorita (Miss). The terms Don (for men) and Doña (for women) are used for high-ranking or respected individuals and senior citizens.

Behavior is dictated by quedar bien—a desire to leave a good impression. Ticos are courteous and easily offended. They prefer to use hidden cues rather than state forthright opinions that might disappoint. Thus they will often conceal the truth to create an immediate good impression as, for example, when visitors ask directions. Society operates on "Tico Time," and punctuality is not a national trait. Verbal commitments are not necessarily meant to be taken at face value. Costa Ricans tend to be fatalistic about events. Si Dios quiere—God willing—is a standard refrain for life's ups and downs.

Bathing suits are frowned on away from the beach.

Life revolves around the family. Personal contacts are the key to success, particularly in business and politics. Individualism is frowned upon; team spirit and cooperation take precedence. Costa Ricans are guarded about their family life and rarely extend invitations to their homes.

Outside the main tourist areas you may not be understood in English, so it is advisable to learn a few Spanish phrases. Most restaurants in tourist areas have menus in English; you may have to ask for them.

HEALTH

The national service, Seguro Social (also known as the "Caja"), offers treatment for tourists for minimal fees. However, the service is not up to North American standards and visitors are advised to seek treatment at private facilities, such as **Clínica Biblica,** tel 257-5252, in San José, or **Hospital CIMA,** tel 231-2781 in Escazú. Most towns have private physicians and clinics.

Take out full travel insurance, which should cover all medical costs—hospitalization, nursing services, doctors' fees, etc. A medical evacuation clause is also important in case sufficient care is not available and you need to return home.

If you require medical help, consult your hotel. Most keep up a list of doctors and medical centers, which can save time. Otherwise, consult the Yellow Pages of the telephone book. Keep any receipts or paperwork for insurance claims. Make a note of the generic name of any prescription medications you take before you leave home. They may be sold by a different trade name in Costa Rica.

Costa Rica's main health hazards relate to its tropical climate, where bacteria and germs breed profusely. Wash all cuts and scrapes with warm water and rubbing alcohol. Although most water is potable, it is wise to regard it as suspect: Drink and brush your teeth with bottled water. Boil water when camping to eliminate giardia, a parasite that thrives in warm water. Avoid uncooked seafood and vegetables, unwashed salads, and unpeeled fruits.

Be liberal with the application of sunscreens and build up your tan, as the tropical sun is intense and severe sunburn or sunstroke can effectively ruin a vacation. Drink plenty of water to guard against dehydration.

Biting insects are common, particularly in the humid lowlands. Malaria is present in the southern Caribbean zone and is spread by mosquitoes: consult your physician for a suitable malaria prophylaxis. Dengue fever is also spread by mosquitoes and occasional outbreaks are

reported in the Caribbean and Pacific Lowlands. There is no preventative medication, so it is wise to try to avoid being bitten.

Use insect repellents liberally, and wear earth-colored clothing with long sleeves and full-length pants. To ward off no-see-ums, tiny biting fleas that strike on beaches at dawn and dusk, apply Avon Skin-so-Soft, a cosmetic that even the U.S. Marine Corps swears by.

Wear long pants when hiking in grasslands, particularly in Guanacaste, to guard against chiggers (coloradillos) and ticks (garrapatas).

HUNTING & FISHING

Hunting is prohibited for foreign visitors and firearms cannot be brought into the country. Fishing is also regulated and visitors must obtain a non-resident permit. This is usually arranged by specialist sportfishing outfitters and lodges. Permits for mountain fishing can be obtained from the Ministry of Agriculture, Antigüo Colegio La Salle, Sabana Sur, San José, tel 231-2344.

MEDIA

NEWSPAPERS

Costa Rica has three national newspapers (each offers a conservative view), published in Spanish: La Nación, La República, and La Prensa Libre, available at newsstands throughout the country. The English-language weekly Tico Times is available in hotel lobbies and gift stores, and offers a well-rounded and often critical perspective of the nation. A number of other English-language publications circulate, including Central America Weekly and the monthly Costa Rica Outdoors. Major U.S. dailies such as USA Today and weekly magazines such as Time and Newsweek are usually available at leading hotel gift stores and select newsstands in major towns and beach resorts.

TELEVISION & RADIO

Television reaches almost everyone, although service is intermittent in remote areas. There are 16 local stations, plus numerous cable channels. Most upscale hotels offer cable TV with U.S. programs.

Costa Rica has about 120 radio stations. All but a few broadcast local and Latin music. The BBC World Service and Voice of America offer English-language news. The granddaddy of English-language stations is Radio 2 (99.5 FM), which plays hits from the 1960s onwards, as does SuperRadio (102.3 FM).

MONEY MATTERS

CURRENCY

The national currency is the colón. U.S. currency is widely accepted (and welcomed, due to the colón's daily devaluation) throughout the country. Most stores, shops, restaurants, and tour companies will accept them, including those in smaller towns. Elsewhere you'll need colones. Exchange rates are notoriously fickle, so check the rate before leaving for your trip.

Bills come in denominations of 1,000 (rojo), 2,000 (dos rojos), and 5,000 (tucán), and 10,000 (jaguar) colones. Coins are issued in 5, 10, 25, 50, 100, and 500 colones.

Banks in larger towns usually have foreign exchange counters. Most hotels exchange currency, as do foreign exchange bureaus (cambios) in the major towns and tourist centers. Check for high commission fees. In remote areas, expect long lines at banks. Limit the amount of currency you exchange, as only $50-worth of colones can be exchanged for dollars on leaving.

Visitors may experience trouble cashing traveler's checks anywhere but banks, due to widespread fraud. Many shops will refuse to accept them.

AUTOMATED TELLER MACHINES

Many banks now have 24-hour automated teller machines (ATMs) for cash advances using credit cards or withdrawals from your account using a bank card. This means your own bank does the exchange. There is usually a small charge for using the ATM.

You will need your personal identification number, or PIN to withdraw cash. Before leaving home, it is wise to check how much you can withdraw at one time or on any one day. Using ATMs during regular banking hours is advisable, in case of problems (e.g., machines not returning cards, etc.).

CREDIT CARDS

Credit cards (tarjetas de crédito) are widely accepted. Visa is the most commonly accepted, followed by MasterCard and American Express.

NATIONAL HOLIDAYS

In addition to Christmas, New Year's Day, and Easter, the following national holidays are observed:

March 19, St. Joseph's Day
April 11, Juan Santamaría Day
May 1, Labor Day
July 25, Guanacaste Day
Aug. 2, Feast of the Virgin of Los
    Angeles
Aug. 15, Feast of the Assumption
Oct. 12, Columbus Day
Dec. 8, Feast of the Immaculate
    Conception

Most tourist sites and services, and many stores stay open for these holidays, but banks and government offices close. Excepting tourist services, the country closes down for Easter week (Wednesday to Sunday), when fiestas and religious processions occur nationwide; Few buses operate on Holy Thursday and Good Friday.

OPENING TIMES

Most stores open from 8 a.m. to 6 p.m., Monday through Saturday, with a one- or two-hour lunch break. Malls, supermarkets, and souvenir stores tend to have longer hours, and also open on Sunday.

Banks hours vary from around 8:15 to 9 a.m. opening to 3 to 3:45 p.m. closing. Some banks have Saturday morning hours. Most businesses and government offices are open Monday to Friday, 8 a.m. to 5 p.m., often with a two-hour lunch break. Some open Saturdays 9 a.m. to noon.

Most restaurants and other tourist-oriented businesses do not close for lunch.

PLACES OF WORSHIP

Every community has at least one Roman Catholic church, and often a Protestant church. Local tourist information offices and leading hotels can usually supply a list of places of worship.

SMOKING

Many Costa Ricans smoke. Smoking is banned on public transport and in taxis, and is restricted in public places, including bars. However, many restaurants lack nonsmoking facilities, and many bars disregard the law.

TAXES

A minimal sales tax is applied to many, but not all purchases. Only full-service restaurants add taxes to your bill, not soda or snack bars. There is a 23 percent sales tax at restaurants and most service industries. Hotels levy a 16.39 percent tourist tax. Be prepared to pay an exit tax of U.S.$26 (payable in colones or U.S. dollars) when leaving the country via air.

TIME ZONES

Costa Rican time is the same as U.S. Central Standard Time (CST), one hour behind Eastern Standard Time (EST), and 6 hours behind Greenwich Mean Time (GMT). There is no daylight saving time, during which the country is 2 hours behind EST, and 7 hours behind British Summer Time.

TIPPING

Tipping is not a fact of life in Costa Rica, except in tourist areas, where many people in service jobs depend on tips to make ends meet. However, a tip is an acknowledgment of good service: If the service is not satisfactory, do not tip.

A 10-15 percent service charge is often added onto restaurant bills, but a tip should be given for good service. Tour guides should be tipped about $2 per person per day for group tours, and more for personalized services.

Hotel porters should be given 50 cents per bag, and room service staff 10 percent of the bill before taxes. Taxi drivers do not expect tips, although those serving the airport generally expect $1 or so.

TRAVELERS WITH DISABILITIES

Costa Rica does not display great sensitivity to the needs of visitors with disabilities, although this is changing. Few buildings have wheelchair access or provide special toilets. Buses are not adapted for wheelchairs, and curb cuts are rare. In fact, most sidewalks are major obstacle courses, with deep fissures, open gutters, etc.

Some modern, upscale hotels have wheelchair access and a few provide special suites. However, older accommodations and restaurants may present difficulties. Fortunately, new compliance codes are coming into effect. Outside San Jose, there are few handicapped-accessible services. New codes are not widely enforced.

The following agencies provide information on tour operators, special guides, and other aspects of traveling abroad for visitors with disabilities:

Vaya Con Sillas de Ruedas, (Go With Wheelchairs), tel 391-5045, tel/fax 454-2810, www.gowithwheelchairs.com. Offers transfers and tours for wheelchair-bound travelers.

Information Center for Individuals with Disabilities, P.O. Box 750119, Arlington Heights, MA 02475, fax 781/860-0673, www.disability.net

Society for the Advancement of Travel for the Handicapped, 347 5th Ave., Ste. 610, New York, NY 10016, tel 212/447-7284, e-mail sathtravel@aol.com

Travelin' Talk, P.O. Box 3534, Clarksville, TN 37043, tel 615/552-6670, fax 616/552-1182.

VISITOR INFORMATION

The Costa Rican government's **Instituto de Costa Rican Tourism** (ICT), tel 800/COSTA-RICA, www.tourism-costarica.com, has several regional tourism bureaus, including the main information bureau situated beneath the Plaza de la Cultura in San José, tel 223-1733, fax 223-5452.

The Costa Rican National Chamber of Tourism, (CANATUR), tel 234-6222, fax 253-8101, www.canatur.org, represents the private tourism sector and publishes brochures and tourist information.

The following all have chambers of tourism:
Alajuela, tel 441-8118
Caribe Sur, tel 272-2024
Cartago, tel 551-0396
Cahuita, tel 755-0017
Dominical, tel 787-0087
Golfito, tel 775-1179
Guanacaste, tel 654-4918

Liberia, tel 378-1972
Limón, tel 758-0978
Monteverde, tel 645-5926
Nicoya, tel 685-5417
Osa, tel 786-6534
Pacífico del Sur, tel 787-0087
Playas del Coco, tel 667-0125
Puerto Jiménez, tel 735-5440
Puntarenas, tel 661-2980
Sarchí, tel 454-1633
Sarapiquí, tel 761-1579
Zona Norte, tel 479-9106

Individual tour operators have Web sites. Costa Rican travel agencies and tour operators are represented by the **Asociación Costarricense de Agencias de Viajes,** tel 257-3285, www.acav.or.cr.

The *Tico Times* maintains a Web site at www.ticotimes.net.

The following conservation groups can provide information on environmental issues:
Fundación Neotrópica, tel 253-2130, www.neotropica.org
Monteverde Conservation League, tel 645-3000, www.mclus.org
Organization for Tropical Studies, Box 90630, Durham, NC 27708, tel 919/684-5774, www.ots.duke.edu, tel 524-0607, www.ots.ac.cr
Rainforest Alliance, tel 212/677-1900, www.rainforest-alliance.org

EMERGENCIES

CRIME & POLICE

Crime in Costa Rica is on the increase. Burglary and petty theft are more prevalent than in most North American cities. Caution should be exercised at all times. In major towns, avoid parks, back streets, and unlit areas after dark. In towns there is a danger of pickpockets, so be wary in crowded areas. Highway robbers target tourists. If you get a flat tire, keep driving to a public place to change the tire.

Never leave anything in cars, don't carry lots of cash or wear expensive-looking jewelry, and keep passports and credit cards out of sight. If anything is stolen, report it immediately to the police and/or your hotel.

For police, fire, and ambulance, call 911. In most areas you can also call 127 for police, or 117 for traffic police; call 128 for the Red Cross, and 118 for the fire department.

The ICT maintains a 24-hour emergency hotline, tel 800/012-3456.

Report crimes to the Judicial Police (OIJ) at Calle 17, Avenidas 16/18, San José, tel 295-3271. Visitors from the U.S. can request a representative of the U.S. Embassy be present.

The traffic police patrol the highways, and a new professionalism belies their reputation for corruption. However, dishonest officials still exist. Never pay a policeman; report any attempts at extortion to the OIJ, tel 295-3272.

EMBASSIES

U.S. Embassy, in front of Centro Comercial, road to Pavas, Rohrmoser, San José, tel 290-4114, http://usembassy.or.cr
Canadian Embassy, Oficentro Ejecutivo La Sabana, Edificio 5, Tercer Piso, Sabana Sur, San José, tel 242-4400, fax 242-4410, www.dfait-maeci.gc.ca/sanjose
British Embassy, Centro Colón, Paseo Colón, Calles 38/40, San José, tel 258-2025, fax 233-9938, www.britishembassycr.com

SNAKE BITES

If a venomous snake bites you, get immediate medical help. Give snakes a wide berth and wear ankle-high shoes when hiking.

HOTELS & RESTAURANTS

HOTELS & RESTAURANTS

Accommodations in Costa Rica are varied and reasonably priced, although standards vary widely. There are great differences between the types of facilities available, and it will help you to understand these differences when deciding where to stay. Remember that large areas of the country are remote, so the available or more desirable accommodations may fill quickly during the busy winter months, particularly during Christmas and Easter holidays.

Eating out can be a great pleasure in San José, which offers a wide variety of possibilities. Elsewhere menus are typically restricted to traditional fare and seafood, with more cosmopolitan options in tourist destinations and upscale hotels.

Accommodations

There are several types of accommodations. While these terms are sometimes used interchangeably, *albergues* (hostels), and *hospedajes* (boarding houses) are among the many choices for budget travelers. Mid-range hotels are widely available, offering minimal service and no frills; standards vary. Top-of-the-range city and resort hotels offer international standards. These range from small, family-run boutique hotels, often in superb settings, that combine intimacy with charm, to large beachside resorts and city hotels owned by international chains. Some of these chains have toll-free numbers:

Best Western International, tel 800/780-7234, www.best western.com

Choice Hotels International, tel 877/424-6423, www.choice hotels.com

Marriott Hotels & Resorts, tel 888/236-2427, http://marriott.com

Radisson Hotels & Resorts, tel 800/333-3333, www.radisson.com

Six superb boutique hotels comprise the Small Distinctive Hotels of Costa Rica, tel 258-0150, www.distinctivehotels.com.

Principally for nature lovers, hikers, and anglers, wilderness lodges range from tent-camps and no-frills wooden lodges with basic family-style meals to more sophisticated options with fine dining, spa pools, and saunas.

Avoid "motels," usually used for short-term sexual trysts.

Apartotels are self-catering units, popular in San José.

In budget hotels, sink plugs may be missing, and showers are often cold. Warm (tepid) water may be provided by an electric element above the shower. Electric elements (aka "suicide showers") are common throughout the country; unless the wiring is damaged, electrocution is no worry. Ensure windows and doors are secure.

Bed-and-breakfast homestays are increasingly popular. Look for advertisements in the *Tico Times,* or try agencies such as:

Bells' Home Hospitality, Dept. 1431, P.O. Box 025216, Miami, FL 33102, tel 225-4752, www.homestay.thebells.org.

The ICT rating system for hotels uses a Sustainable Tourism ranking, taking into account factors such as the retention of natural ecosystems, the use of recyclables, the application of energy-saving devices, etc. A 13 percent sales tax and 3.9 percent ICT tax are added to most bills.

Unless otherwise stated:
1. All hotels have dining rooms and private bathrooms.
2. Hotels are open year-round.
3. All numbers over 8 digits are dialed direct from the U.S.

Restaurants

The vast majority of Costa Rican restaurants serve *comida típica* (see p. 20), and are open from 11 a.m. to 2 p.m., and 6 p.m. to 11 p.m. Make reservations for the more expensive restaurants, particularly on weekends. Service is slow; you may have to ask for your bill.

A selection of good quality restaurants is given below. These are both individual and typical, with notable local associations wherever possible.

Credit cards

Giving a card number is often the only way to reserve rooms in upscale hotels. Many hotels add a fee of up to 6 percent for credit card payments.

Making reservations

Although we have tried to give comprehensive information, please check details before booking. This applies particularly to the availability of facilities for disabled guests or nonsmoking rooms, acceptance of credit cards, and rates. Do not rely on booking by mail: Fax or e-mail your reservation. **Please note that 800 numbers listed do not work within Costa Rica.**

SAN JOSÉ

HOTELS

▦ AUROLA HOLIDAY INN
$$$$
AVE. 5, CALLE 5
TEL 232-2424 OR 800/465-4329
FAX 255-1171

KEY   ▦ Hotel   ▌▌ Restaurant   ① No. of guest rooms   ℗ Parking   ⊕ Closed   ⊟ Elevator   Ⓢ Nonsmoking

www.aurola-holidayinn.com
High-rise elegance overlooking Parque Morazán. Full complement of services including a casino, bars, and 17th-floor restaurant with great views.

🛏 201 ❄ ⬛ ⬛ 📺
🂠 All major cards

🏨 BARCELÓ SAN JOSÉ PALACIO

$$$$
AUTOPISTA GENERAL CAÑAS, 1 MILE NW OF PARQUE SABANA
TEL 220-2034
FAX 220-2036
www.barcelo.com
Elegant, modern high-rise with full services. The upscale casino, sports facilities, and spa are highlights, but the awkward location has little appeal.

🛏 254 🅿 ❄ ⬛ ⬛
📺 🂠 All major cards

🏨 COSTA RICA MARRIOTT

$$$$
1 MILE NW OF CIUDAD CARIARI, 800 YARDS W OF S. ANTONIO DE BELÉN
TEL 298-0000 OR 800/831-1000
FAX 298-0011
www.marriott.com
A rural location on a coffee farm with views to distant mountains. The hacienda-style building has elegant decor, shops, ballroom, golf practice range, and restaurants.

🛏 252 🅿 ❄ ⬛ ⬛ ⬛
📺 ❄ 🂠 All major cards

🏨 HOTEL HERRADURA
🍴 GOLF RESORT & CONFERENCE CENTER

$$$$
CIUDAD CARIARI, 5 MILES NW OF SAN JOSÉ
TEL 239-0033
FAX 293-2713
www.hotelherradura.com
Several very good restaurants (including Spanish and Japanese; see p. 243), a casino, and golf and country club complement the large conference center.

🛏 232 ❄ ⬛ ⬛ 🂠 AE, DC, MC, V

🏨 MELIÁ CARIARI

$$$$
CIUDAD CARIARI, 5 MILES NW OF SAN JOSÉ
TEL 239-0022
FAX 239-2803
www.solmelia.com
A full-service resort with modern decor and full in-room services, midway between the city and the airport. Popular with groups. Tennis courts, two swimming pools, golf course, casino, lively bar, and choice of restaurants.

🛏 220 🅿 ❄ ⬛ 📺
🂠 All major cards

🏨 AMÓN PLAZA

$$$
AVE. 11 & CALLE 3 BIS
TEL 257-0191 OR 800/575-1253
FAX 257-0284
www.hotelamonplaza.com
A modern interpretation of a colonial period style in the historic Barrio Amón district, a 15-minute uphill walk to the city center. Business center, casino, and elegant restaurant.

🛏 90 ❄ ⬛ 📺 🂠 All major cards

🏨 BRITANNIA

$$$
CALLE 3 & AVE. 11
TEL 223-6667, 800/263-2618
FAX 223-6411
E-MAIL britannia@racsa.co.cr
This turn-of-the-20th-century mansion is complete with antiques, colonial tilework, and stained-glass. King-size beds are a new addition. The dining room is located in an old cellar.

🛏 24 ⬛ 🂠 AE, MC, V

(see p. 243)

SOMETHING SPECIAL

🏨 GRANO DE ORO

A Canadian-run hotel off Paseo Colón in a leafy district 20 minutes walk from downtown. Charming decor includes bathrooms adorned with hand-painted tiles. Peruvian artwork abounds and soothing music wafts through the narrow skylit corridors. Impeccable service highlights the top-notch restaurant, where nouvelle Costa Rican dishes are served indoors or on a patio. Reservations essential for rooms. Superb value.

$$$
CALLE 30, AVES. 2/4
TEL 255-3322
FAX 221-2782
www.hotelgranodeoro.com
🛏 32 rooms, 3 suites 🍴
🅿 🂠 AE, MC, V

🏨 HOTEL PALMA REAL

$$$
2 BLOCKS N OF THE I.C.E BUILDING
TEL 290-5060
FAX 290-4160
www.hotelpalmareal.com
This stylish business hotel west of downtown offers such amenities as wireless and high-speed Internet, business center, conference rooms, fitness room, a bar, and two restaurants. There are king-size beds and spa pools in suites.

🛏 65 🅿 ❄ ❄ ⬛
📺 🂠 AE, MC, V

🏨 TRYP COROBICÍ

$$$
CALLE 42, 50 YARDS N OF BULEVAR LAS AMÉRICAS
TEL 232-0618
FAX 231-5698
www.solmelia.com
This high-rise hotel stands on the northeast corner of Parque Sabana. Arranged around a steepled atrium, it has modern facilities including a casino, a nightclub, and spa.

🛏 202 🅿 ❄ ⬛ ⬛
⬛ 📺 ❄ 🂠 AE, MC, V

🏨 BALMORAL

$$
AVE. CENTRAL, CALLES 7/9
TEL 222-5022 OR 800/691-4865
www.balmoral.co.cr
Modern decor, an in-house casino, and on-site car rental and tour desk highlight this modest hotel. Rooms are small and rather noisy, but the location is good for exploring the city core. The restaurant is undistinguished.

🛏 112 ❄ ⬛ 📺 🂠 All major cards

HOTELS & RESTAURANTS

🏨 DON CARLOS
$$
CALLE 9 AT AVE. 9
TEL 221-6707
FAX 255-0828
www.doncarloshotel.com
A rambling converted colonial mansion with a homey ambience, in the heart of Barrio Amón. Stained glass, sculptures, and pre-Columbian treasures abound in public areas. Small restaurant.
ⓘ 36 🚫 All major cards

🏨 HOTEL FLEUR DE LYS
$$
CALLE 13, AVES. 2/6
TEL 223-1206
FAX 257-3637
www.fleurdelyshotel.com
A Swiss-owned hotel in a restored Victorian mansion. Rooms feature wicker and/or wrought-iron beds and pastel walls. Rates include tropical breakfast. French restaurant.
ⓘ 31 🚫 AE, MC, V

🏨 HOTEL 1492
$$
AVE. 1, CALLES 31/33
TEL 225-3752
www.hotel1492.com
A quaint hotel in a charming colonial home in quiet Barrio Escalante. The decor features tile mosaics. Evening wine and cheese on a garden patio.
ⓘ 10 🅿 🚫 🚫 MC, V

🏨 HOTEL OCCIDENTAL TORREMOLINOS
$$
AVE. 5 & CALLE 40
TEL 222-5266
FAX 255-3167
www.occidental-hoteles.com
Well-appointed hotel, with decor on an Egyptian theme, situated near Parque Sabana. Courtesy bus to city center. Italian restaurant.
ⓘ 92 🅿 🚫 🚫 🚫 AE, MC, V

🏨 HOTEL MILVIA
$$
SAN PEDRO
TEL 225-4543
FAX 225-7801

www.hotelmilvia.com
Family-run guest house in a restored 1930s home, replete with antiques, hardwoods, and hand-painted tiles.
ⓘ 9 🚫 MC, V

🏨 HOTEL PRESIDENTE
$$
AVE. CENTRAL, CALLES 7/9
TEL 222-3022
FAX 221-1205
www.hotel-presidente.com
Modern amenities and array of services in this heart-of-downtown hotel make amends for the dowdy decor. Appealing restaurant. Casino.
ⓘ 110 🚫 🚫 🚫
🚫 All major cards

🏨 HOTEL VILLA TOURNON
$$
N BANK OF RÍO TORRES, 200 YARDS E OF CALLE 3
TEL 233-6622
FAX 222-5211
www.hotel-costa-rica.com
This modern hotel near the El Pueblo complex has contemporary art, and pools in the garden. Fireside dining.
ⓘ 80 🚫 🚫 🚫 🚫 AE, MC, V

🍴 LE BERGERAC
$$
CALLE 35, 50 YARDS S OF AVE. CENTRAL, LOS YOSES
TEL 234-7850
FAX 225-9103
www.bergerachotel.com
French provincial style pervades this family-run charmer situated in a quiet eastern suburb. Antique furnishings, modern art, business facilities and gourmet dining on a terrace.
ⓘ 19 🅿 🚫 AE, MC, V

🏨 SANTO TOMÁS
$$
AVE. 7, CALLES 3/5
TEL 255-0448
FAX 222-3950
www.hotelsantotomas..com
A small bed-and-breakfast in a centenarian home between Barrio Amón and downtown.

North American owner maintains high standards.
ⓘ 20 🚫 🚫 🚫 MC, V

🏨 GRAN HOTEL
$
AVE. 2, CALLES 1/3
TEL 256-8585
FAX 256-7575
www.granhotelcr.com
This hotel has a superb location on Plaza de la Cultura, and a lively outdoor café. Rooms are a bit dowdy. It has a 24-hour, no-frills lobby casino.
ⓘ 110 🅿 🚫 🚫 AE, MC, V

🏨 KAP'S PLACE
$
CALLE 19, AVE 11/12
TEL 221-1169
FAX 256-4850
www.kapsplace.com
Colorful, well-kept, and secure budget option is run to high standards. Guests get kitchen privileges in this rambling former home.
ⓘ 16 🅿 🚫 🚫 AE, MC, V

RESTAURANTS

🍴 BAKÉA
$$$$
CALLE 7, AVE. 11
TEL 221-1051
Contemporary decor and creative nouvelle cuisine draw the cognoscenti to this small restaurant with theme rooms. The best of fine dining, albeit small menu and portions.
🕐 Closed Sun., Mon. p.m., & Sat. lunch 🚫 🚫 AE, MC, V

🍴 SAKURA
$$$
HOTEL HERRADURA, CARRETERRA AEROPUERTO
TEL 239-0033, EXT 258
FAX 239-2292
Japanese ambience and acclaimed Teppani-style cuisine. Sushi bar.
🅿 🚫 🚫 🚫 AE, MC, V

🍴 ANTOJITOS
$$
600 YARDS W OF PARQUE SABANA
TEL 225-9525

Classic Mexican staples, such as grilled tenderloin. Mariachis sometimes entertain.

P 🅢 🅢 🅢 AE, MC, V

🍴 LA BASTILLE
$$
PASEO COLÓN AT CALLE 22
TEL 255-4994
This French restaurant is popular with San José's social elite. Elegant ambience and dependable food.
🕐 Closed Sun. P 🅢
🅢 MC, V

🍴 LE CHANDELIER
$$
100 YARDS W & 100 YARDS S OF I.C.E. BUILDING, S. PEDRO
TEL 225-3980
Choose from ten dining areas in this colonial mansion. The nouvelle Costa Rican cuisine is inspired by French classics. Superb artwork decorates the walls.
🕐 Closed Sun. P 🅢
🅢 MC, V

🍴 EL CHICOTE
$$
BULEVAR LAS AMÉRICAS, 400 YARDS W OF I.C.E. BUILDING
TEL 232-0936
Interesting dishes such as shrimp-stuffed tenderloin and honey-basted filet mignon are cooked over an open grill and served amid effusive foliage.
P 🅢 🅢 MC, V

🍴 LUBNAN
$$
PASEO COLÓN, CALLES 22/24
TEL 257-6071
Lebanese specialties such as *kafta naie* (marinated ground beef), kabobs, and falafels. Elegant decor, modest prices.
P 🕐 Closed Sun. 🅢
🅢 MC, V

🍴 JÜRGEN'S GRILL
$$
CALLE 41, 200 METERS N OF AVE. CENTRAL, SAN PEDRO
TEL 283-2239
Hip comes to San José in this upscale, contemporary eatery with a bold aesthetic and

splendid nouvelle cuisine. Celebrate your fine dining experience with a nightcap at the cigar bar.
🕐 Closed Sun. 🅢 🅢 AE, MC, V

🍴 TIN JO
$$
CALLE 11, AVE 6/8
TEL 221-7605
Unpretentious ambience and filling meals at fair prices for Asian fare from sushi and Szechuan to Indian and Thai.
🅢 🅢 🅢 MC, V

🍴 BALCÓN DE EUROPA
$
CALLE 9, AVES. CENTRAL/1
TEL 221-4841
The paneled walls provide a warm ambience for this classic Italian restaurant serving a selection of traditional pastas, steaks, and seafood. Founding Chef Franco died recently, but the standards remain.
🕐 Closed Sat. 🅢 🅢 MC, V

🍴 COCINA DE LEÑA
$
EL PUEBLO COMMERCIAL CENTER
TEL 225-1360 OR 256-5353
The best of traditional *campesino*-style fare such as *olla de carne* soup and *tamales* wrapped in a plantain leaf.
P 🕐 Closed L 🅢
🅢 MC, V

🍴 FLOR DE LOTO
$
CALLE LOISA, 50 YARDS E OF I.C.E. BUILDING, SABANA NORTE
TEL 232-4652
This restaurant serves up a selection of spicy Hunan and Szechuan fare.
P 🅢 🅢 MC, V

🍴 KING'S GARDEN
$
CENTRO COMERCIAL YOAHAN, AUTOPISTA GENERAL CAÑAS
TEL 255-3838
E-MAIL kingsgarden
@orbitcostarica.com
A popular, elegant restaurant

that specializes in Cantonese and Szechuan dishes.
P 🅢 🅢 🅢 AE, MC, V

🍴 MACHU PICHU
$
CALLE 23, AVES. 1/3
TEL 222-7384
E-MAIL machupichu
@orbitcostarica.com
Peruvian seafood such as garlic octopus, *picante de mariscos* (spicy seafood casserole), and ceviches.
P 🕐 Closed Sun. 🅢
🅢 AE, MC, V

🍴 RESTAURANTE LUKAS
$
EL PUEBLO COMMERCIAL CENTER
TEL 257-7124
Traditional Costa Rican fare grilled on an open hearth. Specialties include *corvina* (sea bass) in garlic butter).
P 🕐 Never closes
🅢 MC, V

🍴 RESTAURANTE VISHNU
$
AVE 1, CALLES 1/3
TEL 256-6063
Popular vegetarian restaurant with several other outlets. Salads, veggie burgers, and fruit juices are on the menu.
🕐 Sun. lunch 🅢 🅢 🅢 V

🍴 SPOON
$
AVE CENTRAL, CALLES 5/7
TEL 224-0328
A bargain with various outlets. Salads, submarines, plus delicious baked goods.
🅢 🅢

CENTRAL HIGHLANDS

ALAJUELA

SOMETHING SPECIAL

🏨 XANDARI RESORT AND SPA VILLAGE
Contemporary boutique hotel with villas and an innovative

tropical spa complex sits atop a ridge overlooking coffee fields and the Central Valley. Stunning architecture and stylish furnishings. Trails lead to waterfalls. TV/video lounge. Macrobiotic nouvelle Costa Rican meals served on the dining terrace. The spa village complex includes five jacuzzis, treatment rooms, yoga, and physical fitness room.

$$$$
TACACORI, 3 MILES N OF ALAJUELA
TEL 443-2020 OR 800/686-7879
FAX 442-4847
www.xandari.com
📶 18 villas, 1 studio 🅿
🏊 📺 🚭 AE, MC, V

🏨 PURA VIDA BED & BREAKFAST
$$$
TUETAL NORTE, 3 MILES N OF ALAJUELA
TEL/FAX 441-1157
www.puravidahotel.com
Surrounded by lush gardens, this intimate inn has individually themed cottages. Run by a delightful North American couple, who serve gourmet meals.
📶 7 🅿 🔌 🏊 🚭 MC, V

🏨 ORQUÍDEAS INN
$$
1 MILE W OF S. JOSÉ DE ALAJUELA
TEL 433-9346
FAX 433-9740
www.orquideasinn.com
Set on lush grounds with mountain vistas, this charming, unpretentious boutique hotel has an eclectic choice of rooms, suites, and a skylit geodesic dome. Lively Marilyn Monroe bar.
📶 27 🅿 🔌 🏊 🚭 AE, MC, V

🍴 JAULARES
$
4 MILES N OF ALAJUELA
TEL/FAX 482-2155
E-MAIL restjaulares@racsa.co.cr
Experience a traditional country atmosphere in an alpine setting. Hearty

campesino fare is prepared on an open wood-burning stove, and *refrescos* are created from fresh locally grown fruits.
🅿 🚭 None

ATENAS

🏨 EL CAFETAL INN
$$
SANTA EULALIA, 3 MILES N OF ATENAS
TEL 446-5785
FAX 446-7028
www.cafetal.com
Charming live-in hosts run this homey boutique option on gracious grounds on a working coffee farm. Tours and massages are offered. Inventive meals served in the glass-paneled dining room or on the terrace with fine views.
📶 10 🅿 🏊 🚭 AE, MC, V

🍴 MIRADOR DEL CAFETAL
$$
4 MILES W OF ATENAS
TEL 446-7361
Colorful roadside restaurant splendidly situated over coffee fields with views towards Nicoya. Creative menu offers Central American dishes.
🅿 🔌 🚭 MC, V

ESCAZÚ

🏨 THE ALTA HOTEL
🍴 $$$$$
ALTO LAS PALOMAS, 2 MILES W OF SAN RAFAEL DE ESCAZÚ
TEL 282-4160 OR 888-388-2582
FAX 282-4162
www.thealtahotel.com
A tasteful Mediterranean-style hotel with views over the valley. La Luz Restaurant serves stylish continental/Costa Rican cuisine.
📶 23 🅿 🔌 ⬆ 🏊 📺 🔌 🚭 AE, MC, V

🏨 WHITE HOUSE RESTAURANT CASINO & SPA
$$$$$
SAN ANTONIO DE ESCAZÚ
TEL 288-6362
FAX 288-6365

www.whitehousecostarica.com
This Southern-style plantation above the Central Valley boasts cavernous guest rooms and newer two-bedroom villas filled with gracious furnishings. The Capital Grill restaurant offers spectacular views. Cigar bar. Helicopter tours.
📶 15 rooms 🅿 🏊 📺 🚭 MC, V

🏨 REAL
🍴 INTERCONTINENTAL
$$$$
AUTOPISTA PROSPERO FERNÁNDEZ, 2 MILES NW OF SAN RAFAEL DE ESCAZÚ
TEL 208-2100
FAX 208-2101
www.iccostarica.gruporeal.com
Deluxe hotel with huge rooms and warm, charming decor. Executive floor, business center, travel agency, and upscale shops. The Restaurant Mirage serves French cuisine.
📶 261 🅿 🔌 ⬆ 🏊 📺 🔌 🚭 AE, MC, V

🏨 HOTEL SANGILDAR
🍴 $$$
SAN RAFAEL DE ESCAZÚ
TEL 289-8843
FAX 228-6454
www.hotelsangildar.com
Contemporary Spanish-style

hotel with stylish modern furnishings. Fine continental dining and classical music in the Terraza del Sol restaurant.
1 27 **P** ❄ ⛱ 🚭
💳 AE, MC, V

🏨 CASA DE LAS TÍAS
$$
SAN RAFAEL DE ESCAZÚ
TEL 289-5517
FAX 289-7353
www.hotels.co.cr/casatias.html
Endearing and colorful family-run bed-and-breakfast in a wood-paneled plantation-style home close to central Escazú. Breakfast is served on patio.
1 5 **P** 💳 All major cards

LA GARITA

🏨 MARTINO RESORT & SPA
$$$$
TEL 433-8382
FAX 433-9052
www.hotelmartino.com
Vast grounds with tennis and squash courts, a gym and jogging track surround a Romanesque villa boasting huge rooms, a casino, bars, a spa, and gourmet Italian food.
1 42 **P** ❄ ⛱ 🏋
💳 AE, MC, V

🍴 DELICIAS DEL MAÍZ
$
TEL 433-7206
Traditional corn-based dishes such as tamales and *chorreadas* (corn fritters) from the open grill, are served in atmospheric surroundings based on a traditional theme.
P 💳 None

LOS ANGELES CLOUD FOREST RESERVE

🏨 VILLABLANCA CLOUD 🍴 FOREST HOTEL & SPA
$$$
6 MILES NE OF LOS ANGELES NORTE
TEL 461-0300
FAX 461-0302
www.villablanca-costarica.com
An enchanting ecolodge on the Continental Divide, at the

edge of a cloud forest. Graciously appointed cottages have log fires. Wedding chapel, spa, and nature activities that include guided hikes and horseback riding.
1 42 rooms **P** 🚭
💳 All major cards

MONTE DE LA CRUZ

🏨 HOTEL CHALET TIROL 🍴 $$
TEL 267-6222
FAX 267-6229
E-MAIL info@chalet-tirol.com
Accessed only by horse or by guided hike is a cozy Tyrolean lodge situated on the edge of cloud forest. Choose from modern rooms or rustic cabins. The French restaurant serves dishes such as shrimp in a fennel Pernod sauce.
1 30 **P** ⛱ 🏋 💳 AE, MC, V

PIEDADES

🏨 POSADA CANAL GRANDE
$$
TEL 282-4089 OR 282-4101
FAX 282-5733
www.hotelcanalgrande.com
A luxurious place, with parquet floors in the guest rooms, antiques, leather sofas, and flowers in the lounge. The hotel is surrounded by coffee fields and has an Italian restaurant. Breakfast included.
1 12 **P** ⛱ 💳 AE, MC, V

POÁS

🏨 PEACE LODGE
Stunning, one-of-a-kind decor combines sensually rustic elements with luxury in cavernous rooms on the edge of Braulio Carrillo National Park. Natural stone Jacuzzis and cave-like bathrooms evoke the Flintstones, but the effect is quite romantic enhanced by canopy beds. The amenities and activities of La Paz Waterfall Gardens are at hand.
$$$$$

MONTAÑA AZUL, 3 MILES N OF VARA BLANCA
TEL 225-0643
FAX 225-1082
www.waterfallgardens.com
1 17 **P** ❄ 💳 AE, MC, V

🏨 POÁS VOLCANO LODGE
$$
VARA BLANCA DE HEREDIA
TEL 482-2194
FAX 482-2513
www.poasvolcanolodge.com
Superb location between Barva and Poás volcanoes. This mountain lodge on a cattle farm offers no-frills charm, with a log fire in the timber-beamed lounge. Basic meals; rates include farmhouse breakfast. Some shared baths.
1 9 💳 AE, MC, V

🍴 RESTAURANT COLBERT
$$$
VARA BLANCA DE HEREDIA
TEL 482-2776
Straddling the Continental Divide, with fine views, this airy modern restaurant-bakery serves croissants, pastries, etc., plus nouvelle Costa Rican fare with a French twist.
P 🚭 💳 MC, V

ROSARIO

🏨 VISTA DEL VALLE PLANTATION INN
Hints of Frank Lloyd Wright in a timber-beamed lodge with plate-glass all around, situated at the heart of a citrus and coffee farm overlooking the Río Grande Canyon Preserve. The landscaped grounds feature a stable, and guided hikes are offered. Cottages are tastefully ascetic in Japanese style. Inspired nouvelle dishes are served on an outdoor terrace.
$$$$
ROSARIO, 2 MILES W OF INTER-AMERICAN HWY.

HOTELS & RESTAURANTS

TEL 450-0800
TEL/FAX 451-1165 OR 450-0800
www.vistadelvalle.com
🛈 9 cottages 🅿 ▨ 🚫V

SABANA REDONDA

🍽 LAS FRESAS
$$$
11 MILES N OF ALAJUELA
TEL 482-2620
On the slopes of the Poás
volcano, this elegant
restaurant serves gourmet
Italian. Expansive wine list. The
delightful ambience is
enhanced by a huge log fire.
🅿 🚫 🏷AE, MC, V

SALISPUEDES

🏨 FINCA EDDIE SERRANO
$$
PAN-AM HWY KM 70
TEL 381-8456
Ideal for spotting quetzals, this
rustic lodge with simple cabins
sits on the edge of a cloud
forest. Simple meals are
served. Birding is a specialty.
Fabulous views.
🛈 14 🅿

SAN GERARDO DE DOTA

🏨 TROGON LODGE
$$
TEL 29398-8181
FAX 239-7657
www.grupomawamba.com
Nestled in a deep mountain
valley, this gracious lodge
provides a perfect base for
both birding and trout fishing.
Rustic hardwood cabins sit
over a brook and trout pond.
Simple meals are provided.
🛈 10 🅿 🏷DC, MC, V

SANTA ANA

🍽 LE MONASTÈRE
$$$
IN THE HILLS ABOVE STA. ANA
TEL 289-4404
www.monastere-restaurant.com
The waiters are dressed as

monks in this converted
chapel! The menu offers
French-inspired cuisine such
as grilled lamb chops, together
with a big wine list. Enjoy the
views over the valley.
🅿 🕐 Closed L & all Sun.
🚫 🏷 All major cards

SANTA BARBARA DE HEREDIA

SOMETHING SPECIAL

🏨 FINCA ROSA BLANCA COUNTRY INN
Designed as a private home and
inspired by Gaudí and the
Santa Fe style, this exquisite
boutique hotel offers eclectic
decor. It is set on a working coffee
farm with views over the valley,
and its own stable. The inventive
gourmet cuisine uses local
ingredients. Reservations essential.
Full breakfast included.
$$$$
0.75 MILE NE OF SANTA
BARBARA DE HEREDIA
TEL 269-9392
FAX 269-9555
www.fincarosablanca.com
🛈 7 suites, 2 cottages 🍽
🅿 ▨ 🏷AE, MC, V

SANTO DOMINGO DE HEREDIA

🏨 BOUGAINVILLEA
🍽 $$
0.6 MILE E OF STO. DOMINGO
TEL 244-1414
FAX 244-1313
www.bougainvillea.co.cr
Set on landscaped grounds
containing tennis courts, is this
modern hotel with engaging
modern art. The elegant
restaurant serves popular
Sunday brunch.
🛈 80 🅿 ⬆ 🚫 ▨
🏷AE, MC, V

TURRIALBA

🏨 CASA TURIRE
$$$
8 MILES SE OF TURRIALBA
TEL 531-1111
FAX 531-1075

www.hotelcasaturire.com
Large comfortable rooms in
this clean, award-winning
modern hotel with classical
hints. Situated on a working
plantation, it offers horseback
rides, biking, rafting, and tours.
Edwardian bar. Excellent
cuisine served on the patio.
🛈 16 🅿 🚫 ▨ 🏷AE,
MC, V

GUANACASTE

CAÑAS

🍽 RESTAURANTE RINCÓN COROBICÍ
$
INTER-AMERICAN HWY., 4.5
MILES N OF CAÑAS
TEL 669-6262
Diners can watch rafters far
below floating on the Río
Corobicí. Seafood specialties
include *corvina ajillo* (sea bass
in garlic), and *comida típica* is
also served. Renowned for its
refreshing lemonades.
🅿 🚫 🏷None

LA CRUZ

🏨 LOS INOCENTES LODGE
$$
HWY. 4, 10 MILES E OF INTER-
AMERICAN HWY.
TEL 679-9190
FAX 679-9224
www.losinocenteslodge.com
Volcán Orosí towers over this
ecolodge which specializes in
horseback tours. The meagerly
furnished guest rooms have
shared bathrooms. Lots of
wildlife viewing. Family-style
dining on a veranda.
🛈 11 rooms, 12 bungalows
🅿 🚫 ▨ 🏷AE, MC, V

LAGUNA DE ARENAL

🏨 ARENAL LODGE
$$$$
13 MILES W OF FORTUNA
TEL 460-1881
FAX 460-6119
www.arenallodge.com
Atmospheric mountain lodge

---

with volcano views. Large lounge bar with stone hearth offers the best vistas. Library, TV lounge, and pool table. Sportfishing is offered, as are tours. Rates include buffet breakfast, use of mountain bikes, Jacuzzi, and trails.

1 34 **P** **AE, MC, V**

🏨 HOTEL LA MANSION INN
$$$$
5 MILES N OF NUEVO ARENAL
TEL 692-8018
FAX 692-8019
www.lamaisonarenal.com
A magnificent hillside setting overlooking the lake plus exquisite decor in 14 *cabinas*, a horizon swimming pool, and rustic yet charming bar/restaurant. Horseback rides, rowboats, and canoes offered.

1 14 **P** **S** **≋** **MC, V**

🏨 ARENAL OBSERVATORY LODGE
$$
1.5 MILES SE OF VOLCÁN ARENAL
TEL 692-2070 OR 290-7011
FAX 290-8427
www.arenal-observatory.com
Mountainside lodge offering up-close views of Volcán Arenal. Accommodations vary from no-frills budget dorms to spacious and elegant suites, plus a farmhouse villa. Some rooms are handicapped accessible. Horseback riding, free volcano tour, pool and Jacuzzi, trails. Family-style meals.

1 37 **P** **≋** **AE, MC, V**

🏨 ARENAL VISTA LODGE
$$
S SIDE OF LAKE ARENAL, 1.5 MILES W OF PUEBLO NUEVO
TEL 692-2079
FAX 221-6320
www.arenalvistalodge.com
This quaint lodge has lake views and a private forest. Scandinavian-style cabins have picture windows. Four-wheel drive recommended.

1 25 **P** **S** **≋** **AE, MC, V**

🏨 CHALET NICHOLAS
$$
HWY. 142, 1.5 MILES W OF NUEVO ARENAL
TEL 694-4041
www.chaletnicholas.com
This charming, cozy guest house is run by North American hosts. Rooms boast a combination of orthopedic mattresses and volcano views, and the upstairs bedroom is reached via a spiral staircase. Hiking and horseback rides are offered. Healthy meals a treat.

1 3 **P** **S** **None**

🏨 VILLA DECARY
$$
HWY. 142, 1.5 MILES E OF NUEVO ARENAL
TEL 383-3012
FAX 694-4330
www.villadecary.com
Charming country inn backed by rain forest accessed by trails. Large guest rooms have Guatemalan covers, balconies, and lake views. Gracious North American hosts serve breakfasts, included in rates.

1 5 rooms, 3 bungalows
P **S** **None**

🍴 RESTAURANT WILLY'S CABALLO NEGRO
$$
1 MILE W OF NUEVO ARENAL
TEL 694-4515
This German-run bakery and restaurant sits over a pond with geese. Its European menu runs from sausages and schnitzel to veal, plus some vegetarian options.

P **S** **None**

🍴 TOAD HALL
$
HWY. 142, 3 MILES E OF NUEVO ARENAL
TEL 692-8020
Delicatessen, gift store, and café perched above the lake. Views can be enjoyed from a terrace with granola and banana pancake breakfasts, california lunches" such as grilled sesame chicken salad. Awesome desserts.

P **None**

LIBERIA

🍴 RESTAURANTE PASO REAL
$$
AVENIDA CENTRAL, CALLES CENTRAL & 2
TEL 666-3455
This clean, spacious modern restaurant-sports bar has a huge seafood menu of well-prepared dishes, plus *casados* (set meals). Balcony overlooks plaza. large-screen TV.

S **S** **V**

MONTEVERDE

🏨 MONTEVERDE LODGE
🍴 **$$$**
TEL 257-0766, 645-5057
FAX 257-1665, 645-5129
www.costaricaexpeditions.com
An eccentric modern design maximizes light in this upscale brick-and-timber nature lodge. A mezzanine bar with a fireplace and view of a glass-enclosed spa pool is a lively social center. Spacious guest rooms offer fine vistas. Birds abound on the landscaped grounds. Rates include meals.

1 27 **P** **AE, MC, V**

🏨 BELMAR
$$
TEL 645-5201
FAX 645-5135
www.hotelbelmar.com
This alpine lodge, set on a hillside has clean, wood-paneled guest rooms with wide balconies providing superb sunset views. Dine in or out at the popular continental restaurant.

1 34 **P** **S** **V**

🏨 EL SOL RETREAT & SPA
$$
3 MILES S OF SANTA ELENA
TEL 645-5398
FAX 645-5042
www.elsolnuestro.com
Rustic mountain cottages run by an erudite and charming couple who run this as a holistic retreat. Horizon pool, sauna, and horseback rides.

1 3 **P** **≋**

HOTELS & RESTAURANTS

🏨 HELICONIA
$$
TEL 645-5109
FAX 645-5135
www.hotelhelicona.com
This lodge has modern fixtures in modestly furnished rooms with balconies. Spa pool. Trails into a private reserve. Continental and local favorites in the restaurant.
🛏 33 🅿 🚭V

🏨 EL SAPO DORADO
🍴 **$$**
TEL 645-5010
FAX 645-5180
www.sapodorado.com
Awesome views from stone-and-timber cabins amid landscaped grounds. Units with fireplaces are preferred. Massages offered. Forest trail. Health food restaurant.
🛏 30 🅿 🚭AE, MC, V

RINCÓN DE LA VIEJA

🏨 HOTEL BORINQUEN MOUNTAIN RESORT THERMAE & SPA
$$$
8 MILES NE OF CAÑAS DULCES
TEL 690-1900
FAX 690-1903
www.borinquinresort.com
Mountain resort with cavernous rooms furnished in neocolonial style. A spa offers mud and thermal treatments, plus plunge pools. Horseback rides, ATV safaris, and hikes lead into surrounding forest. Decent restaurant.
🛏 50 🚭 🅿 🚭 🚭 🚭MC, V

🏨 POSADA EL ENCUENTRO INN
$$$
CURRUBANDÉ, 8 MILES NE OF LIBERIA
TEL/FAX 382-0815
Homey bed and breakfast with refreshing pastel decor and comfortable furnishings. Tremendous views over the Guanacaste plains from the pool deck. Closed April.
🛏 6 rooms, 2 bungalows
🅿 🚭 🚭MC, V

🏨 RINCÓN DE LA VIEJA LODGE
$$
OFF INTER-AMERICAN HWY., NEAR NATIONAL PARK
TEL/FAX 661-8198
www.rincondelaviejalodge.com
Perfect for exploring, this remote lodge on the western flank of Rincón has basic furnishings, a serpentarium, dairy, butterfly collection, and canopy tour. Four-wheel drive access. Rates include family-style meals.
🛏 50 🅿 🚭 🚭AE, MC, V

🏨 BUENA VISTA LODGE
$
8 MILES NE OF CAÑAS DULCES
TEL/FAX 661-8158
A real mountain hideaway on the slopes of Rincón. Stone and timber cabins amid lawns, with horseback rides, hikes, a canopy tour, thermal steam bath, and rustic restaurant.
🛏 77 🅿 🚭None

NICOYA

BAHÍA CULEBRA

SOMETHING SPECIAL

🏨 FOUR SEASONS RESORT AT PAPAGAYO PENINSULA
This large-scale deluxe hotel enjoys a dramatic location with spectacular views of the coastline. Sumptuous tropical-themed decor graces public areas and spacious accommodations (rooms or suites available) with balcony views. An Arnold Palmer-designed championship golf course is a major draw, as is the posh spa.
$$$$$
PUNTA MALA
TEL 696-000
FAX 696-0500
www.fourseasons.com/costarica
🛏 165 🅿 🚭 🚭 🚭 🚭 🚭All major credit cards

PRICES

HOTELS
An indication of the cost of a double room without breakfast is given by $ signs.
$$$$$	Over $200
$$$$	$150–$200
$$$	$100–$150
$$	$75–$100
$	Under $75

RESTAURANTS
An indication of the cost of a three-course dinner without drinks is given by $ signs.
$$$$$	Over $75
$$$$	$50–$75
$$$	$35–$50
$$	$20–$35
$	Under $20

🏨 OCCIDENTAL GRAND PAPAGAYO
$$$$
PLAYA BUENA
TEL 672-0193 OR 800/858-2258
FAX 672-0058
www.occidental-hoteles.com
Casually elegant cliffside resort with bungalows stylishly furnished. Suites are worth the premium. Activities include tennis, golf, and diving.
🛏 116 🅿 🚭 🚭 🚭 🚭 🚭All major credit cards

MONTEZUMA

🏨 EL SANO BANANO BEACH HOTEL
$$
0.5 MILE E OF MONTEZUMA
TEL/FAX 642-0068
E-MAIL elbanano@racsa.co.cr
Enjoying a secluded beachfront location, this eclectic place has bungalows and three-story units set amid landscaped foliage.
🛏 14 🚭 🚭

🏨 HOTEL HORIZONTES DE MONTEZUMA
$$$
1 MILE N OF MONTEZUMA
TEL/FAX 642-0534
www.horizontes-montezuma.com

Clinical whites bathe this well-run hilltop, plantation-style hotel with hammocks on broad verandas around an atrium court. Run with German efficiency, you can take Spanish classes here.
[i] 7 P ⊕ ≋ ⊗ MC, V

NOSARA

🏨 LAGARTA LODGE
$$
TEL 682-0035
FAX 682-0135
www.lagarta.com
German-run hilltop lodge with views north over the wetlands and along Ostional beach. Relaxed, no-frills ambience. Several trails lead to the estuary.
[i] 7 P ≋ ⊗ V

🍽 MARLIN BILL'S
$
TEL 682-0458
This unpretentious hillside eatery serves international favorites, from French onion soup and eggplant parmesan to New York strip steak.
⊕ Closed Sun. ⊗ None

PLAYA CARRILLO

🏨 SOUTHLAND GUANAMAR BEACH & SPORTFISHING RESORT
$$$$
TEL 656-0054
FAX 656-0001
www.southlandhotels.com
A dedicated sportfishing resort with hillside cottages. There is no beach, but this is more than compensated for by facilities that include small casino and activities such as watersports and riding.
[i] 41 P ⊕ ⊗ ≋
⊗ AE, MC, V

🏨 EL SUEÑO TROPICAL
🍽 $$
TEL 656-0151
FAX 656-0152
www.elsuenotropical.com
These tasteful bungalows are graced by hardwood touches.

The tropical gardens meld into rain forest teeming with wildlife. Classic Italian favorites such as *ravioli de pescado* are served in the thatched restaurant.
[i] 12 rooms, 3 apartments
P ⊕ ≋ ⊗ ⊗ AE, MC, V

PLAYA COCO

🏨 RANCHO ARMADILLO
$$$
TEL 670-0108
FAX 670-0441
www.ranchoarmadillo.com
Gracious Texan-run colonial hacienda with timber-beamed bungalows. Meals prepared on request by a former Culinary Arts instructor.
[i] 6 P ⊕ ≋ ⊗
⊗ MC, V

🏨 PUESTA DEL SOL
$
TEL 670-0195
FAX 670-0650
E-MAIL hotelsol@racsa.co.cr
A small, simple option with fashionably contemporary decor in Monet colors. Inventive cuisine in a tasteful open-air restaurant/café.
[i] 10 ⊗ P ≋ ⊡
⊗ AE, MC, V

PLAYA CONCHAL

🏨 PARADISUS PLAYA CONCHAL BEACH & GOLF RESORT
$$$$
TEL 654-4123 OR 800/336-3542
FAX 654-4181
www.solmelia.com
Huge upscale resort backing a white-sand beach. Spacious rooms with marble baths. Watersports, entertainment, tour services, restaurants, and great golf course.
[i] 310 P ⊕ ≋ ⊡
⊗ All major cards

PLAYA FLAMINGO

🏨 FLAMINGO BEACH RESORT
$$$$
TEL 654-4444

FAX 654-4060
www.resortflamingobeach.com
This recently upgraded full-service resort on a beach is centered on a vast swimming pool. Car rental and tour services. Modest decor.
[i] 91 P ⊕ ⊟ ⊗ ≋
⊡ ⊗ AE, MC, V

PLAYA GRANDE

🏨 HOTEL BULA BULA
🍽 $$$
TEL 653-0975
FAX 653-0491
www.hotelbulabula.com
Trendily yet simply furnished, with lively pastels, this boutique hotel nestles between the beach and *estero*. Gourmet fusion cuisine served at the Great Waltini's open-air restaurant.
[i] 10 P ≋ ⊗ All major credit cards

🏨 LAS TORTUGAS
🍽 $$$
TEL 653-0423 OR 653-0458
FAX 653-0458
www.tamarindo.com/tortugas
Popular with surfers, this pioneering eco-sensitive hotel is perfect for spotting nesting leatherback turtles at night. The restaurant combines contemporary West Coast cooking with local flavors.
[i] 11 ⊗ P ≋ ⊗ V

PLAYA HERMOSA

🏨 VILLA DEL SUEÑO
$$$$
TEL/FAX 672-0026
www.villasdelsueno.com
An intimate colonial-style hotel with modern touches, arranged around a courtyard pool. The Canadian owners conjure up recherché dishes that are served outside.
[i] 7 P ⊕ ≋ ⊗ AE, MC, V

🏨 LA FINISTERRA
$$
TEL 670-0293
FAX 672-0227
www.finisterra.net

HOTELS & RESTAURANTS

A small contemporary property with live-in owners. The hilltop setting catches the breezes, and rooms open onto a terrace inset with a pool. The restaurant is renown for its cuisine.
🏨 10 🅿 🏊 🚭 🆎 AE, MC, V

PLAYA OCOTAL

🏨 OCOTAL BEACH RESORT
$$$
TEL 670-0321
FAX 670-1122
www.ocotalresort.com
Spacious rooms in a hilltop setting with ocean vistas. A scuba-diving and sportfishing resort with horseback riding, tour services, tennis courts, and a choice of restaurants.
🏨 52 🅿 🚭 🏊 🆎 All major cards

🏨 VILLA CASA BLANCA
$$
TEL 670-0518
FAX 670-0448
E-MAIL vblanca@racsa.co.cr
This deluxe bed-and-breakfast boasts four-poster beds and stenciled murals in the bedrooms. Gleaming bathrooms have wall-to-wall mirrors The garden contains sheltered gazebos where buffets and grills are served.
🏨 15 🅿 🚭 🏊 🆎 All major cards

🍴 FATHER ROOSTER RESTAURANT
$
TEL 670-0321
This is a rustic shore-front eatery serving seafood, burgers, and similar dishes. It has an appealing offbeat ambience, and its own beach volleyball court gets lively.
🚭 None

PLAYA TAMBOR

🏨 TANGO MAR
$$$$
HWY. 160, 3 MILES SW OF TAMBOR

TEL 683-0001
FAX 683-0003
www.tangomar.com
Set splendidly on the water, Tango Mar boasts stilt-legged hardwood cabins, spacious rooms, or villas. There's a nine-hole golf course.
🏨 37 🅿 🚭 🏊 🚭 All major cards

PUNTA ISLITA

🏨 HOTEL PUNTA ISLITA OCEAN RESORT SPA & VILLAS
$$$$
TEL 290-4259
FAX 231-0715
www.hotelpuntaislita.com
Santa Fe-style architecture and luxurious furnishings in individual casitas, which have a commanding hilltop setting. Cliff-face pool, activities, and restaurant serving nouvelle Costa Rican dishes.
🏨 20 bungalows, 9 suites, 5 villas 🅿 🚭 🏊 📺 🆎 All major cards

SAMARÁ

🍴 EL DELPHIN
$$
TEL 656-0418
For a touch of the French Riviera, try this beachfront eatery. Salad niçoise, pastas, pizzas, and tempting desserts. Jazz and candlelight.
🚭 None

SANTA TERESA

🏨 HOTEL FLOR BLANCA
Infused with a Balinese motif, this calming resort sprawls over 7 acres of beachfront. Spacious, romantic villas feature outdoor showers and sumptuous furnishings. The gourmet outdoor Nectar Bar & Restaurant serves Pacific fusion cuisine. Large-screen TV lounge is good for rainy days.
$$$$$
3 MILES N OF MALPAÍS

TEL 640-0232
FAX 640-0226
www.florblanca.com
🏨 10 🅿 🚭 🏊 🆎 All major credit cards

TAMARINDO

🏨 CALA LUNA HOTEL & VILLAS
$$$$
PLAYA LANGOSTA
TEL 653-0214
FAX 653-0213
www.calaluna.com
Regal, intimate property in Southwest style. Choose from rooms or villas with pools. Sportfishing and tours offered.
🏨 20 rooms. 21 villas 🅿 🚭 🏊 🆎 AE, MC, V

🏨 CAPITÁN SUIZO
An elegant resort with rooms and bungalows set round a pool. Howler monkeys live in the treetops. The restaurant serves nouvelle creations.
$$$$
TEL 653-0075
FAX 653-0292
www.captainsuizo.com
🏨 22 rooms, 8 bungalows 🅿 🚭 🏊 🆎 AE, MC, V

🏨🍴 JARDÍN DEL EDÉN
$$$$
TEL 653-0137
FAX 653-0111
www.jardindeleden.com
Stylish, European-run hotel with landscaped gardens studded with artistic pools and a floodlit spa pool. Seafood specialties are served in a thatched-roof restaurant.
🏨 20 🅿 🚭 🏊 📺 🆎 AE, MC

🏨 VILLA ALEGRE BED & BREAKFAST
$$$
TEL 653-0270
FAX 653-0287
E-MAIL vialegre@racsa.co.cr
This beachside villa is a

charming hotel run with style by gregarious North American expats who specialize in arranging and hosting honeymoons. Individually decorated rooms play an international calliope. Pool, honor bar.

🛈 4 🅿 🚫 🛗 🌊 🌊 MC, V

🍴 STELLA'S FINE DINING
$$$
TEL 653-0127
Aptly named, this thatched restaurant serves gourmet nouvelle cuisine.
🕐 Closed Sat. 🅿 🚫 🌊 MC, V

🍴 LAZY WAVE
$$
TEL 653-0737
www.lazywave.com
Rustic wooden decor around a tree-trunk beneath a shade tarp belies the high-standard Pacific fusion fare.
🕐 Closed Sun. 🌊 No credit cards

BRUNCA COAST

🏨 VILLAS GAIA
$$
PLAYA TORTUGA
TEL 363-3929
FAX 256-9996
www.villasgaia.com
Wooden bungalows feature attractive contemporary decor. Trails lead to rain forest and mangroves. Kayaking, snorkeling, and scuba-diving trips, fishing, and hiking.
🛈 12 bungalows 🅿 🌊 🌊 AE, MC, V

DOMINICAL

🏨 HACIENDA BARÚ NWR & ECOLODGE
$$
2 KM N OF RÍO BARÚ BRIDGE, COASTAL HWY.
TEL 787-0003
FAX 787-0057
www.haciendabaru.com

Renowned for its nature reserve, this hacienda is ideal for wildlife viewing. Choose between the simple two-bedroom cabins or house rental. The restaurant serves Italian and local fare. A variety of tours can be arranged.
🛈 6 🅿 🌊 AE, MC, V

JACÓ

🏨 BEST WESTERN JACÓ BEACH RESORT
$$$
AVE. PASTOR DIAZ
TEL 643-1000 OR 800/528-1234
FAX 643-3246
www..bestwestern.com
Large rooms with modern furnishings are situated on the edge of the beach. Full range of services and activities, and adequate fare is served in El Muelle restaurant.
🛈 125 🅿 🚫 🛗 🌊 🌊 All major cards

🍴 LIGHTHOUSE POINT STEAK & SEAFOOD HOUSE
$$
COAST HWY. AT JCT. FOR JACÓ
TEL 643-3083
This lively spot boasts a splendid ambience and a menu spanning the spectrum from hearty American breakfasts to crocodile nuggets. The eclectic decor is straight from a '60s surfing movie. Open 24 hours.
🅿 🌊 MC, V

🍴 PACIFIC BISTRO
$$$
CALLE LAS PALMERAS & AV PASTOR DÍAZ
TEL 643-3083
Mouth-watering Asia-Pacific dishes from a U.S. chef make a visit to this tiny spot worth it.
🕐 Closed Mon. & Tues. 🚫 🌊 None

MANUEL ANTONIO

🏨 LA MARIPOSA
$$$$
2.5 MILES S OF QUEPOS
TEL 777-0355

FAX 777-0050
www.hotelmariposa.com
Unsurpassed coastal vistas. Accommodations range from cottages that hug the cliff's face to junior suites with spa pools, plus contemporary suites and penthouses. available. Creative French cuisine is served.
🛈 22 🅿 🚫 🛗 🌊 MC, V

🏨 MAKANDA BY THE SEA
🍴 $$$$
3.5 MILES S OF QUEPOS
TEL 777-0442
FAX 777-1032
www.makanda.com
Japanese-inspired studios and villas tucked into Japanese gardens. Cliffside pool. The nouvelle cuisine is said to be region's best. Extensive wine list. Reservations essential.
🛈 6 villas, 4 studios 🅿 🌊 🌊 AE, MC, V

🏨 SI COMO NO
🍴 $$$$
2 MILES S OF QUEPOS
TEL 777-0777
FAX 777-1093
www.sicomono.com
Avant-garde design and decor, with split-level, all-suite villas around a dramatic pool and cascade. The state-of-the-art theater shows first-run movies and camp classics. Shops, a conference center, and two acclaimed eateries.
🛈 70 🅿 🚫 🌊 🌊 AE,MC, V

🏨 TULEMAR BUNGALOWS
$$$$
2.5 MILES S OF QUEPOS
TEL 777-0580
FAX 777-1579
www.tulemar.com
A villa, deluxe rooms, and octagonal bungalows with picture windows and modern furnishings in a secluded setting with trails. Breakfast and snacks only, but restaurants are close by.
🛈 14 bungalows, 1 villa 🅿 🌊 🌊 AE, MC, V

⊞ TRES BANDERAS
$$
1 MILE S OF QUEPOS
TEL 777-1521
FAX 777-1478
www.hotel-tres-banderas.com
Popular hotel run by Polish owners, with pleasant decor and both a pool and a spa pool. There is a bar-grill, where ceviche and *bigos* (sauerkraut and meats) are served.
🛏 14 🅿 ⊠ ⊠ ⊠ AE, MC, V

OJOCHAL

🍴 EXÓTICA CAFÉ
$$
2 MILES E OF PLAYA TORTUGA
TEL 369-9261
Surprisingly exotic and accomplished tropical nouvelle cuisine is dished up at this tiny, open-air eatery.
🕘 Closed Sun. ⊠ None

PARRITA

⊞ TIMARI ACTION SPORTS RESORT
$$$
ISLA PLAYA SECO
TEL 200-5335
FAX 779-9426
www.timari.com
Set amid palms, this beachfront resort, constructed of bamboo and hardwood, specializes in adventures. Spacious rooms feature TVs and other modern conveniences. Activities include paragliding, kitesurfing, and kayaking.
🛏 5 🅿 ⊠ ⊠ MC, V

PLAYA HERMOSA

⊞ TERRAZA DEL PACIFICO
$$
HWY. 34, 1 MILE S OF JACÓ
TEL 643-3222
FAX 643-3424
www.terraza-del-pacifico.com
This specialized surf hotel and restaurant is tucked beneath cliffs, with miles of beach to the south. It offers genteel decor combined with a

modicum of facilities, which include a small casino.
🛏 43 🅿 ⊠ ⊠ ⊠ AE, MC, V

PLAYA HERRADURA

⊞ LOS SUEÑOS MARRIOTT OCEAN & GOLF RESORT
$$$$$
TEL 637-8886
FAX 637-8895
www.lossuenosresort.com
This deluxe beachfront resort provides access to an 18-hole golf course, a spa, tennis courts, watersports, a 250-slip marina, and a choice of restaurants, bars, and lounges.
🛏 201 🅿 ⊠ ⊟ ⊠ ⊠ ⊠ All major cards

⊞ VILLA CALETAS
Lavishly furnished rooms and hillside villas in a stunning clifftop setting. The two restaurants serve Costa Rican fare with a French twist. Horizon pool and classical amphitheater for concerts.
$$$$
HWY. 34, 3 MILES N OF JACÓ
TEL 637-0606
FAX 637-0404
www.villacaletas.com
🛏 18 rooms, 11 villas 🅿 ⊠ ⊠ ⊠ AE, MC, V

🍴 STEVE N' LISA'S PARADISE COVE
$
HWY. 34
TEL 637-0168
Burgers, tuna melts, and other favorites in a beachfront setting. Food is served in a friendly atmosphere.
⊠ None

QUEPOS

🍴 EL GRAN ESCAPE RESTAURANT & FISHHEAD BAR
$
TEL 777-0395

PRICES	
HOTELS	

An indication of the cost of a double room without breakfast is given by **$** signs.

$$$$$	Over $200
$$$$	$150–$200
$$$	$100–$150
$$	$75–$100
$	Under $75

RESTAURANTS

An indication of the cost of a three-course dinner without drinks is given by **$** signs.

$$$$$	Over $75
$$$$	$50–$75
$$$	$35–$50
$$	$20–$35
$	Under $20

www.elgranescape.net
Burgers, tuna melts, surf-and-turf, and locally inspired seafood dishes in this open-air restaurant. Sushi upstairs.
⊠ None

SAVEGRE

⊞ RAFIKI SAFARI LODGE
$$$
20 MILES SE OF QUEPOS
TEL 777-2250
www.rafikisafari.com
African-style lodge specializing in nature activities and whitewater adventures. Accommodation is in fully furnished tents with en-suite bathrooms. The South African-run hotel has a traditional *braai* (barbecue) in the Lecker Bar.
🛏 9 🅿 ⊠ ⊠ MC, V

TÁRCOLES

⊞ HOTEL VILLA LAPAS
$$$$
HWY. 34, 0.5 MILES E OF TAMBOR
TEL 663-0811
FAX 663-1516
www.villalapaa
This upscale resort bordering Parque Nacional Carara nestles in a canyon, with bungalows strung out along the

valley. The public areas are decorated on a colonial theme.
① 55 **P** **🔲** 🏊 **S**AE, MC, V

ZONA SUR

BAHÍA DRAKE

🏨 AGUILA DE OSA INN
$$$$$
MOUTH OF RÍO AGUJITAS, 0.5 MILE S OF AGUJITAS
TEL 296-2190 OR 291-0318
FAX 232-7722
www.aguiladeosainn.com
An upscale nature lodge decorated on a native theme, tucked in a canyon. Good for scuba diving and sportfishing. Rates include inventive meals with free-flowing wine.
① 13 **S**AE, MC, V

🏨 LA PALOMA LODGE
$$
0.5 MILES S OF AGUJITAS
TEL 239-2801
FAX 239-0954
www.lapalomalodge.com
Cozy cabins in landscaped grounds facing the Pacific. Family-style meals in an airy restaurant. Tours and activities.
① 10 🏊 **S**MC, V

CORCOVADO

🏨 LAPA RÍOS
🍴 $$$$$
CABO MATOPALO
TEL 735-5130
FAX 735-5179
www.laparios.com
A deluxe nature lodge backed by rain forest. Spacious, airy ranchos sleep up to six. Nature tours, horseback rides, and kayaking. Rates include meals, served in a thatched restaurant with spiraling *mirador*.
① 14 bungalows 🏊 **S**AE, MC, V

🏨 BOSQUE DEL CABO
$$$$$
CABO MATOPALO
TEL/FAX 735-5206
www.bosquedelcabo.com

The Casa Blanca, a clifftop villa on this serene oceanfront property, is the epitome of luxury. Simple meals in a thatched restaurant.
① 8 bungalows, 1 house **P** 🏊 **S**V

🏨 CASA CORCOVADO JUNGLE LODGE
$$$$
N BORDER OF CORCOVADO NATIONAL PARK
TEL 256-3181 OR 888/896-6097
FAX 256-7409
www.casacorcovado.com
This former cacao plantation provides accommodation in graciously appointed thatched cabinas. Watersports, guided hikes, and horseback riding are offered. There is a bar and family-style dining. Two-night minimum stay.
① 10 bungalows 🏊 **S**AE, MC, V

🏨 CORCOVADO LODGE TENT CAMP
$$$$
S BORDER OF CORCOVADO NATIONAL PARK
TEL 257-0766
FAX 257-1665 E-MAIL
www.costaricaexpeditions.com
These unusual tentlike accommodations on wooden platforms appeal to the adventurous traveler. Family-style meals are served in a lofty thatched restaurant. A wide range of adventure activities is offered.
① 20 **S**AE, MC, V

🏨 LUNA LODGE
$$$$
CARATE
TEL 380-5036 OR 888/409-8448
www.lunalodge.com
A dramatic hillside setting and tastefully conceived and decorated thatched cabins that have views into the rain forest. Safari-style tents are also available. A dojo is used for yoga. Access only by four-wheel-drive vehicles.
① 8 cabins, 7 tents **P** 🏊 **S**MC, V

GOLFITO

🏨 BANANA BAY MARINA
$$$
TEL 775-0838
FAX 775-0735
www.bananabaymarina.com
This small hotel and sportfishing resort adjoins its namesake marina. Contemporary rooms. American and nouvelle cuisine served in the Bilge Bar & Grill.
① 4 **P** **🔲** 🏊 **S**MC, V

PAVONES

🏨 CASA SIEMPRE DOMINGO BED & BREAKFAST
$$$$$
TEL/FAX 820-4709
www.casa-domingo.com
This is a deluxe Western-style lodge with a cathedral ceiling. It is set amid landscaped lawns with ocean views to the front and rain forest behind.
① 4 **P** **S**None

🏨 TISKITA LODGE
$$
TEL 298-8125
FAX 296-8133
www.tiskita-lodge.co.cr
Surrounded by rain forest and fruit orchards, this property centers on an old farmhouse where meals are served family style. Accommodation is in wooden cabins with private alfresco showers and toilets. Horseback riding, nature tours, and birding trips.
① 16 **P** 🏊 **🔲** **S**AE, MC, V

PIEDRAS BLANCAS

🏨 ESQUINAS RAINFOREST LODGE
$$$
LAS GAMBAS
TEL/FAX 775-0901
www.esquinaslodge.com
A comfortable albeit simply appointed nature lodge on the edge of Piedras Blancas National Park. Local

---

S Air-conditioning 🏠 Indoor/ 🏊 Outdoor swimming pool 🏋 Health club **S** Credit cards **KEY**

inhabitants lead nature treks, among other activities.
[i] 14 [P] 🛥 🚤 🚭 AE, MC, V

🏨 PLAYA NICUESA RAINFOREST LODGE
$$$
PLAYA NICUESA, 9 MILES NW OF GOLFITO
TEL 735-5237 OR 866/348-7610
www.nicuesalodge.com
This rain forest lodge enjoys a beachfront location, with trails into a private reserve. Simply furnished accommodations have delightful open-air bathrooms. Hammocks abound on broad balconies. Kayaking and windsurfing.
[i] 4 cabins, 4 rooms
🚭 None

PLAYA CATIVO

🏨 RAINBOW ADVENTURES LODGE
$$$$
TEL 831-5677
www.rainbowcostarica.com
A remote waterfront lodge with elegant decor and solar-powered electricity in hardwood cabins. Guided hikes and sportfishing are offered. Accessible by boat.
[i] 4 rooms, 2 cabins 🚭 AE, MC, V

PUERTO JIMÉNEZ

🏨 IGUANA LODGE
$$$
PLAYA PLATANARES
TEL/FAX 735-5205
www.iguanalodge.com
A jungly beachside setting adds allure to this reclusive no-frills lodge with four thatched stilt cabins. A professional chef prepares mackerel dijon and key lime pie, served in the open-air restaurant, open to the public on Tuesdays.
[i] 4 [P] 🚭 None

🍴 JUANITA'S MEXICAN BAR & GRILL
$$
TEL 735-5056

A lively Mexican cantina serving quality burritos, chimichangas, and other staples, including killer margaritas. The tremendous ambience is enlivened by crab races, Hula Hoop contests,and other fun events.
🚭 MC, V

SIERPE

🏨 VERAGUA RIVER HOUSE
$$
RÍO ESTERO AZUL
TEL 788-8111
FAX 786-7460
An exquisite riverside guesthouse surrounded by swampy grasslands good for birding. Charming Italian decor in a choice of rooms, cabins, or a beachfront house.
[i] 8 🚭 None

ZANCUDO

🏨 CABINAS SOL Y MAR
🍴 **$$**
TEL 776-0014
FAX 776-0015
www.zancudo.com
This beachfront property has attractive cabins with skylit bathrooms. The outdoor bar/grill serves dishes such as tuna with capers and burgers.
[i] 5 cabins, 1 house [P]
🚭 No cards

SOUTH CENTRAL

PARQUE INTERNACIONAL LA AMISTAD

🏨 LA AMISTAD LODGE
$$
LAS MELLIZAS
TEL 773-3193 OR 200-5037
FAX 289-7858
www.laamistad.com
On the park's fringe is this mountain lodge with rooms or cabins. Hiking, horseback rides, and camping. Organic meals served family-style. Four-wheel drive access. Rate includes entrance to reserve

and a tour.
[i] 10 [P] 🚭 None

SAN GERARDO DE RIVAS

🏨 RÍO CHIRRIPÓ MOUNTAIN RETREAT B&B
$$
CANAAN
TEL 771-7065
FAX 771-2003
www.riochirripo.com
Inspired by the Santa Fe style, this handsome lodge has homey yet tastefully decorated cabins with balconies overhanging the gorge. Roofed platforms accommodate campers. Airy rancho dining area.
[i] 8 [P] 🚤 🚭 MC, V

SAN VITO

🏨 LAS CRUCES BIOLOGICAL STATION
$$
HWY. 16, 4 MILES S OF S. VITO
TEL 773-4004
FAX 773-3665
www.ots.ac.cr
Attractive contemporary rooms with picture windows, verandas, and modern amenities in the heart of a forest reserve with miles of trails and a stunning garden.
[i] 12 [P] 🚫 🚭 AE, MC, V

NORTHERN LOWLANDS

CHACHAGUA

🏨 CHACHAGUA RAINFOREST LODGE
$$
1 MILE W OF CHACHAGUA
TEL 239-6464
FAX 239-6868
www.chachaguarainforestlodge.com
A working cattle and fruit farm with a private nature reserve at the foot of the Cordillera de Tilarán is the setting for this rustic wilderness lodge. Cabins overlook pond.
[i] 23 [P] 🚤 🚭 AE, MC, V

LA VIRGEN

⊞ CENTRO NEOTRÓPICO SARAPIQUÍS ECOLODGE
$$$$
I MILE S OF LA VIRGEN
TEL 761-1004
FAX 761-1415
www.sarapiquis.org
This upscale stunner nestles in the heart of an ecotourism project adjacent to a rain-forest reserve. Architecture and decor blend contemporary and pre-Columbian styles, with stone floors and tropical pastel colors. The elegant restaurant offers à la carte and buffet options, plus forest views over the canopy.
🛈 36 🅿 🅢 🌊 🅢MC, V

LAS HORQUETAS

⊞ RARA AVIS
$$
9 MILES SW OF LAS HORQUETAS, SARAPIQUI
TEL 764-3131
FAX 764-4187
www.rara-avis.com
A remote wilderness lodge on a private reserve with swimming holes, canopy platforms, butterfly and orchid houses, naturalist guides, trails, and horseback riding. Two-night minimum stay. Simple food; rates include meals. Reservations essential.
🛈 5 cabins, 10 rooms 🅿 🅢AE, MC, V

MUELLE

⊞ TILAJARI RESORT HOTEL
$$$
I MILE W OF MUELLE CROSSROADS
TEL 469-9091
FAX 469-9095
www.tilajari.com
Spacious, modestly furnished rooms on the banks of the Río San Carlos. Adequate meals in a large restaurant. Wildlife abounds, including

crocodiles on the riverbanks. Butterfly garden, squash courts, disco, sauna, and sports facilities. Tours offered.
🛈 76 🅿 🅢 🌊 🅢All major cards

PUERTO VIEJO

⊞ SELVA VERDE
$$$
CHILAMATE DE SARAPIQUÍ, 6 MILES W OF PUERTO VIEJO
TEL 766-6800
FAX 766-6011
www.selvaverde.com
This lodge is set on the edge of rain forest. Choose between rustic accommodations, more upscale cabins, or bungalows. There is a library, lecture room, and communal dining room. Guided hikes and canoe trips can be arranged.
🛈 40 rooms, 5 bungalows 🅿 🅢MC, V

⊞ LA QUINTA DE SARAPIQUÍ COUNTRY INN
$
CHILAMATE, 7 MILES W OF PUERTO VIEJO
TEL 761-1300
FAX 761-1395
www.laquintasarapiqui.com
This cabin complex with modest decor surrounds a colonial hacienda. A butterfly garden, frog garden, and soft adventures to rain forest reserves are highlights. Tasty continental and local dishes are served.
🛈 3o 🌊 🅢 🅢AE, MC, V

TABACÓN

⊞ TABACÓN HOT SPRINGS RESORT & SPA
$$$
TABACÓN, 8 MILES W OF LA FORTUNA
TEL 256-1500 OR 877/277-8291
FAX 221-3075 OR 877/277-8292
www.tabacon.com
This modern lodge with views of Volcán Arenal offers guests direct access to the adjacent

spa. Rooms are tastefully furnished. A choice of restaurants includes an atmospheric eatery directly above the thermal pools.
🛈 106 🅿 🅢 🅥 🅢DC, MC, V

THE CARIBBEAN

BARRA DEL COLORADO

⊞ RÍO COLORADO LODGE
$$$
BARRA DEL COLORADO SUR
TEL 710-6879
FAX 231-5987
www.riocoloradolodge.com
This sportfishing lodge boasts a large fleet plus tackle shop. Simple rooms with modern necessities. Small zoo. Seafood and local dishes are served in the dining room or on the riverside deck.
🛈 18 🅢 🅢AE, MC, V

⊞ SILVER KING LODGE
$$$
BARRA DEL COLORADO SUR
TEL 381-1404 OR 800/847-3474
FAX 381-0849
www.silverkinglodge..com
Well-furnished wooden cabins linked by catwalks on banks of the river from which a fleet of sportfishing boats put out. Tackle shop, TV and video room, indoor spa pool, bar, and restaurant.
🛈 20 🅢 🌊 🅢AE, MC, V

CAHUITA

⊞ MAGELLAN INN
🍴 **$$**
PLAYA NEGRA, 2 MILES N OF CAHUITA
TEL/FAX 755-0035
www.magellaninn.com
Sophisticated style on land-landscaped grounds. Rooms have patios. Shrimp martinique in Creole spice exemplifies the inventive cuisine in the restaurant. Reservations are essential.
🛈 6 🌊 🅢 🅢AE, MC, V

HOTELS & RESTAURANTS

ESTRELLA

🏨 SELVA BANANITO LODGE
$$
9 MILES W OF BANANITO
TEL 253-8118
FAX 280-0820
www.selvabananito.com
A simple, atmospheric lodge on the edge of the rain forest, beside a river. Stilt-legged cabins with solar-heated water add to the jungly appeal. No electricity. Hiking, horseback rides, and family-style dining. Four-wheel drive access.
🛏 11 🅿 🚭 None

🏨 RÍO DANTA RESTAURANT & PRIVATE RESERVE
$
3 MILES W OF GUÁPILES
TEL 710-2626
www.grupomawamba.com
Local cuisine served in airy eatery. decorated with regional icons. Trails lead to rain forest where poison arrow frogs hop about underfoot.
🅿 🕐 Closed D 🚭 AE, MC, V

GUÁPILES

🏨 CASA RÍO BLANCO ECOLODGE
$$
RIO BLANCO, 3 MILES W OF GUÁPILES
TEL/FAX 710-4124
www.casarioblanca.com
A charming little hotel with wooden cabins that have balconies over a river on the edge of rain forest. Delightful albeit simple decor.
🛏 4 cabins, 2 rooms 🅿 🚭 MC, V

PENSHURST

🏨 AVIARIOS DEL CARIBE
$$
TEL/FAX 382-1335
www.ogphoto.com/avarios
Splendidly furnished nature lodge beside a wildlife-rich wetland. Airy library, TV/video

room, and screened restaurant. Hikes and canoe trips offered.
🛏 7 🚭 🚭 MC, V

PUERTO VIEJO

🏨 SHAWANDA LODGE
$$$
PLAYA CHIQUITA, 4 MILES SE OF PUERTO VIEJO
TEL 750-0018
FAX 750-0037, E-MAIL
www.shawandalodge.com
Splendid setting for individual cabins on the fringe of rain forest close to the beach. Tasteful furnishings. Four-poster beds add a touch of romance. The open-air lounge offers similarly contemporary grace. Rates include breakfast.
🛏 12 🅿 🚭 AE, MC, V

🏨 ALMONDS & CORALS LODGE TENT CAMP
$$
PUNTA MANZANILLO, 5 MILES SE OF PUERTO VIEJO
TEL 759-9057
FAX 759-9056
www.almondsandcorals.com
A minimalist, eco-sensitive wilderness lodge with tents on roofed wooden platforms, situated in shore-front jungle. Private bathrooms nearby. Communal restaurant. Tours and outdoor activities.
🛏 24 🅿 🚭 AE, DC, MC

🏨 JARDÍN MIRAFLORES LODGE
$$
PUNTA COCLES, 2.5 MILES SE OF PUERTO VIEJO
TEL/FAX 750-0038
www.mirafloreslodge.com
Charming nature lodge. Accommodations from a basic dorm to suites with king-size beds and lounge. Hikes and boat trips arranged. Breakfasts and dinners served in a thatched roadside café.
🛏 10 🅿 🚭 None

🏨 COCO LOCO
$
400 YARDS SW OF PUERTO VIEJO
TEL 750-0281

www.cocolocolodge.com
Simplicity is the watchword at this back-to-basics retreat amid lawns surrounded by forest. Small Tahitian-style cabins offer few frills but plenty of charm. Mosquito nets over beds. No restaurant.
🛏 4 cottages, 1 four-person bungalow 🅿 🚭 None

🍴 LA PECORA NEGRA
$$$
PLAYA COCLES
TEL 750-0490
Delicious Italian fare of world-class standard at this unpretentious, thatched open-air restaurant. Staples such as calzones, gnocchi, and pizzas are supplemented by superlative daily specials.
🕐 Closed Mon. 🅿 🚭 🚭 AE, MC, V

TORTUGUERO

🏨 TORTUGA LODGE & GARDENS
$$$
2 MILES N OF TORTUGUERO
TEL 257-0766
FAX 257-1665 E-MAIL
www.costaricaexpeditions.com
This comfortable nature lodge on the banks of Tortuguero Lagoon is close to the airstrip. You can eat in the airy dining room or on the riverside terrace. Guided boat tours of Parque Nacional Tortuguero, plus hikes and sportfishing. At night, rockers on verandas prove handy for watching bats scoop fish from the lagoon!
🛏 24 🅿 🚭 🚭 AE, MC, V

🍴 MISS JUNIE'S
$
TEL 711-0683
Down-home cooking by a village elder. Fish platter special comes with beans and rice simmered in coconut milk. Homemade ginger cookies, and *pan bon*, bread laced with caramelized sugar prove to be extremely tempting desserts.
🚭 None

SHOPPING IN COSTA RICA

The tourist boom has spawned a recent outpouring of quality crafts, from beautiful pottery, wooden bowls, and carvings to exquisite gold jewelry and gaily colored miniature wooden *carretas* (traditional oxcarts). San José is filled with crafts stores and art galleries, the latter reflecting an explosion of energy in the art world.

Many crafts use hardwoods, such as lignum vitae, purpleheart, rosewood, satinwood, and tigerwood. Larger items include carved headboards, lathe-turned rockers with leather seats, and decorative mini-carretas for use as liquor bars or garden ornaments and which can be shipped home with relative ease.

The country's renowned coffee is available nationwide. Buy premium export-grade coffee, sold pre-packaged; domestic coffee is notably inferior. Cuban cigars make a popular souvenir (It is illegal for U.S. citizens to purchase them here). Prices are high…about the same as flying to Cuba from Costa Rica *and* buying cigars there. Most upscale hotels have gift stores selling arts and crafts.

OPENING TIMES
See p. 238.

SAN JOSÉ

West of Avenida 2, between Calles 4 and 9 are art and craft stores. Centro Comercial El Pueblo to the northeast of the city center, has alleys lined with galleries, stores, and restaurants. The suburb of Moravia (San Vincente) is known for art, crafts, jewelry, local leatherwork and wicker furniture.

ARTS & ANTIQUES

Andrómeda Gallery, Calle 9, Ave. 9, tel 223-3529. Paintings by Costa Rican and Central American artists. Top local names represented. Works cost as much as $10,000.
Galería de Arte Amir, Ave. 5, Calle 5, tel 221-9128. Broad representation of works by leading artists, including now deceased masters.
Galería Valanti, Avenida 11, Calles 33/35, tel 234-0938. This compact gallery specializes in works from throughout the Americas, with a focus on local artists of note.
Kadinsky, Centro Comercial, Calle Real, San Pedro, tel 234-0478. Stocks artwork by Costa Rica's preeminent artists.

BOOKS & MAPS

7th Street Books, Calle 7, Aves. Central/1, tel 256-8251, e-mail marroca@racsa.co.cr. English-language store stocks novels, nature books, travel guides, and international magazines.
Instituto Geográfica Nacional, Ave. 20, Calles 9/11, tel 257-7798 ext. 2619. Detailed topographic and city maps of the whole country.

CLOTHES & ACCESSORIES

Antic, Edificio las Arcadas, Ave. 2 & Calle 1, tel 233-4630. National costumes, including appliqued *molas* from Drake Bay and the San Blas islands.
Artesanías Malety, Ave. 1, Calles 1/3, tel 221-1670. Pick up a pair of stylish cowboy boots, including alligator skin.
Choza Folclórica, Ave. 3 & Calle 1. Frilly white cotton dresses with colored sashes are Guanacaste's traditional dress.

CRAFTS & JEWELRY

Anda, Ave. 2, Calle 5, tel 233-3340. Indigenous crafts such as balsawood masks, gourds, pottery, musical instruments, ceramics, and weavings.
Boutique Annemarie, Hotel Don Carlos, see p. 242. Arts and crafts, from carved walking sticks to balsawood masks.
La Casona, Calle Central, Aves. Central/1, tel 222-7999. Christmas crèches and tree pendants, textiles.
Esmeraldas & Diseños, Sabana Norte, tel 231-4808.

Choice of good jewelry including gold in pre-Columbian styles.
Galería Namú, Ave. 7, Calles 5/7, tel 256-3412, www.galeria namu.com. High-quality indigenous arts and crafts, including masks, baskets, jade, and paintings from Costa Rica and Panama.
Museo de Oro Precolumbino (see p. 58). Contemporary gold and silver, precious stones. Superb pre-Columbian reproductions.

GIFTS

Arisitide Guzman Mora Ltd., Tibas, tel 235-1603. Classical guitars from precious woods for less than $100.
The Cigar Shoppe, Diana's Inn, Calle 5 & Ave. 3, tel 257-5021. Premium Cuban cigars sold individually and by the box.
Galeriá de Vitrales y Cerámica, Ave. las Americas, Sabana Norte, tel 232-7932. Gorgeous bowls, vases, and contemporary kitchenware plus stained glass items.
Habanos de Costa Rica, Calle 7, Ave. 7/9, tel 383-6835. Operated by Cuba's Habanos S.A., Genuine Cubans at lower prices than the Cigar Shoppe.
Orquídeas del Bosque, Rohrmoser, tel 232-1466, www.costaricaorchids.com. More than 75 species of orchids are sold here for export.

MALLS

San Pedro Mall, Ave. Central Circunvalación, tel 283-7540. The city's largest mall, with dozens of upscale stores. Everything from jewelry and fashion to leathers and books.

MARKETS

Mercado Borbón, Calle 8, Aves. 3/5. Farmer's market on the west side of Plaza Víquez. A great place to buy fresh produce and flowers. Saturday mornings.
Mercado Central, Bet. Calles 6/8 and Aves. Central/1. A maze of tight alleyways where street stalls and shops sell everything from medicinal herbs, flowers, and fresh produce to cowboy

boots, straw hats, and Cuban-style embroidered *guayabero* shirts. Closed Sundays. Beware of pickpockets.

Mercado de Artesanía Las Garzas, Moravia, tel 236-0037. Around 30 craft stores under a single roof.

Mercado de Artesanías Nacionales, Calle 11, Aves. 4/6, tel 223-0122. A daily craft market offering an eclectic choice that includes T-shirts, leather goods, rugs, Guatemalan jackets, and hammocks.

CENTRAL HIGHLANDS

Santa Ana is famous for ceramics: from coffee mugs and small bowls to urns and vases. Sarchí is the nation's undisputed center of crafts, with furniture workshops, fine leatherwork (including satchels, purses, and belts), and is the sole remaining production center in the country for *carretas* (traditional oxcarts). Workshops and craft stores line the main street.

CRAFTS & JEWELRY

Biesanz Woodworks, see p. 70. Biesanz oversees 20 master carvers in the workshop. The store sells bowls and boxes.

Casa El Soñador, see p. 88. Buy primitive-style pieces carved from coffee wood.

Cerámica Santa Ana, Santa Ana, tel 282-6024. Earthenware bowls, vases, and urns, as well as smaller ceramic pieces are made on old-fashioned kick-wheels and fired in an outdoor kiln.

Creaciones Santos, Ave. 3, Calles 1/3, San Miguel de Escazú, tel 228-6747. Exotic stained-glass made on site.

Fábrica de Carretas Joaquín Chaverrí, Sarchí Sur, tel 454-4411. A huge selection of arts and crafts from leatherwork and rockers to hardwood kitch-enware. In the family-run work-shop, you can watch miniature *carretas* being made.

GIFTS

Café Britt, see pp. 82-83. Premium pre-packaged coffees at wholesale prices, plus handcrafted wooden kitchen utensils, bowls, and other gift items on a Costa Rican theme. Café Britt outlets are also located in the José Santamaría International Airport.

Orchid Alley, La Garita, tel 487-7086. Dozens of orchid species ready for export in sealed vials.

Plaza de Artesanías, Sarchí Sur, tel 454-3430. Over 30 stores from leather goods, Guatemalan textiles, and jewelry.

MALLS

Centro Comercial Escazú, San Rafael de Escazú. Boutiques and specialty stores.

Multiplaza, Autopista Prospero Fernández, Escazú, tel 288-1178. Costa Rica's largest mall, with specialty stores ranging from books and fashion to jewelry.

MARKETS

Mercado Central, Bet. Calle 4/6 and Aves. Central/1, Alajuela. A whole block of stalls selling fresh farm produce, meats, fish, spices, leatherwork, and household goods. Be alert for pickpockets and thieves.

Mercado Central, Bet. Calle 2/4 and Aves. 6/8, Heredia. A tight warren of stores offering farm produce, crafts, and general wares. As with all markets, guard your valuables!

GUANACASTE

Monteverde has galleries and gift stores selling some of the most creative works in the country.

CRAFTS & JEWELRY

Committee of Artisans of Santa Elena & Monteverde (CASEM), Monteverde, tel 645-5190. Works by over 100 local artists, from paintings to sculpture and ceramics. Sales benefit the local community.

Extasis Gallery, Monteverde. tel 645-5548. Works by gifted local artist Marco Tulio Brenes.

Jewelry, paintings, and sculptures.

Hummingbird Gallery, Monteverde, tel 645-5030. Wildlife posters and prints, Guatemalan textiles, and crafts from throughout the isthmus, including hand-painted wooden animal figurines. Prints and slides by local photographers, Michael and Patricia Fogden.

Sarah Dodwell Watercolor Gallery, Monteverde, tel 645-5047. Original artwork can be bought at the artist's studio.

Souvenirs La Gran Nicoya, Hwy. 21, nr. Daniel Oduber International Airport., tel 667-0062, http://lagrannicoya.net. A vast range, including ceramics, beachwear, and cigars.

Toad Hall, see p. 247. Quality arts and crafts, books, post-cards, and Cuban cigars.

MARKETS

Mercado Central, Ave. 3 & Calle 2, Puntarenas. Waterfront market crammed with seafood and fresh produce stalls.

NICOYA

Guaitíl is the center of the Indian pottery tradition. Matriarchs work clay into bowls, plates, and vases painted in traditional animal motifs. Feel free to ask for a tour. Expect to pay between $15 and $50 for a trademark three-legged vase in the form of a cow.

CRAFTS & JEWELRY

Cooperativa de Mujeres de Guaitíl, Guaitíl. Artisans sell their handmade pottery.

El Mundo de la Tortuga, see p. 141. Crafts and clothing on an environmental theme; marine turtles are most popular items.

Galeria de las Estrellas, Tamarindo. Stylish gold and silver jewelry, much of it reproductions of pre-Columbian styles.

Iguana Surf, Tamarindo, tel 653-0148, www.iguanasurf.net. Lots of jewelry, woodcarvings, T-shirts, and other souvenirs.

CENTRAL PACIFIC

Quepos has numerous souvenir stores, and Manuel Antonio has beachfront stalls. At Bahía Drake, local women make colorful *molas*, appliqué with animal motifs, that they stitch onto clothes, and wall-hangings. Boruca produces Indian crafts. The men make balsawood masks and decorate gourds.

CLOTHES & ACCESSORIES

Guacamole, Jacó, tel 643-1120. Indonesian-inspired batik beachwear produced at this small clothing store.

CRAFTS & JEWELRY

Buena Nota, Manuel Antonio, tel 777-1002. A selection of resortwear, handicrafts, and general souvenirs as well as books, magazines, and maps.
Boutique Mot Mot, Quepos. Good selection of local crafts. Purchases go to support Fundación Neotrópica.
Galería Arte la Heliconia, Jacó, tel 643-3613. Pottery and artwork, as well as souvenirs.
L'Aventura Multiboutique, Avenida Central & Calle 2, Quepos. tel 777-1019. Great choice of batiks, crafts, jewelry, and leather goods.
Regalame, Si Como No hotel, Manuel Antonio, see p. 252. First-class paintings, sculptures, and handicrafts by local artists and artisans
Villa Caletas, see p. 252. Only juried gold items are sold here.

GIFTS

Lighthouse Point, Jacó, tel 643-3083. Huge stock of souvenirs, T-shirts, cigars, etc.

ZONA SUR

The town of Golfito draws Costa Ricans from afar to its duty-free Depósito Libre zone, although there are few items of interest for tourists. Puerto Jiménez has several small souvenir shops, and many hotel gift shops sell local crafts, highlighted by balsawood masks.

CRAFTS & JEWELRY

Bahía Drake. Community members make and sell brightly colored *molas*.

SOUTH CENTRAL

Shopping is not a strong suit of this region. However the towns of San Isidro and San Vito have many leather shops selling cowboy boots, etc. The indigenous communities of the Talamancas produce crafts, including colorful *molas*.

CRAFTS & JEWELRY

Finca Cántaros, Hwy. 16, at Linda Vista, 2 miles S of San Vito. Quality arts and crafts, including ceramics, jewelry, and South American clothing.

NORTHERN LOWLANDS

The market town of Ciudad Quesada has several *talabarterías* (saddle shops) selling cowboy boots, elaborately decorated saddles, and other leather goods. Fortuna is a popular tourist spot with the usual selection of souvenir shops selling crafts from throughout the nation.

CRAFTS & JEWELRY

Coco Loco Art Gallery & Café, Chachagua, tel 468-0990. Fabulous selection of quality arts and crafts, including indigenous masks. Contemporary sculptures and ceramics too.
Rancho Leona, La Virgen, tel 841-5341. Masterful stained-glass works made to order or bought on-spec for $80–$125 per square foot. Part of the proceeds helps buy endangered forest.

GIFTS & MISCELLANEOUS

MUSA, El Tigre. This women's cooperative sells herbal teas, medicinal herbs, natural aphrodisiacs, toiletries, skin creams, and herbal balms.

MARKETS

Mercado Central, Calle 2 & Ave. Central, Ciudad Quesada. A bustling hive with fresh produce, plus arts and crafts from the local artisans' cooperative.

THE CARIBBEAN

Puerto Viejo has a high-profile expatriate population that is imbued with an entrepreneurial spirit, and both produces and sells a wide selection of simple jewelry, batiks, and a variety of other tourist trinkets.

CLOTHES & ACCESSORIES

Boutique Bombata, Cahuita. A small yet well-stocked shop specializing in resortwear, including batik wraps, as well as jewelry and crafts.
Color Caribe, Puerto Viejo, tel 750-0075. One of the best-stocked souvenir stores in the country. Come here for a selection of jewelry, hand-painted and silk-screened T-shirts, as well as other kinds of clothing.

CRAFTS & JEWELRY

LuluBelu, Puerto Viejo, tel 750-0394. Splendid range of souvenirs, including hammocks, jewelry, embroidered Guatemalan vests, and sandals.
Paraíso Tropical, Tortuguero, tel 710-0323. Surprisingly diverse array of arts and crafts, together with hammocks, swimwear, posters, and more. Ten percent of proceeds are donated to the local school.

MARKETS

Mercado Central, Bet. Calles 3/4 and Aves. 2/3, Limón. Intriguing browsing in this small, crowded market that takes up an entire block and is replete with stalls that sell everything from household goods and crafts to fresh meats and fish. Be on guard for thieves.

ENTERTAINMENT & ACTIVITIES

ENTERTAINMENT & ACTIVITIES

San José has everything from classical concerts to discos. Many casinos are here and in a few resort hotels; most are small, although classier ones have opened recently. Festivals and events are listed in the *Tico Times, Costa Rica Today,* and the "Viva" section of *La Nación.*

The nation supplements its entertainment scene with activities that make the most of the natural diversity. The companies listed may cover additional activities and other areas.

ACTIVITIES

Reading: *A Guide to the Birds of Costa Rica* by Stiles and Skutch.
Cheeseman's Ecology Safaris, tel 408/867-1371, 800/527-5330, fax 408/741-0358, www.cheesemans.com
Costa Rica Expeditions, tel 257-0766, fax 257-1665, www.costaricaexpeditions.com
Costa Rica Temptations, tel 239-9999, fax 239-9990, www.crtinfo.com
Holbrook Travel, tel 352/377-7111, fax 352/371-3710, www.holbrooktravel.com
Horizontes Nature Tours, tel 222-2022, fax 255-4513, www.horizontes.com

CANOEING & KAYAKING

Costa Rica's rivers offer a range of experiences. Contact:
Canoe Costa Rica, tel/fax 282-3579, 732/736-6586, www.canoecostarica.com
Desafío Adventure Company, tel 479-9464, www.desafiocostarica.com

CANOPY TOURING

Get close-up views of wildlife, from narrow walkways between trees, or ziplines that whisk through the treetops. See regional entries.

FISHING

See pp.164–165 for details of the types of fishing available. Boat charters cost $250–400 a half day, and $350–650 a full day (up to four people):
JP Sportfishing Tours, tel 244-6361, 866/620-4188, www.jpsportfishing.com
Papagayo Excursions, tel 653-0227, fax 653-0254, www.papagayoexcursions.com

Rain Goddess, tel 231-4299, fax 231-3816, www.bluwing.com

GOLFING

Half a dozen premier golf courses are concentrated in the Central Highlands and Pacific Northwest. See regional entries.

HORSEBACK RIDING

Horseback riding is available nationwide, notably in Guanacaste, where working cattle farms cater to visitors.
Cross Country International, tel 845/635-2200, 800/828-8768, fax 845/635-3300, www.equestrianvacations.com
Equitour USA, tel 307/455-3363, 800/545-0019, fax 307/455-2354, www.ridingtours.com

MOUNTAIN BIKING

Most tours are one or two days, and a van carries luggage and equipment. Many hotels rent bikes. For tours contact:
Backroads, tel 510/527-1555, 800/462-2848, fax 510/527-1444, www.backroads.com
Coast to Coast Adventures, tel 280-8054, fax 225-6055, www.ctcadventures.com
Experience Plus! Specialty Tours, tel 800/685-4565, fax 970/493-0377, www.experienceplus.com

MOTORCYCLING

Costa Rica's back roads are ideal for motorcycle touring for those who know how to ride.
Costa Rican Trails, tel 221-5800, 888/803-3344, fax 257-4655, www.costaricantrails.com
María Alexandra Tours, tel 289-5552, fax 289-5551, www.mariaalexander.com

Moto-Discovery, tel 830/438-7744, 800/233-0564 fax 830/438-7745, www.motodiscovery.com

NATURE CRUISING

Travel at night, with days spent at wilderness sights. Guides lead hikes. Scuba diving and snorkeling may be available.
Cruise West, 2401 4th Ave., Suite 700, Seattle, WA 98121, tel 888/851-8133, fax 206/441-4757, www.cruisewest.com
Windstar Cruises, 300 Elliott Ave. W., Seattle, WA 98119, tel 281-3535, 800/258-7245, fax 286-3229, www.windstarcruises.com

SCUBA DIVING

Manta rays, groupers, and sharks can be seen on the Pacific coast. Islas Murciélagos (Bat Islands), Catalinas, and Isla del Coco are popular excursions. Caribbean diving focuses on coral reefs, best Feb.–April. Visibility is poor by international standards. Temperatures are above 75°F year-round. See regional entries.

SURFING

The Pacific coast has some of the world's longest rides. You can rent boards at dedicated surf camps such as Tamarindo in Nicoya.
"Costa Rican Surf Report" (233-7386, www.crsurf.com), and **Surf Costa Rica** (201-7139, 888/427-7769, www.surf-costarica.com) give local information.

RAFTING

See pp. 196–197 for information. The industry is regulated by the government. Operators include:
Costa Sol Rafting, tel 431-1183, fax 431-1185, www.costasolrafting.com
Ríos Tropicales, tel 233-6455, fax 255-4354, www.riostropicales.com

WINDSURFING

The two major sites are Laguna de Arenal (see p. 114) and Bahía Salinas (see p. 128). To get on board and go, contact:
Sun Tours and Fun, tel 256-7946, www.suntoursandfun.com

ENTERTAINMENT & ACTIVITIES

SAN JOSÉ

THE ARTS

Little Theater Group, Centro Cultural Eugene O'Neill, tel 289-3910. English-language theater.
National Lyric Opera Company, Teatro Melico Salazar (see p. 60), tel 222-8571. Performances June–Aug.
North American Cultural Center, San Pedro, tel 207-7500, www.cccncr.com. Movies, lectures and more for North American expatriates.
National Symphony Orchestra, Teatro Nacional (see p. 58), tel 236-5395. Weekly, April–Dec.

FESTIVALS

Festival de la Carretas, (Nov.), Paseo Colón & Parque Central. Parade with oxcarts (*carretas*) and traditional dress. Musicians play the *cimarronas*.
Festival de la Luz, (Christmas). A nocturnal parade of dozens of floats decorated with lights, from Parque Sabana straight to downtown.

NIGHTLIFE

Discoteque Infinito, Centro Comercial, El Pueblo, tel 223-2195. Three separate disco environments under one roof.
El Cuartel de la Boca del Monte, Ave 1, Calles 21/23, tel 221-0327. Plenty of live music and dancing.
Fantasía Folclórica, Teatro Popular Melico Salazar (see p. 60). Traditional music and dance. Tues. only.
Jazz Café, Ave Central, Los Yoses, tel 253-8933. The best spot for live jazz and blues.
Key Largo, Calle 7, Avenidas 1/3, tel 221-0277. Raffish bar and dance club in colonial mansion.
Río, Ave Central, San Pedro, tel 225-8371. Packs in chic hipsters; live music and music videos.
Shakespeare Bar, Ave 2, Calle 28, tel 257-1288. Piano bar with occasionally live jazz.
Tabogan, Calle Blancos, tel 257-3396. Popular disco beneath thatch. Occasional live bands.

OTHER ACTIVITIES

BOWLING
Boliche, Calle 37, San Pedro, tel 253-5743

CASINOS
Casino Club Colonial, Ave. 1, Calles 9/11, tel 258-2807
Horseshoe Casino, Ave 1, Calle 9, tel 233-4383

DANCE LESSONS
Kurubandé, tel 234-0682. Locations throughout San José.
Merecumbé, S. Pedro, tel 224-3531

GO-KARTING
Formula 1, Coronado, tel 381-7650

GOLF
Meliá Cariari, see p. 241. 18-hole championship course.

CENTRAL HIGHLANDS

FESTIVALS

Easter Procession, (Easter Sun.), S. Isidro de Heredia. A solemn religious festival with a celebratory theme.
International Music Festival, (July–Aug.), Hotel Chalet Tirol and other venues, see p. 245.
Juan Santamaría Day, (April 11), Alajuela. Festivities to honor the boy hero (see p. 27). Music, parades, and street fairs all week.
La Negrita Pilgrimage, (Aug. 2), see p. 87.
Día de Boyeros, (2nd Sun. in March), S. Rafael de Escazú. Oxcart drivers' (*boyeros*) parade, music, dancing, and folk tales.

NIGHTLIFE

Casino Real, Real Intercontinental, see p. 244.
Q'tal, El Cruce, Escazú, tel 228-4091. Hip club with dancing.

OTHER ACTIVITIES

AUTO RACING
La Guácima Race Track, San Antonio de Belen, tel 293-6359, www.laguacima.com. Go-kart, Formula 3, and motorcycle racing on display.

BUNGEE JUMPING
Tropical Bungee, Rosario, tel 248-2212, www.bungee.co.cr

CASINOS
Fiesta Casino, Garden Court Hotel, Río Segundo de Alajuela, tel 431-1455.

FISHING
Trout farms offer fishing from pools. Bring your own tackle.
Albergue de Montaña Savegre, San Gerardo de Dota, tel 771-1028

GOLF
Parque Valle del Sol, Santa Ana, tel 282-9222, www.vallesol.com. 18-hole course.

HORSEBACK RIDING
Club Hípico la Caraña, Santa Ana, tel 282-6754, www.lacarana.com. Lessons and tours.
Hacienda el Rodeo, Ciudad Colón, tel 249-1013
Rancho San Miguel, La Guácima, see p. 75

MOUNTAIN BIKING
Aventuras Naturales, tel 225-3939, www.adventurecostarica.com.

POLO
Los Reyes Country Club, La Guácima, tel 438-0004

RAFTING
One- or three-day runs with Class III or IV rapids.
Costa Rica Expeditions, San Jose, see p. 260
Ríos Tropicales, San José, see p. 260

SWIMMING
Waterland, Cuidad Cariari, tel 293-2891. Aquatic park. Closed Mon.

GUANACASTE

THE ARTS

Fiesta Brava, Hacienda La Chácara, Liberia, tel 350-1627. Cowboys, rodeo, marimba, traditional food, music. Every Wed. & Sat.

ENTERTAINMENT & ACTIVITIES

FESTIVALS

Día de Guanacaste, (July 25), Liberia. Marimba and mariachi music, parades, and rodeos.
Día del Sabanero, (Nov.), Liberia. Cowboys whoop it up with *topes* and rodeos.
Fiesta Cívica, (May), Cañas. Traditional music and dance, rodeos, and *topes*.
Virgin of the Sea Festival, (July) Puntarenas. Gaily decorated boats, including a dragon boat representing the Chinese community, honor Carmen, the Virgin of the Sea.

NIGHTLIFE

Moon Shiva Café, Bromelias Art Gallery, Monteverde, tel 645-6270. Live music.

OTHER ACTIVITIES

BIRDING
CATA Tours, tel 674-0180, www.catatours.com

CANOPY TOURS
The Original Canopy Tour, Mahogany Park (see p.103) or Santa Elena, tel 291-4465, www.canopytour.com
Rincón de la Vieja Lodge, see p. 248.
Selvatura, see p. 111
Sky Walk, Santa Elena, tel 645-5238, www.skywalk.co.cr

CRUISES
Bay Island Cruises, tel 258-3536, www.bayislandcruises.com
Calypso Cruises, tel 256-2727 or 800/948-3770, fax 256-6767, www.calypsocruises.com. State-of-the-art catamaran.

DIVING
See p. 263 for operators to the Islas Murciélagos.

DRIVING
Tamarindo Adventures, Tamarindo, tel/fax 653-0108, www.tamarindoadventures.net. All terrain four-wheel drive vehicles.
FISHING
Rain Goddess, see p. 260

GUIDED HIKES
Heliconias Lodge, tel 248-2538, www.turismoruralcr.com

HORSEBACK RIDING
Buena Vista Mountain Lodge & Adventure Center, 8 miles NE of Cañas Dulces, tel 661-8158, www.buenavistacr.com
Hacienda Los Innocentes, La Cruz, tel 679-9190, www.losinocenteslodge.com
Hotel Hacienda Guachipelín, Curubandé, tel 666-8075, www.guachipelin.com

MOUNTAIN BIKING
Hotel Hacienda Guachipelín (see Horseback Riding)

RAFTING
Río Corobicí is a calm float, with short rapids, and water all year.
Safaris Corobicí, Hwy. 1, 3 miles N of Cañas, tel 669-6061, www.nicoya.com

SURFING
From Witch's Rock you can ride to Playa Naranjo. Try Playa Portrero Grande (*Endless Summer II*) and Playa Blanca.
Wavehunters Surf Travel, tel 760/433-3078, 888/899-8823, www.wavehunters.com

WINDSURFING
Winds peak at Laguna de Arenal Nov.–April. Bahía Salinas has high winds Nov.–May.
Kitesurfing Center & School, Bahía Salinas, tel 826-5221, www.suntoursandfun.com
Tico Wind Surf Center, Hwy. 142, Laguna de Arenal, tel/fax 695-5387, www.ticowind.com
Tilawa Viento Surf Center, Hwy. 142, Laguna de Arenal, tel 695-5050, http://windsurfcostarica.com

NICOYA

FESTIVALS

Festival of the Virgén de Guadalupe, (Dec. 12), Nicoya. This colorful and often very lively festival combines Catholic and Chorotega traditions in the legend of the Virgin of Guadalupe, or La Yequita (Little Mare). The streets are thronged with crowds who throw fireworks (*bombas*),drink *chicha*, and play traditional music.
Fiesta Cívica, (Late Jan.), Playas del Coco. Beauty pageants, rodeos,and street parties.
Fiesta Cívica, (Jan. 15 & July 25), Santa Cruz. Firecrackers, marimba music, dancing, rodeos.
International Sailfishing Tournament, (July), Flamingo Marina, Playa Flamingo, tel 654-4537, 654-4203
Montezuma Music Festival, (July), Montezuma, tel 642-0090

NIGHTLIFE

Disco Coco Mar, Playas del Coco. Pumped-up Latin beat.
El Sano Banano, Montezuma, tel 642-0638, e-mail elbanano@racsa.co.cr. Health-food café with movies nightly.
Lizard Lounge, Playas del Coco. Theme nights.
Mariner Inn, Flamingo Marina, Playa Flamingo, tel 654-4081. Popular with sailors. Cable TV
Planet Rock, Tamarindo. Live music, large-screen TV.

OTHER ACTIVITIES

For a variety of outdoor activities contact:
Brasilito Excursions, Playa Brasilito, tel 654-4237, www.brasilito.com
Costa Rica Temptations, see p. 260.
Montezuma Expeditions, Montezuma, tel 642-0919, www.montezumaexpeditions .com
Papagayo Excursions, see p. 260.

CANOPY TOURS
Congo Trail Canopy Tour, 9 km W of Sardinal, tel 666-4422
Montezuma Canopy Tour, Montezuma, tel 642-0808, www.montezumatravel adventures.com
Witch's Rock Canopy Tour, Bahía Culebra, tel 666-7546
GOLF
Four Seasons Golf Club, Bahía Culebra, tel 696-0000, www.fourseasons.com
Paradisus Playa Conchal

Beach & Golf Resort, see
p. 249.
Southland Los Delfines Golf
& Country Club, Playa Tambor,
tel 683-0333, fax 683-0304,
www.southlandhotels.com
Tango Mar, see p. 250.

HORSEBACK RIDING
Finca Los Caballos,
Montezuma, tel 642-0124,
www.naturelodge.net

SCUBA DIVING
See eagle rays at Punta Gorda,
or visit the Islas Murciélagos.
Bill Beard's Costa Rica, tel
954/453-5044,
www.billbeardcostarica.com
El Ocotal Diving Safaris,
Playa Ocotal, tel 670-0321, 670-
0321, www.ocotaldiving.com
Resort Divers de Costa Rica,
Playa del Coco, tel 670-0421,
www.resortdivers-cr.com
Rich Coast Diving, Playa del
Coco, tel/fax 670-0176,
www.richcoastdiving.com

SEA KAYAKING
Kayaking grants close-up views
of bird colonies and mangroves.
Gulf Islands Kayaking, S-24
C-34, Galiano Island BC, VON
1PO, Canada, tel/fax 250/539-
2442, www.seakayak.ca

SPELUNKING
Barra Honda's caves are open
Nov.–April. Experienced
spelunkers can enter without a
guide (by permit only).
National Parks Service, tel
686-6760, 671-1455
Proyectos Las Delicias,
Hwy. 18, Barra Honda, tel 685-
5580. A community project,
local guides.

SPORTFISHING
The Gulf of Papagayo delivers
record sailfish and blue marlin.
Asociación de las
Pangueros, Playas del Coco,
tel 670-0228
Billfisher Sportfishing
Charters, Hotel Coco Verde,
Playas del Coco, tel 670-0112,
www.billfishersportfishing.com
Flamingo Bay Pacific
Charters, tel 253-6713,

800/836-7133,
www.fishincostarica.com
Southland Guanamar Beach
& Sportfishing Resort, see
p. 249.
Tamarindo Sportfishing,
Playa Tamarindo, tel/fax 653-
0092,
www.tamarindosportfishing.com

SURFING
Check out Playa Tamarindo,
Santa Teresa, and Malpaís.
Iguana Surf Shop, Playa
Tamarindo, tel/fax 653-0148,
www.iguanasurf.net
Malpaís Surf Camp &
Resort, Malpaís, tel/fax 640-
0061, www.malpaisurfcamp.com

ULTRALIGHT
Flying Crocodile Flying
Center, Sámara, tel 656-0483,
www.flying-crocodile.com

YOGA
Nosara Retreat, Nosara,
tel/fax 682-0071,
www.nosarayoga.com.

CENTRAL PACIFIC

FESTIVALS
International Music Festival,
(July & Aug.), Villa Caletas, see
pp. 170 & 252. Local and
international performers play in
a small amphitheater.

NIGHTLIFE
Barcelo Casino Amapola,
Hotel Amapola, Playa Jacó,
tel 643-2255, www.barcelo
costarica.com/amapola.htm.
Small casino and disco.
Casino Kamuk, Hotel Best
Western Kamuk, Quepos, tel
777-0871, www.kamuk.co.cr
Small, unpretentious spot.
Disco Cocodrilo, Playa Jacó, tel
643-3076. This no-frills disco is
the happening spot in town.
Filthy McNasty's, Playa Jacó.
Lively bar with music.
Rumba's Caribbean Food &
Dance Club, Quepos, tel 777-
0395. Colorful lively bar with live
music. Closed Tues.
San Clemente Bar & Grill,
Dominical, tel 787-0026. Lively

off-beat bar. Disco, live bands,
sports TV, and table football.
Si Como No Movie Theater,
Si Como No hotel, see p. 251.
Thrusters, Dominical. A young
crowd fills this atmospheric bar.
Villa Caletas, see p. 170.

OTHER ACTIVITIES
Local tour operators offer
horseback riding, cruises, and
visits to palm oil plantations.
Estrella Tours, Quepos, tel/fax
777-1286,
www.puertoquepos.com
Lynch Travel, Quepos, tel 777-
1170, fax 777-1571,
www.lynchtravel.com

CANOPY TOURS
Hacienda Barú, see p. 251.
Pacific Rainforest Aerial
Tram, Playa Jacó, tel 257-5961,
www.rainforesttram.com
Rainmaker Conservation
Project, see p. 170.

CROCODILE SAFARIS
Crocodiles are especially prolific
in the Río Tarcoles.
Jungle Crocodile Safari,
Tárcoles, tel 637-0338,
www.costaricanaturetour.com

DIVING
Villas Gaia, see p. 251. PADI
certification and snorkeling.

DOLPHIN SAFARI
Planet Dolphin, Quepos, tel
777-1647,
www.planetdolphin.com

GOLF
Los Sueños Marriott Ocean
& Golf Resort, see p. 252.

HORSEBACK RIDING
Bella Vista Ranch Lodge,
Escaleras, tel 388-0155,
www.bellavistalodge.com
Marlboro Stables, Manuel
Antonio, tel 777-1108
Quepos Trail Rides, Quepos,
tel 777-0566
Rancho Merced National
Wildlife Refuge, Uvita, see
p. 168

KAYAKING
Explore the mangroves of Pacific

river mouths silently by kayak to get close to the critters.
Kayak Joe Tours, Dominical, tel 787-0121

RAFTING
Ríos Naranjo and Savegre.
Amigos del Río, Quepos, tel/fax 777-0082, www.amigosdelrio.com
Ríos Tropicales, Quepos, tel 777-4092

SAILING & CRUISES
Sunset Sails Tours, Quepos, tel 777-1304

SPORTFISHING
Quepos is one of three key centers on the Pacific Coast.
Costa Rican Dreams, Los Sueños Marina, Playa Herradura, tel 637-8942
Bluefin Sportfishing, Quepos, tel 777-4999, www.bluefinsportfishing.com

SURFING
Rent boards and other kinds of surfing equipment are available for rent at Playa Jacó, Playa Hermosa, Esterrillos, Oeste, and Este are also popular.

ULTRALIGHT
Skyline, Uvita, tel 743-8037, www.flyultralight.com

ZONA SUR

NIGHTLIFE
Juanita's Mexican Bar & Grill, Puerto Jimenez, see p. 254

OTHER ACTIVITIES
Land-Sea Tours, Golfito, tel/fax 775-1614, www.landsea-tours.travelland.biz

CANOPY TOURS
Original Canopy Tour, Drake Bay, tel 257-5149

DIVING
Aguila de Osa Inn, Drake Bay, see p. 253
Aventuras Maritimas Okeanos, tel 222-5307, 866/OKEANOS, www.okeanoscocoisland.com

HIKING
Reserva Biólogica Campanario, see p. 175. Treks & ecology courses.

NATURE TOURS
Flying Dutchman River Tours, Ojochal, tel 384-5489. Tours of Terraba-Sierpe Delta.
Vittatus, Sierpe, tel 786-7647. Tours of Terraba-Sierpe.

PANNING FOR GOLD
Asociación de Productores Villa Nueva, Dos Brazos de Río Tigre, tel 775-1422, fax 775-5045
CoopeUnorio, Valle del Río Rincón, tel 225-8966, fax 735-5073. Ex-miners cooperative.

SEA KAYAKING
Kayaking provides a silent entrée into mangrove swamps.
Escondido Trex, Puerto Jiménez, tel 735-5210, www.escondidotrex.com
Zancudo Boat Tours, Playa Zancudo, tel/fax 776-0012, www.loscocos.com/boattours.htm

SPORTFISHING
Crocodile Bay Lodge, Puerto Jiménez, tel 800/733-1115, www.crocodilebay.com
Golfito Sailfish Rancho, Golfo Dulce, tel 813/889-0662, www.golfitosailfish.com
Roy's Zancudo Lodge, Zancudo, tel 776-0008 or 877/529-6980, fax 776-0011, www.royszancudolodge.com (closed Oct.).

WHALE-WATCHING
Delfin Amor Marine Education Center, Drake Bay, tel 527-5558, www.divinedolphin.com

SOUTH CENTRAL

FESTIVALS
Día del Boyeros, (May 15), San Isidro de El General. Traditional oxcarts, rodeos and more.
Festival de los Diablitos, (Dec. 30), Boruca. Masked men disguised as animals and devils

rush through the village creating harmless mayhem, aided by copious amounts of alcohol. The colorful Native American celebration lasts three days, and has an allegorical happy ending.

OTHER ACTIVITIES
Asociación Durika, Buenos Aires, tel 730-0082. This is a farm supporting an ecologically sound reforestation project. Volunteers always needed.
Desafío Adventure Company, La Fortuna, see p. 260

HIKING UP CHIRRIPÓ
This two-day hike can be done solo (see pp. 192–193) or as a guided hike.
Costa Rica Trekking Adventures, San Isidro, tel 771-4582, www.chirripo.com

RAFTING
Ríos General and Chirripó are Class III or IV experiences.
Costa Rica Expeditions, see p. 262.
Ríos Tropicales, see p. 260

NORTHERN LOWLANDS

FESTIVALS
Fería del Ganado, (April), Ciudad Quesada. Costa Rica's largest cattle fair, with a parade (tope), rodeos, and festivities.

NIGHTLIFE
Volcán Look Disco, Fortuna. tel 479-9690. The deafeningly loud music and whirling lights on display draw patrons from miles around. Dance classes offered.

OTHER ACTIVITIES
BALLOONING
Serendipity Adventures, Turrialba, tel 558-1000, 877/507-1358, www.serendipityadventures.com

CANOE TRIPS
Laguna del Lagarto, Lagarto, tel 289-8163, http://lagarto-lodge-costa-rica.com
Rancho Leona, see p. 259.

Selva Verde, see p. 255.
Tilajari Resort Hotel, see p. 255.

CANOPY TOURS
Costa Rica Arenal Canopy Tour, La Fortuna, tel 479-9769, www.crarenalcanopy.com
Termales del Bosque, see p. 212.

CAVE EXPLORATION
Explore the Venado Caverns.
Aventuras Arenal, Fortuna, tel 479-9133, www.arenaladventures.com

FISHING
Inland fishing at Caño Negro lagoon or Laguna de Arenal.
Caño Negro Fishing Club, village of Caño Negro, tel 656-0071, www.canonegro.com
Caño Negro Natural Lodge, village of Caño Negro, tel 265-3302, www.canonegrolodge.com

HORSEBACK RIDING
Desafío Adventures, La Fortuna, see p. 260.
El Gavilán Lodge, Puerto Viejo de Sarapiquí, tel 766-6743, www.gavilanlodge.com
Hotel La Garza, Muelle, tel 475-5222,www.hotellagarza.com
Tilajari Resort Hotel, see p. 255

RAFTING
Ríos Peñas Blancas and Sarapiquí both offer Class II and III trips.
Aguas Bravas, Puerto Viejo de Sarapiquí, tel 292-2072, www.aguas-bravas.co.cr
Desafío Adventures, see p. 260.

RAINFOREST HIKING
Chachagua Rainforest Lodge, see p. 254.
Selva Verde, see p. 255.

THE CARIBBEAN

FESTIVALS
Carnival, (Oct. 12), Puerto Limón. Traditional Caribbean carnival with beauty pageants, parades, and music. Revelers flood the town to celebrate to the beat of calypso and reggae.

Southern Caribbean Music Festival, (March–April), Cahuita, tel 750-0062. Reggae, calypso, and indigenous music, plus jazz and contemporary.

NIGHTLIFE
Johnny's Place, Puerto Viejo. The liveliest dance scene on the Caribbean. Hip-hop and reggae.
Ricky's Bar, Cahuita, tel 755-0228. Colorful restaurant/bar with live music, tropical cocktails, and a beer garden.

OTHER ACTIVITIES
CANOEING
Rent dugout canoes (cayucas) and motorized pangas to explore Tortuguero. Rent kayaks to visit Río Estrella's wetlands and Gandoca-Manzanillo.
Aviarios del Caribe, see p. 256.

DIVING
Cahuita's small coral reef includes the remains of a small wreck. Gandoca-Manzanillo also has a coral reef.
Reef Runner Divers, Puerto Viejo, tel/fax 750-0480, www.reefrunnerdivers.net

DOLPHIN SAFARIS
Talamanca Dolphin Foundation, Manzanillo, tel 759-9115, www.dolphinlink.org

FISHING
Caribbean Expedition Lodge, Parismina, tel 232-8118, www.costaricasportfishing.com
Costa Rica Outdoors, www.costaricaoutdoors.com. Specializes in fishing trips to lakes, rivers, sea, and ocean of Costa Rica.
Río Colorado Lodge, see p. 255.
Río Parismina Lodge, Parismina, tel 292-1207, www.riop.com
Silver King Lodge, see p. 255.
Tortuga Lodge & Gardens, see p. 256.

HIKING
You can hike alone in plenty of places, but a guide is always recommended.
ATEC, (Asociación Talamanca

de Ecoturismo y Conservación) Puerto Viejo, tel/fax 750-0191, www.greencoast.com/atec.htm
Puerto Viejo Tours, Puerto Viejo, tel 755-0082, e-mail puertoviejo@yahoo.com

HORSEBACK RIDING
Cahuita Tours, Cahuita, tel 755-0232
Seahorse Stables, Punta Cocles, tel 750-0468, www.costaricahorsebackriding.com

SURFING
Puerto Viejo's legendary "Salsa Brava" wave kicks up during storm season. Boards can be rented, and there are specialized accommodations. Lesser spots include Playas Bonita and Portrete, north of Puerto Limón.

TURTLE RESEARCH
Sign up as a volunteer, and help guard hatcheries against poaching and predation.
Caribbean Conservation Corps, Tortuguero, tel 224-9215, 800/678-7853, www.cccturtle.org
Marine Turtle Conservation Project, c/o ATEC (see Hiking)
Pacuare Nature Reserve, Pacuare, see p. 224.

ILLUSTRATIONS CREDITS

Abbreviations for terms appearing below: (t) top; (b) bottom;(c) center; (l) left; (r) right:

Cover (l to r): Ian Cumming/Axiom Photographic Agency. Images Colour Library. Images Colour Library. Spine: Images Colour Library. Back cover: (t), Nik Wheeler. (b), Stephen and Fionna O'Meara/Planet Earth Productions.

1, Tom Blagden/Larry Ulrich Stock. 2/3, Michael Melford. 4, Mark Newman/Photo Network. 9, Mike and Corinna Blum/Collection of the pre-Colombian Gold Museum, Museums of the Central Bank of Costa Rica. 11, Nicholas de Vore III/National Geographic Society. 12/13, Alex Webb/Magnum Photos. 14/15, Guido Cozzi/ Bruce Coleman Collection. 16/17, Clive Sawyer/AA Photo Library. 19, Reuters NewMedia, Inc./CORBIS. 20/1, John Skiffington. 2l, Bill Curtsinger/National Geographic Society. 23, William Thompson/National Geographic Society. 24, Mike and Corinna Blum/ Collection of the pre-Colombian Gold Museum, Museums of the Central Bank of Costa Rica. 25, Hulton Getty Collection. 27, Popperfoto. 28, Popperfoto. 29, William Thompson/National Geographic Society. 30, Michael Melford/National Geographic Society. 33, Alantide/ Bruce Coleman Collection. 34/5, Lode Greven/Free Lens Photography. 36/7 Art Directors & Trip Photo Library/Picturesque. 38/9, Buddy Mays/Travel Stock Photography. 40/1, Bill Curtsinger/National Geographic Society. 43, Images Colour Library. 44, Tom Blagden/Larry Ulrich Stock. 47, Tom Blagden/Larry Ulrich Stock. 48, Luiz Claudio Marigo/Bruce Coleman Collection. 50, Amos Nachoum/Corbis UK Ltd. 52/3, Robert Harding Picture Library. 55, Clive Sawyer/AA Photo Library. 58, Mike and Corinna Blum/Collection of the pre-Colombian Gold Museum, Museums of the Central Bank of Costa Rica. 59, Ian Cumming/Axiom Photographic Agency. 60 (t), Ancient Art & Architecture Collection. 60 (b), John Skiffington. 61, Powerstock/Zefa. 62, Powerstock/Zefa. 63, Isabel Cutler. 65, Isabel Cutler. 66, Clive Sawyer/AA Photo Library. 67, Mark Newman/Photo Network. 71, Barry Biesanz. 73 (t), Waina Cheng

Ward/Bruce Coleman Collection. 73 (cl), Jeff Foot/Bruce Coleman Collection. 73 (cr), Stephen J Krassemann/Bruce Coleman Collection. 73 (b), Michael & Patricia Fogden. 74, Clive Sawyer/AA Photo Library. 75, Chris Baker Compositions. 76, Clive Sawyer/AA Photo Library. 77, Robert Fried Photography. 78, Clive Sawyer/AA Photo Library. 79, Gary Braasch/Danita Delimont, Agent. 81 (t), Clive Sawyer/AA Photo Library. 81 (c), J. Feltwell/Garden Matters Photographic Libary. 81 (b), Christer Fredriksson/ Bruce Coleman Collection. 83, Chris Baker Compositions. 84, Christer Fredriksson/Bruce Coleman Collection. 85, Clive Sawyer/AA Photo Library. 86, Guido Cozzi/Bruce Coleman Collection. 87, Clive Sawyer/AA Photo Library. 89 (tl), Clive Sawyer/AA Photo Library. 89 (tr), Clive Sawyer/AA Photo Library. 89 (b), Chris Baker Compositions. 90, Lode Greven/Free Lens Photography. 92/3, Tom Blagden/Larry Ulrich Stock. 95 (t), Mark Newman/Photo Network. 95 (b), John Skiffington. 96, J Feltwell/Garden Matters Photographic Library. 97, Michael & Patricia Fogden. 99, Jon Arnold Images/Alamy. 102/3, Tony Morrison/South American Pictures. 104, Robert Fried Photography. 105 (t), Michael & Patricia Fogden. 105 (b) Clive Sawyer/AA Photo Library. 106, Ian Cumming/Axiom Photographic Agency. 109, M & P Fogden/Bruce Coleman Collection. 110, Lode Greven/Free Lens Photography. 111, Robert Fried Photography. 112, Uwe Walz/Bruce Coleman Collection. 113, Doug Wechsler/BBC Natural History Unit. 114, Macduff Everton/Image Bank. 115 (t), Clive Sawyer/AA Photo Library. 115 (b), John Skiffington. 116, Nik Wheeler. 117, Robert Francis/Robert Harding Picture Library. 118, Nik Wheeler. 119 (t), Kevin Schafer/CORBIS, (b), Nik Wheeler. 120, Kevin Schafer/CORBIS. 121, André Rousseau/Travelvacation.com. 122, Tony Arruza. 123, Kevin Schafer/CORBIS. 125 (br), Larry Ulrich/Larry Ulrich Stock. 126, Gunter Ziesler/Bruce Coleman Collection.127, Ian Cumming/Axiom Photographic Agency. 128, Tom Blagden/Larry Ulrich Stock. 129, Buddy Mays/Travel Stock Photography. 132, Marie Read/ Bruce Coleman Collection. 133, Corey Wise/Alamy. 136, Nik Wheeler. 137, Nik Wheeler. 138, Nik Wheeler. 139, James Davis Travel Photography. 141,

Philip V. D. Berg/Bruce Coleman Collection. 143, David B Fleetham/Oxford Scientific Film Photo Library. 144, Doug Wechsler/BBC Natural History Unit. 145, Macduff Everton/Image Bank. 146, Larry Ulrich/Larry Ulrich Stock. 147, Tim Martin/BBC Natural History Unit. 149 (t), John Skiffington. 149 (c), John Skiffington. 149 (b), Nik Wheeler. 150, John Skiffington. 151, D Maybury/Art Directors & Trip Photo Library. 152, Robert Francis/South American Pictures. 153, Tom Ulrich/Oxford Scientific Film Photo Library. 155, Christer Fredriksson/Bruce Coleman Collection. 156/7, Dietermar Nill/BBC Natural History Unit. 158, Perry Mastrovito/PictureQuest. 159, Isabel Cutler. 160, Nik Wheeler. 161, Clive Sawyer/AA Photo Library. 162, Lode Greven/Free Lens Photography. 165 (t), Tony Arruza. 165 (bl), John Skiffington. 165 (br), John Skiffington. 166/7, Clive Sawyer/AA Photo Library. 167, Michael & Patricia Fogden. 168, Clive Sawyer/AA Photo Library. 169, Paul Sterry/Nature Photographers. 171, Bruce Coleman Collection. 174, Steve Watkins/AA Photo Library. 175, Ian Cumming/Axiom Photographic Agency. 177 (t), Clive Sawyer/AA Photo Library. 177 (b), John Skiffington. 178, Chris Baker Compositions. 179, Bruce Coleman Collection. 182, Gettyone/Stone. 184, Clive Sawyer/AA Photo Library. 185, Gary Braasch/Danita Delimont, Agent. 186, Jim Clare/Oxford Scientific Film Photo Library. 187, Michael & Patricia Fogden. 191, Michael & Patricia Fogden. 192, Clive Sawyer/AA Photo Library. 194/5, Michael & Patricia Fogden. 195, Clive Sawyer/AA Photo Library. 196/7, Steve Watkins/AA Photo Library. 198, Michael & Patricia Fogden. 199, Tom Blagden/Larry Ulrich Stock. 200, Clive Sawyer/ AA Photo Library. 201 (t), John Skiffington. 201 (c), Michael & Patricia Fogden. 201 (b), Clive Sawyer/AA Photo Library. 202, Tom Blagden/Larry Ulrich Stock. 203, Phil Savoie/BBC Natural History Unit. 206, Michael & Patricia Fogden. 207, Phil Savoie/BBC Natural History Unit. 208, Mark Newman/Photo Network. 209, Tom Blagden/Larry Ulrich Stock. 210, Michael & Patricia Fogden. 211 (t), Michael & Patricia Fogden. 211 (c), Michael & Patricia Fogden. 211 (b), Michael Fogden/Oxford Scientific Films Photo Library. 212, Michael & Patricia Fogden. 213, Gary Braasch/Danita Delimont, Agent. 214/5, Ian Cumming/Axiom

Photographic Agency. 216, Steve Watkins/AA Photo Library. 217, Christer Fredriksson/Bruce Coleman Collection. 220, M & P Fogden/BBC Natural History Unit. 221, John Skiffington. 222, Clive Sawyer/AA Photo Library. 225 (t), Gary Braasch/Danita Delimont, Agent. 225 (c), Gary Braasch/Danita Delimont, Agent. 225 (b) Michael & Patricia Fogden. 226 (t), Danny Lehman/CORBIS. 226 (b), Ian Cumming/Axiom Photographic Agency. 228/9, Chris Baker Compositions. 230, Buddy Mays/Travel Stock Photography. 231, Nancy Sefton/Bruce Coleman Collection. 233, Michael Melford.

The world's largest nonprofit scientific and educational organization, the National Geographic Society was founded in 1888 "for the increase and diffusion of geographic knowledge." Since then it has supported scientific exploration and spread information to its more than nine million members worldwide.

The National Geographic Society educates and inspires millions every day through magazines, books, television programs, videos, maps and atlases, research grants, the National Geography Bee, teacher workshops, and innovative classroom materials.

The Society is supported through membership dues, charitable gifts, and income from the sale of its educational products. Members receive NATIONAL GEOGRAPHIC magazine—the Society's official journal—discounts on Society products, and other benefits.

For more information about the National Geographic Society, its educational programs, publications, or how to support its work, call 1-800-NGS-LINE (647-5463), or write to: National Geographic Society, 1145 17th Street, N.W., Washington, D.C. 20036 U.S.A.

Printed in Spain.

Published by the National Geographic Society

John M. Fahey, Jr., *President and Chief Executive Officer*
Gilbert M. Grosvenor, *Chairman of the Board*
Nina D. Hoffman, *Executive Vice President,*
      President, Books and School Publishing
Kevin Mulroy, *Senior Vice President and Publisher*
Marianne Koszorus, *Design Director*
Kristin Hanneman, *Illustrations Director*
Elizabeth L. Newhouse, *Director of Travel Publishing*
Barbara A. Noe, *Senior Editor and Series Editor*
Cinda Rose, *Art Director*
Carl Mehler, *Director of Maps*
Nicholas P. Rosenbach, *Map Coordinator*
Carol B. Lutyk, Lise Sajewski, Jane Sunderland, *Editorial Consultants*
R. Gary Colbert, *Production Director*
Richard S. Wain, *Production Project Manager*
Joy Rothke, *Contributor*
Robin Reid, *Project Manager for 2006 edition*
Jennifer Davis, Steven D. Gardner, Rebecca Gross, Carol Stroud, Teresa Neva Tate, Ruth Thompson, Mapping Specialists *Contributors to 2006 edition*

First edition: Edited and designed by AA Publishing (a trading name of Automobile Association Developments Limited, whose registered office is Norfolk House, Priestley Road, Basingstoke, Hampshire, England RG24 9NY. Registered number: 1878835).

Rachel Alder, *Project Manager*
David Austin, *Senior Art Editor*
Victoria Barber, *Editor*
David Austin, *Designer*
Inna Nogeste, *Senior Cartographic Editor*
Richard Firth, *Production Director*
Steve Gilchrist, *Prepress Production Controller*
Cartography by AA Cartographic Production
Picture Research by Wyn Voysey
Area maps drawn by Chris Orr Associates, Southampton, England
Illustrations drawn by Ann Winterbotham

Second Edition 2006
ISBN: 0-7922-5368-X

The Library of Congress catalogued the first edition as follows:
Library of Congress Cataloging-in- Publication Data
Baker, Christopher
        National Geographic Traveler. Costa Rica
                        p   cm
              Includes index.
              ISBN 0-7922-7946-8 (alk. paper)
              1. Costa Rica—Guidebooks. 1. National Geographic Society (U.S.)
      11. Title: Costa Rica
      DC16.N37 2000
      914.404'839—dc21 98-54974
                                                              CIP

Printed and bound by Cayfosa Quebecor, Barcelona, Spain. Color separations by Leo Reprographic Ltd., Hong Kong. Cover separations by L.C. Repro, Aldermaston, U.K.

Visit the society's Web site at http://www.nationalgeographic.com

The information in this book has been carefully checked and to the best of our knowledge is accurate. However, details are subject to change, and the National Geographic Society cannot be responsible for such changes, or for errors or omissions. Assessments of sites, hotels, and restaurants are based on the author's subjective opinions, which do not necessarily reflect the publisher's opinion. The publisher cannot be responsible for any consequences arising from the use of this book.

NATIONAL GEOGRAPHIC
TRAVELER

A Century of Travel Expertise in Every Guide

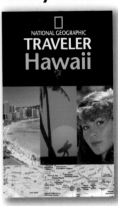

- **Amsterdam** ISBN: 0-7922-7900-X
- **Arizona** (2nd Edition) ISBN: 0-7922-3888-5
- **Australia** (2nd Edition) ISBN: 0-7922-3893-1
- **Barcelona** (2nd Edition) ISBN: 0-7922-5365-5
- **Boston & Environs** ISBN: 0-7922-7926-3
- **California** (2nd Edition) ISBN: 0-7922-3885-0
- **Canada** ISBN: 0-7922-7427-X
- **The Caribbean** ISBN: 0-7922-7434-2
- **China** ISBN: 0-7922-7921-2
- **Costa Rica** (2nd Edition) ISBN: 0-7922-5368-X
- **Cuba** ISBN: 0-7922-6931-4
- **Egypt** ISBN: 0-7922-7896-8
- **Florence & Tuscany** (2nd Ed.) ISBN: 0-7922-5318-3
- **Florida** ISBN: 0-7922-7432-6
- **France** ISBN: 0-7922-7426-1
- **Germany** ISBN: 0-7922-4146-0
- **Great Britain** ISBN: 0-7922-7425-3
- **Greece** ISBN: 0-7922-7923-9
- **Hawaii** ISBN: 0-7922-7944-1
- **Hong Kong** (2nd Edition) ISBN: 0-7922-5369-8
- **India** ISBN: 0-7922-7898-4
- **Ireland** ISBN: 0-7922-4145-20
- **Italy** (2nd Edition) ISBN: 0-7922-3889-3

- **Japan** (2nd Edition) ISBN: 0-7922-3894-X
- **London** ISBN: 0-7922-7428-8
- **Los Angeles** ISBN: 0-7922-7947-6
- **Mexico** (2nd Edition) ISBN: 0-7922-5319-1
- **Miami and the Keys** (2nd Edition) ISBN: 0-7922-3886-9
- **New Orleans** (2nd Edition) ISBN: 0-7922-3892-3
- **New York** (2nd Edition) ISBN: 0-7922-5370-1
- **Paris** ISBN: 0-7922-7429-6
- **Piedmont & Northwest Italy** ISBN: 0-7922-4198-3
- **Portugal** ISBN: 0-7922-4199-1
- **Prague & Czech Republic** ISBN: 0-7922-414
- **Provence & the Côte d'Azur** ISBN: 0-7922-9542-0
- **Rome** ISBN: 0-7922-7566-7
- **San Diego** ISBN: 0-7922-6933-0
- **San Francisco** (2nd Edition) ISBN: 0-7922-3883-4
- **Sicily** ISBN: 0-7922-9541-2
- **Spain** (2nd Edition) ISBN: 0-7922-3884-2
- **Sydney** ISBN: 0-7922-7435-0
- **Taiwan** ISBN: 0-7922-6555-6
- **Thailand** (2nd Edition) ISBN: 0-7922-5321-3
- **Venice** ISBN: 0-7922-7917-4
- **Washington, D.C.** (2nd Edition) ISBN: 0-7922-38

AVAILABLE WHEREVER BOOKS ARE SOLD